As I read through *Gospel-Centered Counseling*, I kept finding myself responding to the words I was reading . . . and that response was vocal. I was amazed. *Blessed. Enlightened. Encouraged. Reminded.* Bob Kellemen understands grace and the gospel in ways that are profound, beautiful, and astonishing. I love this book and the gospel that is so beautifully portrayed here where the rubber meets the road, in our daily lives, in our struggle to believe and to live in the light of all he's done. What a blessing!

ELYSE FITZPATRICK, author of *Good News for Weary Women*
and *Give Them Grace*

Gospel-Centered Counseling is an immense help to both counselors and counselees. Bob frames every counseling issue within the drama of redemption and in the hope of the gospel. The result? A book that belongs on every pastor's shelf! It is *wise*, filled with exegetical insights that flower into rich, everyday counsel. It is *deep*, addressing the whole person, mind, body, and spirit. It is *broad*, deftly moving from Scripture, into the soul, and back out into real life with wonderful clarity. It is *compassionate*. I felt loved and understood by Bob, the sign of a good counselor. Most of all, it is *true*, imparting the hope of Christ into the heart of people — "Behold, I am making all things new!"

JONATHAN K. DODSON, Lead Pastor, City Life Church,
author of *Gospel-Centered Discipleship*

Counseling is not biblical unless it is driven by the gospel in theory and reflects the gospel in practice. Bob Kellemen shows us how gospel-centered counseling flows from the Scriptures and aims at "growth in Christlikeness for the glory of Christ." But he also shows us how we, as counselors, journey alongside others with the very same gospel that we *all* desperately need. *Gospel-Centered Counseling* reflects the deep layers of experience and wisdom forged over three decades as Bob has served faithfully as a shepherd and teacher. Bob understands the deep dynamic struggles of body and soul in our suffering and sin, and he rightfully addresses our affections and imagination in ways that few others do. *Gospel-Centered Counseling* is a "must-have" as you seek to care for and equip others to minister with the gospel as a church.

ROBERT K. CHEONG, Pastor of Care, Sojourn Community Church,
author of *God Redeeming His Bride*

In *Gospel-Centered Counseling*, Bob Kellemen demonstrates convincingly that biblical theology and systematic theology are indeed *practical* theology. Embedding his methodology in the unfolding redemptive narrative of the Bible, he works out the practical implications of our multifaceted salvation in Jesus Christ and shows their impact for interpersonal ministry. Full of rich biblical insight and examples from Bob's many years of pastoral and biblical counseling ministry, *Gospel-Centered Counseling* will benefit anyone who longs to help others live with joyful fidelity to our triune God.

> MICHAEL R. EMLET, M.Div., M.D., Faculty and Counselor at CCEF; author of
> *CrossTalk: Where Life and Scripture Meet*

What a gift Bob Kellemen is to the church today! Bob has been in the counseling trenches for three decades now, and in *Gospel-Centered Counseling* he weaves together a practical approach to helping real people with real problems. He never forgets that these are people who are suffering and don't just need counsel, they need compassion. The compassion at the heart of his counsel is rooted in a verse he weaves through the counseling process, showing us what it would look like to apply 1 Thessalonians 2:8, which says, "We loved you so much that we were delighted to share with you not only the gospel of God but our own lives as well, because you had become so dear to us." Get this book if you love God, love people, and really want to help.

> BRAD BIGNEY, Sr. Pastor, Grace Fellowship Church, author of *Gospel Treason*

Gospel-Centered Counseling is more than a book on how to counsel others. It is a clear and compelling presentation of how the gospel changes everything. Bob has weaved the grand narrative of Scripture with practical application for everyday life. He has called us to be wise counselors who care about orthodoxy while bringing the Word to hurting people with love and care in such a way that grace is not compromised on the road to truth. I would recommend this book first for your personal edification and second as a guide to helping others grow and change.

> GARRETT HIGBEE, Executive Director of Biblical Soul Care,
> Harvest Bible Chapel

Insightful and practical, Dr. Kellemen's *Gospel-Centered Counseling* provides a comprehensive guide for leading readers deep into the contours of genuine biblical soul care. His ability to effectively apply rich gospel-saturated theology to the here-and-now struggles of the human soul is impressive. This is an excellent read for anyone wanting to enhance their understanding of Scripture and how it applies to the complexities of the human estate.

JEREMY LELEK, Ph.D., LPC-S, President, Association of Biblical Counselors

Bob's heart for other people to know and understand the true heart behind biblical counseling is clearly articulated in this book. With so many competing voices and ideas as to where life change and healing come from, Bob has captured the heart and essence of the grand narrative of grace and redemption with this work. *Gospel-Centered Counseling* challenges the professional minister, pastor, counselor, and lay person to remember what they have been saved from and what they have been saved to through the gospel. This book encourages me as it can be so easy, as a minister of the gospel, to forget what should propel our work in the ministry.

LEE LEWIS, Biblical Counselor, Council Board Member,
Biblical Counseling Coalition

Gospel-Centered Counseling is like a smartphone. That is, it can be helpful in multiple ways. Beginning biblical counselors will benefit from the case studies, which model how to minister the Word rather than just dispensing it. Experienced counselors will be prompted to evaluate whether or not their counseling truly reflects the major themes of the Scripture with appropriate application to the problems of life and living. Leaders seeking to disciple others will find in *Gospel-Centered Counseling* a book that teaches theology in a warm, equipping-for-life fashion. Preachers will find seeds of helpful sermon series. Every reader will be more thankful for Christ and the good news of the gospel.

RANDY PATTEN, Director of Training and Advancement,
Association of Certified Biblical Counselors

Gospel-Centered Counseling comprehensively applies our theology to our counseling — it's a theology for life. It will be a vital resource for those who want to be equipped to use God's Word to help people in community. The extensive use of cases makes the book easy and enjoyable to read while also showing how key principles work in practical, real-life situations. The frequent "tweet-size" summaries are helpful and memorable. They also keep the reader on track with the book's main message: the gospel of grace is the foundation for change. Theology matters.

JIM NEWHEISER, Executive Director,
Institute for Biblical Counseling and Discipleship

Gospel-Centered Counseling is a book that ought to be in every biblical counselor's library. Bob Kellemen has dedicated his life to thinking deeply about the way the Good News of Jesus Christ intersects all of life and ministry. Bob writes as both a careful theologian and a compassionate counselor. His love for Jesus coupled with careful scholarship will help readers gain a greater understanding of the grand story of redemption. This book will change you for the better and equip you to help others in that same marvelous process. These are exciting days for the biblical counseling movement because there are more great resources than ever before. This book is more evidence that Jesus is carefully building his church. To him be the glory.

STEVE VIARS, Sr. Pastor, Faith Church, author of *Putting Your Past in its Place*

The Scriptures were never intended to be a weekend medication to dull the pain of the weekly real-life questions that confuse, burden, depress, and weaken us. Rather, God gave us the Scriptures to provide daily practical discernment and nourishment, centered in the cross, that enables us to treat deadly diseases originating from unbiblical worldviews. Sounds fine for the professionals, but how does an ordinary nonprofessional answer life's most critical questions for himself and others? Dr. Kellemen in *Gospel-Centered Counseling* provides a seven-days-a-week cohesive perspective of Christian living and heart transformation that will help you and those you counsel to experience healthy heart transformation. Written in a style that combines stories, theology, and practical application, *Gospel-Centered Counseling* keeps you engaged! For a thoughtful, creative, practical, memorable, and scriptural answer to life's most critical questions read this book.

DR. A. CHARLES WARE, President, Crossroads Bible College,
coauthor of *One Race One Blood*

Gospel-Centered Counseling

EQUIPPING BIBLICAL COUNSELORS

HOW CHRIST CHANGES LIVES

Robert W. Kellemen

Foreword by Deepak Reju

ZONDERVAN®

ZONDERVAN

Gospel-Centered Counseling
Copyright © 2014 by Robert W. Kellemen

This title is also available as a Zondervan ebook.
Visit www.zondervan.com/ebooks.

Requests for information should be addressed to:

Zondervan, 3900 *Sparks Drive SE, Grand Rapids, Michigan 49546*

Library of Congress Cataloging-in-Publication Data

Kellemen, Robert W.
    Gospel-centered counseling : how Christ changes lives / Robert W. Kellemen.
        pages cm. — (Equipping biblical counselors)
    Includes bibliographical references and index.
    ISBN 978-0-310-51613-2
    1. Counseling—Religious aspects—Christianity. 2. Bible—Psychology. I. Title.
    BR115.C69K44 2014
    253.5—dc23   2014019296

Published in association with the literary agency of Wolgemuth & Associates, Inc.

Cover design: Christopher Tobias
Cover photo: Fotalia
Image concept: Mike Costanzo
Interior design & composition: Greg Johnson/Textbook Perfect

Printed in the United States of America

14 15 16 17 18 19 20 /DCI/ 22 21 20 19 18 17 16 15 14 13 12 11 10 9 8 7 6 5 4 3 2 1

Contents

Foreword

Bob Kellemen's *Gospel-Centered Counseling* is a masterpiece. It clearly and compellingly sets out a theological framework in which to build our counseling practice. And it makes the connection to Christian concepts and the Bible very clear. But it also sets forth with every theological concept a way to see how it relates to the nitty-gritty, real-life, real-time elements of counseling. Theology shapes and defines how we do counseling.

Here's some backstory: I love people, and I love helping people. But for years all I ever ran into in the evangelical publishing world was psychology books written by well-meaning Christians who told me a lot about people but not much about God. The connection to God, the Bible, Christ, sin, suffering, human motivation, the world, the flesh, the devil was well-intentioned but often superficial. As a young seminary student, I wrote in my journal a list of biblical concepts that I had never seen in a counseling textbook. I was craving for someone to show me how to relate the Bible to the care of souls. That was the 1990s. Little did I know at the time that there was something called the Biblical Counseling Movement.

As a pastoral intern, fresh off my first year of seminary, a stack of books were handed to me by the senior pastor on my first day. I don't remember much of what I read, except for one book that really stood out to me that summer — Jay Adam's *A Theology of Christian Counseling*. It was bit like a bomb, sitting at the foot of a mountain, that when detonated, shattered my needs-based worldview. All that was left was a huge crevice on the side of the mountainside of my soul.

Reading Adam's *A Theology of Christian Counseling* instilled several principles that have stayed true to this day. And Bob Kellemen's *Gospel-Centered Counseling* instills those same principles today.

Here's the first one: *Theology matters.* Theology is literally "the study of God" (*theos* — God; *ology* — study of). It is essentially the study of all things related to God. Because the Bible is God's Word, we come to understand God most clearly through his Word. We come to understand Jesus, humanity, sin, suffering, hope, and every category that matters to human living through the Bible. God has revealed himself in the Bible and told us everything we need to know him and to grow in our relationship with him. Theology matters because *a careful study of the Bible will help us know God and rightly understand all that he has made.*

Here's the second principle: *Sound theology leads to sound practice.* If counseling is the care of souls, it leads to a lot of talking, crying, complaining, helping, sorting, thinking, praying, and doing. Underneath every counseling practice lies some form of theology; that is, some understanding of God, sin, suffering, Christ, humanity, etc. Even if you don't consider yourself a theologian, you are one. You have adopted some view of these things that leads you to do what you do in the counseling office. Again, theology matters. It's an inescapable reality. But now we see even more why it matters — our theology is the foundational cornerstone on which we build our counseling theory and practice.

Fast forward to 2014. A few weeks ago, a copy of Bob Kellemen's *Gospel-Centered Counseling* arrives. Not since my reading of Adams' book have I found something this good — a solid biblical foundation on which we can build our counseling philosophy and practice. Suffice it to say, I'm not trying to make Bob Kellemen into the next Jay Adams. Far be it from me! Jay is unique as the founder of the modern biblical counseling movement. The writing of his first book *Competent to Counsel* and his formation of the Christian Counseling Education Foundation (C.C.E.F.), both in the late 1960s, and then later on, his formation of the National Association of Nouthetic Counselors (recently renamed the Association of Certified Biblical Counselors), all set him apart as a giant figure of whom we are all in a huge amount of debt.

Probably a better way to state things — Bob's book *Gospel-Centered Counseling* is built on the shoulders of Jay's work. It is a theologically rich counseling guide for the next generation. It starts out by setting a thorough theological framework, which Bob works through over the course of the book:

- The Word: Where do we find wisdom for life in a broken world?

- The Trinity/Community: What comes into our mind when we think about God? Whose view of God will we believe — Christ or Satan's?

- Creation: Whose are we? In what story do we find ourselves?

- Fall: What's the root source of our problems? What went wrong?

- Redemption: How does Christ bring us peace with God? How does Christ change people?

- Church: Where can we find a place to belong and become?

- Consummation: How does our future destiny with Christ make a difference in our lives today as saints who struggle against suffering and sin?

- Sanctification: Why are we here? How do we become like Jesus? How can our inner life increasingly reflect the inner life of God?

Theologically-rich, isn't it? Hand this book to a young seminary student or counselor who is pining away, trying to figure out the connection between the Bible, faith, and counseling, and you will hand that young person a goldmine.

Bob understands that *theology matters* and that *sound theology leads to sound practice*. And he makes that clear in this outstanding book.

Patiently read. Consider. Absorb the theological concepts. Find a friend and share these ideas — use the companion discussion/application guide. Share in church. Pray about it. Put your theology into practice. Then praise God and thank him for giving us his Word and a rich theology that helps us understand how to care for hurting souls.

Deepak Reju, Ph. D., Pastor of Biblical Counseling and Families at Capitol Hill Baptist Church (Washington, DC), President of the Biblical Counseling Coalition, Author of *The Pastor and Counseling* and *On Guard: Protecting and Responding to Child Abuse at Church*

Acknowledgments

I penned *Gospel-Centered Counseling* while serving on the board of directors of the Biblical Counseling Coalition (BCC) and as the BCC's executive director. It has been my honor to serve on the board with seven significant leaders of the modern biblical counseling movement: Nicolas Ellen, John Henderson, Garrett Higbee, Randy Patten, David Powlison, Deepak Reju, and Steve Viars. These men are more than colleagues; they are friends — spiritual friends — who have built into my life and ministry. Thank you, Nicolas, John, Garrett, Randy, David, Deepak, and Steve for your gospel-centered friendship and ministry in my life.

Over the years, I've worked with several publishers and editors and have enjoyed each working relationship. Ryan Pazdur of Zondervan has not only been an editor but a sounding-board and a friend. Thank you, Ryan, for the work you and your team have done to make *Gospel-Centered Counseling* a much better book than it would have been without your help.

My agent, Andrew Wolgemuth, of Wolgemuth & Associates, Inc., has truly become a great friend. We pray for each other. We care about each other's lives and families. Andrew has the rare blend of a sharp mind, business acumen, and a loving heart. Thanks, Andrew!

I reserve my greatest appreciation for my wife, Shirley. Shirley, we're well into our fourth decade of marriage — and by God's grace and your patient love, we're closer than ever. Thank you for embodying gospel-centered relationships in our marriage. No one I have ever met more fully displays Christ's grace than you do.

INTRODUCTION

Changing Lives with Christ's Changeless Gospel Truth

We've all heard of brilliant surgeons with horrific bedside manners. We've likely known some scholarly people whose relational skills could use a little development. On the other hand, many people know what it's like to care deeply, but do not know what to do after the hug. Perhaps we've experienced friends who can cry with us, but seem unsure how to offer much additional help.

God calls us to love well and wisely. That's why, in biblical counseling, we must weave together truth *and* love — comprehensive biblical wisdom *and* compassionate Christlike care.

That's the design of the Equipping Biblical Counselors series. In *Gospel-Centered Counseling* and *Gospel Conversations*, I unite Paul's ministry theme of Scripture *and* soul in 1 Thessalonians 2:8: "We loved you so much that we were delighted to share with you not only the gospel of God but our lives as well, because you had become so dear to us."

My prayer for this two-book series follows Paul's wisdom *and* relationship prayer in Philippians 1:9 – 10: "And this is my prayer: that your love may abound more and more in knowledge and depth of insight, so that you may be able to discern what is best and may be pure and blameless until the day of Christ."

My passion follows Paul's truth *and* love passion in Ephesians 4:15 – 16: "Instead, speaking the truth in love, we will in all things grow up into him who is the Head, that is, Christ. From him the whole body, joined and held together by every supporting ligament, grows and builds itself up in love, as each part does its work."

Equipping in biblical counseling is not either/or: *either* be a brilliant but uncaring soul physician, *or* be a loving but unwise spiritual friend. God calls us to be wise *and* loving biblical counselors. *Gospel-Centered Counseling* and *Gospel Conversations* offer you a comprehensive and compassionate approach to one-another ministry — to using God's Word in your personal ministry to God's people.

Keep Reading If . . .

Keep reading if you see yourself in any of the following portraits . . .

Picture with me a committed Christian sitting at Starbucks with her best friend and fellow church member. Her heart is pounding as she silently prays, "Lord, please give me wisdom." Her friend has finally opened up about the fear, anxiety, and panic she experiences daily and said, "I know the Bible talks about trusting the Lord and taking all my anxiety to him. But how in the world do I relate who God is and what his Word says to my fears?" I'm writing *Gospel-Centered Counseling* and *Gospel Conversations* for this committed Christian friend and thousands like her — for folks like *you* — who want to know what to do after the hug.

Picture with me a pastor stepping out from behind the pulpit. He's just finished confidently preaching on James 4:1 – 4 and the source of relationship problems. During the meet-and-greet time after the service, a visitor, not knowing that this is typically time for casual chitchat, asks the pastor, "How could my wife and I apply your message to our marriage? We've seen a divorce attorney, but we'd like to save our marriage. Could you help?" While looking poised on the outside, inside the pastor is thinking, "They taught me how to preach in seminary, but not how to help a struggling couple to change." I'm writing *Gospel-Centered Counseling* and *Gospel Conversations* for this pastor and thousands of others — for folks like *you* — who long for the same confidence and competence in the personal ministry of the Word that you have in the pulpit ministry of the Word.

Picture with me a couple called by their church to lead their congregation's new biblical counseling equipping ministry. It's designed to train "the average person in the church" to be "competent to counsel." Sorting through literally hundreds of excellent books on counseling, the husband says to his wife, "So much great material. But where do we begin? My head is swimming with information, but at the same time drowning with overload." His wife, nodding in agreement, replies, "We need something that ties this all together, that guides us from the big picture to the nightly lesson. You know, like the *Evangelism Explosion* training manuals do for sharing our faith." I'm writing *Gospel-Centered Counseling* and *Gospel Conversations* for this couple and thousands like them — for folks like *you* — who long for a focused local church counseling curriculum. For folks who want a best-practice approach for equipping God's people to change lives with Christ's changeless truth so they can care like Christ.

Not "Smurfy" or Trendy, but Eternal and Daily

In *Gospel Wakefulness*, Jared Wilson tells about a gospel-loving friend who asked him, "Do you remember *The Smurfs*? Do you remember how they used the word 'smurfy' for everything? If something was great, the Smurfs said it was smurfy." His friend then wondered whether "all the gospel-centered *this* and gospel-driven *that* is just our version of 'smurfy.' "[1]

It's a legitimate concern. Is "gospel-centered" like "smurfy"? Are we just jumping on the proverbial bandwagon? Mimicking the popular lingo? Enjoying being trendy by dropping a gospel buzzword into every other sentence?

I'd prefer to think gospel centeredness reflects Paul, who said, "I am not ashamed of the gospel, because it is the power of God for the salvation of everyone who believes" (Rom. 1:16). Gospel centeredness echoes the author of Hebrews, who penned every sentence in Hebrews as a word of gospel encouragement (Heb. 13:22) applied to the life of believers enduring suffering and battling besetting sins.

The King James Version captures well our potential attitude toward gospel centeredness: "Not with eyeservice, as menpleasers; but as the servants of Christ, doing the will of God from the heart" (Eph. 6:6, KJV). We could be gospel centered in a way that's trendy, or in a way that's eternal. We could be gospel centered in a way that's "smurfy," or in a way that applies Christ's changeless truth in our changing times to change lives.

I've been equipping biblical counselors in the local church and seminary settings for three decades. I summarized those thirty years in my book *Soul Physicians*:

> I have doggedly pursued the fundamental question: *What would a model of biblical counseling and discipleship look like that was built solely upon Christ's gospel of grace? What does the gospel offer? What difference does the gospel make in how we live, how we relate, and how we offer help?*[2]

I have had a lifelong passion for gospel-centered counseling — applying God's eternal plan of salvation and sanctification in Christ to our daily lives and relationships.

What does gospel-centered counseling mean? When I joined three-dozen counseling leaders in a year-long process to craft the "Confessional Statement" of the Biblical Counseling Coalition, we united to describe counseling centered on Christ and the gospel.

> We believe that wise counseling centers on Jesus Christ — His sinless life, death on the cross, burial, resurrection, present reign, and promised return. Through the Gospel, God reveals the depths of sin, the scope of suffering, and the breadth, length, height, and depth of grace. Wise counseling gets to the heart of personal and interpersonal problems by bringing to bear the truth, mercy, and power of Christ's grace. There is no true restoration of the soul and there are no truly God-honoring relationships without understanding the desperate condition we are in without Christ and apart from experiencing the joy of progressive deliverance from that condition through God's mercies. We point people to a person, Jesus our Redeemer, and not to a program, theory, or experience.[3]

What does gospel-centered counseling look like? It will take me two books — *Gospel-Centered Counseling* and *Gospel Conversations* — to answer that question. But here's a one-sentence summary:

> Gospel-centered counseling promotes personal change centered on the Person of Christ through the personal ministry of the Word.

The Résumé of the Gospel-Centered Counselor

We not only need to know what gospel-centered *counseling* looks like. We also need to know what the gospel-centered *counselor* looks like and what equipping in gospel-centered counseling includes.

Imagine that you're forwarding your résumé to the divine Counselor. What characteristics would you highlight to demonstrate your qualifications to be a gospel-centered biblical counselor?

Fortunately for us, the apostle Paul has already completed the résumé of an equipped gospel-centered counselor. "I myself am convinced, my brothers, that you yourselves are full of goodness, complete in knowledge and competent to instruct one another" (Rom. 15:14). Building on this verse, *Gospel-Centered Counseling* and *Gospel Conversations* seek to equip you to mature in the "4Cs" of Character, Content, Competence, and Community:

- Christlike *Character*: Full of Goodness — Spiritual Maturity (Being)
- Biblical *Content*: Complete in Knowledge — Wisdom Applied to Life (Knowing)
- Counseling *Competence*: Competent to Instruct — Christlike Ministry (Doing)
- Christian *Community*: Brothers/One Another — Biblical Community (Loving)

I'll weave this four-dimensional equipping map throughout both books. However, *Gospel-Centered Counseling* will especially help you to develop the biblical *content* — wisdom applied to life — necessary to counsel effectively. It offers you theology for life.

Theology for Life: *Gospel-Centered Counseling*

I present full-day seminars on "How to Care Like Christ." The morning sessions highlight a theology of biblical counseling where we explore life's eight ultimate questions from a biblical perspective. The afternoon sessions emphasize a methodology of biblical counseling, where I introduce four core biblical counseling relational competencies. I recently had a pastor at an evangelical church say, "Could you either skip the theology part or rush through it, so that we can spend the bulk of our time on the *practical* stuff?"

I wasn't shocked because I understood where he was coming from. We often teach theology in such a way that it separates truth from life. So I began to illustrate for him a few of the ways I would help his people see that theology is practical and relevant, that truth *is* for life, that God's Word *is* robust, real, raw, relevant, and relational. I was grateful when he said, "Well, if *that's* what you mean by theology, then don't you dare skip it!"

His fear was a valid fear — that equipping in biblical counseling would just be a "brain dump" — all about information transfer. He wanted the assurance that when I equipped his people, it would be content related to life — all about transformation in Christ.

Making Biblical Counseling Truly Biblical

Everybody talks about the personal ministry of the Word, but how do we make biblical counseling truly biblical? How do we design equipping in one-another ministry so that it is truly transformational? In three decades of equipping,

I've found that a crucial way to move from information to transformation is to probe the Bible's wisdom about life's ultimate questions.

Michael Horton, in *The Gospel-Driven Life*, notes that the working assumption of contemporary Christianity is that modern culture — whether sociology, education, or psychology — properly interprets human identity and the ideals of proper human function, but lacks the methods for obtaining those goals.[4] In other words, we assume the world at least gets the questions right, even if they fumble the answers. Horton questions whether the world even gets the questions right:

> This is where we typically introduce the Bible as the "answer to life's questions." This is where the Bible becomes relevant to people "where they are" in their experience. Accordingly, it is often said that we must *apply* the Scriptures *to daily living*. But this is to invoke the Bible too late, as if we already knew what "life" or "daily living" meant. The problem is not merely that we lack the right answers, but that we don't even have the right questions until God introduces us to his interpretation of reality.[5]

In *Gospel-Centered Counseling*, we turn to God's Word not only to find answers for daily living but first to discover God's ultimate questions about life. This forces us to address the question, "Do I define the Jesus story or does it define me?"[6]

The Bible's Eight Ultimate Life Questions

In my study of Scripture, I've found that the Bible's grand gospel narrative defines for us eight ultimate life questions. Here's how these questions are typically ordered and often worded by students of the Bible and life:

- The Word: "What is truth?" "Where can we find answers?"
- The Trinity: "Who is God?" "How can we know him personally?"
- Creation/Understanding People: "Who are we?" "What makes people tick?"
- Fall/Diagnosing Problems: "What went wrong?" "Why do we do the things we do?"
- Redemption/Prescribing God's Soul-u-tion: "How do we find peace with God?" "How do people change?"
- Sanctification: "How does the change process occur?" "How does change happen?"

+ The Church: "What is God doing in the world today through his people?" "How can we help one another to change?"
+ Consummation: "Where are we headed?" "How does our future destiny impact our present reality?"

These are excellent biblically derived questions about life. Through my study of a gospel-centered approach to biblical counseling, I've tweaked the ordering and the wording. Together, these eight ultimate-life questions seek to answer the biblical counselor's foundational question: "What would a model of biblical counseling and discipleship look like that was built solely upon Christ's gospel of grace?"

+ The Word: "Where do we find wisdom for life in a broken world?"
+ The Trinity/Community: "What comes into our mind when we think about God?" "Whose view of God will we believe — Christ's or Satan's?"
+ Creation: "Whose are we?" "In what story do we find ourselves?"
+ Fall: "What's the root source of our problem?" "What went wrong?"
+ Redemption: "How does Christ bring us peace with God?" "How does Christ change people?"
+ Church: "Where can we find a place to belong and become?"
+ Consummation: "How does our future destiny with Christ make a difference in our lives today as saints who struggle against suffering and sin?"
+ Sanctification: "Why are we here?" "How do we become like Jesus?" "How can our inner life increasingly reflect the inner life of Christ?"

Two hallmarks of the modern biblical counseling movement have always been the *sufficiency of Scripture* and *progressive sanctification*. In my outline of life's eight ultimate questions, those two issues serve as bookends. By starting with the Word of God, we humbly submit to God's wisdom about life in our broken world. By ending with sanctification, we acknowledge that we build our answer to the question, "How do we become like Jesus?" upon God's answers to all the preceding questions — upon God's grand redemptive narrative.

Many theologians and biblical counselors have summarized the Bible as a CFR Narrative: Creation, Fall, Redemption. This summary offers a wonderful picture of the grand movement of the Bible's gospel story.

My six questions between the two bookends offer an expanded, robust portrait of the biblical narrative for biblical counseling. Instead of CFR, it is the "CCFRCC Narrative of the Drama of Redemption."

- Bookend One: The Word — The Sufficiency of Scripture for Biblical Counseling
  - Prologue: Community — Before the Beginning/Eternity Past
  - Act I: Creation — In the Beginning
  - Act II: Fall — The End of the Beginning
  - Act III: Redemption — Eternity Invades Time
  - Act IV: Church — In the Fullness of Time
  - Epilogue: Consummation — After the End/Eternity Future
- Bookend Two: Progressive Sanctification — The Goal of Biblical Counseling

In *Gospel-Centered Counseling* we will explore, chapter by chapter, each of life's ultimate questions as they relate to your life and ministry as a biblical counselor. At the end of each chapter, we'll provide you with a tweet-size summary that captures God's gospel answer to life's ultimate questions.

How to Care Like Christ: *Gospel Conversations*

I began by saying that the comprehensive biblical wisdom of the soul physician must morph together with the compassionate Christian care of the spiritual friend. *Gospel-Centered Counseling* seeks to equip you to become a wise physician of the soul who understands people, diagnoses problems, and prescribes God's soul-u-tions — biblically.

But we can't stop there. Ministry is always about truth *and* love because Jesus is full of grace *and* truth. The second book in this series, *Gospel Conversations*, provides an intensive, relational, hands-on equipping manual. Through it you will develop twenty-two biblical counseling relational skills so you can care like Christ. It provides four biblical/church history compass points for speaking truth in love — gospel conversations:

- *Sustaining: "It's Normal to Hurt"* — Learning how to weep with those who weep by offering biblical sustaining care for hurting people.
- *Healing: "It's Possible to Hope"* — Learning how to give hope to the hurting by offering biblical healing comfort and encouragement for suffering people.

- *Reconciling: "It's Horrible to Sin, but Wonderful to Be Forgiven"* — Learning how to be a dispenser of Christ's grace by offering biblical reconciling care-fronting for people struggling against besetting sins.
- *Guiding: "It's Supernatural to Mature"* — Learning how to disciple, coach, and mentor by offering biblical guiding wisdom for people growing in the grace and knowledge of Christ.

Together, these two books explore how *Christ changes lives* as the foundation for *how to care like Christ.* The goal of *Gospel-Centered Counseling* and *Gospel Conversations* is to further equip you for the gospel-centered process of seeing lives changed through the changeless truth of Christ's gospel of grace.

Welcome to the journey. Let's jump in!

CHAPTER 1

Mining the Richness of God's Word: God's Treasures of Wisdom

Ashley and her husband, Nate, met with me at church the day after their twin sons' eleventh birthday. With tears streaming down her face, Ashley shared that twenty-five years earlier, not long after *her* eleventh birthday, a relative had begun sexually abusing her.

Those who knew Ashley would have been shocked. She grew up in a Christian home, was active at church as an adult, served as a leader in the women's ministry, and was always "pleasant."

As Ashley described herself, "Yes, I'm the good girl from the good home. The good mom; the good wife. But nobody knows the ugliness I feel inside. Nobody knows how I've pretended and denied all these years. I just can't keep faking it any longer. I'm a mess. Depressed to the point that at times I've thought about suicide. Always fearful and anxious — terrified I'll displease someone. Terrified someone will find out what an empty but evil thing I am …"

As Ashley's voice trailed off, Nate asked, "Pastor Bob, can you *help*? Does the Bible offer any *hope* for my wife?"[1]

How you or I respond to Ashley's soul struggles and to Nate's life questions depends on how we answer several other foundational questions:

+ *Truth Questions:* "Where do we find wisdom for life in a broken world? How do we view God's Word for the personal ministry of the Word?"

+ *Life Questions:* "What does it look like to live a whole life in a broken world? What is the purpose of life?"
+ *Counseling Questions:* "What is the ultimate focus of wise and loving counseling in a broken world — what does *help* look like? How can gospel-centered counselors minister to saints who are facing suffering and fighting besetting sins — what does *hope* look like?"

I've written this chapter and this book to address these vital questions. In particular, in chapters 1 – 2, we're seeking to ask and answer the question, "Where do we find wisdom for life in a broken world?"

You *Can* Handle the Truth

When dear folks like Ashley and Nate courageously share their raw concerns with people in the church, I've noticed that we tend to respond in one of three typical ways. First, some *refer.* The stereotype goes something like this: "I'm a committed Christian. I want to help you with your struggle. However, we have to understand that while the Bible provides insight for our 'spiritual lives,' God never intended that we use his Word to address 'emotional and mental' struggles. For relevant help for those issues, we need outside experts." While this perspective shows some confidence in God, there is a corresponding conviction that for "non-spiritual issues," God's Word is not the most appropriate resource.

Second, some follow a *sprinkling* approach. The stereotype goes something like this: "I'm a committed Christian. I want to help you with your struggles. To the insights I've gleaned from the world's wisdom about your issue, I'll add Christian concern, prayer, and some occasional biblical principles where they seem pertinent." There's confidence in God's Word as important in helping hurting people, but its application lacks an understanding of the vital, comprehensive, and robust nature of God's Word for life in a broken world.

Third, some follow the *concordance* approach. The stereotype goes something like this: "I'm a committed Christian. I want to help you with your struggle. You have a problem. I'll use my Bible concordance to find God's answer." Some have called this the "one-problem, one-verse, one-solution" approach. There's confidence in the Bible, but its application lacks an understanding of the complexity of life and the rich nature of God's Word.

In each case, I have purposefully prefaced my comments with "the stereotype ..." Life and counseling are infinitely more complex than three paragraphs can encapsulate. Further, it is not my intent to promote an "us against them" or a "good guys/bad guys" mind-set. Rather than accuse or antagonize, I hope to invite, encourage, and equip.

Instead of just saying, "Don't do it that way," I desire to increase our confidence in God's Word for life in a broken world and increase our competence in applying Christ's changeless truth to change lives. I believe we follow other approaches — like the *refer*, *sprinkle*, and *concordance* approaches — and turn to other sources because:

- No one has equipped us to understand the richness and robustness of God's sufficient Word for life in a broken world — helping us to develop *confidence* in how we *view* the Bible for real life.
- No one has equipped us to apply God's authoritative truth to life relevantly and relationally — helping us to develop the *competence* to *use* God's words for real-life issues.

I want to equip you to *view* and *use* the Bible in a "fourth way" — the gospel narrative way. If we are to view the Bible accurately and use the Bible competently, then we must understand the Bible's story the way God tells it. In chapters 1 – 2, we'll listen in as God tells his story and ours as the drama of redemption. It is a gospel narrative of relationship.

The Bible presents a grand narrative in which God is both the Author and the Hero, with the story climaxing in Christ. God begins by telling the story of relationship initiated in Genesis 1 – 2 and relationship rejected in Genesis 3. After those first three chapters, the rest of the Bible tells the story of God wooing us back to his holy and loving arms, all the while fighting the Evil One who wants to seduce us away from our first love.

Ever since Genesis 3, life is a battle for our love — the ageless question of who captures our heart — Christ or Satan. In *Soul Physicians*, I encapsulated all of life as *a war and a wedding*.[2] Others have described it picturesquely as *slay the dragon; marry the damsel*. The Bible calls it "the gospel."

Our counseling is sterile and dead if we see the Bible as an academic textbook. But if we view and use the Bible as the story — the gospel-centered drama — of the battle to win our hearts, then our biblical counseling ministry comes alive.

To help you to grow in confidence and competence, to help you to handle God's Word skillfully and artfully, I'll follow Paul's approach in Colossians. While he did not hesitate to caution people against being taken captive by false approaches (Col. 2:4, 8), and while he did not hesitate to lovingly confront those who followed false approaches (Col. 2:16 – 23), Paul emphasized the incomparable supremacy of Christ and the unparalleled sufficiency of Christianity. Like Paul, we'll focus on stirring up our confidence in Christ's gospel of grace (Col. 1:3 – 23), Christ-dependent ministry (Col. 1:24 – 2:2), Christ's wisdom (Col. 2:3 – 23), our salvation and sanctification in Christ (Col. 3:1 – 11), and the body of Christ ministering the Word to one another (Col. 3:12 – 4:18). When people asked Paul, "Where do we turn for life wisdom among many fiercely competitive worldview options?" he responded with an infinite answer in one word: *"Christ!"*

Looking for Answers in All the Wrong Places

As Paul wrote to the believers in Colosse, their situation mirrored ours. Like us, they were saints — "holy and faithful brothers in Christ" (Col. 1:2). They were sons and daughters of "God our Father" (Col. 1:2). Though forgiven and welcomed home by God through Christ (Col. 1:13, 22), they were facing suffering — condemnation from Satan (Col. 1:22), judgment by others (Col. 2:16), interpersonal grievances and struggles (Col. 3:13, 15), and family discord (Col. 3:19 – 21). They also battled the same temptations to sin that we face — sexual immorality, impurity, lust, evil desires, greed, anger, rage, malice, slander, and lying (Col. 3:5 – 9). And just like us, many voices were clamoring for their attention, claiming to have cornered the market on the secret steps to wholeness (Col. 2:4, 8). I imagine Paul receiving a letter something like this from one of these saints, sons, sufferers, and sinners ...

> Dear Brother Paul,
>
> I'm confused. No. Not about my salvation. I know I'm saved. I've received Christ's grace by faith. What I'm confused about is life. Not only mine, but the Christians around me. I look around and see saints who struggle just like sinners. Our relationships are not just messy, but often a mess. Our homes are sometimes harsh and cold places. At times we seem to handle suffering little differently than those who do not know Christ. I see Christians who have no sense of who they are in Christ. They seem to sway between self-hatred and self-sufficiency.
>
> What gives? What is the gospel sufficient for? Heaven only? If grace is so sufficient, then why do we seem to be so ineffectual in our lives and relationships?
>
> But here's where I really get confused. It seems like some folks feel as if the church doesn't have wisdom for real life, yet the world sure claims it does! Every time I turn around, I hear about some new answer, some new approach to life, some new philosophy of life claiming to tell me

what life is all about, how to live the good life, and how to make sense of my messed-up life.

One day it's a group alleging to have some special corner on the truth, some secret success sauce that they've been initiated into that I must learn. The next day it's another group saying I have to work harder, follow all their rules and regulations. The third day it's the philosopher types with all their fine-sounding arguments about emotions, relationships, and right thinking.

While they all contradict each other, they all have one message in common. They all seem to be saying that my Christianity is not enough. They all demand that I mix Christ's wisdom for living with their wisdom for living. It's like I can keep my Christianity, but I have to *add* their secrets. I need Christianity *plus* their new way of thinking. I need Christianity *plus* their new way of living. I'm supposed to use my Christianity and plug in their steps.

So, Brother Paul, is Christianity all I need or what? If Christ is sufficient, do I really need something more? And if the gospel is sufficient not only for eternal life but for daily life now, then why doesn't it seem sufficient to me and the rest of us? I know you're busy, but if you could find time to reply, I sure would appreciate it.

Brother Theophilus

God's Word: Relational and Relevant

Though the letter is imaginary, it captures the real and raw life situation that motivated Paul to craft the letter that we know as Colossians. Using our imaginations again, perhaps we picture Paul, in response to this letter, stoically pondering his response, as if this is an academic exercise. Nothing could be farther from the truth as Paul himself describes it. In his desire to care for their souls, Paul is struggling to the point of weariness, laboring to the point of exhaustion, and agonizing like an athlete wrestling in the Olympics. The whole time he's clinging to Christ's supernatural power working mightily within him (Col. 1:29 – 2:1). Paul models for us counseling that is passionate and compassionate, other centered and Christ dependent.

Paul's mission in this life-and-death contest is to relate gospel truth to the Colossians' relationship: with God — that they would be mature in Christ, with one another — that they would be united in love, and with themselves — that they would be encouraged in heart (Col. 1:28; 2:2). Paul models counseling that sees God's Word as relational and relevant to life in our broken world.

God's Word: Rich and Robust

Paul also models counseling that is gospel centered and Christ focused. Instead of allowing the pressure to provide a quick answer to drive him to simplistic solutions, Paul goes "big picture" by focusing on the larger story — the largest story — "Christ in you, the hope of glory" (Col. 1:27). Rather than offering "steps" or "keys," Paul invites his Colossian friends to journey with him on a treasure hunt so "they may have the full riches of complete understanding, in order that they may know the mystery of God, namely, Christ, in whom are hidden all the treasures of wisdom and knowledge" (Col. 2:2 – 3).

Pie in the sky? Too heavenly minded to be of any earthly good? That's what the Colossians were being told. And it's what the world tells us today. The gospel might be good for "spiritual stuff," for heaven, but for life today you need Christ +, or the gospel +, or Scripture +, or Christianity + the world's wisdom. We might call this "the deficiency of Christ view" or "the deficiency of Scripture view."

Paul, like the apostle John, counters this deficient worldview by pointing people to the all-sufficient Christ who not only offers the amazing grace of eternal life but also the amazing grace of life lived to the fullest — *today* (John 10:10). Jesus does not make the false promise of a trouble-free life, but the hopeful promise of peace in the midst of a troubled and troubling world (John 16:33).

It was this Christ-centered worldview that led the Biblical Counseling Coalition to explain gospel-centered counseling as:

> We point people to a person, Jesus our Redeemer, and not to a program, theory, or experience. We place our trust in the transforming power of the Redeemer as the only hope to change people's hearts, not in any human system of change. People need a personal and dynamic relationship with Jesus, not a system of self-salvation, self-management, or self-actualization. Wise counselors seek to lead struggling, hurting, sinning, and confused people to the hope, resources, strength, and life that are available only in Christ.[3]

This is the hope that we offer Ashley and Nate. This is the hope that Christ offers us. This is the hope that Paul offered the Colossians.

The Gospel for Real Life: Heaven Invading Earth

Paul's purpose in responding to the real-life concerns of the Colossian believers was to call them back to the supremacy and sufficiency of Christ, the gospel, Scripture, and Christianity for salvation *and for life today* — rich wisdom for life in a broken world. He does so by helping them and us to understand the gospel narrative — the drama of redemption — that I summarized in the introduction.

Remember where he is as he writes — in prison. What keeps him going when life knocks him down? What keeps him serving freely when life locks him up? What keeps him pursuing righteousness when he's the recipient of injustice?

Paul Tripp words these questions like this: "What is the best news you can imagine? What is your reason for getting up in the morning? What is so significant that you will build your whole life around it?"[4] The apostle Paul's answer is "the good news — the gospel."

The Good News as the Epicenter of the Good Book

When people come to us as biblical counselors, we don't shout, "Gospel!" as if it's some magic wand. Instead, we first understand the gospel story, then we seek to understand our friend's story, then we journey together to intersect God's eternal story and their temporal story. I picture it as pivoting back and forth with our friends between the larger story of the gospel and the smaller (but real and meaningful) story of their life.[5] We earn the right to bring God's perspective to bear on our friends' lives by first listening well to their life story. Gospel-centered counseling means that together with our counselees we derive our understanding of earthly life from heaven's viewpoint.

Paul helped the Colossians and us to understand the gospel narrative by placing it within the context of eternity and time. In Colossians, he developed what I called in the introduction the "CCFRCC Narrative," or "The Drama of Redemption."

+ Prologue: Community — Before the Beginning/Eternity Past
+ Act I: Creation — In the Beginning
+ Act II: Fall — The End of the Beginning
+ Act III: Redemption — Eternity Invades Time
+ Act IV: Church — In the Fullness of Time
+ Epilogue: Consummation — After the End/Eternity Future

Community: Listen to the Creator of Life for Wisdom for Living

Secular psychology by its very definition must begin with us — who are we? Gospel-centered counseling begins *before the beginning* with God — who is

God and what difference does he make in how we look at and live life in a broken world? That's why Paul doesn't start with "once upon a time;" he begins before time, in eternity past by reintroducing the Colossians to the cosmic Christ (Col. 1:15 – 19).

If you have a problem understanding yourself, others, and life, who is sufficient for understanding people and life if not the Creator? It's as if Paul says, "Okay, you could try to understand the creature by the creature (worldly wisdom), or you could turn to the Creator to understand the creature." Since "all things were created by him and for him" (Col. 1:16), turn to him.

And it's as if Paul is saying, "Is your life falling apart? Do you feel like you're coming unglued? Then turn to the One in whom 'all things hold together'" (Col. 1:17).

It's also as if Paul is saying, "You want to know how relationships work? Then turn to the Eternal Community of Oneness — Father, Son, and Holy Spirit." Paul describes it beautifully in Colossians 1:13 when he speaks of the Father bringing us into the kingdom "of the Son he loves."

Before God created, what was he doing? This vital question exposes the vital quest in the human soul created in the image of God. Before God created; he related. "In the beginning was the Word, and the Word was *with* God" (John 1:1, emphasis added). The Trinity always enjoys the sheer delight of eternal, unbroken communion, connection, and community. Their love teaches us how to love — even in a broken world.

Creation: The Way Things Were Meant to Be

In describing the Creator, Paul teaches us about creation and the creature — about us. We were not made to live for ourselves or by ourselves. All things, especially image bearers, were made "for him" (Col. 1:16). All things, especially image bearers, were made to be dependent on him — "in him all things hold together" (Col. 1:17).

What a perfect picture of the garden — Adam and Eve as dependent worshiping beings living in a perfect paradise where everything is held together — shalom, peace, oneness, wholeness, holiness, health, unity. No separation, division, shame, fear, mixed motives, or false love.

The Father, Son, and Holy Spirit did not need to create, did not need us, did not need anything (Col. 1:19 — the Trinity is infinitely full and complete). Not only is our salvation by a loving grace gift ("God so loved the world that he gave" — John 3:16), even our very creation is a loving grace gift from our Trinitarian God who chose to invite us into relationship with their divine community. The essence of life is not only relational, it is a certain type of relational living — mutual self-giving, self-sacrificing, other-centered living.

In the flow of God's grand narrative, Paul's creation narrative teaches us how we were meant to live life with God and with each other. His other-centered worldview guides us in unique directions when we seek to help Ashley and Nate answer central life questions like, "What does it look like to live a whole life in a broken world? What is the purpose of life?"

Fall: Not the Way Things Are Supposed to Be

Tragically, it all fell apart when Adam and Eve attempted to live life apart from the Creator of life. As a result of their rebellion, they moved from other-centered, dependent God-worshipers experiencing shalom to self-centered, independent self-worshipers experiencing shame. Paul captures it in a sentence: "Once you were alienated from God and were enemies in your minds because of your evil behavior" (Col. 1:21).

As a loving soul shepherd, Paul speaks the truth to the Colossians and to us. He informs us that apart from Christ, our wills are bent only toward Satan's *sub-version* of God's grand narrative because our minds are under "the dominion of darkness" (Col. 1:13).

We can trace every inch and each ounce of separation, shame, sadness, and selfishness to Adam and Eve's willful choice to choose Satan's counsel over God's counsel — to choose Satan over God. The Colossians were facing that same choice. It is the choice we and our counselees face every day — to whose counsel will we commit our hearts and minds?

Since the Fall, life is not just *one* grand narrative — it is a competition between *two* grand narratives that each vie for our attention and commitment. As we'll see in chapter 5, Satan's grand narrative is filled with lies, self (self-sufficiency, selfishness, self-effort), works, and condemnation, while Christ's grand narrative is filled with truth, God (Christ-sufficiency), other (other centered), faith, grace, and forgiveness.

How we respond to Ashley's and Nate's plea for help and hope depends on how we answer the question, "Where do we find wisdom for life in a broken world?" Throughout God's Word, he invites us to make a choice between two clear paths — the path of wisdom or the path of folly. Gospel-centered counseling seeks to follow humbly the wisdom path of Christ's grand grace/gospel narrative rather than arrogantly following the foolish path of Satan's grand works/condemnation narrative. Our imaginations are held captive to Satan's lying, condemning narrative (2 Cor. 10:4 – 7). Gospel-centered counseling is part of God's frontal assault on mind-sets surrendered to secular stories — the wisdom of the world.

Redemption: Experiencing Abundant Life Today and Eternal Life Forever

Can you imagine if Paul had ended with the Fall — with alienation from God, domination by Satan, and our hearts, minds, wills, and emotions surrendered to evil beliefs and behaviors? We would have no hope or help to offer Ashley and Nate. But God's grand gospel narrative is a resurrection narrative. Death dies. Hope lives. Christ rises and we rise with him.

The epicenter of the Book of God — the Gospels — is nothing less than a victory narrative. Gospels were a common literary form in the ancient Near East. Whenever a great king won a major victory, he commissioned the writing of a gospel — a vivid retelling of the good news of the vanquished enemy and the victorious king. This glorious good news was told again and again, often from multiple points of views, to exalt the king and encourage his people.

To the Colossians, struggling to know how to live well and wisely, Paul opens the curtain to the main movement in the drama of redemption — victory, resurrection. Then Paul points the spotlight on the main character in the drama of redemption — *Christ*. He rejoices with the Colossians that they have "faith in Christ Jesus" (Col. 1:4). He points their attention to the life, death, and resurrection of Christ, reminding them what they had embraced "the word of truth, the gospel that has come to you. All over the world this gospel is bearing fruit and growing, just as it has been doing among you since the day you heard it and understood God's grace in all its truth" (Col. 1:5 – 6).

In Jay Adams's classic work, *A Theology of Christian Counseling*, he accurately noted that "all counselors have one goal in common: change."[6] But what type of change and how does it happen? This is the counseling question that we must answer before we answer Nate's questions about hope and help: "What is the ultimate focus of wise and loving counseling in a broken world — what does help look like? How can gospel-centered counselors minister to saints who are facing suffering and fighting besetting sins — what does hope look like?"

When the Colossians asked Paul about the best route to change, it's no contest. It is Christ's gospel of grace that is bearing fruit all over the world and in the heart of each believer in Colosse.

Paul says, "You want to know about change? About victory? Listen to the gospel announcement of Christ's victory! And I'm not talking only about past victory over sin, as amazing as that is. I'm also talking about ongoing victory in our daily battles as we face suffering and struggle against sin." That's why Paul reminds them — as believers — that this gospel is continuing to bear fruit and grow "just as it has been doing … since the day you heard it and understood [it]" (Col. 1:6).

Of course, Paul is not in any way minimizing, nor am I, the eternal significance of the gospel. In Christ "we have redemption, the forgiveness of sins" (Col. 1:14). In Christ we have been reconciled to God (Col. 1:22).

For a long time I applied only half the picture of my salvation. Here's how I pictured it. God is a holy and righteous Judge. I'm on trial before him because of my sins. God is about to pronounce me guilty when Christ steps up and says, "Charge me instead. Put Bob's sins on me, and put my righteousness on Bob." God the Judge accepts his Holy Son's payment on my behalf and declares me "not guilty. Pardoned. Forgiven."

That's pretty amazing. But my picture used to stop there. God is the Judge; he forgives me; then he sends me away on my own and says, "Next case."

But that's not the full picture of our salvation. That's not the picture painted by Paul in Colossians 1. In the biblical picture, Christ takes me by the hand from the courtroom and leads me into the Father's house, walking me into God's presence. When we enter the living room, the Father, my Father, is not in his judge's robes. He's in his family attire. When he sees me, it is just like Luke 15 and the prodigal son. My Father runs to me, throws his arms around me, and kisses me. He puts the family ring on my finger and ushers me back home!

Through Christ, God is not only the Judge who forgives you. He is your Father who welcomes you. He has always loved you. That's why he sent his Son to die for you. And now with the barrier of sin demolished, nothing stands between you and your loving heavenly Father. You can meet God person to Person, son or daughter to loving Father. It's not simply, "Come on in, the water's fine!" It's, "Come on home, everything is fine between us!"

Talk about addressing life's ultimate questions! Life's overarching question is, "How do I find peace with God?" Paul answers, "In Christ!"

Of course, embracing Christ doesn't stop a fallen world from falling on us — we still face suffering. And embracing Christ doesn't end our battle against the world, the flesh, and the Devil — we still wrestle against sin. However, embracing Christ does empower us so that we "may live a life worthy of the Lord and may please him in every way: bearing fruit in every good work, growing in the knowledge of God, being strengthened with all power according to his glorious might so that you may have great endurance and patience, and joyfully giving thanks to the Father" (Col. 1:10 – 12). That's the type of real-life gospel change we can promise folks like Nate and Ashley.

Church: Love Poised between Faith and Hope

As Paul provides spiritual counsel for the troubled and confused Colossian Christians, he doesn't envision them alone. Instead, he envisions them together "as God's chosen people" (Col. 3:12) and "as members of one body" (Col. 3:15) — the church. Paul includes these words of one-another ministry in the context of growth in grace (Col. 3:1 – 11) because sanctification is a Christ-centered community journey. "We proclaim him, admonishing and teaching everyone with all wisdom, so that we may present everyone perfect in Christ" (Col. 1:28).

In Paul's letter of spiritual counsel, he does not move directly from Redemption to Consummation. Instead, he teaches that we find ourselves as the church living between two comings — the first and the second coming of Christ. We are poised between looking back with *faith* in our Redeemer and looking forward with *hope* as we await his return as Conquering Groom. What is our role in this dramatic waiting epoch?[7] God calls us to speak and live truth in love.

> *Therefore, as God's chosen people, holy and dearly loved, clothe yourselves with compassion, kindness, humility, gentleness and patience. Bear with each other and forgive whatever grievances you may have against one another. Forgive as the Lord forgave you. And over all these virtues put on love, which binds them all together in perfect unity.* (Col. 3:12 – 14, emphasis added)

And how is the church to love one another? "Let the word of Christ dwell in you richly as you teach and admonish one another with all wisdom" (Col. 3:16). Where does the church find wisdom for life in a broken world? In God's Word, where the grand gospel narrative is told. We are to build wisdom's house together as the redemptive narrative dwells deeply within each of us and overflows lovingly between us.

What has the church to say and do that no other human institution can say and do? We are the Jesus-centered community that speaks gospel truth in love to one another in such a way that it opens a door for sharing the gospel message (Col. 4:3). In God's grand narrative drama, the church is, as Kevin Vanhoozer pictures it, *the theater of the gospel*.[8] We are to perform the gospel in our one-another relationships with the world as our audience so that they will ask us for a reason for the faith, hope, and love they witness (Col. 4:4 – 7; 1 Peter 3:15). As the church we are to embody communion with God and one another in a manner that entices and invites others to join in.

Consummation: The War Is Won; The Bride Is Wed

The Bible's narrative presents life as a war and a wedding, that we can capture the Bible's drama as "slay the dragon, marry the damsel." To people beaten down by sin and beaten up by suffering, Paul says, "Let me tell you the rest of the story — the end of the story. We were under Satan's domain of utter darkness. Helpless and hopeless, Christ has rescued us. Just as earthly rulers transplant a conquered people from one country to another, so Christ has transplanted us from our earthly citizenship to our heavenly citizenship. But he transplants us not from liberty into slavery, but from slavery into liberty. He transplants us not out of darkness into semi-darkness, but out of dismal blindness into marvelous light. He's disarmed his enemies and ours, triumphing over them by the cross" (Col. 1:13; 2:14 – 15).

Paul not only pulls back the curtain to show us the end of the war, he also shows us the beginning of the wedding. "But now he has reconciled you by Christ's physical body through death to present you holy in his sight, without blemish and free from accusation" (Col. 1:22). This is almost identical to Paul's wording in Ephesians 5:25 – 27 where his focus is on Christ's love for the church, providing the example for a husband's love for his wife. This is wedding language!

Paul is letting us eavesdrop on eternity. Just like John does. "Hallelujah! For our Lord God Almighty reigns. Let us rejoice and be glad and give him glory! For the wedding of the Lamb has come, and his bride has made herself ready. Fine linen, bright and clean, was given her to wear" (Rev. 19:6 – 8). The victory is announced. God reigns! The wedding march starts. All the scars and blemishes of sin are cleansed. The bride wears white!

Paul and John share the same message: *The war is won! The bride is wed!* Both messages communicate the same point: the gospel is about God radically changing people. The war Christ wins for us provides victory over sin and Satan where once we were their slaves. The wedding Christ prepares us for produces purity where there once was sin and shame. And it is all for God's glory.

This victory narrative forms the foundation of our counsel and changes the agenda of our counseling. Typically we ask God and seek help from each other to change our feelings and our circumstances. God is in the change business, but a very different type of change — heart change, Christlikeness — presenting everyone "perfect," or mature, in Christ (Col. 1:28).

Listen to the song of eternity — it's about celebrating Christ's victory and the Bride's purity for God's glory! We look at our lives and want instructions or explanations. What we need is imagination and vision to see life today in light of eternity.

Gospel-centered counseling highlights both Good Friday and Easter — the cross and the resurrection. The gospel message is not like the White Witch's evil rule over Narnia, where it is always winter and never Christmas. The gospel narrative is Christ's holy and loving shepherding of the universe where it is always spring and always Easter!

Confidence as a counselor begins with how we *view* the Bible. The central message of the Bible is God's announcement of our past, present, and future victory in Christ. Because God so loved us, he sent his Son to slay the dragon and marry the damsel — the Bride of Christ — us!

The Good News as the End of the Story

Though the outcome of the war is sure, skirmishes continue. When our current dreams are dashed, when we surrender yet again to another temptation, we must remind ourselves that we've read the end of the story.

The grand narrative of the Bible shows that life makes sense. History is moving toward a God-ordained purpose. More than that, the stories of our lives have purpose. God is directing all of history toward the final defeat of evil, toward happily ever after, toward his people ruling with him and in relationship with him.

Christ's triumph in the drama of redemption guides our interactions in our one-another ministry. We engage one another in gospel conversations, encouraging each other to ponder: "Why give up when we lose one battle, since we know we have won the war?" "Why choose mere survival, when we are more than conquerors?" "Why choose the cheap thrills of the pleasure of sin for a season when in the end we rule the universe forever dressed in pure white robes?"

Where We've Been and Where We're Headed

I've summarized life's first ultimate question as, "Where do we find wisdom for life in a broken world?" Of course, we all would agree on a two-word answer: "God's Word." In chapter 1, I've developed that answer further, but can still condense it into a tweet-size summary: *To view the Bible accurately and use the Bible competently, we must understand the Bible's story the way God tells it — as a gospel victory narrative.*

So when folks like Ashley and Nate ask for help and hope, the church does not have to feel inferior and *refer* them to "outside experts." We don't have to simply *sprinkle* in a few Christian principles alongside the world's wisdom. We don't have to follow the shallow *concordance* approach of one problem, one verse, one answer.

Remedying these approaches involves understanding the Bible's grand narrative and connecting it with wisdom to our daily lives. The Bible's drama of redemption provides the context from which we offer wise biblical counsel. Our imaginations must become captive to Scripture so that the Bible's CCFRCC narrative becomes the governing framework for how we speak truth in love. Our role is to help one another to re-narrate our lives in light of the good news of Jesus Christ.

However, this still leaves some questions: "Does the gospel narrative approach mean that we ignore everything the world has to say about life struggles? Do we disregard valid scientific research? Do we refuse to consider medication if and when life struggles may have a physiological component?" We might imagine that we are the first generation of Christians to have to sift through complex questions like this, but that's not true. In chapter 2, we'll explore Colossians 2 to address these important issues that we must not and cannot ignore.

CHAPTER 2

Discovering Wisdom for Life in a Broken World: Our Treasure Hunt for Wisdom

Ashley's situation was anything but simple, but what is simple when it comes to the human soul in a broken world? Ashley was facing external suffering — the horrors of the abuse she suffered. She was also dealing with internal suffering — her responses to her abuse — depression, suicidal thoughts, fear, anxiety, shame ... And Ashley was dealing with heart sin — perfectionism, people pleasing, self-trust, believing Satan's lies ...

In response to her depression and suicidal thoughts, would it be helpful if she saw a doctor? A psychiatrist? Could there be biochemical issues? Could medicine be an option? These are vital and valid questions related to the complex mind-body connection.

In response to Ashley's fear and anxiety, would it help if I were aware of the latest research on trauma and post-traumatic stress? This is a vital and valid question related to descriptive research.

In thinking through causes and cures, symptoms and prescriptions, would it be acceptable for me to blend my biblical worldview — the gospel narrative — with a secular worldview? Would it be wise to merge my biblical understanding of people, problems, and solutions with a secular psychology understanding of those issues? These are vital and valid questions related to counseling theory and prescriptive therapy.

These specific questions raise broader questions. Is gospel-centered biblical counseling "Bible only" counseling that naively ignores resources that God has lovingly put at our disposal? Does the use of any resource other than the Bible involve capitulation to the "wisdom of the world"?

Good people disagree on how to answer these complex questions. I've found that rather than examining Scripture to explore these questions, we often use reason and logic to discern to what extent, if any, we should blend the world's reason and logic with our biblical interpretations. We tend to do this because we assume that prior to the advent of modern secular psychology, Christians did not have to ponder these questions; therefore, the Bible does not address them. Colossians teaches otherwise.

A Shepherd's Concern for His Sheep

Recall the issues that motivated Paul to write to the Colossians from his prison cell. The Christians in Colosse were facing suffering — condemnation from Satan (Col. 1:22), judgment by others (Col. 2:16), interpersonal grievances and struggles (Col. 3:13, 15), and family discord (Col. 3:19 – 21). They were also battling sinful temptations — sexual immorality, impurity, lust, evil desires, greed, anger, rage, malice, slander, and lying (Col. 3:5 – 9). In today's world, these are the types of life issues that cause us to grab our smartphone and schedule a counseling appointment.

In Paul's world, these were also the types of life issues that caused people to visit first-century soul experts.[1] Paul forged Colossians in the heart of active controversy about which source of wisdom could address perplexing life issues.[2] Like today, first-century Christians engaged in heated debates about where they could find wisdom for life in a broken world.[3]

Paul steps onto the debate platform in Colossians to point people to Christ's all-sufficient wisdom because in him "are hidden all the treasures of wisdom and knowledge" (Col. 2:3). What's the context for Paul's reference to Christ's wisdom? It's the same context that brings folks to counseling sessions today: relationship with God — that they would be mature in Christ and in relationships with one another — that they would be united in love and in inner-life issues — that they would be encouraged in heart (Col. 1:28; 2:2).

What's the motivation behind Paul's emphasis on Christ's all-sufficient wisdom? He's concerned that his flock will turn to the world's pseudo-wisdom instead of to the wisdom of the Word. "I tell you this so that no one may deceive you by fine-sounding arguments" (Col. 2:4). "See to it that no one takes you captive through hollow and deceptive *philosophy*, which depends on human tradition and the basic principles of this world rather than on Christ" (Col. 2:8, emphasis added).

Ancient Philosophy Equals Modern Psychology

Here's the word that confuses us — *philosophy*. We hear that word and we assume it means abstract, esoteric, academic reasoning about theoretical issues unrelated to life. That's not how Paul uses the word or how Paul's readers understood the word *philosophy*.

Philosophy in Paul's day focused on diagnosing and healing diseases of the soul produced by false beliefs and mishandled desires that were cured by expert talk based on a systematic theory of human well-being.[4] Clearly, *ancient philosophy and modern psychology cover the same terrain*. In fact, ancient philosophy, modern psychology, *and* gospel-centered counseling all cover the same terrain — but with a very different source of wisdom. So, Paul's first-century caution to beware of deceptive philosophy is also Paul's twenty-first-century caution for us to beware of deceptive psychology that depends on human wisdom and not on Christ's all-sufficient wisdom.[5]

These "expert talkers" of Paul's day claimed they were elite thinkers who possessed superior insight necessary for overcoming suffering and defeating sin. They argued that without their advanced teaching, progressive wisdom, and special knowledge, no one could handle life maturely.[6] Paul's shepherd's heart was angered by such elitism. Three times in Colossians 1:28 he repeats that Christ's wisdom is for everyone. His message is that "there is no part of Christian teaching that is to be reserved for a spiritual elite. All the truth of God is for all the people of God."[7]

William Hendriksen paraphrases the message the counselors of Paul's day were giving the Colossians. "Are you putting up a tremendous but losing battle against the temptations of your evil nature? We can help you. Faith in Christ, though fine as far as it goes, is not sufficient, for Christ is not a complete Savior."[8] F. F. Bruce describes it as a "syncretism" (blending, mixing) of Jewish religious ritual with Hellenistic philosophy of living that was fine with adding in elements of Christianity.[9] Paul's shepherd's concern was alarmed by this message of "Christ + human wisdom." It is as if Paul is saying in Colossians 2:1 – 9, *"Strangely, we seem prepared to learn how to live from almost anyone but Christ."*

That's exactly what these first-century counselors were touting—how to live the good life out of a good heart for the good of society.[10] Though their models of the good life and their theories about how to achieve it varied (just as today we have hundreds of counseling models and theories), these first-century soul physicians all sought to help people to live a flourishing life where they could fulfill their unique purpose by making a meaningful contribution to society. And they sought to accomplish this goal by talk therapy—using human reasoning, argumentation, dialogue, discourse, instruction, confrontation, and reproof to change their counselees' beliefs and behaviors.[11]

Beware!

Ever since Satan's temptation of Adam and Eve in Genesis 3, we have faced two competing sources of wisdom about people, problems, and solutions—and Paul provides wise counsel on how to respond. In fact, Paul's counsel about counseling in Colossians 2:4 would have been excellent guidance for Eve: "Don't be deceived by fine-sounding arguments!" Paul pictures these first-century counselors as communicators, teachers, and debaters who wooed and wowed people with style that lacked substance. They deceived or beguiled people through false reasoning—human reason apart from divine revelation. They had an appealing sales pitch with an appalling product.

Paul is so concerned that he tells the Colossians to "Beware!" He's saying, "Wake up! Pay attention. Danger! Danger! Don't be duped or caught off guard." That would have been excellent counsel for Adam when he failed to guard the garden. Paul uses military language when he warns the Colossians against being taken captive—carried away as booty in the spoils of war. He describes the weapons of warfare as hollow philosophy—human reasonings that are empty, proud, and lacking content and worth for real-life change. They're also deceptive—designed to trick or con, to entice through a pleasant illusion.

Paul is so fiercely against such counsel because it is according to human tradition and the basic principles of the world, not according to Christ. This is once again military language—"basic principles" was used of military units organized for warfare in columns. The term became used for foundational systems of belief upon which people patterned their lives. Paul's saying, "Don't be duped by the enemy or your allegiance will be stolen by secular, sin-distorted human reasoning used to try to cure souls. Don't even think of following people who are separated from the life of God because they can only teach you how to live life separated from God!"

Wisdom from the Wisest Person Who Ever Lived

Paul is not shy about expressing pastoral concern when his flock is tempted to learn how to live life from anyone but the Creator and Sustainer of life — the one who is the Way, the Truth, and the Life. However, most of Paul's focus in Colossians is decidedly positive. Colossians 1 is all about the supremacy of Christ and the sufficiency of Christ's gospel of grace for relational living now and forever. Colossians 2 is all about Christ's all-sufficient wisdom to live the good life (life abundant and eternal) out of a good heart (a renewed heart) for the good of society (a life of love for God and others) for the glory of God.

Paul writes Colossians 2 to help the Colossians to ponder, "Who is the wisest person who ever lived?" Not just the most brilliant person who ever lived (though that would also be Christ) who might give the Colossians information. But the wisest person who ever lived who offers the Colossians transformation. Paul doesn't just want the Colossians to know about the wisest person who ever lived; he wants them to know him. He wants them, and us, to have the full riches of complete understanding that we might know Christ — in whom are hidden all the treasures of wisdom and knowledge (Col. 2:2 – 3).

Paul's excited. He is saying, "Let me tell you about the truly purpose-driven church. It's a community of believers on a search-and-discovery mission, a treasure hunt, to find and uncover the greatest treasure ever — Christ who embodies wisdom, who *is* wisdom for life."

Jesus Knows People

Paul's fascination with Christ reminds us of the apostle John's captivation with Christ. At the end of John 2 we find a "textual marker" — like a blazing, blinking neon light demanding our attention. That neon light proclaims, "Jesus Knows People!" Everyone was enamored with Jesus because of his many miraculous signs (John 2:23). But Jesus would not entrust himself to the fickle crowd because "he knew all men. He did not need man's testimony about man, for he knew what was in a man" (John 2:24 – 25). Jesus knows people intensively and extensively — he knows everything about everybody. He wasn't googling the latest pop psychology book at Amazon because *Jesus knows people.*

John 3 – 4 seems to have been penned, in part, to address folks who might have been thinking, "Yeah, right, John. Prove it. Prove that Jesus knows everything about everybody." In those two chapters, Jesus counsels the two most different people imaginable in John's day — Nicodemus and the woman at the well. Consider their differences: Nicodemus, Jewish, male, self-righteous, insider, religious leader; and the nameless Samaritan, female, unrighteous, outcast, irreligious follower.

Trace Jesus' soul-care ministry to these two individuals, and you'll see many "methods" but one message communicated in numerous person-specific ways. He meets both where they are, but he leaves neither where they were. To Nicodemus the Pharisee, Jesus speaks of the kingdom of God, being born again, of Moses, and of God's love. To the Samaritan woman at the well, Jesus connects through their common humanity — they thirst. Then he speaks to her of living water, of her husband who is not her husband, and of worship in spirit and in truth.

And it is the nameless Samaritan woman who rightly names Christ. Her words are like the second bookend around these chapters. "He told me everything I ever did" (John 4:39). That's simply another way of saying, *Jesus Knows People!*

Jesus is the Wonderful Counselor. He's the ultimate Soul Physician. His personal ministry with Nicodemus and the Samaritan woman depicts his understanding of people — thoroughly; his diagnosis of root problems — precisely; and his prescription of soul-u-tions — perfectly.

Impact the Babylonians, Don't Spoil the Egyptians

It is to this Wonderful Counselor that Paul points us when he exalts Christ as the only One in whom are hidden *all* the treasures of *wisdom* and knowledge. To understand Paul's point, we have to understand the biblical portrayal of wisdom. Throughout the Bible, wisdom and folly relate to the whole person living a godly or ungodly life in every area of relationship, thinking, motivation, behavior, and emotions. Wise living from God's perspective is not "Sunday living"; wise living emphasizes practical reality 24/7.[12]

Wisdom is shrewd, never simplistic. Rather than offering a mathematical formula or an exact science in every situation, it offers eternal perspective that we are responsible to apply daily as we think deeply and love intimately. Studying the Old Testament's primary word for wisdom (*hocmah*) and the primary New Testament word for wisdom (*sophia*) reveals a very practical definition: God has given us in his Son, his Word, his Spirit, and his people all things we need to live sanely in this insane world in light of the world to come. We have what we need to live this life — relating, thinking, choosing, doing, feeling — in light of the life to come. Christ, who is wisdom, offers us all we need to move toward spiritual, relational, mental, behavioral, and emotional healing and health.

This definition of biblical wisdom is important because we're often told that pastoral counseling, one-another ministry, and biblical counseling are fine for "spiritual matters" — for our eternal relationship with God. However, we're told that how we relate to one another — how we handle our mental and emotional life — that's primarily the domain of psychology, not the domain of the Bible. That's like saying some things are not the domain of Christ. That's in direct opposition to what Paul has communicated throughout Colossians. In everything Christ has the supremacy (Col. 1:18), and for everything we have Christ's sufficiency (Col. 2:3).

It is an unbiblical secular-sacred dichotomy to proclaim that Christ is supreme over "spiritual matters," but not over daily-life issues of relating, thinking, choosing, behaving, and feeling. Those are spiritual matters — everything is spiritual — in relationship to God.[13]

This is certainly Paul's view as he encourages us to apply Christ's wisdom to our daily lives and relationships. "Just as you received Christ Jesus as Lord, *continue to live in him*" (Col. 2:6, emphasis added). Paul then applies Christ's wisdom for daily living to restraining sensual indulgence (Col. 2:23). Think about that. When most people think of what to include in the category of "spiritual," the last item that would enter their mind is the physical body and sexuality. Paul is saying, "Everything, including our sexuality, our sensuality, is under the Lordship of Christ and is redeemable by grace — salvation grace and sanctification grace."

Paul urges us to apply Christ's wisdom to our emotional life — how we deal with anger, rage, and malice (Col. 3:8). When most people think of what to include in the category of "spiritual," the second-to-last item they would think of is emotions and feelings. Paul says, "Everything, including our emotionality, our 'emotional intelligence,' is under the lordship of Christ and is redeemable by grace — salvation grace and sanctification grace."

Paul teaches us to apply Christ's wisdom to our relational struggles — to husbands who are harsh and fathers who embitter their children through discouragement. Abusive husbands and fathers — is that the domain of only the secular social worker, or is even that under the domain of the lordship and wisdom of Christ?

You may be wondering about the header to this section: "Impact the Babylonians, Don't Spoil the Egyptians." In the counseling world, the phrase "spoil the Egyptians" has been used frequently to picture the idea of blending the best of what the world has to offer with the best Christ has to offer. It comes from an incident in Exodus: "Every woman is to ask her neighbor and any woman living in her house for articles of silver and gold and for clothing, which you will put on your sons and daughters. And so you will plunder the Egyptians" (Ex. 3:22; see also Ex. 12:36).

Connecting that verse to counseling theory and practice involves an inaccurate analogy and an incorrect application. In Exodus, God's people were leaving a pagan nation and were told to spoil them, not of their wisdom, but of their material possessions. The more apt analogy for counseling would be Daniel in Babylon. Here we have a spiritual analogy of God's people entering a pagan nation and impacting it with God's wisdom. Thus, Paul's analogy in Colossians 2 could be called "Impact the Babylonians." As the church, we are to be salt and light, taking Christ's all-sufficient wisdom into our hurting, broken, and confused world.

This is exactly Paul's prayer request for himself: "And pray for us, too, that God may open a door for our message, so that we may proclaim the mystery of Christ, for which I am in chains. Pray that I may proclaim it clearly as I should" (Col. 4:3 – 4). And it is Paul's prayer for the Colossians and for us that we would impact the Babylonians — impact our world for Christ with Christ's wisdom. "Be wise in the way you act toward outsiders; make the most of every opportunity. Let your conversation be always full of grace, seasoned with salt, so that you may know how to answer everyone" (Col. 4:5 – 6).

What a beautiful portrait of gospel conversations. The Colossians were surrounded by people who were floundering and listening to the "wisdom of the world," to the philosopher-counselors of their day. Paul said that such worldly counselors lacked wisdom and any value in restraining sensual indulgence. Into this confused world, Paul didn't say, "Spoil the Egyptians." Instead, he said, "The Egyptians are spoiled — their so-called wisdom is folly! Impact the Babylonians — pray for wisdom to share gospel conversations that are full of Christ's grace so that you will offer wisdom for fellow believers and for unbelievers as they face life in a broken world."

Don't Take a Backseat to Anyone!

Chapters 1 – 2 of this book and Colossians 1 – 2 are both about confidence in the resources we have in Christ. We've explored how to view the Bible — the written Word — with confidence for life. We can have confidence in the supremacy of Christ's gospel of grace for relational living now and forever. We've also explored how to view Christ — the Living Word — with confidence for life. We can have confidence in the sufficiency of Christ's wisdom for living the good life out of a good heart for the good of society and for the glory of God.

The Superiority of the Body of Christ

Paul has one more major message for the Colossians. It's also about confidence — this time confidence in the body of Christ, the church, for equipping one another to grow in Christ. We can have confidence in the superiority of the body of Christ for helping the whole person to become whole, healthy, and holy in Christ.

Paul doesn't choose his topic in a vacuum. The Colossians were being told that they needed community in addition to their Christian community. Their community in Christ was being judged as insufficient (Col. 2:16, 18, 20). There was a long history of this mind-set in the ancient Near East. Philosopher-counselors like Epicurus presented themselves as the only savior — the correct guide of correct speech and deed.[14] He invited his pupil-disciples into his "Epicurean Garden," which was an enclosed therapeutic community. "Its members became her new family. And there can be no question as to who the head of this family is: for its members even wear images of Epicurus on their rings and put his portrait on their drinking cups."[15]

Likewise, the Stoic philosopher-counselor invited disciples into a community where they became lifelong members of a family participating in a way of life ordered by reason. Their god was the god within — the god of rational argument and human reason. They saw the commitment to God and divine revelation to be foolish and illogical.[16]

There is nothing new under the sun. Today the world seeks to cause the church to feel inferior, communicating that we have to send the "hard cases" to the professionals, to the experts. For far too long, we've been sold the lie and bought the propaganda that when the messy issues of life strike a member of our church family, we should hug, pray, and refer.

That's certainly not Paul's message to members of the body of Christ:

> *Let the peace of Christ rule in your hearts, since as members of one body you were called to peace. And be thankful. Let the word of Christ dwell in you richly as you teach and admonish one another with all wisdom. (Col. 3:15 – 16)*

We quote these verses often, but frequently out of context. Notice what Paul sandwiches around his encouragement for us to let Christ's treasure of wisdom richly dwell in us as we engage with one another in the personal ministry of the Word. On the one side it is deep heart/affection change and mind renewal that leads to lives transformed from sexual immorality, lust, greed, anger, rage, malice, slander, and lying. On the other side it is lasting relational change in how husbands and wives, parents and children relate to one another.

Where does Paul send people when they need to address counseling issues? To the church! Where does Paul place his confidence for growth in grace, for progressive sanctification, for deep heart change? To the body of Christ! And with what resource does Paul arm his flock? The wisdom of the Word of Christ applied first to our lives and then to each other's lives. Paul says to the Colossians and to us, "When it comes to helping people deal with difficult life issues, don't take a backseat to anyone!"

A Comprehensive Definition of Biblical Counseling

When we discuss who is equipped to address which types of life issues, part of our struggle is that we typically maintain a shallow definition of the personal ministry of the Word, whether we call it pastoral counseling, one-another ministry, biblical counseling, or gospel-centered counseling. We need a definition of biblical counseling that encompasses all of life. Here's one such working definition:

> Christ-centered, church-based, comprehensive, compassionate, and culturally informed biblical counseling depends upon the Holy Spirit to relate God's Word to suffering and sin by speaking and living God's truth in love to equip people to love God and one another (Matt. 22:35 – 40). It cultivates conformity to Christ (the whole person becoming whole in Christ — our inner life increasingly reflecting the inner life of Christ) and communion with Christ and the body of Christ leading to a community of one-another disciple-makers (Matt. 28:18 – 20).

In this definition, the "spiritual stuff" is everything related to who we are as everlasting, embedded, embodied, emotional, volitional, rational, relational, self-aware, social, and spiritual beings.[17] Biblical counseling focuses on everything related to how the whole person deals with all of life — sin and suffering — with the goal of sanctification — growth in Christlikeness. This gospel-centered one-another ministry is what Paul calls the body of Christ in Colossians.[18]

Yes, But

We began this chapter pondering three issues related to Ashley and dear people like her:

+ Question 1: Questions related to the complex mind-body connection.
+ Question 2: Questions related to descriptive research.
+ Question 3: Questions related to counseling theory and prescriptive therapy.

We'll briefly examine question 3 first as a foundation for the first two questions.

What about Counseling Theory and Prescriptive Therapy?

Everything in this chapter has addressed the third question: Is it acceptable to blend our biblical worldview about people, causes and cures, and symptoms and prescriptions with a secular worldview? Would it be wise to merge our biblical understanding of people, problems, and solutions with a secular psychology understanding of these issues?

My conviction related to counseling theory and prescriptive therapy should be clear. Paul warns us against "integrating" secular counseling *theory* with biblical counseling *theology*. He warns us against integrating secular counseling therapy with biblical counseling soul care.

I believe that the supremacy of Christ's gospel, the sufficiency of Christ's wisdom, and the superiority of Christ's church provide us with all the treasures of wisdom we need to develop a comprehensive biblical theology and methodology of biblical counseling. That's exactly what *Gospel-Centered Counseling* and *Gospel Conversations* seek to offer — a rich, robust, relevant approach to real-life issues built on Christ's gospel of grace.

What about the Complex Mind-Body Connection?

But what about questions 1 and 2? Does the Bible address the complex mind-body connection and issues of medication? Does the Bible give us guidance about whether Christians could or should use the latest descriptive research about life struggles?

I'm convinced it does. Paul more than hints at it when he highlights Christ as Creator of everything, Lord of all. As Abraham Kuyper explained, "There is not a square inch in the whole domain of our existence over which Christ, who is sovereign over all, does not cry, 'Mine!'"[19]

Paul's words and Kuyper's echo Genesis 1:26 – 28 and what some have called the "Creation Mandate" or the "Cultural Mandate."

> *Then God said, "Let us make man in our image, in our likeness, and let them rule over the fish of the sea and the birds of the air, over the livestock, over all the earth, and over all the creatures that move along the ground." So God created man in his own image, in the image of God he created him; male and female he created them. God blessed them and said to them, "Be fruitful and increase in number; fill the earth and subdue it. Rule over the fish of the sea and the birds of the air and over every living creature that moves on the ground." (Gen. 1:26 – 28)*

I define the Creation Mandate as the God-given, repeated command that image bearers subdue and rule the earth as God's vice-regents, under-shepherds, and under-scientists. We are to love God with all our being, including our physical brain and body, thus exalting God by exploring, enjoying, and expanding the physical realm. The scientist analyzing rocks can glorify God just as much as the preacher preaching about the Rock of ages or the songwriter writing "Rock of Ages."

God created us in his image with the capacities necessary to relate and rule as he relates and rules. When God commanded us to subdue and rule the earth, he was encouraging us to exercise our under-sovereignty over the entire physical universe. We are to be co-creators who tread and knead what God has created — advancing civilization, regulating natural forces, and exploring natural resources. The Creation Mandate is our calling, our vocation, to work like God works — in his power for his glory.

God created and ordered the material universe. Science investigates the material universe and affirms that order. Logically, then, as Christians we should embrace science, research, and medicine as disciplines that examine God's creation in obedience to the Creation Mandate. As Steve Viars states, "Those ministering the Word through counseling should be friends of good science and desire to promote the research and development of hard data in every area of human existence."[20]

Studying and treating the complex mind-body connection is part of the Creation Mandate. Neurological psychology, rightly undertaken, involves the scientific study of the physical brain, its normal functioning, abnormal functioning, and physical cures leading to a restoration of normal functioning.

Such scientific research done in submission to the Creation Mandate has great potential for addressing these complex mind-body issues.

The Biblical Counseling Coalition's "Confessional Statement" nuances the complex mind-body issue as follows:

> We believe that biblical counseling should focus on the full range of human nature created in the image of God (Genesis 1:26 – 28). A comprehensive biblical understanding sees human beings as relational (spiritual and social), rational, volitional, emotional, and physical. Wise counseling takes the whole person seriously in his or her whole life context. It helps people to embrace all of life face to face with Christ so they become more like Christ in their relationships, thoughts, motivations, behaviors, and emotions.
>
> We recognize the complexity of the relationship between the body and soul (Genesis 2:7). Because of this, we seek to remain sensitive to physical factors and organic issues that affect people's lives. In our desire to help people comprehensively, we seek to apply God's Word to people's lives amid bodily strengths and weaknesses. We encourage a thorough assessment and sound treatment for any suspected physical problems.

A biblically based, holistic approach to counseling respects all dimensions of personhood[21] created by God in the full context of the Bible's grand narrative. It is naive and potentially harmful to treat people as one-dimensional beings. While this means that we must take into account possible physiological contributions to life struggles, it also means that we should never view psychotropic interventions as the sole solution for life issues. Sadly in a fallen world, fallen scientists tend to see us simply as material beings, soulless machines. Thus, what could be part of the curative process can be used as justification to ignore the inner-life issues that may well be connected to various emotional and mental struggles.[22]

In addition to legitimate concern with a materialistic worldview, it is also wise to acknowledge that psychotropic medication is still in its infancy. We would be naive not to take into account their side effects and the low current success rate in actually helping troubled people.[23]

Still, as part of the Creation Mandate, psychotropic medication and neurological psychology as part of a comprehensive, whole-person approach has biblical legitimacy. Psychotropic medication is an issue of Christian liberty and wisdom. Therefore, if Ashley were to decide to take medication for her depression, God's people should respond with compassionate understanding, not with guilt-inducing attitudes.[24]

What about Descriptive Research?

What about descriptive research or what we might call research psychology? Consider a working definition of research psychology done under the Creation Mandate:

> Research psychology is the empirical exploration that describes how people typically tend to respond to life events. It examines how things are, not how things were meant to be. It describes observable trends, categorizes clusters of responses, and organizes clusters of symptoms. It does not interpret reasons or causes. It does not prescribe cure or care. It avoids theoretical models, problem diagnosis, and treatment plans.

Christian research psychologists would explore God's world with a confidence that though chaos exists, God has given us the tools to discover order and explore disorder in the physical realm. Christian research psychologists would humbly and respectfully remain within the expertise of their field. They would practice descriptively, describing what they find. They would not practice interpretatively. They turn to the Scriptures when they want to ponder the question of why we are the way we are. They will not practice prescriptively regarding matters of the soul. While they might recommend physical interventions, they would return to the Scriptures to prescribe soul cures.

The Biblical Counseling Coalition's "Confessional Statement" provides a helpful summary of the role of descriptive research in a comprehensive biblical approach:

> When we say that Scripture is comprehensive in wisdom, we mean that the Bible makes sense of all things, not that it contains all the information people could ever know about all topics. God's common grace brings many good things to human life. However, common grace cannot save us from our struggles with sin or from the troubles that beset us. Common grace cannot sanctify or cure the soul of all that ails the human condition. We affirm that numerous sources (such as scientific research, organized observations about human behavior, those we counsel, reflection on our own life experience, literature, film, and history) can contribute to our knowledge of people, and many sources can contribute some relief for the troubles of life. However, none can constitute a comprehensive system of counseling principles and practices. When systems of thought and practice claim to prescribe a cure for the human condition, they compete with Christ (Colossians 2:1 – 15). Scripture alone teaches a perspective and way of looking at life by which we

can think biblically about and critically evaluate information and actions from any source (Colossians 2:2 – 10; 2 Timothy 3:16 – 17).

In my book *God's Healing for Life's Losses*, I examined the descriptive research done by Elisabeth Kübler-Ross and others on the stages of grief.[25] I saw those five stages as one way of categorizing how people in a fallen world typically journey through their grief process. However, such descriptive research cannot assess whether that typical journey is a healthy one. Nor can it assess, simply through research, whether these responses correspond to God's process for hurting (grieving) and hoping (growing). I used the descriptive pattern as a catalyst to take me back to the Scriptures to explore interpretive and prescriptive issues and then developed a biblically based process for journeying through grief to growth.

But What about "General Revelation"?

Some may raise a final question: "If you allow for neurological psychology and research psychology humbly practiced under the Creation Mandate, then why not allow for theoretical psychology and counseling psychology (understanding people, diagnosing problems, and prescribing solutions for matters of the soul) under the principle of general revelation?"

This is a legitimate question that unfortunately often includes an inaccurate understanding and definition of "general revelation." In these discussions, people tend to equate human reasoning with general revelation. That's a category mistake. Rather than being a subset of general revelation, human reasoning is part of our creation in God's image. Our reasoning has become distorted by our rebellion against God, which is why Paul warns us against blending human reasoning with Christ's wisdom. For matters of the soul, Paul points us to special revelation, which is a term theologians use to describe God's inspired, inerrant Word authoritatively and sufficiently setting forth God's standards for human life.[26]

The purpose of general revelation is to declare the existence of the Creator of the natural order — to know *about* the Creator (Ps. 19:1 – 6; Rom. 1:18 – 20). The purpose of special revelation is to draw us to *know* the Creator, to reveal how to love like the Creator, and how to live for the Creator (Ps. 19:7 – 14; Matt. 22:35 – 40).

The general revelation that people perceive through creation is cursed and fallen — the data people interpret is not pristine (Rom. 8:19 – 25). Special revelation, on the other hand, is inspired and inerrant — the data we interpret is supernaturally blocked from error (though, of course, our interpretations are not inerrant).

Additionally, special revelation — the Word of God — is living and active, powerfully capable of exposing heart issues, cleansing the heart, and changing the heart (Heb. 4:12 – 13). Special revelation — Scripture — "is God-breathed and is useful for teaching, rebuking, correcting and training in righteousness, so that the man of God may be thoroughly equipped for every good work" (2 Tim. 3:16 – 17). The Word of God, studied by the people of God, under the guidance of the Spirit of God is authoritative and sufficient for matters of the soul — for building a theory/theology of people, problems, solutions, and care of souls.

Where We've Been and Where We're Headed

Where do we find wisdom for life in a broken world? Here are two tweet-size answers from chapter 2: *The supremacy of Christ's gospel, the sufficiency of Christ's wisdom, and the superiority of Christ's church provide the wisdom we need for counseling in a broken world.* And: *We discover wisdom for how to live life in a broken world from the wisest person who ever lived — Christ!*

My prayer as you've read chapters 1 – 2 is that your *confidence* in God's Word for real-life issues would grow. I want us to have a *view* of God's Word that leads to the conviction that the body of Christ does not have to take a backseat to anyone in ministering to folks like Ashley and Nate. I also want us to grow in *competence* in how we *use* God's Word to understand people, diagnose problems, and prescribe soul-u-tions. I've designed the rest of this book, along with the second book in this series, *Gospel Conversations*, to equip us to grow as competent biblical counselors.

In addressing life's first ultimate question, we've probed: "Where do we find wisdom for life in a broken world?" Life's second ultimate question transitions us from the *written* Word of God to the *living* Word of God. Here we answer the question, "What comes into our mind when we think about God?" The most important thing about us is our view of God. What is the biblical view of God, and what difference does that make in how we do biblical counseling?

CHAPTER 3

Knowing the Creator of the Soul: Our Great Soul Physician

A generation ago, A. W. Tozer penned the classic words that form the foundation for our focus in chapters 3 – 5. "What comes into our minds when we think about God is the most important thing about us." Tozer continued, "The most portentous fact about any man is not what he at a given time may say or do, but what he in his deep heart conceives God to be like. We tend by a secret law of the soul to move toward our mental image of God."[1]

"Amen!" or "What!?"

I'm sure we would all share a mental "Amen!" to Tozer's thoughts related to life in general. However, my prayer is that the next three chapters would lead us to say a mental "Amen!" to Tozer's quote related to biblical counseling for life in a broken world. To put it another way, when life comes crashing down on us, I want our first thought to be, "What is my image of God?"

In Psalm 27, when war broke out against David and he was besieged by an army, he sandwiched around his situation his view of God. He began by praying to his personal God: "The LORD is *my* light and *my* salvation — whom shall I fear?" (Ps. 27:1, emphasis added). He concluded by communicating the one thing he would ask. If an army surrounded me, the one thing I would ask for would be rescue! Not David. His request was that he could "gaze upon the beauty of the LORD" (Ps. 27:4). Long before Tozer, David understood that the most important thing about us in the midst of suffering and sin is our image of God.

As counselors, when we're confused by how to respond to the broken person sitting in front of us, I want to make the radical suggestion that our first thought should be about *our triune God*. I'm assuming that many are now voicing a mental "What!?" instead of a mental "Amen!" I understand how my counsel goes against everything our world teaches us about helping people. Alexander Pope's famous line sums up the world's view: "Know then thyself, presume not God to scan, the proper study of mankind is man."[2]

Secular psychology begins with us — who are we? Biblical counseling begins *before the beginning* with our triune God — who is God and what difference does he make in how we perceive and live life in a broken world?

Even the most spiritual among us might be wondering, "Bob, how in the world is the complicated doctrine of the Trinity going to help me when I'm already confused about broken people in a broken world?" I'm not talking about an abstract doctrine of the Trinity; I'm talking about our personal understanding of and relationship to our triune God. Saying "God is love" and "God is Trinitarian" communicate the same message, but the first seems alive and real, while the latter seems, to us, aloof and academic, cold and stodgy. But God is love because God is a Trinity.[3] As C. S. Lewis explained:

> All sorts of people are fond of repeating the Christian statement that "God is love." But they seem not to notice that the words, "God is love" have no real meaning unless God contains at least two Persons. Love is something that one person has for another. If God was a single person, then before the world was made, he was not love.[4]

Perhaps three illustrations — two biblical and one personal — might help us understand the relevance of the Trinity to life in a broken world ...

The Upper Room

Imagine yourself as one of the twelve disciples — you've placed all your hope and trust in Jesus the Messiah. Now he tells you he's leaving. You'll be persecuted and this world will be a life of persistent trouble.

Now imagine Jesus, the divine Counselor, is counseling you. He tells you not to let your heart be troubled. He reminds you that he has overcome the world and that in him you can find peace. Sounds like counsel you and I might share with one another. But then in John 17, Jesus puts his exclamation point on his practical counsel by pointing his troubled followers to — the Trinity. He takes them back *before the beginning* to unveil for them the eternally shared love and glory that he and the Father (and the Spirit) continuously enjoy.

In their sight and in their hearing, Jesus prays for his disciples that their troubled hearts — hearts that feel like abandoned orphans — will grasp that the Father loves them *with the same love as he loves the Son* (John 17:23). To hearts that feel like their every dream has been dashed and every purpose shattered, Jesus prays that they will grasp that he has given them the glory that his Father gave him (John 17:22).

Sinclair Ferguson pointedly captures how this Trinitarian narrative summarizes the essence of practical counseling:

> I've often reflected on the rather obvious thought that when his disciples were about to have the world collapse on them, our Lord spent so much time in the Upper Room speaking to them about the mystery of the Trinity. If anything could underline the necessity of Trinitarianism for practical Christianity, that must surely be it![5]

A Broken Culture

When Paul writes to the saints in Ephesus, he is addressing people in a broken culture. It's a culture where people have lost all sensitivity and have given themselves over to sensuality to indulge in every kind of impurity, with a continual lust for more (Eph. 4:19). It's a decaying culture where people lie, cheat, mishandle their anger in fits of rage, steal, speak destructive words to one another, fight, slander each other, hold onto malice, and withhold forgiveness (Eph. 4:25 – 32).

It's a godless culture where there is no legal procedure for divorce since wives are simply for cleaning the house and bearing children. Men find their sexual enjoyment outside of marriage, so they don't bother divorcing their wives. The Athenian orator Demosthenes explains, "We have courtesans for the sake of pleasure, we have concubines for the sake of daily cohabitation, and we have wives for the purpose of having children legitimately and being faithful guardians of our household affairs."[6]

"Family life" in "the good old days" was just as bad. When writing about parenting, Paul confronts a society gone mad. Selfishness is the word *du jure*. Attitudes persist that make life perilous for children. Rome has a law called *patria potestas*, literally meaning "the father's power." This law allows the father absolute control over every member of his family. He can sell them all as slaves; make them work in his fields in chains; even punish any member of his family as severely as he wants, including the imposition of the death penalty.[7] A letter dated 1 BC provides insight into how children, girls in particular, are viewed in the Greco-Roman world of Paul's day:

> Hilarion to Alis, His Wife: Know that we are still even now in Alexandria. I beg and beseech you to take care of the little child.... If — good luck to you — you have another child, if it is a boy, let it live; if it is a girl, throw it out."[8]

No wonder Paul exhorts husbands to love their wives like Christ loves the church. No wonder he exhorts fathers not to be harsh with their children, but to bring them up in the loving nurture and discipleship of Christ.

However, Paul does not start his family counsel with husband-wife and parent-child exhortations. Where does Paul begin? You guessed it. Paul begins before the beginning with the Trinity. After greeting the saints in Ephesus, Paul immediately focuses their attention on a three-stanza hymn of praise to Father, Son, and Holy Spirit (Eph. 1:3 – 14).

That's so unlike what we're tempted to do. If we were counseling a couple with a cruel, dictatorial husband, we'd race to the exhortation in Ephesians 5:25 – 33 about Christlike love. If a family comes to see us with a harsh, demanding, unloving, verbally abusive father, we'd turn to Ephesians 6:4 about Christlike parenting. Both are great places to turn, but neither is the first place where Paul turns.

The All-American Family

I know how futile it is to turn first to exhortations before turning to the gospel of grace freely given to us by our triune God. By God's grace, he taught me another way when I was counseling Steve and Alexis.

At first glance, Steve and Alexis were the all-American couple living the American dream. Married over two decades, three teenage children who would make any parent proud, great jobs, beautiful home, active in their previous church ...

But look beneath the surface and you would see another story, as I did the day their oldest son, Eric, knocked on my office door. Hesitantly, he unfolded a family narrative that revealed how their American dream had become a family nightmare. One child physically abused. Another child depressed. A mom who was fearful and in denial. A dad who was angry and controlling. Infidelity had previously rocked the family.

A church our size (about 275 at the time) — we should refer, right? An average-size congregation, surely we did not have the resources to meet such an immense and complicated crisis, right?[9] That's not how we perceived it. Our entire congregation was prepared to unite as a family, as the body of Christ, to minister to this young man, his parents, and his siblings. Even before Eric walked out of my office, biblical, relational, relevant plans were in place to begin to address not only the immediate crisis but also the ongoing heart issues.[10]

Steve met with me for biblical counseling (while a trainee participated in our sessions). Steve and Alexis met for biblical marriage counseling with one of our trained biblical counselors (and also with me). One of our elders began an informal but intensive mentoring relationship with Eric. One of our deacons began the same with Eric's younger brother. One female biblical counselor met with Eric's younger sister in a mentoring relationship, and another met for formal biblical counseling with Alexis.

A Model of Counseling Modeled After the Trinity

As I began meeting with Steve, I made it clear that his abusive behavior had to stop — immediately. However, that was not the extent of my counsel. First, Steve knew this already and he truly wanted to change. Second, "Stop it!" counseling is not gospel-centered, Trinitarian-focused counseling. If my understanding of and my relationship to the Trinity mean anything in my life and ministry, then my ministry to Steve could not be sterile, aloof, stiff-arm counseling from a distance.

I needed to practice what I preached — I must know the Trinitarian Soul Physician personally to be a powerful soul physician. And if I know God personally as the eternal community of Oneness, then my life and my counseling will be forever changed.

I needed to practice what Paul practiced — intense relational ministry, face-to-face, soul-to-soul ministry. Recall the background to Ephesians. When Paul was saying good-bye to the Ephesian elders, knowing he would never return to Ephesus, he had to wrench himself away. They all wept as they embraced and kissed one another, grieving that they would never see each other again (Acts 20:13 – 21:1). Like Paul in Ephesus, my personal relationship to the all-loving Trinity had to shape my personal relationship to Steve.

Saint, Sinner, and Sufferer

As I related intensely and intimately with Steve, I followed the gospel-centered, Trinitarian-focused path that Paul journeyed in helping broken families in a broken culture. I started exactly where Paul started — with *saints* in their life *situation*: "To the saints in Ephesus" (Eph. 1:1). Steve and I explored his salvation testimony, and I was confident that he had committed his life to Christ. We also explored his life situation — upbringing, background, family culture, and dating and marital history. Because I'm committed to counseling that seeks to follow the model of the relational connection of the Trinity, I wanted to know Steve well — as saint, sinner, and sufferer.

As Steve and I relationally explored the Word, we pivoted between his story and God's story. In counseling that reflects the relationship within the Trinity, that "pivoting" is not simply teaching, as if counseling is a *monologue*. Instead, I invited Steve to journey with me in a *trialogue* — Steve, me, and the Holy Spirit through God's Word — journeying together in relating Christ's gospel story to Steve's life story.

Father, Son, and Spirit

As Steve and I traveled together, I had to keep fighting the temptation to skip ahead to Ephesians 5:21 – 6:4 and "teach" Steve how to be a loving husband and father. Instead, we explored together the greatest example of love ever — the Father, Son, and Holy Spirit's love for one another that overflows in their Trinitarian grace-love for us (Eph. 1:3 – 14).

By beginning with the glory of our Trinitarian God and the gospel-grace salvation we have through the Father, Son, and Spirit, Paul sends a clear message. Out of gratitude for grace we live our lives — including our marriage and parenting — to bring praise and glory to the Trinity. Paul models that the first duty of a biblical counselor is to define reality — and reality begins with our Trinitarian God who chose us, adopted us, redeemed us, cleansed us, forgave us, sealed us, and guarantees our eternal inheritance. By starting here with Steve, he shifted his mind-set, reality, and focus regarding what it means to be loved with grace and about what it means to be a husband and father who glorifies God by loving with grace.

Everything that follows in Ephesians has a Trinitarian shape to it. Who God is drives everything. According to Robert Letham, "Paul sees Christian experience as thoroughly Trinitarian."[11] Knowing the Trinity richly, deeply, and personally is of first importance on Paul's agenda for the church (Eph. 1:17). Letham notes, "It is the first category on his prayer list, the single most important thing he mentions."[12] That's why, having laid this Trinitarian foundation, Paul then prays a biblical counseling prayer (Eph. 1:15 – 23). I prayed it like this for Steve:

I keep asking that the God of our Lord Jesus Christ, the glorious Father, may give you, Steve — a father and husband who is a saint — the Spirit of wisdom so that you may know our Trinitarian God better, deeply, personally, in a life-changing way. I pray, Steve, that the eyes of your redeemed heart may be enlightened to know your hope, your inheritance, and the Trinity's incomparably great power that is at work in you. Steve, it's the same almighty power that raised Christ from the dead! I pray this, Steve, so that through Christ and for Christ you can love your family with love that flows from the eternal love of the Father, Son, and Spirit.

But God: The Fallen Condition Focus

Paul is still not ready to move to the passage we would have run to first — Ephesians 5:21 – 6:4. No, before that Paul wants us to see our guilt before our triune God (Eph. 2:1 – 3). Paul is once again reshaping reality through his fallen-condition focus.

That's what I wanted to do with Steve. In his thinking, his need for grace was a "back then" need before he was saved. He needed to understand that he not only needed salvation grace but also sanctification grace. Steve had been trying to change in his own power. We turned him to where Paul turns people — to our total depravity and also to our total dependence on grace — on our triune God. We turned to two of the most important words in the English language — "but God" (Eph. 2:4).

Steve began to understand that he could not change himself; he began to understand that before he even has a desire to change, the Father, Son, and Holy Spirit share the overflow of their eternal love with him. Our triune God is rich in mercy, and because of his great love for Steve, by grace made him alive with Christ, raised him with Christ, and seated him with Christ. I could look Steve in the eyes and say, "By grace, you are God's workmanship, his poem. The triune God created you in Christ Jesus to minister beautifully and powerfully to your wife and children."

Which God?

"But God" is powerful and meaningful only if the God we worship is the one true Trinitarian God. Steve, like every person who has ever lived, seeks to answer three vital identity questions:

+ What is my image of God?
+ What is my identity in Christ?

‣ What do Christlike relationships with others look like?"

As we explored Ephesians together, I asked Steve, "When you think of God, what first comes into your mind?" In his most honest moments, Steve would answer, "I know what I should say. But to be honest, sometimes it seems like God is like the Deist God — the uninvolved Creator, the Watchmaker who wound this thing up and now leaves us alone."

Perhaps Melville was peering into Steve's heart when he wrote, "The reason the mass of men fear God and at bottom dislike him is because they rather distrust his heart, and fancy him all brain, like a watch."[13] Before we jump on some Steve-bashing bandwagon, perhaps we might admit that we have fallen prey to such insidious thoughts at various points along our journey. With "eyeballs only," we do a little spiritual calculation. "Let's see, when my life is unfair, when I suffer unjustly, when the wicked prosper, the options are: God doesn't care or God is not in control. He's either not strong enough or not loving enough."

This is exactly the argument of the "New Atheists" like Christopher Hitchens, author of *God Is Not Great.* In an interview, Hitchens stated:

> I think it would be rather awful if it was true. If there was a permanent, total, round-the-clock divine supervision and invigilation of everything you did, you would never have a waking or sleeping moment when you weren't being watched and controlled and supervised by some celestial entity from the moment of your conception to the moment of your death.... It would be like living in North Korea.[14]

Michael Reeves explains that, "For Hitchens, God is The Ruler, and so must by definition be a Stalin-in-the-sky, a Big Brother. And who in their right mind would ever want such a being to exist?"[15] When people describe the God they don't believe in, he "sounds more like Satan than like the loving Father of Jesus Christ: greedy, selfish, trigger-happy and entirely devoid of love. And if God is not Father, Son, and Spirit, aren't they right?"[16]

But our triune God is not that God! The picture changes entirely if God is fundamentally the most kind and loving Father and only exercises his rule as who he is — the eternal loving community of Father, Son, and Spirit. "In that case, living under his roof is not like living in North Korea at all, but like living in the household of the sort of caring father Hitchens himself wished for."[17]

We often talk, rightfully so, in biblical counseling about "idols of the heart." The Bible talks even more frequently about false lovers of the soul and spiritual adultery (see chapters 8 and 9). The human mind is a perpetual forge of idols, *and* the human heart is a perpetual forge of false lovers. So what needed to change in Steve? His worshiping heart needed to change. He needed to repent of his sinful unbelief about God, the Spring of Living Water (Jer. 2:13). God is looking for true worshipers (John 4:23 – 24), but Steve was a false worshiper believing Satan's lies about God. Everybody is a theologian. Everybody has an idea about who God is and how he works. Steve needed to repent of a heart captured by Satan's lie instead of captivated by God's beauty.

With a cleansed heart and a renewed mind, Steve was able to see the Wonderful Counselor in high definition. As he did, Steve began to see God as rich in mercy, overflowing with great grace-love, and powerfully and personally at work in *his* life.

So yes, I talked to Steve about the Trinity. "Steve, the issue of the Trinity is not simply a philosophical debate. The issue is which God you will believe or reject. At least believe or reject the one true triune Father, Son, and Spirit God. The God who invites you into his eternal family of joy and love. The Trinity is the secret to God's beauty. Love and worship the God and Father of all who draws you into his eternal love and fellowship."

Who Am I in Christ?

Over time, Steve began to live according to new heart answers to the question, "What is my image of God?" In turn, he began to put on new answers to the question, "What is my identity in Christ?" Steve got "stuck" in a good way on the phrase "his great love for us" (Eph. 2:4). Couldn't get it out of his head. Didn't want to. We explored specifically the Father's great love (Eph. 1:3 – 6) for him, the Son's great love for him (Eph. 1:7 – 12), and the Spirit's great love for him (Eph. 1:13 – 14).

Steve not only saw himself as loved by the Trinity, but as empowered by the Trinity (Eph. 1:15 – 23; 2:9 – 10). As he put it, "I can be the new person I already am through God's powerful work in me."

What Do Christlike Relationships Look Like?

With a renewing image of God and renewing identity of himself in Christ, Steve was ready to explore the question, "What do Christlike relationships with others look like?" Answering that question now came naturally, or shall I say, supernaturally, for Steve. His way of relating to Alexis and his children had been much like his false image of God — uncaring dictator. Steve was struck by a phrase tucked away between Ephesians 1:6 and 7 — "the One he loves." As Steve put it, "That's a description of the Father's relationship to his Son! I want that to be a description of my relationship to my wife, my sons, and my daughter — they are the ones I love."

How does Jesus change people? By dealing with life's ultimate question — "What comes into our mind when we think about God?" Jesus changes us by changing our very nature (regeneration), which changes our view of God, which in turn changes our identity in Christ. Before Paul ever mentions the *gospel imperatives* (commands about how to live like Christ), he provides *gospel indicatives* (what has already happened through the grace of our triune God), and he highlights *gospel identity* (who we are in Christ), which leads to *gospel increase* (the fruit of maturing Christlikeness).

Sanctification Grace

There's still the question of how this change in Steve's life would be empowered. So we kept exploring Ephesians, and we saw more about sanctification grace — growth in Christlikeness through the power of our triune God (Eph. 3:14 – 21; 5:18; 6:10 – 18). We also learned together about the role of the body of Christ in growth in grace (Eph. 3:18; 4:11 – 16; 5:19). Steve brought both of these ideas together in his prayer for his family from Ephesians 3:14 – 21.

> *Father, I pray that out of your glorious riches you would strengthen me, Alexis, Eric, Joel, and Bethany with power through your Spirit so that your Son would dwell in each of our hearts by faith. Root and establish our home, beginning with me, in love so that together with all the church — our whole congregation, because we can't do this alone — we would grasp how wide, long, high, and deep is the love of Christ.*

Then, just before we finally explored the Ephesians 5:21 – 6:4 gospel imperatives about marriage and family, Steve and I saw how God sandwiched Spirit-dependence around marriage and family living. Right before Ephesians 5:21, Paul tells us that we must be *Spirit-filled* (Eph. 5:18). Just after Ephesians 6:9, he informs us that we must be *Spirit-empowered* (Eph. 6:10 – 18). Steve even picked up the Trinitarian references in Ephesians 6:10 – 18: "Be strong in the Lord ... put on the full armor of God ... pray in the Spirit." Steve jumped for hope. "I know I can't change on my own. But with the Spirit's filling and the empowerment of the Trinity, God can, is, and will change me as I depend upon him!"

Trusting the Story Author

I see two threads in Steve's life story. First, regarding the *written* Word of God, Steve would have confidently answered the question, "What is truth?" by saying, "God's Word is truth!" However, if you had asked him, "Where do you find wisdom for life in a broken world?" Steve would have looked at you with a blank stare of desperation. While Steve could have walked you through the "Roman's Road" process for coming to Christ, he saw the gospel story as something he needed *before* he came to Christ. Part of my role as I came alongside Steve was to help him have confidence in the rich relevance of the written Word of God to his daily life and relationships *after* he came to Christ.

The second thread in Steve's life story relates to the *Living* Word of God. If asked, "Who is God?" Steve could have blurted out theology answers like Creator, Lord, Savior, Shepherd, and King. But we know his response was quite different when I asked him to answer honestly, "What comes into your mind when you first think about God?"

We can tie together these two themes from Steve's life. Yes, we must get the gospel story right. However, we also must trust the story Author. The gospel is not only a message to believe; it is a Person to follow. That Person is our triune God.

And, as we'll see in more detail in chapter 5, there is a battle for our minds and hearts. So we must ask ourselves another question: "Whose view of God will I believe — Christ's or Satan's?" How we answer that question determines how our lives answer questions from Christ, like, "Will you follow me?" "Who do you love and worship?" The Bible's drama of redemption forces us to answer the questions, "Who do you say that I am?" "Will I acknowledge God for who he is?"[18] As with Adam and Eve, God comes to each of us and asks, "Where are you? Where are you in your heart relationship to me?"[19]

John Stott has rightly written that, "All true worship is a response to the self-revelation of God in Christ and Scripture, and arises from our reflection on who he is and what he has done.... The worship of God is evoked, informed, and inspired by the vision of God."[20] Since God reveals himself as our triune God, we must pursue a Scripture-driven, Spirit-led vision of the Father, Son, and Holy Spirit.

Such a vision has rich relevance to biblical counseling and Christian living because the state of our soul depends on what occupies our mind. As biblical counselors, we seek to reorient our counselees' perspective from a self-focus to a God-focus — putting God at the center where he belongs and where life makes sense. Thus our counsel becomes Trinity-centric. Everyone puts something in the center of counseling. I am proposing that counseling must be gospel-centered (chapters 1 – 2) and Trinity-centric (chapters 3 – 4).

Knowing Our Triune God

Think for a moment about that infinite stretch of "time" before anything was created. Let your imagination contemplate what it must have been like for the Trinity to exist together with no one and nothing else. Now try to reduce to a single word whatever comes to your mind.

Here's my best attempt:

+ In the Beginning God *Created*
+ Before the Beginning God *Related*

Before they created, the Trinity related. What were the Father, Son, and Holy Spirit "doing" before they created? Jesus answers that question. "Father … you loved me before the creation of the world" (John 17:24). They were experiencing constant, uninterrupted, intimate relationship. They were together in harmony, giving, sharing, relating — loving.

Some counseling models begin at the beginning with Creation — God's original design, intent, and Genesis 1 – 2. Some start with the Fall — sin, depravity, and Genesis 3. Others begin with Redemption — salvation, sanctification, and the New Testament. While all of these are essential, if we are to proceed chronologically, we will begin with eternity past — John 1:1 – 18; 17:1 – 26.

I propose that we construct a biblical counseling model that begins before the beginning. I suggest that we build our model of counseling on the foundation of the triune relationship that existed before the foundations of the earth. If we are going to learn spiritual friendship, then let's look to the ultimate Spiritual Friend and the eternal Spiritual Friendship: the Trinity. The relationship within the Trinity models how we ought to relate. Father, Son, and Holy Spirit demonstrate how love lives.

Intimacy beyond Our Wildest Imagination

The god of the Muslims is a monad — the Alone with the Alone. He exists in sterile oneness. Not so the Trinity. "In the beginning was the Word, and the Word was with God, and the Word was God. He was with God in the beginning" (John 1:1 – 2).

In *The Book of God*, Jack Miles surmises that God has no history. Before he created us, since he had no one to relate to, Miles blasphemously claims that God had failed to develop any personality.[21] He was a God alone and a lonely God in need of companions. Not so the Trinity. "No one has ever seen God, but God the One and Only, who is at the Father's side, has made him known" (John 1:18).

In his gospel, John styles his introduction to echo the Genesis account of the beginning. Then he takes us time traveling back before the beginning of time. As we arrive, we find that the Word *was* with God in the beginning. In using the Greek word for "was," John could have chosen a tense that would have pictured a snapshot where we happen to travel back in time to a moment when the Son happened to be in the Father's presence. Instead, John selects a tense picturing an ongoing video. *Whenever* we might travel back in time, at *whatever* point we would arrive, we would *always* find Father and Son (and Spirit) together. We might translate John's phrase the way his first-century readers would have heard it. "The Word was continually, without interruption, with the Father always and forever."

As the Bible's narrative begins, we do not find the Author alone at his desk. We discover the Author in relationship. The everlasting, intimate connection shared within the Trinity demonstrates that relationship is the gravity that holds our universe together — reality is relational.

Notice again where the Word was: "And the Word was *with* God" (John 1:1, emphasis added). The Greek preposition signifies "before, in the presence of, face-to-face with." When my children were young, we played a game called "Eye Contact." I would bellow, "Josh! Marie! Let's play 'Eye Contact!'" They'd race to me, shove their eye sockets into my eye sockets, press their eyeballs into my eyeballs, and we would make eye contact.

Father and Son (and Spirit) play an eternal game of "Eye Contact." The Trinity always enjoys the sheer delight of eternal, unbroken communion, connection, and community.

How intimate is their fellowship? John shows us by describing Jesus "in the beginning," at the Father's side; "in the bosom of the Father" (John 1:18 KJV). "Bosom" stresses the closest, most intimate, relaxed, and comfortable shared relationship imaginable. John uses the same word later in his gospel to describe himself sharing a meal with Jesus, leaning on Christ's bosom (John 13:23 KJV). Without being disrespectful, we might say that the Trinity enjoys an eternal hug, an endless embrace. They dwell together, they make their home together, and their home is the home that we all long for and dream of. Not an empty, massive mansion, but a place of welcoming embrace.

We must realize something that's not easy for our modern mind to hear. *God does not need us.* We are unnecessary to the existence and happiness of the Trinity — the Father, Son, and Spirit were perfectly happy without us. But because God is not a hoarder, he chose to share. And his sharing is extravagant. "The Word became flesh and made his dwelling among us" (John 1:14). Jesus left his Father's glory, moved out of his heavenly home, and built a home here with us.

Though God could never need us, it is within his very nature to communicate himself to us. "No one has ever seen God, but God the One and Only, who is at the Father's side, *has made him known*" (John 1:18, emphasis added). Jesus exegetes the Father — he explains, makes clear, and reveals the very nature of God to us. The Trinity teaches us, Thomas Torrance wrote, that "God is not alien and unknowable. He has communicated with us. He himself is a living, dynamic, personal being and has revealed himself to be so. He loves us and has enabled us to know him."[22]

Before God created, he related. However, he did create, and he created in order to invite us into the relationship shared by the Trinity. Not out of need, but out of love, out of grace.

Admiration beyond Our Grandest Dream

In John 1, John carries us back before time began, and in John 17, Jesus is our time-traveling guide. In his prayer, Jesus transports us to that infinite stretch before time so we can sense the unbounded esteem the Trinity shares as Father, Son, and Holy Spirit marvel at one another. "Father, the time has come. Glorify your Son, that your Son may glorify you" (John 17:1). From before the foundation of the world, the Trinity has shared intimacy beyond our wildest imagination *and* shared admiration beyond our grandest dreams. "You loved me before the creation of the world" (John 17:24). "And now, Father, glorify me in your presence with the glory I had with you before the world began" (John 17:5).

The Trinity is a mutual admiration and adoration society of shared glory. Five times in the first five verses, Jesus speaks of "glory." The Greeks used this word, *doxa*, to denote reputation and good standing. The Old Testament equivalent, *kâbôd*, has the root sense of something weighty that gives importance and honor. In relationship to God it expresses what makes God impressive. He's a heavyweight, not a lightweight. Both words refer to the splendor of God's majesty. Glory embraces the divine honor, splendor, power, and radiance that are the essence of God's being. To glorify God means to acknowledge or extol what is already a reality. It includes praising, valuing, and honoring God for who he is.

In high school our youth group took a bus trip from the flat lands of Indiana to the mountains of Pennsylvania. Amber and her mom had never been out of Indiana, and they had never seen mountains before. We reached Pennsylvania and they were amazed. When Mom would spot another mountain peak on the horizon, she would yell, "Hey, Amber, look out the window!" Soon every time we encountered another glorious vista, the entire bus would yell, "Hey, Amber, look out the window!" That's how the Trinity relates. They never get over the thrill of delighting in the glory they see in one another.

Shared Sheer Delight

So what did the Trinity "do" before they created? They enjoyed each other and bragged on each other. They were thrilled with each other. They shared sheer delight. The Trinity is radically other-centered and entirely unselfish. "Father, you are incredible!" "Son, you are amazing!" "Spirit, you are awesome!" There never was a time when the Trinity was denied the pleasure of delighting in their mutual glory.

And none of this changed when Jesus came to earth. "I have brought you glory on earth by completing the work you gave me to do" (John 17:4). As John 1:18 and 17:6 teach, Jesus came to reveal, to unveil, and to display his Father's glorious nature. Jesus is the Father's press agent and biographer. According to Hebrews 1:1 – 3, Jesus is the eloquence of God, the dazzling outshining, God's mirror image. He's the clean, clear, crisp imprint of God. "Anyone who has seen me has seen the Father" (John 14:9).

As remarkable as God's glory is, Jesus thrills us even more when he prays, "I have given them the glory that you gave me, that they may be one as we are one" (John 17:22). We participate in God's glory! Jesus makes it clear that the goal of our salvation is our glorification (see also 1 John 3:1 – 3). What is sown in dishonor is raised in glory.

God could have hoarded his glory. From eternity past, the one reality that has always existed is God. Yet the ever-living God has never been alone. God chose to share, but not because he had to or needed to. God acts in sovereign freedom. His acts do not spring from the need to make up deficiencies, but from the passion to express the abundance of his delight. Because he is good and generous, God delights to give us the very delight that he has in himself. Jonathan Edwards explained it like this: "Part of God's fullness which he communicates, is his happiness. This happiness consists in enjoying and rejoicing in himself; so does also the creature's happiness."[23] No one would want to spend eternity with an unhappy God. Instead, God invites us to enjoy what is most enjoyable with unbounded energy and passion forever.

It's All about Him

John, like Paul, teaches us that counseling is not about us as the counselor and not ultimately about our counselee. Counseling is about relating in Christlike ways so that we give people a glimpse of the wonder of our God. It is about helping people to grow in grace so that they glorify God in their lives — spreading his fame.

At the back of the auditorium in a church where I've ministered hangs a simple but profound sign. It is a constant reminder to anyone in the pulpit and everyone in the church. It reads: "It's All About Him!" Life and ministry, whether the pulpit ministry of the Word or the personal ministry of the Word, are all about him, about God, about glorifying his name and spreading his fame.

Where We've Been and Where We're Headed

So where do we turn when "the all-American couple" walk into our lives with their dashed dreams and shattered hopes? Do we turn to the world's supposed wisdom? Do we race to a biblical exhortation to "try harder"? Or do we run first, last, and always to the Trinity because we know that our view of God determines everything?

How does Jesus change people? By first dealing with life's ultimate question — "What comes into our mind when we think about God?" We've seen here in chapter 3 that the one true God is a God of love — our Trinitarian God of interpersonal relationships. We can summarize this chapter's Christian living lessons and principles of biblical counseling with this tweet-size statement: *We must know the Trinitarian Soul Physician personally to be a powerful soul physician.*

But who is this Trinitarian God? When we say that "God is good; he's good *all* the time," what exactly do we mean? More importantly, what does the Bible mean? In chapter 4, we'll explore a consistent biblical summary image of God as a God of *holy love* — our *affectionate Sovereign*, the *Lion and the Lamb*.

CHAPTER 4

Recognizing the Most Important Fact about Us: Our View of God

As two women in our church, Shelly and Connie, were ministering to Bethany, the teenage daughter of Alexis and Steve, they kept in view our focus from chapter 3. What comes into Bethany's mind when she thinks about God is the most important fact about her.

This did not mean that the first interactions they had with Bethany involved a Sunday school lesson on the Trinity. It did mean that they listened compassionately to Bethany's story of suffering in her relationship with her father. As they listened, they listened *theologically* — they listened with biblical ears and saw Bethany's life story through biblical lenses.

Bethany's caring church counselors understood that the state of her soul depended on what occupied her mind — especially what occupied her mind about God and her relationship to him. I vividly recall the first supervision meeting I facilitated with Shelly and Connie as they told me about their interactions with Bethany. Shelly explained, "I'm not surprised that Bethany's image of God as her Father is skewed — given some of the parenting failures of her earthly father." Reflecting on that observation, the three of us discussed the importance of a profound concept from J. I. Packer.

> If you want to judge how well a person understands Christianity, find out how much he makes of the thought of *being God's child, and having God as his Father.* If this is not the thought that prompts and controls his worship and

prayers and his whole outlook on life, it means that he does not understand Christianity very well at all.... Our understanding of Christianity cannot be better than our grasp of adoption.[1]

As our supervision time continued, Connie reminded us of a point I had made in one of our recent counselor equipping classes. "Pastor Bob, it strikes me that your comment a couple of weeks ago applies here. You said that 'one of the primary callings of a biblical counselor is to help people to define reality biblically.' And you're always reminding us that *reality is relational because God is Trinitarian.*'"

Shelly and Connie had to laugh when they said that last line in unison since they had heard me repeat it so frequently.

Connie continued, "Our study last week is so vital as we move forward with Bethany. Our whole focus on God as our Father of holy love, our sovereign Shepherd, our affectionate Sovereign has to be part of the reality that reshapes how Bethany sees God and relates to God."

Our God Questions

The observations we made regarding Bethany are equally true for each of us. Recall the three core identity questions that every person seeks to answer:

+ What is my image of God?
+ What is my identity in Christ?
+ What do Christlike relationships with others look like?"

Our tendency is to ask the second question first and to ask it without reference to a biblical understanding of God. So instead of thinking about our identity "in Christ," we focus on our own identity and ask, "Who am I?" Our modern wording of the question, while sounding so deep, is actually quite impoverished.

As Matt Chandler explains, "Often the question of 'Who am I?' should be answered with 'Whose am I?' The gospel provides the greatest identity one can ever find."[2]

Justin and Lindsey Holcomb apply this gospel perspective specifically to sexual abuse counseling.

We can't avoid the question, "Who am I really?" And we can only answer that by answering the prior question, "In what story do I find myself a part?" Story is powerful. The link between story and identity cannot be understated....

There is another story different from the victim story and the self-affirmation story. God offers the redemptive story told in Scripture. The identity from that story is founded on grace."[3]

This is why biblical counselors help people to probe the question, "What is my image of God?" Then we explore with them the question, "What is my identity in Christ?" It's also why biblical counselors explore these questions within the context of the gospel story and within the context of knowing and trusting the story Author.

In helping people to see the intersection between their life story, the gospel story, and the Author of the story, I've found that we all ask two central questions about God:

+ *"God, do you care?"* — Questions about God's love.
+ *"God, are you in control?"* — Questions about God's holiness.

Every problem of the soul includes a distorted, unbalanced answer to these two questions about God's infinitely perfect character. To know the God of peace and the peace of God, we must know God in the fullness of his *holy love*, in the perfection of his *affectionate sovereignty*, in the beauty of who he is as *the Lion and the Lamb*. Our biblical vision of God as a Trinitarian God of holy love is central to biblical counseling and Christian living.

The Battle for Our Hearts and Minds

In our fallen world, there is a battle for our affection and attention, for our love and loyalty. In this battle, Satan says, "The world is ugly so God must be ugly too. Live an ugly life." Christ says something very different to us: "Life in a fallen world is bad and ugly. But God is good and beautiful — he alone is good and he is good all the time. Live a beautiful life for his beautiful glory."

The battle for our minds and hearts is won or lost according to our image of God. Since we reflect what we revel in and become like what we worship, we must know God in all his majesty and beauty if we are to become like him. When life's struggles hit, we don't simply help one another with *solutions* to problems. Instead, we help one another with *soul-u-tions* (change at the heart level) by helping one another to grasp who God is and encouraging one another to respond like Christ.

Biblical counselors know God. They enlighten their spiritual friends to grasp the holy love of God. They expose Satan's deceitful veiling of God's glory and grace that invades their spiritual friends' lives. They teach that God is good even when life is bad. He is not only the author of our story, God is the protagonist in the story — the good guy, our loving hero. Jared Wilson says it well in *Gospel Wakefulness*: "The Bible may be an epic love story, but we are not the protagonists in it. The Bible's story is about God. He is its chief character. He is the hero."[4]

But what do we mean when we say, "God is good"? What is the essence of God's goodness?

The Holy Love of God

When we say that "God is good" and "God has a good heart," we mean that God is a God of beauty and majesty — of holy love. A vision of God's holy love delivers us from caricatures of our triune God. John Stott reminds us: "We must picture him neither as an indulgent God who compromises his holiness in order to spare and spoil us, nor as a harsh, vindictive God who suppresses his love in order to crush and destroy us."[5]

That God is holy and loving is foundational to biblical Christianity and to biblical counseling. The Scriptures express the oneness or unity of God in terms of the complementary nature of his holiness and love — his holy love.

Stott refers his readers to ten passages (Ex. 34:6 – 7; Ps. 85:10; Isa. 45:21; Hab. 3:2; Mic. 7:18; John 1:14; Rom. 11:22; 3:26; Eph. 2:3 – 4; and 1 John 1:9) that highlight God's holiness and love. He then concludes: "Here are ten couplets, in each of which two complementary truths about God are brought together, as if to remind us that we must beware of speaking of one aspect of God's character without remembering its counterpart."[6]

I've identified my own list of couplets of God's holy love: Exodus 33:14 – 23 with Exodus 34:5 – 7; Psalm 26:3; 40:10 – 11; 62:11 – 12; 63:2 – 3; 85:10; Isaiah 40:10 – 11; John 1:14; Romans 2:4 – 5; 11:22; and 1 Peter 1:16 with 1 John 4:8. In these passages, God's love and holiness are simultaneously displayed. They are equally infinite; he maintains them in perfect harmony.

The psalmist noted this when he described the God in whom his soul found rest. "One thing God has spoken, two things have I heard: that you, O God, are strong, and that you, O Lord, are loving" (Ps. 62:11 – 12). The poet divinely attests to two great summarizing truths about God. They are the two grand truths that God's revelation declares through every page: *God is holy; God is loving.* He is filled with majesty and beauty. He is King and Shepherd, full of grace and truth, transcendent (far above us) and yet immanent (near us), just and merciful, uncompromising and kind, in control and caring.

So What?

What difference does it make whether or not we see God as a God of holy love? Thomas Chalmers, in his sermon "The Expulsive Power of a New Affection," captures well the historic Christian thinking on the connection between our image of God and our Christlike character. "The best way to overcome the world is not with morality or self-discipline. Christians overcome the world by seeing the beauty and excellence of Christ. They overcome the world by seeing something more attractive than the world: Christ."[7] Even as the perfect heavenly vision will purify us from our sin (1 John 3:2 – 3) and wipe away every tear in our suffering (Rev. 7:17), so a growing vision of God *now* will strengthen us against sin (1 John 3:3) and sustain us in our suffering (Rom. 8:17 – 18).

In two "God is" passages, the Bible summarizes the vision we desire our spiritual friends to see: 1 John 4:8, "God is love," and 1 Peter 1:16, "[God is] holy." Biblical soul care enables people to see that "life is bad, but God is good — *holy and loving*." In the midst of suffering, when life is ugly, we sustain our spiritual friends with the truth that God is loving: beautiful, caring, kind, generous, extravagant, comforting. We help them to know that "it's normal to hurt," and that "God cares about your suffering." They find healing in their suffering as they realize that "it's possible to hope" because "God is in control." Because God is holy, sovereign, and omnipotent, nothing can thwart his good purposes in their lives.

In the midst of battles against besetting sin, we help our spiritual friends to acknowledge that "even when I give in to sin, God is gracious and forgiving." Such conviction requires that they perceive both God's holiness and love. Biblical counselors assist people trapped in Satan's snare by exposing how horrible it is to sin against a holy God. However, we don't leave people there. We take them to the cross, to Christ's grace, love, and forgiveness. We expose people to the truth that "it's horrible to sin, but wonderful to be forgiven." Through the Word of God, the Spirit of God, and the people of God, we empower our repentant, forgiven spiritual friends to know that "it's supernatural to mature." Why? Because God is holy and, therefore, all-powerful and all-capable of empowering us. And God is loving. Therefore, his love is what empowers us to change. Regular exposure to the holy and loving heart of God ignites love for God in the heart of the believer, which is the only right and effective relational motivation for Christian living.

Portraits of Our Sovereign Shepherd

Isaiah 40:10 – 11 presents a captivating couplet communicating God's holy love. Isaiah invites us to gaze upon our sovereign Shepherd.

- "See, the Sovereign LORD comes with power, and his arm rules for him. See, his reward is with him, and his recompense accompanies him" (Isa. 40:10). Here we see the majesty of God's holiness — his sovereignty, his power, and his commitment to justice, to always rule in a way that is right.
- "He tends his flock like a shepherd: He gathers the lambs in his arms and carries them close to his heart; he gently leads those that have young" (Isa. 40:11). Here we see the beauty of God's love as he cares for his people, leading them with a gentle touch.

This couplet summarizes Israel's relationship with God. They had known him both in his sovereignty and his sweetness, in his sternness and his kindness, in his judgment and his mercy. He is their sovereign Shepherd — the Lion and the Lamb.

Join me on a guided tour of two exhibit halls in Isaiah's art gallery. One is filled with grand drawings of Yahweh — the Sovereign LORD — in all his majesty. In the other hall, we marvel at tender images of God — our Good Shepherd — in all his beauty.

Portraits of God's Holiness: Majesty and Glory — Our Hero

Isaiah begins his tour with the startling words, "Behold your God!" (Isa. 40:9, KJV). His words are intended to stun. No one can behold God and live. His words are also meant to remind — to remind us that Isaiah himself saw the LORD high and lifted up, the train of his robe filling the temple. "Above him were seraphs, each with six wings: With two wings they covered their faces, with two they covered their feet, and with two they were flying. And they were calling to one another: 'Holy, holy, holy is the LORD Almighty; the whole earth is full of his glory'" (Isa. 6:2 – 3).

In the Hebrew language, if you want to emphasize the perfection or the infinite nature of something, you use the same descriptor twice in a row. Isaiah does this when he tells us that God will keep us in perfect peace (Isa. 26:3). The Hebrew simply says *shalom, shalom* — peace, peace. In Isaiah 6:3, Isaiah repeats the word for holy not once, but twice. Once God is holy. Twice he is perfectly holy. Three times and Yahweh is perfect holiness squared!

By saying that God is perfectly holy, Isaiah is telling us that all of God's character is an infinite cut above. Holiness involves the perfection of all his attributes so that when we say God is merciful, we are saying that he is perfectly, infinitely merciful. When we say he is just, we mean he is perfectly, infinitely just.

The incomparability of God is essential to his holiness, as Eric Rust explains:

> God is the most unique and separate being who stands apart from men. He is transcendent in his splendor and majesty, towering in his enthroned glory above the temple, the prophets, and the people. He is not like other holy ones and his holiness takes its unique quality from his own exalted character. Indeed, the other gods are idols. Such deities shall pass away, but men will flee in fear before the terror of Yahweh.[8]

Isaiah's response to God's holiness reveals another nuance to the word *holy*. "'Woe to me!' I cried. 'I am ruined! For I am a man of unclean lips, and I live among a people of unclean lips, and my eyes have seen the King, the LORD Almighty'" (Isa. 6:5). God is perfect, he is infinitely above us, and he is absolutely pure. The biblical viewpoint relates the holiness of God to his character as totally good and entirely without evil.

Isaiah's encounter with God's holiness was no boring lecture on God's attributes. Isaiah models the response that God's holiness ought to produce in each of us: *awe*. Throughout the Old Testament, holiness is used alongside words like splendor, glory, and majesty. Psalm 96:9 speaks of the splendor of God's holiness, while Psalm 21:5 pictures God's splendor and majesty, and Psalm 113:4–7 emphasizes the radiance of God's glory. God's holiness inspires awe. He is weighty beyond all measurement. He is admired beyond all beings.

When our children were teens, our family enjoyed a three-day canoe trip in West Virginia. I was delighted each time my daughter, Marie, expressed her amazement at the scenery. "It's won-der-ful," she'd exclaim, stretching out each syllable as long as possible. When we "see" God, our souls exclaim, "Won-der-ful! Incredible! Amazing! Awesome. Magnificent. 'Hey, Amber, look out the window and behold God!'"

God is our pristine hero. We swell up with pride and want to brag about him to everyone we know. Isaiah says it like this: "Look! Sovereign Yahweh. He's coming with infinite power, his omnipotent arms ruling the universe for him. His justice riding alongside" (author paraphrase of Isa. 40:10). To a discouraged people, this was grand news. The grandest! "Our holy God will right all wrongs. Though we have suffered, he has not left us. Though evil seems to reign, in reality our good God reigns. Entrust yourself to him. Behold your hero. Your rescuer. Your white knight on his glorious steed. More powerful than Superman. More timely than the Lone Ranger. God, your sovereign hero."

Portraits of God's Love: Beauty and Grace—Our Loving Husband and Father

Isaiah goes on to describe this tender warrior: "He tends his flock like a shepherd: He gathers the lambs in his arms and carries them close to his heart; he gently leads those that have young" (Isa. 40:11). Isaiah shuttles us into the second section of his spiritual art gallery. This one marked "Portraits of God's Love: Beauty and Grace — Our Loving Husband and Father." Isaiah shows us pictures of our loving Shepherd smiling, taking care of his sheep. We view rustic images of a rugged, yet sensitive, Shepherd leading his flock to quench their thirsts beside still waters.

The same hero with the huge arms from our first gallery now scoops up a baby lamb in his caring arms. The canvas displays a series of scenes. First the scooping, then the holding, then the carrying close to his heart. All the women on our tour "Oooohh" and "Aaahhh." "So sweet." "So cute." Then they nudge the men. "Why can't *you* be like that!"

In defense of males, we can't be exactly like this because only God is perfectly good. The primary word that New Testament authors use to describe God's goodness (*agathos*) emphasizes God's relational beauty. That is, out of the goodness of God's heart overflows his generous, kind, liberal, loving way of relating to us. My Aunt Dorothy used to say, "He's such a beautiful person." She was talking about the person's soul — the way he related to others was beautiful and attractive. God's style of relating to us is beautiful.

This is why Isaiah insists that we behold the beauty of God's shepherding love. That is why David makes it his ultimate life goal, as we saw in chapter 3, to gaze upon God's beauty. "One thing I ask of the LORD, this is what I seek: that I may dwell in the house of the LORD all the days of my life, *to gaze upon the beauty of the LORD* and to seek him in his temple" (Ps. 27:4, emphasis added).

Isaiah directs our gaze to an even more attractive picture. We see a compassionate Father tenderly receiving his prodigal son back home. This is exactly what the original readers of Isaiah 40 would have seen. Isaiah begins chapter 40 with the words, "Comfort, comfort my people, says your God. Speak tenderly to Jerusalem, and proclaim to her that her hard service has been completed, that her sin has been paid for" (Isa. 40:1 – 2). Israel's suffering was just suffering sent from the holy God. Now her comfort is gracious comfort delivered by her loving God.

When we say, "God has a good heart," what we are really saying is that he has a gracious heart. Grace is the cosmic ethic — God gives generously, extravagantly. Grace is not a husband loving his attractive wife. Grace is not even a husband seeing attractiveness where others might see only ugliness. Grace is the loyal love of our divine Husband transforming our ugliness into beauty. God is the noble Husband wanting only the best for his faithless wife. He woos her and pursues her, and when she returns, he cleanses her from all her impurity. He beautifies her and then compliments her on her beauty. "You are so beautiful!" Out of his good heart God reconciles rebels, receives prodigals, and beautifies the faithless bride. He takes joy in being beautiful to the ugly.

The Christ of the Cross

If the sovereign Shepherd of Isaiah 40 is one of the clearest Old Testament pictures of God's holy love, then the Christ of the cross is *the* clearest New Testament picture. We find it difficult, John Stott writes, "to hold in our minds simultaneously the images of God as Judge who must punish evil-doers and of the Lover who must find a way to forgive them."[9] G. C. Berkouwer succinctly states the answer to our mental dilemma: "In the cross of Christ God's justice and love are *simultaneously* revealed."[10]

The cross of Christ "is the event in which God makes known his holiness and his love simultaneously, in one event, in an absolute manner," Emil Brunner writes in *The Mediator*. The cross "is the only place where the loving, forgiving merciful God is revealed in such a way that we perceive that his holiness and his love are equally infinite."[11] The Christ of the cross, Stott says, answers the question, "How can the holy love of God come to terms with the unholy lovelessness of man?"[12] The cross is where the kindness and severity of God meet. "Divine love triumphs over divine wrath by divine self-sacrifice."[13]

Work to Be Done ... Based on Work Already Done by Christ

As Shelly and Connie worked with Bethany, they realized there was a lot of work to be done. Shelly used the phrase "horizontal work based upon vertical work." By that she meant that she would be addressing only secondary issues if all she and Connie did was address the horizontal relationship between Bethany and her earthly father without also addressing the vertical relationship between Bethany and her heavenly Father. Yes, it was essential to rebuild a safe, trusting father-daughter relationship between Bethany and Steve — that horizontal relationship. But Shelly and Connie were convinced that they also needed to help Bethany to rebuild her Father-daughter relationship with God — the vertical relationship.

This did not mean that they started preaching messages on Isaiah 40 and on Christ. It meant that Shelly and Connie listened compassionately to the pain in Bethany's heart related to her father's behavior. It also meant that they started listening to and for messages (out of the heart the mouth speaks) that evidenced any breach in Bethany's relationship with Christ and any distorted views of God as Father based on Bethany's relationship to her earthly father.

Over the course of this relational process, Shelly, Connie, and Bethany did explore Isaiah 40. Bethany was able, slowly, to renew her mind with biblical images of God as her sovereign Shepherd.

As Steve and I met, we also explored Isaiah 40. Steve wept as he came to realize how his behavior as a father was warping Bethany's image of her heavenly Father. His sincere repentance, along with a humble request for forgiveness, and dramatically altered behavior (the horizontal relationship) coupled with Bethany's application of Isaiah 40 to her life (the vertical relationship) were all used by God's Spirit to reshape Bethany's view of God and to renew her trust in God as her loving and holy heavenly Father.

Taking Her to the Cross

As powerful as Isaiah 40 was in Bethany's life (and Steve's life), nothing was as powerful as taking her to the cross. Stott, in *The Cross of Christ*, writes, "The cross revolutionizes our attitude to ourselves as well as to God."[14] This is true in all areas of life, but it is especially pertinent to suffering.

The worst pain of suffering is not simply what happens *to* us, as horrific as that can be in our fallen world. The worst pain of suffering is what happens *in* us as we reflect on our suffering and as Satan tempts us to doubt God's good heart — his holiness and love. Stott captures this reality powerfully:

> The cross of Christ is *the proof of God's solidary love*, that is, of his personal, loving solidarity with us in our pain. For the real sting of suffering is not misfortune itself, nor even the pain of it or the injustice of it, but the apparent God-forsakenness of it. Pain is endurable, but the seeming indifference of God is not.[15]

The cross of Christ and the Christ of the cross smash to bits the caricature of God either as an uncaring despot (unloving) or as an impotent grandpa (unholy). Where was God when Bethany was being abused? He was not lounging on some celestial deck chair nor rocking in some celestial rocking chair. He was not forsaking Bethany. He was forsaking his Son! Stott writes, "The God who allows us to suffer, once suffered himself in Christ, and continues to suffer with us and for us today."[16]

In wrestling through these issues, Shelly and Bethany trialogued[17] about a Stott quote from *The Cross of Christ*: "I could never myself believe in God if it were not for the cross.... In the real world of pain, how could one worship a God who was immune to it?"[18] Later, Connie and Bethany trialogued about a Sinclair Ferguson quote:

> When we think of Christ dying on the cross we are shown the lengths to which God's love goes in order to win us back to Himself. We would almost think God loved us more than he loves His son. We cannot measure His love by any other standard. He is saying to us, "I love you this much." The cross is the heart of the gospel; it makes the gospel good news. Christ died for us; He has stood in our place before God's judgment seat; He has borne our sins. God has done something on the cross which we could never do for ourselves. But God does something *to* us as well as *for* us through the cross. He persuades us that He loves us.[19]

Connie wanted to help Bethany explore the place of Jesus Christ as her real, functional Savior. She wanted to help Bethany grasp the height, depth, breadth, and width of God's love for her in Christ. She wanted Bethany to ponder, in the midst of her earthly suffering, how the words "You are my beloved daughter in whom I delight" could be an endless source of joy and strength. She wanted Bethany to ponder, "What comes into my mind when I think of myself? Is it loved by God?" She wanted Bethany to understand that her affliction does not establish her identity, but her identity in Christ will sustain her through her affliction.

Good Advice or Good News?

What did Bethany need? Well, it certainly was important that her dad repent, ask forgiveness, and truly change. And, by God's grace, little by little (progressive sanctification), he did. As amazing and important as that was, for lasting personal healing and lasting heart change, Bethany needed even more than having her relationships and circumstances change.

What did Bethany need? The compassionate listening and empathetic care of her counselors — Shelly and Connie — were major aspects of the

Spirit's work in providing Bethany with healing hope. However, Shelly and Connie never pointed Bethany to themselves. They kept pointing her to who she really needed — her triune God — to Christ her Wonderful Counselor, to the Spirit her caring Comforter, and to God her heavenly Father.

What did Bethany need? The "gospel imperatives," like renewing her mind and forgiving others as Christ had forgiven her, were vital. However, the gospel is not good advice; it's good news. For lasting healing and lasting personal change, Bethany needed "together with all the saints, to grasp how wide and long and high and deep is the love of Christ, and to know this love that surpasses knowledge" (Eph. 3:18 – 19).

What did Bethany need? *Bethany needed the good news of God's good heart of holy love.*

Where We've Been and Where We're Headed

In this chapter we've made even more personal the question, "What comes into our mind when we think about God?" We said that we all ask two central questions about God: "God, do you care?" (questions about God's love), and "God, are you in control?" (questions about God's holiness). We can summarize the Christian living lessons and the biblical counseling principles of this chapter with this tweet-size statement: *To know the God of peace and the peace of God we must know our triune God in the fullness of his holy love demonstrated in the cross of Christ.*

Since God has an infinitely, eternally good heart of holy love, why does it seem so hard at times to trust his good heart? Peter addresses that question when he writes, "Cast all your anxiety on him because he cares for you" (1 Peter 5:7). Having shared the good news of God's good and caring heart, Peter then gives the bad news of Satan's lying narrative: "Your enemy the devil prowls around like a roaring lion looking for someone to devour" (1 Peter 5:8).

God cares; Satan devours. God tells the true narrative of his good heart; Satan whispers the deceitful narrative that calls God's goodness into question. In chapter 5, we'll see that the Bible, like every story, has a protagonist — God, *and* an antagonist — Satan. Every counseling contact has four main characters — the divine Counselor, the human counselor, the counselee, and the anti-counselor — Satan. We need to understand the battle for the soul in order to answer the question, "Whose version of the story will we believe — God's or Satan's?" In chapter 5, we learn the role of spiritual warfare in the process of biblical counseling and spiritual friendship.

CHAPTER 5

Engaging the Battle for Our Soul: Our Spiritual Warfare in Spiritual Friendship

You've detected by now that our congregation's ministry to Steve, Alexis, and their children was multifaceted. Part of that ministry included marriage counseling for Steve and Alexis with Roger (one of our trained biblical counselors) and me. As we prepared to counsel this hurting and hurtful couple, Roger and I kept our focus on the connection between Ephesians 5:22 – 6:9 and Ephesians 6:10 – 18.

We knew that it was no accident that Paul concludes his section on household relationships with the ominous but indispensable reminder that when it comes to family living, "our struggle is not against flesh and blood, but against the rulers, against the authorities, against the powers of this dark world and against the spiritual forces of evil in the heavenly realms" (Eph. 6:12). Paul chooses a word — *struggle* — that empathically communicates a life-and-death battle. Wrestling matches in the Greco-Roman world were won when the victor was able to press and hold down his prostrate antagonist by the neck — pinning his opponent to the ground by strangling. At times, the loser had his eyes gouged out, resulting in lifelong blindness.[1]

Roger and I knew that our counseling could not be surface and world focused because then we would act as if Steve's and Alexis's problems were only flesh-and-blood problems. According to Paul, their problems — their root struggles — were spiritual life-and-death struggles against spiritual darkness. So Roger and I pondered the role of spiritual warfare in the process of spiritual friendship and biblical marriage counseling.

Because we understood the bigger picture of the purpose of the written Word (chapters 1 – 2) and the triune holy love of the Living Word (chapters 3 – 4), we knew that Satan's unspiritual warfare emphasizes planting seeds of doubt about God's good heart. There is a battle for our view of God that governs whether we trust God's good heart. With Steve and Alexis, we wanted to explore whose view of God they would believe — Christ's or Satan's?

So over the course of much compassionate listening and seeking to know the marital story of Steve and Alexis, Roger looked first at Alexis and then at Steve and said, "Alexis, I know that right now you sometimes feel like Steve is your enemy. And Steve, sometimes you feel like Alexis is your opponent. But I want you both to consider who your real enemy is — Satan. My prayer for you is that as the four of us counsel together, you'll begin to see each other once again as partners, as teammates, as soul mates as you stand firm together against your common enemy — Satan. As Paul says in Ephesians 6:11, I pray that together you will 'stand against the devil's schemes.'"

As you read Roger's words, you're likely wondering what Roger and I had in mind as we related Satan's schemes to biblical marriage counseling. When many of us think about "spiritual warfare" and "overcoming the adversary," our minds move to eerie thoughts of demons and exorcisms. Rather than eerie thoughts, Paul and the rest of the biblical authors focus on:

- Renewed minds that understand Satan's strategy.
- Renewed hearts that apply Christ's counterstrategy.

As we connect spiritual warfare to spiritual friendship and spiritual growth, we'll follow this biblical pattern by exposing the Evil One's crafty schemes and by disclosing Christ's victorious plan for demolishing Satan's strongholds. Put simply, spiritual warfare is the battle for our minds and hearts to believe and trust the truth from God instead of lies from the Devil.

Tempted to Rebel

The Bible exposes the two-pronged attack in Satan's basic "bait-and-switch" scheme:

- First Satan tempts us to rebel against God.
- Then Satan condemns us for rebelling against God.

Satan mounts his mutiny against God through a deceitful stronghold: *God is untrustworthy*. In subtle and not-so-subtle ways, Satan places God's heart on trial, whispering insidious lies. "God is holding back on you. He wants you to jump through hoops in order to earn his love. He's stingy. He doesn't have your best interest in mind. You're better off trusting in yourself. Your resources work better than waiting on and trusting in him." To counteract Satan's challenge to God's good heart, we need to expose his seducing strategies.

Seducing Strategy 1: Enticing Us to Distrust God's Good Heart

Just as kryptonite rendered Superman powerless, so Satan's kryptonite against the believer is separation through slander. He slanders God to us and us to God. His devious design lures us away from God and tempts us to rely on ourselves. The original lie reveals the nature of all his lies — Satan wants us to doubt God's generous goodness (Gen. 3:1 – 6). As Jay Adams explains:

> The first question in history was asked by Satan: "Has God said . . . ?" By this question, Satan attacked God's Word, i.e., God's good counsel. "Perhaps His counsel is not so simple, so plain or so beneficent as it seems," he intimated.[2]

Moses warns his readers with his opening words, "Now the serpent was more *crafty* than any of the wild animals the LORD God had made" (Gen. 3:1, emphasis added). "Crafty" suggests shrewd, brilliant malevolence — a being who is clever enough to package his venomous hatred in a sugar coating. He simply wants some information, right? "Did God actually say . . . ?" He is only after a little conversation, right? "Hath God said . . . ?" He seeks simple clarification, right? "You must not eat from any tree in the garden?"

"Hath God said" seduces Eve to ask, "Why is God a 'Must Not God?'" The serpent is not simply saying, "Do I have it right?" He is implying, "God said what!?"

God, of course, had said, "You are *free* to eat from *any* tree in the garden; but you must not eat from the tree of the knowledge of good and evil, for when you eat of it you will surely die" (Gen. 2:16 – 17, emphasis added). The serpent sidesteps, alludes, and ultimately ignores God's generous benevolence and twists his one prohibition — a protective prohibition meant to teach God-dependence and intended to spare us from the consequences of self-sufficiency.

The serpent is not finished. He blatantly calls God a liar: "You will not surely die" (Gen. 3:4). Then he shoots the poisoned arrow. "For God knows that when you eat of it your eyes will be opened, and you will be like God, knowing good and evil" (Gen. 3:5). "God is withholding! God is terrified that he might have to share some of his glory. God hoards his gifts so he alone can enjoy them." Michael Horton captures Satan's scheme well. "Satan's first strategy was to persuade Eve that God was stingy and narrow-minded.... The assumption is that God is just keeping us down, holding us back from realizing our own inner potential and divinity."[3]

Satan wants us to see God as our enemy, thus disconnecting us from God. Thwarting the pursuit of supreme joy, delight, and provision is his aim. Rather than seeing God as our gracious Creator who creates beings in his image with a will empowered either to obey or rebel, Satan deludes us into seeing God as our cruel taskmaster who suppresses our freedom and demands that we grovel. The marquee scrolling across our minds trying to reinterpret life reads: *God Against Us*. This becomes the dominant lens through which our flesh interprets life. We no longer give our loving Father the benefit of the doubt. We view every event as conclusive proof that God is not for us.

Sin is like a malicious virus that relentlessly seeks to erase our memory of our trusting relationship with our trustworthy God. What if Adam and Eve had reminded each other that every good and gracious gift comes down from the Father of lights? What if they had recalled that God gives us richly everything to enjoy? Because they did not, they became susceptible to Satan's second seducing strategy.

Seducing Strategy 2: Enticing Us to Trust Our Own Heart

Doubting God inevitably leads to trusting self. Michael Horton again insightfully explains that Satan was tempting Eve to interpret reality instead of trusting God's revealed interpretation. The end result then and now is that we all must answer the question, "Do I define the Jesus story or does it define me?"[4]

In Genesis 3:6, Adam and Eve eat the forbidden fruit and their fall is complete. In Genesis 3:7, they realize their nakedness and cover their shame on their own. Imagine what might have happened had Adam and Eve cried out to God between Genesis 3:6 and 3:7:

> Then the eyes of both of them were opened, and they realized they were naked, standing exposed as failed and flawed male and female, naked before him with whom they have to deal.
>
> Then the naked man and the naked woman heard the song of the Lord God as he was walking in the garden in the cool of the day, as he always did for fellowship. And they stayed.

Adam cried out to God, "I am unworthy to be called your son, for I have sinned against you in my self-sufficiency. I have failed to be the courageous and responsible male you designed and called me to be. I have been a coward rather than a guardian. Make me like one of your animals, for I am soulless."

Eve cried out to God, "I am unworthy to be called your daughter, for I have sinned against you in my self-sufficiency. I have failed to be the completing female you designed and called me to be. I have poisoned rather than nourished and cultivated. Make me like one of your animals, for I am soulless."

Instead, the LORD God slew the innocent animals he had handcrafted. He shed blood. Carefully, tenderly, he handcrafted robes of righteousness for his son and his daughter.

Then he ran to them, threw his arms around them, kissed them repeatedly, and whispered gracious assurances of his love in their ears. The Father said to his angelic servants, "Quick, bring the robes that I have handcrafted and put them on my son and my daughter. Put rings on their fingers and sandals of peace on their feet. Bring the fatted calf and kill it. Let's have a feast and celebrate. For this son of mine and this daughter of mine were dead and they are alive again." So they began to celebrate!

Grace means never having to cover our sin ourselves. But Adam and Eve, having doubted God's goodness, do not embrace his grace. Instead of depending on God, they depend on themselves. Naked and afraid, they ashamedly hide. As terrified rebels, they turn their backs on and run from God. Seeking righteousness through their own efforts, they sew fig leaves together to make coverings for themselves. They attempt to make themselves attractive and acceptable by trying to beautify their ugliness.

In the flesh we use every strategy at our disposal, every scheme we can imagine, to not need God's grace. Whenever we mistrust God's good heart, we always trust our own fallen hearts. What fig leaves do you and I sew to cover our shame? What view of God does such shame and hiding suggest?

Condemned for Rebelling

Once we succumb to Satan's scheme, we might imagine that he would applaud us. "Atta boy! Now you're getting it. You're on my team now." But instead, once we bite his bait, he lures us in, fries us, and eats us alive. "You fool! You sinner! How could you have disowned God? Now he hates you. You're ugly, unwanted, filthy, puny, and putrid. What a mess you're in. Run. Hide. Be ashamed. Be afraid."

Condemning Tactic 1: Accusing Us to God

First Satan tempts us to sin, and then he taunts us for having sinned. Puritan writer Thomas Brooks explains how Satan presents the pleasure and profit of sin, but hides the misery that follows.

> Satan's first device to draw the soul into sin is to present the bait and hide the hook. He paints sin with virtuous colors. After having tempted us to sin and to mind sin more than Christ, then he makes us believe that we are not good because we were beset by temptation and cannot enjoy God as we once did. The moment we give into temptation, Satan immediately changes his strategy and becomes the accuser.[5]

Consider three passages picturing Satan's condemning narrative: Job 1 – 2; Zechariah 3:1 – 10; and Revelation 12:7 – 10. In Job, Satan accuses Job of being a fair-weather follower of God. In Zechariah, he slanders the filthy-attired priest, Joshua. In Revelation 12:10, he is rightly labeled "the accuser of our brothers." Satan not only accuses God to us, he accuses us to God.

And how does God respond? He looks to the cross; he looks at his Son. "Who will bring any charge against those whom God has chosen?" (Rom. 8:33). The answer, of course, is Satan brings the charges. However, the answer is much more than that. God is saying, "No one can bring charges *that stick*, charges *that condemn*." "If God is for us, who can be against us? He who did not spare his own Son, but gave him up for us all — how will he not also, along with him, graciously give us all things?" (Rom. 8:31 – 32).

Satan is always working against us, but is never victorious. Since Christ died for us while we were his enemies, certainly now that we are his family, his grace covers our sin. His grace covers our disgrace. Therefore, nothing in all creation, including the powerfully evil creature Satan, can ever "separate us from the love of God that is in Christ Jesus our Lord" (Rom. 8:38 – 39).

Condemning Tactic 2: Accusing Us to Ourselves

So Satan fights a futile battle to persuade God to condemn us. Unfortunately, he's more successful with his attempts to convince *us* that we are contemptible. The great Reformer, Martin Luther, experienced these attacks and fought to overcome these demonic character assassinations:

> The Deceiver can magnify a little sin for the purpose of causing one to worry, torture, and kill oneself with it. That is why a Christian should learn not to let anyone easily create an evil conscience in him. Rather let him say, "Let this

error and this failing pass away with my other imperfections and sins, which I must include in the article of faith: I believe in the forgiveness of sins, and the Fifth Petition of the Lord's Prayer: Forgive us our trespasses."[6]

Satan seeks to fill our souls with shame that separates us from God. "Give up on life. Throw in the towel." Paul labels this "worldly sorrow" that produces death (2 Cor. 7:10). Satanic shame involves self-contempt and self-disgust that cause us to despair of all hope that God could love a sinner like us. Condemning shame convinces us that God has forever justly rejected us. Godly sorrow, on the other hand, is guilt that leads us to return to God. It is guilt that escorts us to grace. It reminds us of our absolute dependence on Christ's grace and invites us to return home to our forgiving Father. Shame separates; sorrow connects.

Condemning Tactic 3: Accusing Us to and through One Another

If we have faith like Luther, we can overcome Satan's second condemning methodology. However, before we celebrate prematurely, we should remember Satan's persistence and remind ourselves of his third condemning methodology. He not only accuses us to God, and to ourselves, but he also accuses us to and through others.

James is aghast that out of the same mouth we release words that praise our Creator and words that curse those made in his image (James 3:9 – 10). He calls this a "restless evil, full of deadly poison" (James 3:8). More than that, he identifies the source of our bitter envy, selfish ambition, and divisive speech — it "is earthly, unspiritual, of the devil" (James 3:15).

Luther's practical eye, trained by his lifelong battle against Satan, helps us to see the connection between our devouring words and Satan's diabolical methodology.

> There is no person on earth so bad that he does not have something about him that is praiseworthy. Why is it, then, that we leave the good things out of sight and feast our eyes on the unclean things? It is as though we enjoyed only looking at — if you will pardon the expression — a man's behind. The devil gets his name from doing this. He is called Diabolos, that is, a slanderer and reviler, who takes pleasure in shaming us most miserably and embittering us among ourselves, causing nothing but murder and misery and tolerating no peace or concord between brothers, between neighbors, or between husband and wife.[7]

Diabolos, the Devil, loves division. He attempts to separate us from God through shame that tempts us to run, hide, and cover; he strives to separate us from ourselves through shame that produces self-contempt and the disintegration of our shalom; and he toils to separate us from one another through shame that divides and conquers.

In the midst of Satan's insidious seductions and shrewd tactics, we could be tempted to give up, to raise the white flag of surrender to our enemy. Yet God calls us to be "more than conquerors" (Rom. 8:37). But how? What is Christ's victorious counterstrategy in our spiritual warfare against the Prince of Darkness?

Christ's Counterstrategy

We've seen that God is the eternal community of selfless love who graciously created us to revel in and reveal his goodness (Gen. 1; John 1; John 17; Eph. 1). Could any script be better written? Could any lead actor or actress ever receive a better role?

What's the problem then? A great liar, the great Liar attempts to rewrite the script. Satan, the sinister antagonist, sneaks in his revisions. Paul warns us about them. "See to it that no one takes you captive by philosophy and empty deceit, according to human tradition, according to the elemental spirits of the world, and not according to Christ" (Col. 2:8, ESV). It is an alluring script with vicious hooks to captivate our soul's attention.

At the end of life, each of us must answer the question, "Whose story has captured my soul?" Our role in the story is to counter Satan's subversion. "We demolish arguments and every pretension that sets itself up against the knowledge of God, and we take captive every thought to make it obedient to Christ" (2 Cor. 10:5).

We live our lives amidst two competing interpretations of life. In this competition, this warfare, "We do not wage war as the world does. The weapons we fight with are not the weapons of the world. On the contrary, they have divine power to demolish strongholds" (2 Cor. 10:3 – 4). So how do we wage war? What is Christ's counterstrategy, and what is our role in it?

Victorious Strategy 1: The Battlefield Scouts

When suffering comes our way and besetting sins assault us, how do we interpret the circumstances of our life? When life's expectations take a painful

U-turn, leaving us with a new reality, how do we perceive life? Paul informs us how *not* to interpret our life story: "You are looking only on the surface of things," he warns the Corinthian church (2 Cor. 10:7). "Surface" literally means "according to facial expression," or what we might call "with eyeballs only." When suffering happens, we tend to see only what the flesh can see — mere external appearance, what is outward, only on the surface, skin deep.

Yet God has given us all that we need to see life with spiritual eyes. When Paul and Barnabas heal a man lame from birth, the citizens of Lystra and Derbe shout, "The gods have come down to us in human form!" (Acts 14:11). Paul and Barnabas respond with outrage and embarrassment.

> *We also are men, of like nature with you, and we bring you good news, that you should turn from these vain things to a living God, who made the heaven and the earth and the sea and all that is in them. In past generations he allowed all the nations to walk in their own ways. Yet he did not leave himself without witness, for he did good by giving you rains from heaven and fruitful seasons, satisfying your hearts with food and gladness.* (Acts 14:15 – 17, ESV, emphasis added)

Our God has not left us without witness. No one can look at life's gifts and doubt the goodness of the giver. No one, that is, with spiritual eyes. When we interpret life with eyeballs only, God holds us without excuse. And justly so.

> *The wrath of God is being revealed from heaven against all the godlessness and wickedness of men who suppress the truth by their wickedness, since what may be known about God is* plain to them, *because* God has made it plain to them. *For since the creation of the world God's invisible qualities — his eternal power and divine nature —* have been clearly seen, being understood *from what has been made, so that men are without excuse.* (Rom. 1:18 – 20, emphasis added)

When we observe life with eyeballs only, we will not see God's goodness, especially when life is bad. *When life stinks, our God-perspective shrinks, and when our God-perspective shrinks, our hearts stink.* And our God-perspective shrinks because Satan *crops Christ out of the picture.* Just like we can do with digital photography when we crop unwanted blemishes out of a picture, so Satan crops the holy love of God out of the picture.

But even when we are blind to God's holy love, Christ still moves toward us with holy love (Rom. 1:16 – 17). God has not abandoned us in our evil world. With spiritual eyes, with faith eyes, we see him and his goodness every-where — his fingerprints are visible and detectible (Acts 17:24 – 31).

Faith is the assurance of things we can't see with eyeballs only. Without faith it is impossible to please God, because anyone who comes to him must believe that he exists and that he graciously rewards those who earnestly seek him (compare Heb. 11:1 – 6).

The role of biblical counselors is to facilitate the discovery of a greater God awareness through spiritual eyes that look at life through scriptural lenses. Put another way, our role is to *crop Christ and his holy love back into the picture*. We help one another to look at life with faith-eyes that perceive that God in Christ is graciously good — forgiving those who deserve judgment (2 Cor. 5:21).

Victorious Strategy 2: The Battlefield Weapon

Life, then, is a battle for our minds. How do we fight the battle? What's our strategy? When Paul explains that we do not "wage war" as the world does (2 Cor. 10:3), he uses a word that means "strategy." In Paul's day, strategy was inseparably linked to "generalmanship" — the tactics and war plans of the highest-ranking military officer. Two generals hand us our marching orders. Which general's strategy will win our minds?

Satan's grand strategy is to blind us to God's true nature. Being the father of lies, the creator of the lying narrative, he attempts to cause us to see God as the Evil Emperor, Darth Vader, or Ming the Merciless. He wants us to view God as malevolent.

Biblical counselors scout his subterfuge. Satan tempts us to reinterpret our image of God — God is a bully, Christ is our prison warden, and the Holy Spirit is an impersonal force. Satan also deludes us into reinterpreting our relationship to God — God is now our enemy.

Yet biblical counselors know Christ's counterstrategy. He opens our eyes to the true nature of life. God is our pursuing Father, and we are his adult sons and daughters. Christ is our forgiving Groom, and we are his virgin brides. The Holy Spirit is our comforting Mentor, and we are his best friends and disciples.

Two very different generals present us with two strategies — this is the battle for our minds. When Satan's lying salvos assault our position, what weapons should we use to fight back? The word "weapons" pictures a siege implement, a battering ram. These are not defensive weapons. They are offensive. Our weapons are our Father's weapons — far superior to human weapons, abilities, traditions, and philosophies (2 Cor. 10:4). The very gates — the protective walls that guard a city on a hill — of hell shall never stand against them. They will fall. What sort of weapons can demolish demonic reasoning? Truth. The Word. The Truth about who Christ is and who we are in and to Christ.

In C. S. Lewis's novel *The Chronicles of Narnia*, Aslan, the great lion, is the Christ-figure. The evil White Witch captures him, binds him, and kills him. The four children, Lucy, Edmond, Susan, and Peter, forfeit hope. Exhausted from battle and weeping, they sleep. Upon waking they're horrified to see mice gnawing on Aslan's dead body. But upon further, closer, inspection they realize that the mice are actually eating away the ropes that bind the great lion king. Before their eyes, they see him rise. With their own ears they hear him roar. They're ecstatic, yet confused. *"How? Why? What?"* they stammer.

Aslan hushes them. He explains the evil, finite, temporal magic of the White Witch. With a twinkle in his eyes, he tells them, "But she did not know of the deeper magic from before the dawn of time."[8] The White Witch, Satan, and all who follow them, perceive life with eyeballs only so they know only of the evil magic *in* time. We, with faith eyes, see the deeper magic from *before* the dawn of time. We perceive the eternal power and gracious goodness of God, who raises the dead.

The weapon of our warfare is the gospel story itself, the "magic" announcement — "Behold your God!" — that echoes from before the dawn of time. It's the power of God's love that raised Christ from the dead. This resurrection power, Paul tells us in Ephesians 1:18 – 23, is the same power that is at work now within us.

Jesus' incarnation launched God's full and final counteroffensive against Satan and sin. His death, resurrection, and ascension assure his victory. As the church, we are the outpost of God's kingdom in the world where God showcases the glory of the gospel.[9] The gospel is the wartime announcement of the victory of our king and hero who has come to slay the dragon and free his bride![10] It is our calling to remind one another daily of the wisdom, beauty, and power of Christ's gospel of grace.

Victorious Strategy 3: The Battlefield Soldiers

Our role as biblical counselors is to remind broken people of this gospel script. We're soldiers in a battle standing back-to-back as spiritual friends speaking God's truth in love. We provide grace relationships of compassion and present grace narratives with discernment using the weapon of truth — God's Word. We take down enemy lies and take captive enemy plans.

Our general commands us to demolish strongholds, arguments, and every pretension that sets itself up against the knowledge of God (2 Cor. 10:4 – 5). The word "demolish" means to take down by force by destroying the foundation. It pictures knocking the props out from under someone, knocking them off their feet.

In high school wrestling, the best wrestlers are those with the best take-downs. As a wrestling coach, when I teach young wrestlers to do takedowns, I teach them that their opponent's arms are like a moat or a gate preventing them from reaching the castle. The castle's foundations are their legs. To take someone down, they have to take control of their opponent's legs by knocking them out from under them.

In a similar way, the Bible tells us that we wrestle against principalities and powers. We must take down and dethrone their foundational strong-holds, arguments, and pretensions. "Strongholds" is a military term referring to a fortress or fortified place. The word came to be used metaphorically for anything on which someone relies for strength or security. In 2 Samuel 22:3, God holds the title of our stronghold.

We must rip the foundations out from under all bastions of human reasoning that say, "I don't need God!" We must demolish every non-God story of life. We must pulverize every God-is-not-good life narrative.

And in place of these lies and deceptions, these false stories, biblical counselors apply the victorious gospel narrative: You were buried with Christ in baptism and raised with him through the powerful working of God. You have been made alive together with Christ, your sins forgiven and your debt canceled — nailed to the cross. He disarmed the rulers and authorities and made a public spectacle of them, triumphing over them by the cross (compare Col. 2:12 – 15).

A Grace Beginning

As Roger and I began counseling with Alexis and Steve, our understanding of the written Word of God, the living Word of God, and of spiritual warfare each served as a GPS for our thoughts.

- *The Written Word*: God tells his story as a gospel/grace victory narrative: his Word is richly relevant for eternal life and daily life.

- *The Living Word*: What comes into our minds when we think about God is the most important thing about us: God is our triune God of holy love.

- *Spiritual Warfare*: Satan plants seeds of doubt about God's good heart: In the battle for our hearts, whose view of God do we trust — Christ's or Satan's?

When I introduced this family to you, I mentioned a mom who was fearful and in denial, a dad who was angry and controlling, and infidelity that had previously rocked the family. I wouldn't be surprised if many of you assumed that Steve had been guilty of the infidelity. He had not. Alexis had.

Alexis was fearful because she had never truly received God's forgiveness. She told us in counseling, "I live in constant dread that the other shoe will drop — and God's hand will be on the other end of that shoe, squashing me like a bug that's pestering him." She was in denial about the true state of her family because ever since her affair, again in her words, "I have clung to the god of a perfect family with me as the perfect wife and mother."

Alexis was relying on her perfectionistic self-sufficiency as her stronghold — her place to find life, her fortified safety zone. Elyse Fitzpatrick helps us to see the connection between these strongholds and our arguments and imaginations. "Our beliefs about the sources of joy (through finding a spouse or success, for instance) are frequently experienced as colorful imaginations that captivate our hearts."[11]

Alexis does not imagine in black and white. She imagines in living color, Technicolor, big screen, Jumbotron. Her thoughts of a perfect life, a perfect family — the all-American family — are incredibly attractive. This is exactly what Paul pictured when he used the word "arguments" (2 Cor. 10:5). It's the same word that is used in Hebrews 11:19 when referring to Abraham's reasoning process — his mental calculations.

In her moments of despair, Alexis is adding up reality without factoring God into her equation. "I can't trust God to fix the messes in my life because I made such a mess of my life that he's given up on me. I either have to fix every mess myself or, when that fails, pretend the messes don't exist." In those instances, she shuts her thoughts off from God. Her deliberations are warped, out of joint, sinful.

According to the apostle Paul, all such thoughts smack of arrogance. They're pretentious images that ascend like the Tower of Babel over the landscape of our minds, shouting, "We have vaulted above God! We can make life work apart from him!" Paul insists that we implode these top-most perches of audacious pride. Such pride rises above and against the knowledge of God, acting as if he is unworthy to be retained in our thoughts.

Alexis began to experience lasting victory when she recognized the horrors of her sin. "I'm saying that God is unforgiving! My perfectionism is one constant penance — my effort to pay my own ransom, to pay the price that only Christ can pay, to pay the price that Christ *already paid*." Her God was all holiness and no love — and in the end her God was neither holy nor loving — just condemning.

As biblical counselors interacting with Alexis, Roger and I wanted to help her to see with spiritual eyes who God is and who she is in Christ. This follows the passion of our Commander in Chief, who orders us to take captive enemy plans (2 Cor. 10:5). Literally, we are to make our thoughts prisoners of war without any rights or power. When Paul wrote of "thought[s]," he used a word that means plans, plots, and schemes. He chose the identical word in 2 Corinthians 2:11 for Satan's thoughts, his schemes, designs, and plots. Satan's scheme is simple. His plot goes like this: "You don't need God. He's not so hot (not so loving, not so holy), anyway. You can make it on your own." At root, all sin follows this same plot line, this same story line — to minimize God by blinding us to the glory and beauty of his triune holy love. John Piper expresses this well:

> Sin is what you do when your heart is not satisfied with God. No one sins out of duty. We sin because it holds out some promise of happiness. That promise enslaves us until we believe that God is more to be desired than life itself (Ps. 63:3). Which means that the power of sin's promise is broken by the power of God's. All that God promises to be for us in Jesus stands over against what sin promises to be for us without him.[12]

As Alexis's biblical counselors, we wanted to help her to pluck out her eyeballs-only thinking, and we wanted to do it in a creatively powerful and uniquely personal way. "Alexis, here's the picture that I'm sensing. You've been handed two blueprints for your life. One instructs you to rebuild your broken life just like Adam and Eve did — with your own creation, your own fig leaves. Your fig leaf starts with trying to construct the perfect home by being the perfect wife and mom. When that doesn't work, and it never can, then you try on the fig leaf of denial — turning a blind eye to the very real and serious troubles in your home. But beneath both fig leaves is a root — it's a root that's crept into every crevice of your heart. You named it well earlier — 'God is unforgiving.' Until we uproot that root, you'll never find peace, and you'll never experience the forgiveness your heart longs for.

"The other blueprint terrifies you, yet attracts you. Before the architect even thinks about handing it to you, he reaches out his hands to wrap you in his embrace. Those hands are nail-scarred. And the scars scare you. For if you accept the embrace of his nail-scarred hands, you have to truly face your sin-marred heart. And you have to lift up your hands in utter dependence, no longer trusting in your goodness, but in his."

Alexis needed to apply Christ's gospel of grace to her personal life and her family life. To defeat Satan, she needed the joy of the Lord's holy love. Matthew Henry, in his commentary on the Bible, wrote: "The joy of the Lord will arm us against the assaults of our spiritual enemies and put our mouths out of taste for those pleasures with which the tempter baits his hooks."[13] Of course, this was not the end of our counseling with Alexis or of our marriage counseling with Alexis and Steve. But it was a beginning — a grace beginning.

Where We've Been and Where We're Headed

Every biblical counselor must ponder the question, "Whose view of God does my counselee believe — Christ's or Satan's?" Here's our tweet-size summary of the biblical counselor's spiritual warfare calling in response to that question: *Because Satan attempts to plant seeds of doubt about God's good heart, God calls us to crop the Christ of the cross back into the picture.*

Having built a biblical counseling foundation of knowing the written Word of God (chapters 1 – 2) and the living Word of God (chapters 3 – 5), we are ready to learn together in chapters 6 – 7 about "Creation: Understanding People." In seeking to answer the questions, "Who am I?" and "Whose am I?" we can either trust what the creature says about the creature, or we can trust what the Creator says about the creature.

Believing that Jesus knows people, we will seek to understand people biblically by examining a spiritual anatomy of the soul. In chapter 6, we'll consider a comprehensive understanding of people that leads to people helping that helps the whole person to become whole in Christ — our inner life increasingly reflecting the inner life of Christ.

CHAPTER 6

Examining the Spiritual Anatomy of the Soul: Our View of People

Picture Mike seated across from you. He's just begun unfolding his story of struggles with fear, anxiety, worry, and panic. How you respond and how you relate to Mike depend on several factors.[1]

First, every counselor has a theory of knowledge. We may not all be aware of ours, or even know that we have one, but we all trust some *source of insight for living*. Sitting down to minister to Mike, we're all asking ourselves the questions, "Where can I find answers for Mike? Where do I find wisdom for life in a broken world?" I maintained in chapters 1 – 2 that for the Christian, our sufficient source of knowledge about matters of the soul is God's rich, robust, relevant revelation in Scripture.

Second, how we respond and relate to Mike is conditioned by our *view of reality*. The ultimate reality question revolves around our view of God. "Who is God? Do I even believe he exists? Is he caring and in control?" What comes into our mind when we think about God is the most important factor, not only about our counselee, but *also about ourselves as counselors*. In helping others, how the counselor answers this question makes a huge difference: "Whose view of God will I believe — Christ's or Satan's?" I developed the thesis in chapters 3 – 5 that reality is relational because God is a Trinitarian God of holy love.

We unite our theory of knowledge and our view of reality by pondering another ultimate life question, "In what story do I find myself?" How we answer that question as Mike's counselor is just as important as how Mike answers that question. Are we part of a story where we're our own source of wisdom for living and where reality is the result of a chance evolutionary process? Or are we part of a grand gospel story that is sovereignly and affectionately guided by a God who has a good heart and whose Word is our loving source of wisdom for living?

There is a third factor that determines how we respond and relate to Mike. It includes three aspects wrapped into one question that every counselor must ask and answer, "What is my view of people, problems, and solutions?" We'll explore biblical answers to this threefold question throughout chapters 6 – 12 and 15 – 16.

- *Creation: Understanding People* (chapters 6 – 7) — Whose am I? Who am I? What is the nature of human nature? What is the shape/design of the soul? What does a healthy human being look like?

- *Fall: Diagnosing Problems* (chapters 8 – 10) — What's the root source of our problems? What went wrong? Why do we do the things we do?

- *Redemption/Sanctification: Prescribing God's "Soul-u-tions"* (chapters 11 – 12 and 15 – 16) — How does Christ bring us peace with God? How does Christ change people? How do we find peace with God? Why are we here? How do we become like Jesus?

A counselor's answers to these questions shape every aspect of his or her response and relationship to Mike. They shape how the counselor views Mike (understanding people), how the counselor assesses the root causes of Mike's core issue(s) (diagnosing problems), and how the counselor perceives and presents the route to change with Mike (prescribing solutions).

While I understand that as biblical counselors we get nervous with words like "psychology," "psychopathology," and "psychotherapy," every counseling model addresses these categories. Think of it like this:

- "Is my *psychology* model — my understanding of people (Creation) — biblical?"

- "Is my *psychopathology* model — my diagnosis of root causes/problems (Fall) — biblical?"

- "Is my *psychotherapy* model — my approach to caring and prescribing cures (Redemption/Sanctification) — biblical?"

I'm not suggesting that biblical counselors start using these terms or that we start calling what we do "psychotherapy." I'm simply highlighting that every counselor, pastor, people-helper, and spiritual friend must examine these three ultimate life questions. In chapters 6 – 12 and 15 – 16, we'll probe these questions *scripturally* by seeking to understand the nature of human nature as designed by God, marred by sin, and redeemed by grace.

In chapters 6 – 7, we start with the age-old question every human being has always asked and that Mike is asking, "Who am I?" We'll place that question into the context of God by asking it as, "Whose am I?" And we'll place that question into the context of God's grand narrative by asking, "In what story do I find myself?"

Pursuing God's Target: The Image of God — God's Design of the Soul

In developing a biblical understanding of people, we could begin at the Fall and highlight human depravity. Some biblical/Christian approaches to counseling seem to start here, which is understandable, given our desire to address the deep impact of sin. While we'll thoroughly address sin in *Gospel-Centered Counseling*, we won't start there. That would be like a medical student examining diseased cadavers before ever learning the basic anatomy of the *healthy* human body. We'll begin at the beginning, where we'll learn from the One who made us in his image as we examine the spiritual anatomy of the soul. In doing so, we'll discover that life as we now find it is not the way it was supposed to be.

In the film *Grand Canyon*, an attorney attempts to bypass a traffic jam. His route takes him along streets that are progressively darker and more deserted. His expensive car stalls on a secluded street patrolled by a local gang. The attorney manages to phone for a tow truck, but before it arrives, three young thugs surround his disabled car and threaten his life. Then, just in the nick of time, the tow truck driver arrives. Savvy enough to understand what is about to go down, the driver takes the leader of the group aside to introduce him to metaphysics.

"Man," he says, "the world ain't supposed to work like this. Maybe you don't know that, but *this ain't the way it's supposed to be*. I'm supposed to be able to do my job without askin' you if I can. And that dude is supposed to be able to wait with his car without you rippin' him off. Everything's supposed to be different than what it is here."

The creation narrative teaches us how things were *supposed to be* — including how we were meant to live life with God and with each other. It teaches us God's *original* design for the soul — the nature of human nature as bearers of God's image — the *imago Dei*. It enables us to answer the questions, "What is health? What does a healthy image bearer look like?"

"Very Good!"

While our triune God did not *need* relationship with us, he did create us for relationship with him. What sort of being could be fitted for intimate relationship with our Trinitarian God? Only a being created in the image of God. Our first parents entered the universe by cosmic conception marvelously fashioned to reflect God, relate to God, rule under God, and rest in God (Gen. 1:26 – 28).[2]

God takes great care to assure that he has our attention before he announces his intention to create us in his image. The literary and theological arrangement of Genesis 1 builds to a crescendo. Day after day, the hovering Spirit nurtures a home fit for a king and a queen. Reading the creation account for the first time, we are left with the nagging question, "Who is all of this for? Who is worthy to rule this blue sphere?"

Every day for five days God said, "Let there be" and "Let the . . ." Abruptly, as day six dawns, the Trinity communes together, "Let *us*." The angelic hosts stop. They take note. Something very personal is afoot.

Every day for five days God had reflected on his handiwork and declared, "It is good." On the evening of day six, the Trinity boasts, "It is *very* good." Angels draw near. Hushed. Listening. Hearing.

"Very good!" A shout of exultation. "My sculpture is beautiful! I'm delighted."

"Very good!" The Trinity savors humanity. Spectacular. Superb. Wholeness. Harmonious. Pleasing.

The angels crowd closer. Amazed for five days by the luster of material creation and physical beings, Adam and Eve leave them speechless, take their breath away.

What is the essence of human nature as originally created by God? It is very good. Dignity. The apex of creation. The *imago Dei*.

Don't get nervous. We will address sin and depravity. The very fact that I need to calm our concerns highlights how easily we forget the beauty and purity of God's original design of humanity. If we're going to be helpful to

Mike, we first have to glimpse what a healthy, whole, and holy Mike was designed to look like, live like, and love like.

Soul-u-tion-Focused

There are three important reasons why we must biblically understand God's original design of people. First, the world has more than 250 different models of the human personality. Human reason seeks to understand humanity from humanity — knowing the creature through the creature. The Bible provides us with the inspired understanding of the nature of human beings. Through God's revelation, we come to understand humanity from Deity — knowing the creature through the Creator.

Second, even within Scripture-based approaches to counseling, we have a tendency to emphasize one aspect of the human personality over others. I am suggesting an approach that offers a *comprehensive* understanding leading to people helping that helps the whole person to become a whole person in Christ.

Third, knowing who God designed us to be provides us with our target or goal in counseling. The end goal of biblical counseling is our inner life increasingly reflecting the inner life of Christ (the relational, rational, volitional, and emotional capacities discussed throughout this chapter). Christ is not only the exact image of God (Heb. 1:3); he is the perfect image of the healthy and holy image bearer. As Philip Butin notes, "Calvin's most complete definition of the *imago Dei* in the *Institutes* is based on the assumption that 'the true nature of the image of God is to be derived from what scripture says of its renewal through Christ.'"[3] Our goal is not simply symptom relief, but Christlikeness. We are not solution focused; we are *soul-u-tion focused* — we focus on inner change at the heart level, at the soul level.

For us to move others toward this goal, we must grasp God's comprehensive original design for the human personality. Biblical counselors rightly talk frequently about the heart. But what is a comprehensive biblical understanding of the heart? In order to reflect God, relate to God, rule under God, and rest in God (Gen. 1:26 – 28), God designed image bearers as one comprehensive being with the following interrelated capacities of personhood:

+ Relational Beings: Loving with Passion — Affections
  + Spiritual Beings: Communion/Worship
  + Social Beings: Community/Fellowship
  + Self-Aware Beings: Conscience/Shalom

- Rational Beings: Thinking with Wisdom — Mind-Sets
  - Rational Beings: Thinking in Images
  - Rational Beings: Thinking in Ideas/Beliefs
- Volitional Beings: Choosing with Courage — Purposes/Pathways
  - Volitional Beings: Heart Motivations
  - Volitional Beings: Actions/Behaviors
- Emotional Beings: Experiencing with Depth — Mood States
- Embodied Physical Beings: Living with Power — Embodied Personality
- Embedded Life-Situational Beings: Engaging Our World — Embedded Socially
- Everlasting Beings: Created By, Like, and for God — *Coram Deo* Existence[4]

Figure 6:1 helps to capture the essence of our comprehensive nature. Notice that the innermost *core* of our being is our spirituality — our capacity for relationship with God. Note also that the entire *circumference* of our existence is God-focused — we are *coram Deo* (living face-to-face with God) beings created by, like, and for God. Everything about us shouts that we are in-relationship-to-God beings.

Figure 6:1

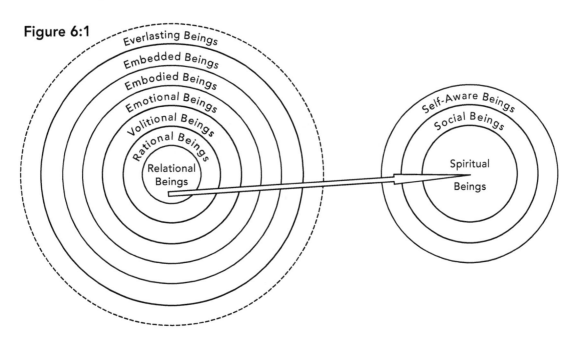

In seeking to understand people biblically and relationally, we'll journey "from the inside out." We'll trace the relational movement from our spiritual relationship with God outward toward our social, self-aware, rational, volitional, and emotional capacities. We'll then explore how we interact with our world as embodied beings and embedded beings. Finally, we'll explore the significance for counseling of the reality that we are everlasting beings whose ultimate "environment" is God.

We Are Relational Beings: Created to Love Passionately/Sacrificially—Affections

Created in the image of our loving, Trinitarian God who eternally relates in the unity and diversity of Father, Son, and Holy Spirit, we are *relational* beings. God designed us as *spiritual* beings who relate to him, *social* beings who relate to one another, and *self-aware* beings who relate to our own selves.

As relational beings, God designed us to love passionately. By passion, I do not mean romantic passion, but passion as in "Passion Week" and the "Paschal Lamb"—loving sacrifice. God made us to love sacrificially, to put others first. As God is a God of *agape* love, which initiates love for the benefit of another, so in our original design we are initiators of sacrificial love. God created us to love him wholeheartedly and to care intimately about and to connect deeply with others.

According to Jesus, love is the core of our being and our central calling: to love God and to love others (Matt. 22:35 – 40). Biblically and in church history, our relational affections have been emphasized as a key component, even *the* key component that makes us human.[5] If we are to counsel Mike powerfully, we need to understand that in the very core of his being, he has deep *affections, longings,* and *desires* (Pss. 62:5; 63:1, 8; 84:2; 143:6). God designed Mike and us to *thirst* for relationship. Without relationships we shrivel, shrink, and dry up.

Relational Longings and Desires

Thirst was God's idea. He created us with a soul that thirsts for what only relationships can quench. The Hebrew word for soul derives from a root that means "throat" and "gullet"—the organ through which we take in nourishment, fill our hunger, and quench our thirst.[6] The Hebrews used physical body parts to represent the immaterial aspects of the human personality.[7]

Psalm 63:1 is one example: "O God, you are my God, earnestly I seek you; my soul thirsts for you, my body longs for you, in a dry and weary land where there is no water."

As the throat craves physical satisfaction, so the soul craves personal, relational connection. We long for and are motivated by a thirst for intimate involvement and union with fellow personal beings (Gen. 2:18; 1 Sam. 18:1 – 3; Pss. 42:1 – 2; 62:5; 63:1, 8; 107:8 – 9; 130:6; 143:6). These longings for relationship are part of our essential being as image bearers. Speaking of both the Hebrew and Greek words for soul, nineteenth-century theologian Franz Delitzsch wrote, "As Scripture uses it, it is altogether manifest in the character of desire, predominant over everything and pervading everything."[8]

Relational Motivation

Love is to the soul what breathing is to the lungs and food to the stomach. Without connection, we shrivel; we starve to death. With mutual, giving, grace relationships, we thrive. The exact center of our being is our capacity to give and receive in relationships.

What motivates Mike to do what he does? What impels him? In training counselors, I like to tell them, "Go where the action is." The action is relational because image bearers are relationally motivated. John Piper notes, "We have an immense void inside that craves satisfaction from powers and persons and pleasures outside ourselves. Yearning and longing and desire are the very stuff of our nature."[9] Puritan writer, Henry Scougal, reminds us, "The soul of man has in it a raging and inextinguishable thirst."[10] We're motivated to quench our relational thirsts — as spiritual beings, social beings, and self-aware beings.

Spiritual Relational Beings: Created to Exalt and Enjoy Our Triune God

In Psalm 42:1 – 6, we see the threefold longing of our soul. Verses 1 – 2 highlight our *spiritual* longing. "As the deer pants for streams of water, so my soul pants for you, O God. My soul thirsts for God, for the living God. When can I go and meet with God?" David pictures a deer panting with thirst for the flowing stream of refreshing water. The word for "pant" indicates a strong, audible breathing, gasping, and panting caused by a prevailing drought. As the deer's throat thirsts for water, so David's soul thirsts for communion with God. His soul, designed by God and for God, is parched, empty, thirsty — desperate for God.

104   Gospel-Centered Counseling

God designed us as spiritual beings to worship and commune with him. The "Holy of Holies" of our soul is our capacity to love and worship God. As the deer pants for the water, so we thirst and long for God. That's our target, our GPS, our measuring rod. We help Mike, in the midst of his struggles with anxiety, to address the questions, "How well am I worshiping God? Am I thirsting after God with all my soul?"

We Are Motivated by Religious Affections

The Puritans called these spiritual longings "religious affections." By "affections" they did not mean our emotions, but something deeper. Emotions are *reactive*; affections are *directive*. As Jonathan Edwards explains: "Affections are the main-spring of human actions. The Author of human nature not only gave affections to man, but he made them the basis of human actions."[11] Earlier he wrote:

> The affections are the spring of men's actions. All activity ceases unless he is moved by some affection — take away desire and the world would be motion-less and dead — there would be no such thing as activity or any earnest pursuit whatsoever. Everywhere the Scriptures place much emphasis on the affections.[12]

The energy behind life is relational/spiritual. Relationships are fundamentally what move us. John Owen describes it this way:

> Relational affections motivate the soul to cleave to and to seek relationships. The affections are in the soul as the helm is in the ship; if it be laid hold on by a skillful hand, he turneth the whole vessel which way he pleaseth.[13]

Like God, as image bearers, we are persons in relationship. Spiritual relationships are the "Holy of Holies" of the soul because there truly is a God-shaped vacuum in the human soul.

Social Relational Beings: Created for Mutual Loving Connection

David mingles his spiritual thirst with his *social* thirst in Psalm 42:3 – 4. "My tears have been my food day and night, while men say to me all day long, 'Where is your God?' These things I remember as I pour out my soul: how I used to go with the multitude, leading the procession to the house of God, with shouts of joy and thanksgiving among the festive throng." Where once David joined with others in worship, now others mock him. Where he once was a leader of people, now he flees from the people he led. It is not good for David to be alone. He hungers for fellowship with the festive throng.

God designed us for both worship and for fellowship — to hunger for communion with him and connection with one another. The God who created us for relationship with himself also said that it was not good to be alone (Gen. 2:18). We are social beings created for community — to love our neighbor as ourselves. We help Mike to evaluate how well he is loving others. That's our counseling target: "Mike, even in the midst of your battles with fear, how are you clinging to God so he can empower you to love others well?"

Self-Aware Relational Beings: Created for Shalom

David's hunger includes a third dish. "Why are you downcast, O my soul? Why so disturbed within me? Put your hope in God, for I will yet praise him, my Savior and my God" (Ps. 42:5 – 6). David has *self-aware* longings. He speaks to himself, to his soul. Disturbed and downcast, he longs for inner peace, for shalom. He's thirsty for his original design — which is to be unashamed before God and others, at peace and rest in his identity in the triune God (Gen. 2:25). Human beings are unique among God's creation in their ability to reflect upon their inner experience.

God designed us with the capacity to relate to ourselves: We are self-aware beings. We are not computers or androids with artificial intelligence. We are not animals living on instincts. We can reflect on our own existence. In fact, Romans 12:3 commands us to reflect on ourselves accurately according to who we are in Christ. Our target with Mike is a deep self-awareness of who he is *in Christ* — and how his Christ-identity can provide peace that passes understanding.

We Are Rational Beings: Created to Think Wisely — Mind-Sets

Created in the image of our all-knowing, wise God, we are *rational* beings. We think in words (beliefs) and pictures (images) as Adam did when he gave each animal a creative name that expressed and portrayed that animal's unique nature (Gen. 2:19 – 20). God designed us with minds that can perceive his world and advance his kingdom. In that original design, God empowered us to think wisely — to think God's thoughts after him, to understand life from his perspective.

We can summarize our rational capacity with the concept of mind-sets. In counseling, we don't simply help people to change one thought; we help people to understand the pattern of their thinking — their mind-sets. This is what Paul emphasizes in Romans 12:1 – 2 when he commands us to renew our minds — our deeply held and characteristic ways of thinking about God, self, and others.

"Spiritual eyes" is an image we can use to capture our original rational nature. We are not to look at life with "eyeballs only" (from a merely earthly, temporal perspective), but with 20/20 spiritual vision (2 Cor. 10:3 – 7). God designed us to use our imagination (Isa. 26:3), our spiritual vision to see our world, our relationships, our situations, our past, present, and future from God's perspective (2 Cor. 4:16 – 18). We are to be visionaries dreaming big dreams for God's kingdom and God's people (Eph. 3:20 – 21).

Our goal as counselors and counselees is to interpret life through eternal lenses with spiritual eyes. With Mike, we pursue and target wisdom: rational maturity which God defines as being transformed by the renewing of our minds as we look at life from an eternal perspective (Ps. 1; Rom. 12:1 – 2).

Rational Direction

The Puritans understood how the soul operates. "The choice of the mind never departs from that which, at the time appears most agreeable and pleasing."[14] "The will never desires evil as evil, but as seeming good."[15]

Eve had God, she had Adam, and she had a pleasing and good earth. Yet she still sinned. Why? "When the woman *saw* (rational direction) that the fruit of the tree was *good* (relational motivation) for food and *pleasing* (relational motivation) to the eye, and also *desirable* (relational motivation) for gaining wisdom, she *took* (volitional action) some and *ate* (volitional action) it. She also *gave* (volitional action) some to her husband, who was with her, and he *ate* (volitional action) it" (Gen. 3:6, emphasis and parentheses added). Eve chose what she concluded was good, pleasing, and desirable.

We can outline how our complex heart capacities work together.

+ I pursue (volitional action) what I perceive (rational direction) to be pleasing (relational motivation).

+ What I believe (rational direction) about what satisfies my longings for relationship (relational motivation) provides the direction that I choose to pursue (volitional action) and determines my response (emotional reaction) to my inner and outer world.

+ I do (volitional) what I determine/decide (rational) I delight in (relational).

Our Relational Imagination: Pictures of Reality

We are captured by what captures our imagination. "And God saw that the wickedness of man was great in the earth, and that every imagination (*yçser* — to fashion, form, and frame) of the thoughts of his heart was only evil continually" (Gen. 6:5, KJV, parenthesis added). Notice that it is not simply the heart, nor even the thoughts of the heart, but the *imagination* of the thoughts of the heart that God identifies as the root source of wickedness and, therefore, the root source of righteous, wise thinking.

What is this mysterious imagination? In a physical sense, the Hebrew word pictures the potter fashioning and shaping clay. In an abstract, internal sense, the word depicts how we fashion, frame, devise, and purpose in our minds, how we form a summary picture of reality as we perceive it. Thus, the Bible can employ *imagination* for our mind's ability to fashion idols of the heart. However, it can also use *imagination* in a very positive sense. "You will keep in perfect peace (*shalom, shalom*) him whose mind (*yçser*) is steadfast, because he trusts in you" (Isa. 26:3, parentheses added). With our imagination, we can form mental pictures of life where Yahweh is our Tower of Power or where pieces of wood and stone are our place of safety.

Our imagination consists of summarizing pictures, images, stories, and narratives that control our convictions. Mike might be captured by an image such as, "Life is filled with giants and I'm a loser with no slingshot and no smooth stones. I'll do what I always do — run away with my tail tucked between my legs." Or Mike might be captivated by an image like, "While I don't have a single rock to fight with, Christ is my Rock of Ages! I'll guard the garden because Christ guards my soul." Simply telling Mike, "Be anxious for nothing," is correct, but insufficient. We would want to help him decipher which images control his affections, cognitions, interactions, actions, and reactions.

The Puritans developed an entire biblical psychology based on the imagination. Consider Timothy Keller's summary of their psychology of the imagination:

> One of the earliest Puritans to define the "imagination" was Richard Sibbes (1577 – 1635). He wrote that imagination was a "power of the soul" which is "bordering between our senses on the one side and our understanding on the other." The office of imagination "is to minister matter to our understanding to work upon." However, sinful imagination usurps and misleads the understanding. Charnock is more specific, for in a sermon he states that the imagination is the place of the "first motion or formation of thoughts." The imagination was not a power designed for thinking, but only to receive

the images impressed upon the sense, and concoct them, that they might be fit matter for thoughts; and so it is the exchequer (bank account) wherein all the acquisitions of sense are deposited, and from thence received by the intellective faculty. Thought engenders opinion in the mind; thought spurs the will to consent or dissent; it is thought also which spirits the affections.

Let us pause for a moment to summarize what is being said. Modern cognitive therapists see "thinking" as fundamental to behavior and feeling. If we change the thinking, we can change the feelings and thus behavior, so goes this approach. However, the Puritans considered imagination, even more fundamentally than thinking, as the control of the behavior. Imagine two thoughts sitting on the intellect: "This sin will feel good if I do it" and "This sin will displease God if I do it." Both are facts in the mind. You believe both to be true. But which one will control your heart? That is, which one will capture your thinking, your will, and your emotions?[16]

The Puritans answered: the one that possesses the imagination will control the soul, mind, will, and emotions. The imagination makes a thought real or vivid. It is the faculty for appreciation and value. It conjures up pictures which create thoughts that direct our longings, illuminate our minds, move our wills to choose, and stir our emotions.

In summary, the imagination is more basic, base, and rudimentary than language. Our imagination is our ability to think in pictures — pictures that summarize our basic view of life. Originally used of the cast, mold, or form used for shaping or framing something, the imagination relates to the framing of thoughts ingrained in the heart.[17] It is thinking in parables — representative, symbolic thinking, thinking that makes comparisons (co-pare, co-parable, to make a corresponding picture of a verbal reality).

Remember elementary school "show-and-tell"? Wasn't it one of your favorite times of the school week? You or a classmate could bring in some treasured possession, show it, describe it, touch it, feel it, and see it. You loved concrete, pictorial thinking. The imagination is the show-and-tell of our minds.

Our minds do not simply react to sensory input instinctively like animals, nor do we store input like computer chips. We *story* input. We do something with it; we have a say in forming, shaping, molding, and organizing input. We are meaning-makers. More than that, we must do something with it. To survive, we organize. We pattern truth. We "theme" our perceptions. In this, we are like God — in his imagining image (Ps. 139:15 – 18; Is. 46:10 – 11; Jer. 18:11 – 12).

The imagination is God's gift of the capacity to organize input into images that lead to interpretations and result in ideas (beliefs). We form the multitude of our life events into a comprehensive narrative by "storying" reality. We weave together a theme from the individual events of our lives in order to make sense of life and to have a sense of control/mastery over life.

The imagination is like the editor of, say, a liberal newspaper. This editor edits in and out and constructs the final shape of the article of belief. This slant filters how I perceive reality. If it filters out God, grace, generosity, goodness, relationship, being my brother's keeper, etc., then I am competitive rather than cooperative, a hoarder rather than a sharer, self-sufficient rather than dependent on God and interdependent with others. The mind set on the flesh allows the fleshly brain to continue to edit my new perceptions so that they fit with the current mind-set of the world, the flesh, and the Devil. The mind set on the Spirit rejects the lies of the world (Satan's law meta-narrative, his diabolical imaginations) and is transformed by receiving the mind of Christ and the grace meta-narrative.

We Are Volitional Beings: Created to Choose Courageously—Pathways/Purposes

Created in the image of our all-powerful God who creates out of nothing and whose purposes no one can ever thwart, we are *volitional* beings who act purposefully. God created us not as robots, but as sons and daughters with a will to choose his will. We are not animals who react on instinct, nor are we computers that act on input. We are human beings with a motivational capacity to act on the basis of our beliefs about what quenches our relational thirsts (Gen. 3:6).

God designed us to relate, to think, and to choose. We have a will to set and pursue goals (Prov. 20:5). We are motivated by what we believe will satisfy the deepest thirsts in our soul. So in counseling we don't only encourage people to change their behavior; we empower people through Christ to make changes at the level of deep heart motivation (Prov. 16:1–2).

As originally designed by God, we are capable of choosing courageously instead of selfishly or cowardly. Like William Wallace in *Braveheart* when he was being tortured, our will shouts *Freedom!* We fight bravely to free others.

Just as we can summarize our longings with *affections* and our thoughts with *mind-sets*, so we can summarize our ability to choose with the words *pathways or purposes*. We tread a path in our actions as we habitually train ourselves either toward righteousness or toward evil. Joshua recognized our capacity to choose a certain life direction when he exhorted God's people to "choose for yourselves this day whom you will serve" (Josh. 24:15).

In Paradise, God gave humanity dominion (Gen. 1:26 – 28). Adam and Eve were to subdue the planet, expanding the reign of Paradise until all was Edenic. They were to be faithful stewards serving their Creator by being co-creators, vice-regents, and under-shepherds. Satan came to heist their reign, our reign. In our fallen state we declare, "My will be done! My kingdom come!" We are still willful, but stubbornly and rebelliously so. Christ came to restore us to our original state. In our redemption we can say, "Not my will, but yours be done."

Thus, we have our next target. We are called to be a part of the amazing process of helping Mike to pursue the purpose/motivation of courageously and unselfishly loving others for God's glory — even while struggling against fear and worry.

We Are Emotional Beings: Created to Experience Deeply—Mood States

Created in the image of our passionate and compassionate God, we are *emotional* beings who experience life deeply and internally. God created us to feel. Though the Christian world sometimes makes emotions "the black sheep of the image-bearing family," God loves emotions. Jesus wept, and so do we. The Spirit grieves, as we do. The Father rejoices, like we do. We have the emotional capacity to respond to our outer world based on our inner actions, choices, goals, beliefs, images, longings, and desires.

Like God, we relate, think, choose, and feel. We experience life deeply, responding and reacting to our external situations based on our internal affections, mind-sets, and pathways.

We can summarize our emotional capacity with the phrase *mood states*. In helping a hurting person, we don't simply try to address one emotion; instead we work with people to manage their moods — to grow in their ability to handle painful, messy, complex feelings in a godly way — to soothe their soul in their Savior.

Like a gospel choir or the composers of the spirituals, we are built to sing — to express our deeply felt emotions — both positive and negative. Like the psalmists, we are designed by God to express our inner feelings both with candid psalms of lament and with joyful psalms of thanks.

Our next counseling target is to help Mike to assess how well he is managing his moods. Is he stuffing his feelings, trying to handle them on his own, or using them like spears to harm others? Or is Mike maturely taking all his feelings to God and handling his emotions in a God-honoring way that ministers to others?

We Are Embodied Beings: Created to Live Fully — Embodied Personalities

We have been discussing the comprehensive capacities of the *heart* — our inner person. While we must focus here, we can't ignore the relationship between the heart and two central arenas of influence: the body (we are embodied beings) and our social environment (we are embedded beings).

God, who is spirit, created us as embodied beings. He is infinite; we are finite. He is divinity; we are dust made a living being (Gen. 2:7). He is noncontingent; we are contingent. He is needless; we are needy. He is independent; we are dependent. He is without limits; we are limited.

God created us to entrust us, body and soul, to his care, to enjoy embodied existence, to appreciate thankfully every good and perfect gift, and to use the members of our bodies as servants of righteousness (Rom. 6:12 – 13). The body — the flesh, our skin and bones — is God's great gift to us.

We are one holistic being with physical (body) and metaphysical (soul) capacities. The Bible clearly highlights the complex inter-working of body and soul, brain and mind. We are physical beings designed by God to live fully — to express our personhood through our physical body. God gave us a physical body and a physical brain so that we could discipline ourselves to righteousness, as Paul explains in Romans 6 — offering the parts of his body as instruments of righteousness. Like Samson, we can choose to surrender our physical body to lusts of the flesh or to works of righteousness.

In biblical counseling with Mike, we must take into account this complex inter-working and connection of the mind and body.[18] We must relate to Mike as a holistic relational, rational, volitional, emotional, *and* physical being.[19]

We Are Embedded Beings: Created to Engage Our World — Embedded Socially

Who we are is not a question we can ask without also seeking to understand the context in which we live. Biblical counselors seek to understand the influences that shape the responses of the human heart.

As biblical counselors, we seek to recognize the complexity of the connection between people and their social environment. Thus, we seek to remain sensitive to the impact of suffering and of the great variety of significant social-cultural factors (1 Peter 3:8 – 22) people have experienced. In our desire to help comprehensively, we seek to apply God's Word to people's lives amid both positive and negative social experiences — both now and in their past.

Taken together, the embodied personality and the socially embedded soul address the age-old issues of nature/nurture. As biblical counselors addressing the complex mind/body connection, we are asking the *nature* question: "To what extent does the body affect how our heart/the inner person responds to life?" As biblical counselors addressing the past and present relational experiences of our counselee, we are asking the *nurture* question: "To what extent do relationships affect how our heart/the inner person responds to life?"

While the Bible steers us away from genetic determinism (that biology is the primary cause of our behavior), it does recognize that what happens in the body can affect us spiritually (e.g., Job 2:4 – 6), and what happens in the soul can affect us physically (e.g., Pss. 32:3 – 4; 38:1 – 8). While the Bible steers us away from social determinism (that our relational situation is the primary cause of our behavior), it does clearly recognize the influence of other people on our lifestyle choices (Deut. 7:1 – 4; Prov. 13:20; Luke 6:40; Acts 4:13; 1 Cor. 15:33) and it compassionately identifies with the impact of suffering on the soul (Rom. 12:15; 2 Cor. 1:3 – 11). As biblical counselors we seek to discern how Mike — as one complex, comprehensive person (body and soul/heart) — operates in a network of personal relationships situated within a society because we understand that he is a *socially embedded being.*[20]

We Are Everlasting Beings: Created by, like, and for God — *Coram Deo* Existence

We have come "full circle." We began with the core of our being, the "Holy of Holies" of the soul — we are spiritual beings designed to enjoy and exalt our triune God. We "commence" with the circumference of the embodied, embedded soul — we are everlasting beings. We are *"coram Deo"* (in the presence of God) beings created by, like, and for God. As Ed Welch notes, properly comprehending the image of God leads "naturally to seeing that people are, at their very root, people-who-live-*before*-God and people-who-are-to-live-*for*-God."[21]

Jay Adams says it succinctly: *"God is man's Environment."*[22] Sam Williams further develops this important concept:

The Bible's take on mental health and mental disorder is theocentric. We are not just responsible for ourselves — we are responsible to Someone.... People are not the center of this mental health system. God is the only star in the system and our counselees are like moons, intended to revolve around this Son-God and to reflect His light.[23]

Thus, worship is central to the counseling process. Every counselee is a worshiper and, at the end of the day (and session), their problems are a function of what or whom and how they worship. To counsel persons made by, like, and for God means that there are no God-free zones in the counselee's life or in counseling.

Where We've Been and Where We're Headed

Each of us asks the question, "Who am I?" Because we were created for relationship with God, deep in our hearts we ask the further questions, "Whose am I?" "In what story do I find myself?" As biblical counselors, we begin to ask that question by returning to the beginning and asking, "What is health? What does a healthy image bearer look like?"

In this chapter, we learned that a healthy image bearer looks like Christ — our inner life (relational, rational, volitional, and emotional) increasingly reflecting the inner life of Christ. We've described biblically what the inner life — the heart — is. So we can capture our tweet-size summary of this chapter like this: *The whole, healthy, holy person's inner life increasingly reflects the inner life of Christ — relationally, rationally, volitionally, and emotionally.*

As a biblical counselor, you are a *biblical cardiologist*. Relational affections, rational mind-sets, volitional pathways, and emotional mood states become your diagnostic categories as you minister to people. How does a skillful biblical cardiologist, an artful soul physician "pull all of this together" when connecting with real people with real struggles? In chapter 7, we'll journey with Mike in order to answer that question in a real-life way.

CHAPTER 7

Journeying into the Heart: Our Role as Soul Physicians and Biblical Cardiologists

I was a good wrestler in high school — winning on natural ability without knowing a great deal of wrestling moves or techniques. When I went to college, my coach was one of the best wrestling coaches in the country — and a stickler on precise technique. We would drill and drill the same moves every practice. Coach Spates broke down every move into small components. His philosophy was to build a great foundation through repetition so that we increased "muscle memory" and eventually didn't have to think about the move; we hit it spontaneously, naturally, even artfully.

Well, that was the theory, but in reality, I got worse before I got better. Initially, it was all so mechanical for me. I was like the Tin Man in *The Wizard of Oz* whose immobilized joints needed to be oiled. While I was thinking about the next part of the wrestling move, my super-quick opponent had already countered my move and completed his own move.

However, in time, theory turned into practice. It was so much fun the first time my muscle memory and hours of drilling moves took over and I slickly and quickly hit a move on my opponent. I eventually became much better than I ever was in high school. I went from naturally good without proper technique, to unnaturally mechanical as I learned proper technique, to spontaneously very good with a proper foundation built.

Does this have anything to do with counseling, or do I simply like to talk about my college wrestling prowess? I always share this illustration before I start teaching the connection between counseling theory and methods. Understanding and putting into practice a biblical theory of people, though absolutely foundational, can at first make counseling seem unnatural and clinical. Instead of simply caring, your care seems forced and technical. However, with patience, your supernatural desire to care becomes blended with a biblical understanding of how to care well and wisely. In time, you become not just an effective biblical counselor but an artful soul physician, a soulful biblical counselor.

In this chapter, I'm going to be like Coach Spates — breaking down the fundamentals of a biblical understanding of people. As we build this foundation together, remember that *reality is relational* (yes, I repeat that often). Although the explanation may read like a technical process, in reality counseling is *soul-to-soul relating*. By connecting and counseling according to God's design of the soul, we become an answer to Paul's biblical counseling prayer: "And this is my prayer: that your love may abound more and more in knowledge and depth of insight" (Phil. 1:9). Our society teaches us that love is just a romantic feeling and that counseling is all about feeling compassion for our counselee. The Bible teaches that counseling is all about wise compassion — love founded on truth and grounded in biblical wisdom about the heart.

A Biblical X-Ray of the Heart in the World

Like Coach Spates, we'll start this chapter's practice session with some review as well as some further development. Thinking back to Mike and his anxiety struggles, we know that God designed Mike as an image bearer who is one comprehensive being with the following interrelated heart capacities:

- EV: Everlasting Being: Created by, like, and for God — *Coram Deo* Existence
- LS: Embedded Life-Situational Being: Engaging Our World — Embedded Socially
- P: Embodied Physical Being: Living with Power — Embodied Personality
- E: Emotional Being: Experiencing with Depth — Mood States
- V: Volitional Being: Choosing with Courage — Purposes/Pathways
  - V1: Volitional Being: Actions/Behaviors
  - V2: Volitional Being: Heart Motivations

- RT: Rational Being: Thinking with Wisdom — Mind-Sets
  - RT1: Rational Being: Beliefs
  - RT2: Rational Being: Images
- RL: Relational Being: Loving with Passion — Affections
  - SP: Spiritual Being: Communion/Worship
  - SO: Social Being: Community/Fellowship
  - SA: Self-Aware Being: Conscience/Shalom

The abbreviations at the beginning of each bullet point will help us as we track together through biblical counseling trialogues with Mike. While it can look like an abstract outline, in reality it is a biblical X-ray of the heart in the world that guides us as we seek to speak the truth in love with Mike. For teaching purposes we started in chapter 6 from the inside out — from the "holy of holies" of the soul, working outward toward the soul in the world. With Mike, we start from the outside in — moving from what he is facing externally toward how he is facing life with God internally.

Life is never nearly as linear as what we are about to present. It is helpful to think of counseling as "spaghetti relationships." It's messy. It weaves all over the place, moving back and forth and back again. So while the trialogues in this chapter are brief and linear for the sake of logical development, please understand that they represent a complex relational process that would occur over many times of counseling connection.

Journeying *In* Together: Listening to and Entering Mike's Earthly Story — Heart Probes

As Mike comes to us, we want to start by listening well to his earthly story. Mike is dealing with a fallen world that often falls on him, and he's battling against the world, the flesh, and the Devil as he seeks to respond in godly ways. We want to enter Mike's story compassionately and wisely by journeying in as we move from Mike's outer world (what happened *to* Mike) toward his inner world (what is occurring *in* Mike *with* God). As we journey in, we're engaging and entering Mike's earthly story with robust relational depth.

To sense the relational nature of our interaction with Mike, think of what follows as the skeletal outline of a journey taken with Mike. Picture it as your side of a sample spiritual conversation with Mike that is guided by a comprehensive biblical understanding of the heart. Imagine yourself connecting soul to soul with Mike as you listen to his earthly story in light of Christ's gospel story. Don't think of it simply as data collection or information gathering. Rather, think of it as soul connecting and story sharing.

Before performing open-heart surgery, a heart surgeon orders a battery of tests to probe the condition of the heart. What follows is a series of heart probes that a soul physician engages in to better diagnose the spiritual condition of Mike's heart as he responds to his world.

While we would never say these exact words in this exact way, our side of the conversation might sound something like this as we journey in, seeking to understand and explore Mike's story:

- LS: Exploring Mike's *Current* Life Situation as a Socially Embedded Being

  "Mike, what brought you here today?" Or "Mike, How can I help?" Or "Please tell me what you're facing ..."

- LS: Exploring Mike's *Past* Life Situation

  "Mike, if you were writing your life story in one chapter, what would you write to highlight what you've been through?" And "What would the title be?" Or "How would you summarize your life story in ten minutes?"

- P: Exploring Mike's Life as a Physical Embodied Being

  "How is all of this impacting you physically, Mike?" Or "Mike, as you've faced all of this, have you experienced any physical responses or symptoms, any health issues?"

- E: Exploring Mike's Life as an Emotional Being

  "How are you feeling about all of this, Mike?" Or "When that happened, how did you feel?" Or "How did you respond emotionally, Mike?"

- V1: Exploring Mike's Life as a Volitional Being — Behavioral/Actions

  "When that happened, Mike, how did you respond?" Or "When you felt like that, what did you do?"

- V2: Exploring Mike's Life as a Volitional Being — Motivational/Goals

  "What would you have liked to happen when you responded like that, Mike?" Or "Mike, what were you hoping would happen when you did that?" Or "What do you think your goal might have been?"

- RT1: Exploring Mike's Life as a Rational Being — Beliefs

  "Mike, if we played an MP3 of your thoughts right then, what would we have heard?" Or "Where do you think that perspective comes from?" Or "Mike, where do you think you might have learned that way of looking at this?"

- RT2: Exploring Mike's Life as a Rational Being — Images

  "Mike, if you were to summarize your thinking right then in one picture or image, what would it be?" Or "Mike, if you were to summarize how you see your situation right now with a book or song title, what would the title be?"

- SA: Exploring Mike's Life as a Self-Aware Being

  "Mike, if you took a smartphone pic of how you saw yourself in that split second, what would the image be?" Or "Reflecting back on it now, how do you think you saw yourself in that second?"

- SO: Exploring Mike's Life as a Social Being

  "Mike, how did all of this impact your relationships with your family members?" Or "What do you think you were wanting the most from your son/daughter/spouse right then, Mike?"

- SP: Exploring Mike's Life as a Spiritual Being

  "Where is God in all of this, Mike?" Or "Mike, what do you think you were longing for from God right then?" Or "Mike, if you wrote a 'thirst psalm' like Psalm 42, how would you word it?"

Counseling, of course, is not a series of questions and answers. The preceding dialogue simply seeks to capture in sentence summaries the essence of probing each aspect of the heart in the world. The trialogues illustrate theologically guided questions — our biblical theology of the heart is what guides our biblical counseling journey with Mike.[1]

A GPS for Our Journey with Mike

Consider chapter 6 and the first part of chapter 7 to be like the first week of college wrestling practice. Lots of new terms and techniques thrown our way ... but so far they can feel a tad disjointed, mechanical, even forced. We need a GPS to guide us as we journey with Mike.

In the introduction to *Gospel-Centered Counseling*, I outlined four biblical compass points (that we explore in detail in *Gospel Conversations*) for speaking the truth in love:

- *Sustaining: "It's Normal to Hurt"* — Learning how to weep with those who weep by offering sustaining care for hurting people — biblical empathy for the *troubling* story.

+ *Healing: "It's Possible to Hope"* — Learning how to give hope to the hurting by offering healing comfort for suffering people — biblical encouragement for the *faith* story.

+ *Reconciling: "It's Horrible to Sin, but Wonderful to Be Forgiven"* — Learning how to be a dispenser of Christ's grace by offering reconciling care-fronting for people struggling against besetting sins — biblical exposure in the *redemptive* story.

+ *Guiding: "It's Supernatural to Mature"* — Learning how to disciple, coach, and mentor by offering guiding wisdom for people growing in the grace and knowledge of Christ — biblical equipping in the *growth-in-grace* story.

Throughout the rest of this chapter, I provide sample trialogues to picture, in summary form, what you might hear if you were the proverbial "fly on the wall" listening in as Mike and I journeyed together. Our journey combines our biblical understanding of the heart with our four biblical compass points of sustaining, healing, reconciling, and guiding.

Journeying In Together: Entering Mike's Troubling Story— Biblical Sustaining

"Mike, I understand that I'm the third counselor you've seen. I respect your tenacity and persistence. Thank you for the privilege of being a part of your journey. Could you put into words *what you're facing?* Take me back as far as you think you need to go to *help me to know you* and to *begin to understand what you're going through …*" (SE).

Mike says he is thirty-five; he's been married for twelve years. He and his wife have three children, ranging in age from four to ten. Mike has a master's degree in business, has been very successful in the work world, and has advanced to a high level in the company where he works.

Mike says he was raised in a Christian home and came to Christ as a pre-teen. His father was a successful businessman who owned his own company. His mother was an elementary school principal. Mike is an only child who describes his parents as being "very driven" and as having set "incredibly high standards for me." He describes himself as "the good kid who always did what he was told and always strove for excellence and even perfectionism in sports and school."

Mike notes that he's always faced some low-grade anxiety when stress was high — "my way of coping was to work harder, faster, wiser." He calls himself a "lifelong worrier." But he added, "From one perspective, it worked! My hard work paid off—I was an all-state baseball player; I graduated second in my class in high school. But from another perspective, it never worked for me in that I've never had peace. Everyone sees me as altogether, but I always feel like I'm one failure away from falling apart."

By Mike's own admission, he's a "helicopter parent" who hovers over his three children much the way his parents did with him. However, he sees himself and his wife as "much more encouraging and affirming than my parents ever were with me."

Mike said that a year before he started to see anyone for counseling, he was in an automobile accident caused by a drunk driver. Mike was the only one in the car and sustained a concussion, several broken bones, and has had serious back problems ever since. He missed three months of work, which "were the hardest three months of my life. I worried constantly about the pile of work that I would face upon my return. I worried even more about whether I'd be replaced — if they would find out that they could manage just fine without me."

When Mike returned to work, he discovered that "some of my concerns were valid. The pile of work was almost insurmountable. And a coworker who had come up the ranks with me had been given a promotion I had worked my entire career for." In response, Mike drove himself to new heights of "both worry and work." The stress became "almost unbearable. I couldn't sleep. I was agitated and impatient. I had two occurrences of what I guess you would call panic attacks. I finally went to my doctor for some help ... I also saw two counselors from a local agency, but neither was able to help me."

After we explored the type of help he wanted from his first two counselors and the type of help he received, Mike said he is taking an antianxiety medication, "which I took reluctantly and secretly — only my wife knows — because I'm embarrassed that I can't handle this on my own." Mike says he is "praying and fasting regularly, devouring the Word, and trying to apply it to everything in my life." As he pictures it, "It's almost like I'm an OCD Christian — driven to be a perfect Christian so I can manage my anxiety better."

When I asked Mike during our first meeting what he hopes for from counseling, he responded, in part, "I want my joy back. I want my peace back. In fact, I want joy and peace for the first time in my life. I also want to be a better husband and parent — I'm so focused on my work worries that I feel I'm a distracted spouse and dad. And I want a right relationship with God. I've read my Bible enough to know that I'm pretty much like the older son in the parable of the prodigal son — it's all about *works* for me ... which I know is not what Christianity is all about."

Picture yourself having engaged Mike as you've listened and empathized with his story. He's introduced you to his life story from his perspective. Now where do you go? There are numerous legitimate options, but if we're following our biblical counseling GPS, then we could journey in, starting by exploring how all of this is impacting Mike as an embodied being.

"Mike, as I reflect on all you've shared, first I want to say, 'Thank you' for your courage in opening up like this. With everything you're going through, I'm especially encouraged that your goals are so Christ centered and other focused. Honestly, that's not always the case when hurting folks talk with me. Even with all you've shared, I can't begin to imagine what this has been like for you. But I want to. Given everything you've been through, it might be helpful to me initially to hear a little more about *how all of this may be impacting you health-wise. You've mentioned you couldn't sleep, your back problems, and that you've had two panic attacks ... Could you help me to understand more about these physical concerns?*" (P).

"Well, I've had some not-so-great reactions to the medication — at first it made me more anxious than ever. But lately I think the meds may be taking some of the edge off my anxiety. The two panic attacks were terrifying, and now I worry that my worry might cause another one! And the back pain sometimes is almost debilitating, but I just have to keep working."

After some back and forth exploring of Mike's physical concerns, I say, "That's a lot of stuff all crashing down on you at once, Mike. Your 'worry about your worry' is not uncommon at all. *How are you doing with all of this? I'd like to try to understand more about your feelings of worry about worry and the pressure you feel to keep working even when your body is screaming to stop*" (E).

"I guess it's all interrelated. I worry about my work, my back, my worry. Like I said, I've always had this low-grade anxiousness, but this is *way* different. Recently, after an hour drive to work in rush-hour traffic, my back was aching, my mind was racing, and I didn't know if I could even get out of the car to go to work."

"That had to be really difficult, Mike — physically, emotionally, mentally — every way." After interacting about how difficult this was for Mike, I said, "You had some hard choices to make in that moment as you sat in your car, didn't you. *So paint me a picture of what you did that morning*" (V1 — focused on behavior/actions).

"Well, it wasn't just that moment — I'd been prayin' the whole commute! The sweatier my palms got, the harder I gripped the steering wheel, the more I prayed."

"I can believe that! What was the gist of your prayer? *What were you asking God to do?*" (V2 — focused on goals, purposes, heart motivation, and SP — focused on Mike's walk with God).

"It was like a mantra. 'Fix it, God. Fix me, God!' I just wanted the anxiety, fear, and worry to go away with the snap of a finger. Well, it didn't go away. I sat in the car a couple minutes and then just forced myself to get out and go to work."

"Mike, that had to take a lot of self-discipline, and perhaps in a bit we could talk about where you found that strength. But right now I'm wondering *what was going on in your mind as you left your car and trekked to the office*" (RT1 with a focus on beliefs/mind-sets).

"Honestly, I was disappointed in God. I can even picture myself shaking my head as I walked to the elevator. I was thinking, 'What's the use praying? God doesn't care.' I know that's not true, but you asked what I was thinking."

"Yes, I did, and I appreciate your honesty." After further interaction about Mike's thoughts about God, I ask, "So, as you're in that elevator, *if I could somehow look at an X-ray of your mind, what MRI would I see of you, of God, of life?*" (RT2 with a focus on images).

"Funny you should ask that, because I was the only person in the elevator and I thought at the time, 'That's typical. *I'm all alone, again.* God is outside, or up there, or somewhere, just forcing me to buck up and work harder.' I don't want to go all 'psycho-babble' or blame everything on my past, but it felt like God was just like my parents had been — expecting the world of me, but not entering my world at all."

I lean forward. "Wow. First, I want you to know you're not all alone. I'm here — as a small taste of Christ always being here for you/with you. I don't say that to deny that you felt totally alone, but just to provide a context for what we both know deep in our hearts is true" (SA, SO, and SP — entering Mike's troubling inner/outer story, accepting Mike's story, and gently inviting Mike to allow God's story to invade and pervade his story).

"Second, if I could summarize, *your self-portrait* at that point was *one-part loner and one-part worker. Almost like someone exiled to a deserted island and made to work on a chain gang, but you're the only member of the chain gang! You've been given no resources, but told you have to finish a bridge back to the mainland by yourself if you ever want to join the rest of us.* And the *one giving you your marching orders is none other than God* (SA, SO, and SP — with a focus on Mike's view of himself, others, his world, and God). Where is that on-target, off-target?"

"That's not just my portrait *at that point*. You've captured well the story line I've been telling myself most of my life. I know it's not true, but yeah, that sums it up. No wonder I never have any peace."

The preceding trialogue is a sample spiritual conversation that encapsulates what could take several weeks of interaction. It illustrates movement from Mike's outer troubling world to his inner troubling world. It highlights that Mike's greatest issue is not simply what's happening *to* him, but what's happening *in* him. By joining Mike's troubling story with empathy and understanding, you've helped him to crystallize his heart issues and to see that *it's normal to hurt*.

Journeying Out Together: Entering Mike's Faith Story— Biblical Healing

Now what? We could move in a host of directions with Mike. One direction would involve an exploration of Mike's unbiblical, dishonoring views of God. This would shift our focus to *Christ's redemptive story*. Our emphasis would be on issues of repentance and forgiveness. We'll illustrate that absolutely necessary process under our *reconciling* header. Right now, we'll focus on biblical encouragement for Mike's *faith* story — biblical healing hope where we help Mike to see God and life from a biblical perspective — seeing that *it's possible to hope*. As we'll see, this faith journey *also* leads Mike to repentance.

As nice as it would be if Mike's circumstances changed, that's not his greatest need — he needs *heart* change. He needs a change in his faith relationship with God. Changed circumstances won't bring Mike lasting peace, but heart change in his view of and relationship to the God of peace will bring Mike the peace of God. Biblical peace is not the promise that the troubling story will disappear, but that Christ will appear in the midst of all our troubles (John 16:33).

Now we journey *out* with Mike. When we left our trialogue, we had just broached the holy of holies — *Mike and God*. We'll return there, exploring biblical images of Christ that can help Mike to renew his relationship to God. Then we'll travel outward as the new hope-filled, Christ-dependent Mike still has to face the same troubling world.

"Mike, last week when we wrapped up, I mentioned that the passage everyone talks about when it comes to anxiety — Philippians 4:6 — has to be applied in context. *Given your view of God as an uncaring boss who leaves you all alone, I said that it could help if you explored Philippians for different portraits of God* (SP — with a focus on renewed relationship/images of God). What did you see this week?"

"To be honest, at first it was a battle even to sit down and explore the Word — my agitation and angst were so high. So I went for a run and used my phone's Bible app and eventually saw a ton right in Philippians 4. The Lord is *near* (Phil. 4:5). The God of peace *will be with you* (Phil. 4:9). The peace of God *will guard* your hearts and minds in Christ Jesus (Phil. 4:7). When anxiety attacks me, I tend to focus so much on my situation and feelings that I lose my focus on God or accept a skewed view of him. Frankly, I've seen how sinful that is, and I've found myself receiving God's forgiveness this week."

"That's awesome, Mike! Your new view *of* God is leading to a new way of relating *to God in Christ*. Rather than being a God who leaves you alone; *he's the God who invites you to come home*" (SP).

"I was thinking too, as you quoted those verses about God guarding your heart, that what you've done this week is *guard your relationship to God your guard* (SP). I wonder if in the past you've felt alone and like you had to expend all your energy guarding yourself, but now you can 'let your guard down' and *cast all your care upon God because you know he cares for you*" (SP — with a focus on putting off and putting on).

Mike leans back in his chair and, after a reflective pause, responds, "I like that image of 'guarding my relationship to God my guard.' I think I'd been focusing on 'winning God over' and 'earning a relationship with God,' but back when we talked about Romans 8 and the truth that there's no condemnation for those who are in Christ, and that nothing can separate me from God, that launched me on a path toward some victory in my anxiety. If we had only focused on my 'earthly fears,' we never would have hit the heart issue. With that big issue of my acceptance in Christ settled, every other fear — while not wiped away — is starting to fall into place, a place I can begin to handle *with Christ*."

"I like that, Mike. It's like *you needed the assurance of your eternally secure relationship with the God of peace before you could even begin to experience the peace of God in your daily struggles*" (SP, SA, and ES — who God is and who Mike is in Christ, all related to Mike's inner fears and outer situation).

"Mike, we've talked a good deal about you and Christ — which is foundational — but we've not talked very much about you and others. Right here in the context of Philippians 4:6, Paul talks about "brothers" (v. 1), about how he "love[s] and long[s] for" the Philippians (v. 1), about how they are to "stand firm in the Lord [as] dear friends" (v. 1), and about how they are to be contending together as teammates and "fellow workers" (v. 3). *How could you invite others into your struggles?*" (SO — focused on Mike and his relationships to others).

"I've been thinking about that. I've barely even let Sandra in — she's the only one who knows I'm on medication. And even with Sandra, I feel like 'I'm the man; I need to take care of myself.' I guess I don't know how to balance being a godly, strong man who guards my wife and being a humble man who opens up to her."

"I don't think any of us have that one totally figured out, Mike. But maybe there are some clues in this passage. That term 'loyal workfellow' in 4:3 pictures people who are united by a relational bond as close as family. It pictures comrades, partners, spiritual friends — a band of brothers. The other phrase, 'fellow workers,' is *sun atheleo* — athletes together, teammates. In your case with Sandra — soul mates. *Let's talk a bit about what it would be like for you to invite Sandra in to be your teammate and soul mate*" (SO).

After some extended discussion of Mike and Sandra, Mike's focus shifts. "This has been helpful for me to think about inviting Sandra into my struggle, but she has her own struggles with mild depression. So last week I tried to share Philippians 4:7 with her, but it came across more like a quick fix or a biblical Band-Aid. My anxiety pervades everything — I was so *anxious* that she respond to my *help* that I was focused on me and not really on her."

"That's some good insight into your heart, Mike. I wonder if that indicates that before you apply Philippians 4:7 to Sandra, we need more application to your life." As Mike and I explore Philippians 4:7 together, we note that the passage doesn't promise that Mike will never feel any more anxiety, or that Sandra will never again battle depression. Nor does it promise that Mike's and Sandra's external situation would change. Instead, God is saying that through it all, God's peace will put a sentinel around their hearts and minds. I said it like this to Mike: "*God will garrison your beliefs and images so that in the midst of external stress and internal distress, you and Sandra can experience peace and rest*" (RT — with a focus on images *and* beliefs).

"*So, Mike, with your mind not focused on protecting yourself but on trusting God's protection, and with your heart now focused on being there for Sandra, what would it look like for you to journey with Sandra in an other-centered way?*" (V2 and V1 — renewed heart motivation leading to Christ-like ministry).

"First, I would ask her forgiveness for not listening well and for trying to fix her so I felt good. Then, I'd listen. And as we talked, if I sensed that sharing Philippians 4:7 could be helpful *to Sandra*, I'd share how it could apply to *both of us*. Maybe I'd try to paraphrase how you explained it to me last week. Our threat detector discerns a threat and screams, 'Incoming missile! Take cover!' Our emotions and flesh scream, 'Take control! Trust yourself!' But our new mind in Christ whispers, '*Shh*. Quiet. Rest. Trust. Look at this threat with spiritual eyes.' The threat is real; our feelings are real. There is a battle. But Christ has overcome the world. He has won the fight, so we don't have to fight in our own power. Then I'd ask Sandra how I could help her to fight her battle with depression in Christ's power."

Mike pauses. "It's easy for me to say that now with you. But thinking about really coming through for Sandra like that is, frankly, terrifying. I've barely been taking care of myself, and now I'm thinking — like I should be — of taking care of my wife."

"You're right, Mike, you're moving out of your comfort zone, and this is a lot in a few weeks. It's like you're applying Philippians 4:9, where Paul says, 'Whatever you have learned [about trusting Christ] … put it into practice' (V1). But it's right after that where Paul says, 'And the God of peace will be with you' (v. 9). And 'You can do all things through Christ who strengthens you' (paraphrase of v. 13) (SP). It's like in 1 Peter 5:7, where Peter says we cast our care on Christ because we know he cares for us. *So we take our fears to our Father. We soothe our soul in our Savior* (E). Then Peter says we do it by resisting the Devil — *the Bible never pretends that life is easy* (ES). You do it by *standing firm in the faith — gospel faith that trusts that God is with you and for you, empowering you to love others for him and through him* (SP). How could that *mind-set* (RT) impact your *fears* (E) as you think about *ministering to Sandra?*" (SO).

Journeying In Together: Entering Christ's Redemptive Story with Mike — Biblical Reconciling

In the back and forth, messy "spaghetti relationships" of biblical counseling, we'll find that sustaining, healing, reconciling, and guiding mingle together all over the place. Our illustrative vignettes so far have focused predominantly on facing suffering face-to-face with Christ — sustaining and healing. We look now at sample gospel conversations that more overtly address Mike's sin, Christ's grace, and Mike's growth in grace — reconciling and guiding.

"Mike, when we wrapped up last week, you said you wanted to talk about your relationship to your youngest son, Greg. *Where would you like to start our focus?*" (ES).

"Two weeks ago Greg, who is in middle school, brought up a struggle with a bully at school. I really blew it when I responded. I let my fears get the best of me."

"Tell me about *your fears as you talked to Greg*" (ES/E).

"I was terrified that I wouldn't have the answers for Greg. And then the terror just spiraled. If I don't have the answer, then Greg will be bullied all his life, and then Greg will be fearful all his life, and then I'll pass my pattern on to Greg."

"I can see even now that just thinking about it again brings up a lot of *those same spiraling feelings* (E). So this whirlwind of those old fearful patterns attacked you again. *Paint me a picture, as if I were there, of how you responded to your feelings and to Greg*" (V1).

Mike doesn't hesitate. "In a nutshell, out of fearing that I wouldn't know what to do, I minimized the situation and ended up basically communicating to Greg, 'Just buck up and be a man!'"

"Mike, I can tell by your voice and your words that you feel horrible about how you related to Greg. And we'll want to spend some time talking about moving back into Greg's life. But first, as you've had some distance between that now, *what do you think was going on inside? What do you think you hoped would happen as a result of how you responded* to Greg?" (V2 — focused on goals, purposes, heart motivation).

"I didn't want Greg to see how helpless and weak I felt. So I guess my goal was to *act* strong." Almost in mid-sentence, Mike realized, "Wow. I bullied *him* because I felt like the situation was bullying *me*. How sinful is that!?"

"Wow is right, Mike, but I have a different 'wow.' Wow — that's courageous insight to acknowledge that sin to yourself and to me. Makes me think of Romans 2:4 and how the kindness of God leads us to repentance. Life may have been bullying you, but right this second you're not seeing God as your bully.

"*So, it's like I hear two mind-sets — one where you protect yourself because life's been bullying you* (RT1 — with a focus on sinful mind-sets) *and one where you protect others because you experience the kindness of God and say, 'Life may bully me, but God never does'* (RT1 — with a focus on godly mind-sets). *Where do you think those two very different mind-sets come from?*" (RT — with a focus on mind-sets/beliefs).

This leads to some lengthy interaction about two very different sources of Mike's beliefs about life, God, and others. Mike concludes, "It's like I was recruited into two different armies or something."

"That's a fascinating way to put it, Mike. So, *picture for me the two generals who recruited you*" (RT2 — with a focus on images).

Mike smiles and says, "Hmm. This weird image just went through my mind. It's like the two generals are Saul and Paul. The first one is Saul before he became the apostle Paul. Rule-keeper. Finger-pointer. Condemner. Based on what we've discussed about Satan's lying, condemning, works-based narrative, it's clear now that General Saul — the five-star finger-wagging general — is me believing Satan. But the second general is Paul after he's humbled, forgiven, cleansed, and grace-focused. The Paul who says in Romans, 'Who condemns you?' That's me trusting Christ's good heart."

"Mike, I like how you say that it's you either believing Satan or trusting Christ. *So who are those 'two yous'?*" (SA).

"Well, you asked me before about the title of my life story. I guess in the first story my title, as far as how I see myself, is 'Unprotected.'"

"So, Mike, to use Greg's situation, it sounds almost like just the mention of Greg being bullied conjured up all these images where *you view yourself as bullied and God as the bully, or at least as the one who refuses to protect you and Greg from life's bullies*" (SA, SO, and SP — with a focus on Mike's view of himself, others, his world, and God).

After much intense interaction, Mike comes to grips with what he describes as his "warped, sinful, self-protective view of myself and God. It goes back to what we've said before. When I refuse to believe that God is my Guard, then I guard myself, and then I go off guard duty of ministering to Sandra and the kids."

"In Christ, you know the Father is calling you to come home to him, Mike. When the prodigal son returned home, *the Father ran to him, threw his arms around him, kissed him impetuously, and insisted that he be robed in the family clothes*" (SP — with a grace invitation to come home).

After interacting further, it is obvious that God was working on Mike's heart. I asked him if he wanted to pray. Mike didn't hesitate, leaning forward and praying, "Father, I confess as sin my dishonoring beliefs about you, my doubts about your care and control. I confess as sin protecting myself because I doubt that you lovingly guard me. I thank you that you're faithful even when I'm unfaithful, even when I refuse to fear you and choose to fear life. But I never need to fear that you will refuse to forgive me. I accept your grace and forgiveness in Christ. Empower me by your grace to stop believing these lies and to start living by gospel truth. Empower me to ask for Greg's forgiveness. Empower me to give him a taste of what it's like to have a father who guards him like you guard us. In Jesus name, amen."

A thousand words can never capture all that went into the relational process of helping Mike to see that *"It's horrible to sin, but wonderful to be forgiven."* But prayerfully, the words can offer you a taste of speaking truth in love — of compassionate counseling based on a biblical understanding of people — of the heart.

Journeying Out Together: Entering Mike's Growth-in-Grace Story — Biblical Guiding

You've listened in as I've journeyed with Mike through sustaining, healing, and reconciling. Mike still has a desire to move back into Greg's life with Christlike love. Here's a sample trialogue that seeks to summarize biblical guiding that communicates that *"It's supernatural to mature in Christ."*

"Mike, last week was powerful. I went home and did some soul-searching, repenting, and receiving Christ's forgiveness in my own life. Thank you for being an example to me.

"What was this past week like for you? When I ask that, *I'm wondering in particular, what it's been like for you and your heavenly Father?"* (SP — picking up on last week's "return of the prodigal son").

"I was telling Sandra that there's this 'sweet trajectory.' That's the only way I can describe it. It's not like there's 100 percent movement all the time where I'm 'getting grace' and running to my heavenly Father. But it *is* like this magnet drawing me back to my Father. I *want him.* I want to *know him.* I'm drawn not only to 'God my Guard' but to 'God my Father.' It may sound trite, but when I say 'God my Father,' there's a different meaning to that than I've ever grasped in my life."

Mike looks and sees my tears. Tears of joy and celebration. We both sit in silence for a bit. Savoring it all. Taking it all in.

"Whew!" I finally say. "We could wrap up right now — the briefest counseling session ever!"

We both laugh.

"But, what do you say we keep going ... I'm wondering, given how you've experienced God as your Father this week, *how have you seen yourself in Christ?"* (SA).

"I guess the obvious answer would be 'as son,' " Mike responds. "And that's certainly true. 'Loved son. Protected son. Forgiven son. Wanted son.' But even more it's 'empowered son' and so it's 'brave dad.'

"I had some trepidation about revisiting the bullying issue with Greg — especially my sinful response to him. But it was really cool to *feel the fear and face it with Christ and march into Greg's room to ask for his forgiveness"* (SO based on SP and SA — I didn't even have to bring up Mike's relationship to others ... he brought it up; I journeyed with him).

Mike continues, "Things had been lukewarm at best between us since our last intense conversation. When I asked Greg if we could talk again about the kid who was bullying him, I could almost see the hairs go up on the back of his neck. When he hesitantly said, 'Yes,' I sat down on the side of his bed. He was at his desk, and he scooted somewhat so he was facing me.

"As I started asking his forgiveness, he kept turning more and more toward me in his chair." Mike's voice cracked. "It was a sweet time. At the end, I asked if we could pray together. We hadn't done that, just the two of us, in a couple years. Greg wasn't totally comfortable praying right then, but he said, 'It'd be okay if you prayed for us, Dad.'"

After some time of celebrating with Mike, I say, "I looked up the meaning of your name this week. It means *who resembles God*' (SA/RT — Images). That's how I see you, Mike. As God is your Father with all the special meaning that is coming to have for you, you are a Christlike father to Greg. Through Christ, you are increasingly resembling the Father's holy love."

"Coming from someone I've really come to appreciate and respect, that means a lot to me," Mike said.

We both take it in.

After some time, I summarize: "By God's grace — *grace you've tasted in your own life* — *you've been moving into Sandra's life and Greg's life and your other kids' lives* (V1 — relational actions motivated by SP — God's grace). I don't picture it like you're doing it because the 'finger-wagging God' is scolding you or guilting you into it. I picture you doing it *because the grace of God is teaching you to want to say 'Yes!' to godliness and to be eager to do what is good*" (Titus 2:11 – 14) (V2 — heart motivation encouraged by SP — relational affections).

"I want that to be true of my heart more and more," Mike said. "I want it to be true because it glorifies God and because it ministers to my family. But I also want it to be true because it sure feels good! I'm feeling some of that peace that I talked about never having. Is it okay to enjoy that and want that?"

"Sure it is, Mike. First, you've highlighted Christ-centered and other-centered motives — so that's a fantastic foundation. There's nothing wrong and everything right about longing to experience peace, shalom, wholeness, and holiness. *Celebrate those feelings and those affections.* We don't demand them or live for them, and we know we will only fully experience them in heaven, but *we sure can celebrate them when God blesses us with peace now*" (SA, SP, and E in the midst of ES).

Where We've Been and Where We're Headed

Here are three tweet-size summaries of our journey with Mike in this chapter: *Theology matters. Understanding people biblically matters. Biblical counselors pursue compassionate and wise counseling where our love abounds in depth of knowledge about the heart in the world.*

Our depth of knowledge of people starts with knowing and applying the written Word and knowing personally the living Word. It then moves to knowing people as originally designed — Creation.

We could wish that we did not need to know the fallen nature of people — the Fall. However, we must turn our attention there now. We need to understand people as originally designed by God, as marred by sin, and as restored by grace. So we turn our attention to a theology of sin that leads to biblical diagnosis of heart issues — the fallen personality structure. We start with an exploration of serpentine seduction to sin.

CHAPTER 8

Exploring Serpentine Seduction to Sin: Our Spiritual Adultery

Of all people, Christians should be the most realistic. We should be people who refuse to deny the tragedy of sin because we understand that we will never grasp the good news if we don't understand the bad news. As J. C. Ryle explains, "Christ is never fully valued, until sin is clearly seen. We must know the depth and malignity of our disease, in order to appreciate the great Physician."[1]

Though sad and tragic, without the narrative of the Fall, we could never make sense of life. As important as it is to return to our original design (creation), we would be naive to end our journey there. God didn't. The true story of life must include the sad story of our descent into the abyss of sin and the untold suffering that accompanies it.

The Fall is the only reasonable explanation for sin and suffering — life as it now exists is inexplicable apart from understanding the entrance of sin. By dissecting the fallen *soul*, we're able to diagnose the impact of sin on the human personality (chapters 8 – 9). By dissecting the fallen *planet*, we're able to diagnose the reasons for suffering and a biblical approach to grieving with hope (chapter 10).

Biblical counselors must deal thoroughly *both* with the *sins* we have *committed and* with the *evils* we have *suffered*. Skip the Fall, and we skip relevant answers to real-life questions about both sin and suffering. The Fall teaches us that life as we now find it is not the way it was meant to be. We either face this tragic reality, or we become irrelevant and so heavenly minded that we are of no earthly good.

People all around us are asking, "How do you explain life today?" "What went wrong?" "What's the root source of our problem?" They may not word it quite like that. Perhaps it sounds more like, "Why do I keep doing the same foolish things again and again?" "Why are the world and my life in such a mess?" "If a good God made the world, why has it gone so wrong?" "If God is so good, then why did he allow my daughter to be accidentally run over and killed by my husband in our driveway?"

We view the scriptural answers to these vital questions in chapters 8 – 10:

- Chapter 8: Exploring Serpentine Seduction to Sin — What went wrong? What are the dynamics of seduction and temptation?

- Chapter 9: Diagnosing the Fallen Condition of the Soul — What's the root source of our problem? Why do we do what we do?

- Chapter 10: Applying the Gospel to Suffering — How does the gospel address the evils we have suffered?

The Dynamics of Spiritual Seduction

To answer the question, "What's the root source of our problem?" we have to understand the nature of Satan's seduction of Adam and Eve and what was involved in their first sin. Learning this, we learn how Satan seduces us and the despicable nature of our sinful allegiance to him rather than our loving faithfulness to God.

"Adam and Eve were both naked and unashamed" (Gen. 2:25, author's translation). "Now the serpent was more naked than any of the wild animals the Lord God had made" (Gen. 3:1, author's translation). You read that right. Moses chooses the same Hebrew root word that we can translate either as "naked" or as "crafty."[2] The serpent was naked. Open. Transparent. The Angel of Darkness clothed himself with light. The Lying One masqueraded as integrity, openness, transparency, and genuineness.

The Scripture tells us that the serpent was more cunning, subtler, craftier than any creature made by God. This is hypocrisy shrewdly disguised as integrity. A fake portrayed as genuine. A counterfeit camouflaged as authentic. Satan is at work behind the scenes of every seduction. In this first scene,

Moses draws back the curtains to expose Satan's serpentine seduction — to expose the entrance of *another counselor*.

Seduction to Doubt God's Good Heart

Digging into the dialogue between Satan and Eve, we discover the divine diagnosis of temptation. "Hath God said?" This is the first question in the Bible. Seeds of doubt are planted. "Is it really so? Did God really say *that?*" Satan implies that what God says is open to human judgment. He invites Eve to be her own counselor and to live according to autonomous personal wisdom.

"You must not." In truth, God had said, "You are *free* to eat from *any* tree in the garden" (Gen. 2:16, emphasis added). But now Satan counters that freedom. "He said *what!?* He commanded you *not* to eat from *any* tree in the garden?" God, according to the serpent, is a Must-Not God! A Shalt-Not God. He is suggesting, as is the essence of all sin, that we should distrust God's heart.

Eve, rather than calling on Yahweh, rather than involving Adam who heard God's command, rather than resisting the Devil, dialogues with the seductive serpent. Attempting to correct his glaring misrepresentations, she still gets it wrong. God emphasized their scandalous freedom. "You are *free* to eat from *any* tree in the garden." But Eve minimizes it. "We *may* eat fruit from *the* trees in the garden."

Eve continues, "We must not eat *fruit* from the tree that is *in the middle of the garden*. And we must not *touch* it or we *will* die." She highlights the delicacy that God withholds — the fruit. She makes it a geographic rather than a moral issue — in the middle of the garden, instead of the *tree of the knowledge of good and evil*. She adds restrictions — or *touch* it. She subtracts seriousness — you will die, instead of you will *surely* die.

The serpent hardly has to do any work at this point. Deceived, Eve is doing his work for him. Speaking again to Eve, the serpent deceitfully assures her, "You will *not* surely die!" Cunning. Then he drives the foul knife deep. "God jealously hoards his Deity. His best gift he withholds — godlike wisdom."

When Satan tempted Eve, he accused God, intimating that God commanded his restriction out of envy, because he would have none so great, wise, and happy as he is. The serpent could be saying, "God is needlessly restrictive. There's something in his character causing him to deprive you. What is it about God that motivates him to limit your pleasure? Is he cruel? Unkind? Lacking generosity?"

While God was being generous and protective, Satan portrays him as punitive and jealous. "Your so-called 'loving God' is selfish! He's holding back.

He withholds what you need because he is jealous and insecure. God restricts you because he does not love you. God has a character flaw!"

John Murray notes that the pivot of Satan's attack is not simply a denial of God's power. It is much more diabolical. Satan directly assails God's veracity and integrity, accusing God of deliberate falsehood and deception; accusing him of being jealous of and selfish with his exclusive possession of the knowledge of good and evil.[3] Jay Adams concurs. "These three attacks — doubt, distortion and denial — were designed to lead to distrust."[4]

The Fall introduced a competing story line that called into question God's good heart. Milton Vincent describes it like this: "Every time I deliberately disobey a command of God, it is because I am in that moment doubtful as to God's true intentions in giving me that command. Does He really have my best interest at heart?"[5]

Satan attempts to minimize Eve's perspective of God by claiming that God minimizes her freedom. He poisons Eve's view of God. He emails a virus into her system that seduces her to see God in a punitive, rather than a protective way. He tempts Eve to see herself as sufficient rather than trust God as her sufficient Shepherd.

Eve was innocent and uncorrupted, living in simple dependence on and enjoyment of God. The only being she knew had been only kind to her. The whole creation formed a symphony singing God's goodness. Then someone else appeared suggesting that God might not be as good as she supposed. "Have you ever wondered why God won't let you at that tree? Have you asked yourself if there might be something good outside of God that you could enjoy if you had the sense to go for it?" Eve is ensnared by "worldly wisdom" instead of clinging to the wise and Wonderful Counselor.

Seduced in the realm of *desire*, Eve is deceived in the sphere of *imagination*. Moses informs us that she *saw* the fruit (Gen. 3:6). The Hebrew word means to perceive with the imagination and to believe with the heart. Eve looks intently upon and purposely at the fruit, touching it with her eyes before touching it with her fingers and lips.

Her rational imagination is intricately connected to her relational motivation. She pursues what she perceives to be pleasing. She seeks what she senses is satisfying. "When the woman saw that the fruit of the tree was good for food and pleasing to the eye, and also desirable for gaining wisdom, she took some and ate it" (Gen. 3:6). Elyse Fitzpatrick summarizes Eve's unhappy choice:

> Why did Eve choose to disobey God? Look again at three words in the verse: *good, delight, desirable*. These are words that illustrate the motivation behind

actions. Our choices are predicated upon what we think is "good," what we "delight in," what we find most "desirable." The truth about our choices is that we always choose what we believe to be our best good. We always choose what we believe will bring us the most delight.[6]

There is nothing wrong with desire. God made the trees "pleasing to the eye and good for food" (Gen. 2:9). However, Eve was seduced *through* her desires. Temptation lurks around desire's highway. She perceives that the fruit is good — beneficial, favorable, pleasant, beautiful, precious, delightful, able to make one happy. She perceives that the fruit is pleasing — beautiful, strongly desirable, delightful, precious, pleasant. She perceives that the fruit is desirable — fulfilling, craving, satisfying, earnest desire, strong affection, appetite, delight.

Desire itself was not the problem. Desiring anything more than God was the problem. The Puritans called this "overmuch love." Satan instigated a titanic tug-of-war in her soul. "Choose you this day whom you will love, whom you will desire. Decide who satisfies your soul most deeply. Who is altogether lovely? Who and what is most dear to you? Who do you hold supreme? Who do you love with all your heart, soul, mind, and strength? What do you crave more than life itself?" Eve chose the creature over the Creator. Choosing the forbidden fruit, she chose the serpent and herself. "She took some and ate it" (Gen. 3:6).

Seduction to Love Anyone or Anything More than God

And what of Adam? "She also gave some to her husband who was with her, and he ate it" (Gen. 3:6). Eve was beguiled and deceived (Gen. 3:13; 1 Tim. 2:14); Adam was not deceived (1 Tim. 2:14). He sinned knowingly. He was undeceived by the serpent's lies about God's goodness and good intent in his one protective prohibition. Then why did he sin? How was *he* seduced?

Biblical interpreters before and after Augustine have agreed with his interpretation that, "The first man did not yield to his wife in this transgression of God's precept, as if he thought she spoke the truth: but only compelled to it by his social love to her, for the apostle says: 'Adam was not deceived but the woman was deceived.'"[7]

Moses provides the inspired interpretation of the nature of Adam's sinful choice. "To Adam [God] said, 'Because you listened (hearkened) to your wife and ate from the tree about which I commanded you, "You must not eat of it," Cursed is the ground because of you; through painful toil you will eat of it all the days of your life'" (Gen. 3:17, parenthesis added).

"Listen" means to loyally obey — listen diligently to, give heed to, pay attention to, hearken to. Adam's sin? He knowingly chose Eve over God. The seduction in Adam's sin? In his desires. The reason for Adam's sin? His imagination. As Eve chose the goodness of the fruit over God's goodness, so Adam chose the goodness of the female over God's goodness (Rom. 1:25). Seeing God as the great Forbidder, Adam chose the one who ate the forbidden fruit. More precious was she in his sight than God. More wise his wisdom than God's. More precious his will than God's.

It is no coincidence that Moses uses the same word for "hear/hearken" in Deuteronomy 6:4–5. "Hear, O Israel: The Lord our God, the Lord is one. Love the Lord your God with all your heart and with all your soul and with all your strength." In other words, "Don't be like Adam, who hearkened to and loved his wife with all his heart, soul, and strength."

Living in fellowship with God is the natural state of humanity. The temptation was Satan's enticement to compel Adam and Eve to exercise their wills in *independence* of God. They tried the impossible and contemptible — to live outside their design as worshiping beings of the one true God.

God designed Adam and Eve to recoil at ugly and rejoice in beauty. Their first sin, and every sin thereafter, includes the failure to discern good (beautiful) and evil (ugly). The tree of the knowledge of good and evil was Adam and Eve's opportunity to discern between God's goodness and Satan's evil. As image bearers, they had the capacities necessary to recoil at the ugliness of desiring and choosing anything or anyone more than God. They had the capacities to rejoice in the beauty of God's good heart.

Had they recoiled, God would have "confirmed them in holiness." They would permanently be "like God" as perfect bearers of his beautiful image. Instead, they became like Satan — his ugly image bearers. They chose the ugliness of doubting God's good heart over the beauty of trusting God's generous soul. They could have "known" good and evil without ever having to experience evil. Instead, they and all their descendants become filled only with evil all the time continually (Gen. 6:5).

Divine Commentary Tracing the Tracks of Temptation

Numerous later passages divinely decipher the tangled web of deceived desires woven in every temptation to sin. In these divine commentaries, God exposes the heart dynamics and traces the tracks of every temptation that we and our counselees face.

- Enticed in Our Affections: False Lovers of Our Soul
- Deceived in Our Imagination: Foolish Idols of Our Heart
- Blinded in Our Perception: Arrogant Suppression of Our Mind-Set
- Enslaved in Our Volition: Contemptuous Purposes/Pathways of Our Will
- Ungoverned in Our Emotions: Fleshly Surrender of Our Mood States

A Personal Heart Checkup

As biblical counselors, we seek to be soul physicians who use the Bible to examine and diagnose the heart. Seeking to be counselors with integrity, we start with ourselves so that we change the adage "Physician, heal thyself." Instead we say, "Soul physician, go to the great Soul Physician for ongoing healing from sin before you seek to share Christ's healing hope with others."

With that in mind, as you read the divine commentary tracing the tracks of sin, prayerfully reflect on a personal besetting sin or remember a time when you (like all of us) caved into temptation. Ask the Holy Spirit to apply his truth to your life. At the end of each of the following sections, you'll find heart exam questions that you can use to trace the tracks of temptation to sin.

As you read, if God moves in your heart to prompt confession and repentance, I'd encourage you to take some time to pray. You also may want to read through a passage such as Hosea 14; Luke 15:11 – 32; Psalm 32; or Psalm 51. Each of these passages not only involves confession and repentance ("it's horrible to sin"), but also receiving God's gracious forgiveness ("it's wonderful to be forgiven"). As you pray, receive and enjoy God's forgiving grace.

Enticed in Our Affections: False Lovers of Our Soul

Sin begins its enticement in our desires. "Each one is tempted when, by his own evil desire, he is dragged away and enticed" (James 1:14). Though the NIV translates the Greek word for desire (*epithumias*) as "evil desire," it is actually a neutral term. For example, Luke 22:15 tells us that Jesus desired with great desire to eat the Passover with his disciples — using *epithumias* twice. Paul uses the same word for his desire to depart and be with Christ (Phil. 1:23) and for a person's desire to be an elder (1 Tim. 3:1).

So what is desire, according to the Scriptures? The Greek root word *thumos* means passion, movement, motivation, vital force, and impulse. With the prefix *epi*, it expresses a yearning, craving, boiling passion, a bubbling want. In other contexts it connotes concepts like pleasure, cherish, value, relish, deem, esteem, and appreciate. When used toward God, it pictures supreme devotion or a driving hunger and thirst. Desires are God's idea. It is the distortion of desire that underlies our temptations, and this is Satan's province. Evil allures us to pursue God-designed desires in God-prohibited ways.

Each of us is seduced through our appetites, affections, delights, and desires. We are relational beings created with the capacity for relational motivation — designed to desire and pursue what we perceive will satisfy our soul. Satanic seduction always tempts us toward spiritual separation, toward spiritual adultery where we pursue false lovers of the soul.

Jeremiah 2 provides a classic divine commentary on seduction. Jehovah, the Husband of Israel, reflects on days gone by when his wife was faithful. "I remember the devotion of your youth, how as a bride you loved me and followed me through the desert, through a land not sown" (Jer. 2:2). Sadly, Jehovah has other memories of this unfaithfulness. "My people have committed two sins: They have forsaken me, the spring of living water, and have dug their own cisterns, broken cisterns that cannot hold water" (Jer. 2:13). God summarizes the essence of seduction to sin. It is unfaithful awayness — spiritual adultery. Sin seduces us to love false lovers. "Long ago you broke off your yoke and tore off your bonds; you said, 'I will not serve you!' Indeed, on every high hill and under every spreading tree you lay down as a prostitute" (Jer. 2:20). Sin is spiritual prostitution.

Where does sin seek its entry point into our hearts and lives? Through our cravings — in our legitimate relational longings for intimacy. Jehovah puts it rather bluntly: "You are a swift she-camel running here and there, a wild donkey accustomed to the desert, sniffing the wind in her craving — in her heat who can restrain her? Any males that pursue her need not tire themselves; at mating time they will find her" (Jer. 2:23 – 24).

Our desire to love and be loved is core to our *imago*. Like God, we are relational, communal beings. Unlike God, we are finite beings. So we hunger and thirst for relationship. We satisfy our hungry souls either *coram Deo* — face-to-face with God, or *coram Diabolos* — face-to-face with Satan.

Examining My Affections: Thirsts, Desires

Thinking about your affections and a current besetting sin or a past time of surrender to temptation, prayerfully ponder and apply to your life the following heart probes:

+ "At the moment of temptation, what do I believe is most satisfying — God or this sin? Why? In what ways?"

+ "What thirst, hunger, affection, delight, appetite, or desire am I attempting to satisfy?"

+ "In what ways does God satisfy the legitimate aspects of this affection?"

+ "What am I hoping for when I give in to this sin?"

+ "What does Scripture say about this longing?"

Deceived in Our Imagination: Foolish Idols of Our Heart

Why do we choose sin? Why do we follow Satan over God? Why savor the fruit the Creator made over the Creator? As we have suggested, sin seduces us through our affections while it deceives us through our imagination. James informs us that we are tempted through our desires as we are dragged away and enticed (James 1:14). It's like a fishing and hunting analogy of bait and snares. The delicious worm is tantalizing to the hungry fish. The bloody scent mesmerizes the ravenous bear. We're allured by bait — deceptive bait that blinds us to God's goodness.

While explaining the nature of satanic seduction, James uses these memorable words: "Don't be deceived, my dear brothers. Every good and perfect gift is from above, coming down from the Father of the heavenly lights, who does not change like shifting shadows" (James 1:16 – 17). In other words, don't be deceived about the source of every good and every perfect gift. God is *not* a Shalt-Not God! He is the Gift-Giving God.

To allure and ensnare us, Satan must deceive us by blinding us to our God's worth. Jehovah says exactly this when he asks and answers the age-old question concerning why we sin. "This is what the Lord says: 'What fault did your fathers find in me, that they strayed so far from me?'" (Jer. 2:5). "Fault" is a startling word. The KJV accurately translates it as "iniquity." We turn from God when we perceive some iniquity in him. Specifically, "fault" means to act in a deceitful way, tricking, an insidious manner of relating, dishonest and unfair dealings, injustice, and even perverseness. It suggests a remarkable accumulation of unrighteousness — a contemptuous view of God.

Sound familiar? Satan deceived Eve into thinking that God was deceptive and unfair. How does Satan snare us? He captures our imagination as we interpret our situation. When Jehovah asked about the fault that they *found* in him, he chose a word for "found" that means a conclusion reached by interpreting experience. Here they are in the desert seeing God in their imagination as their beloved who provides for and protects them (Jer. 2:2 – 3). They correctly imagine him as their "spring of living water" (Jer. 2:13). Though life is bad (living in a desert), their loving God is altogether lovely.

But then something tragic happens. They interpret their desert experience through a new grid, the grid of blinded imagination. Notice how they view God now. "You of this generation, consider the word of the LORD: Have I been a desert to Israel or a land of great darkness? Why do my people say, 'We are free to roam; we will come to you no more'? Does a maiden forget her jewelry, a bride her wedding ornaments? Yet my people have forgotten me, days without number. How skilled you are at pursuing love! Even the worst of women can learn from your ways" (Jer. 2:31 – 33).

Jehovah, who had been worthy of following in a desert, they now imagine to be a desert! Jehovah, who illuminated their path, they now fancy a land of great darkness. Satan captured and blinded their imagination. "Your so-called 'Husband' is the cosmic Killjoy! Take a look at all his shortcomings."

We move far from God when we think little of God. Don't take my word for it. Take God's. "'Your wickedness will punish you; your backsliding will rebuke you. Consider then and realize how evil and bitter it is for you when you forsake the LORD your God and have no awe of me,' declares the Lord, the LORD Almighty" (Jer. 2:19). We forsake God when we lose our awe of him — when we lose all respect for God. In our inner attitude, we no longer detect the Trinity's awesome holy love; we no longer appreciate the majestic beauty of the Trinity.

Examining My Imagination: Images, Idols

Thinking about your imagination/images and a current besetting sin or a past time of surrender to temptation, prayerfully ponder and apply to your life the following heart probes:

+ "What controlling false images of God cloud my thinking when I'm struggling against this sin? What lowly views of God capture my attention?"

+ "How is Satan cropping God out of the picture? How is Satan cropping in false images of deceptive beauty and seductive temptation?"

+ "As I face this sin, what faulty, but seductive, views of relational reality fill my mind?"

◆ "As I face this sin, what compelling sinful images captivate my soul
while capturing my mind?"

Blinded in Our Perception: Arrogant Suppression of Our Mind-Set

Satan *entices* us through our *desires*, *deceives* us in our *imagination*, and *blinds* us in our *perception*. We discover this third aspect in yet another divine commentary on the dynamics of seduction — Romans 1:18 – 31. Paul introduces the process. "The wrath of God is being revealed from heaven against all the godlessness and wickedness of men who suppress the truth by their wickedness" (Rom. 1:18). The essential idea of godlessness is irreverence, disregard, indifference, and insult that results in paying little attention to God and results from suppressing the truth about God's nature.

According to Paul, God's glorious nature is as plain as the nose on our face. His invisible attributes are manifested in his visible creation. Those with eyes to see may observe God by observing the world around them (Rom. 1:19 – 20; Ps. 19:1 – 3). It does not take a CSI team to detect the fingerprints of God. Through creation, we can see his eternal power and Godhead — the sum total of his glorious divine attributes.

Adam and Eve not only saw God's goodness through creation, they walked with their Creator and experienced his goodness — his holy love. So what went wrong? How could they sin? They had to *suppress* the awareness of what they saw, knew, and experienced. For sin to conceive, we must push away from our awareness all signs of God's goodness. "For although they knew God, they neither glorified him as God nor gave thanks to him, but their thinking became futile and their foolish hearts were darkened" (Rom. 1:21).

When Satan tempts us, he crops Christ out of the picture. He presents us with digital images of life where Christ, the cross, and the gospel story are suppressed from our perception. This is what he did to Eve in the garden. Eve, reflecting on God, must have thought to herself: "Glorious? I thought so, but it doesn't seem like it now. The fruit seems more desirable than God." "Good?" Adam wonders. "I thought so, but Eve seems better for me than the Creator."

Isn't this what Paul is saying? "They exchanged the truth of God for a lie, and worshiped and served created things rather than the Creator — who is forever praised. Amen" (Rom. 1:25). Paul is careful with his Greek. They bartered *the truth* for *a lie*. The truth is that God is forever worthy of praise. The lie is that God is not worthy to be retained in our thinking (Rom. 1:28).

Paul continues in verse 25: "[They] worshiped and served created things *rather than* the Creator" (emphasis added). Literally, when placed side by side — Creator and creature, Creator and fruit, Creator and the female — they *preferred* the creature, fruit, and female to the Creator. Eve and Adam worship substitute lovers; they pass by the Creator altogether because they are blinded to the truth that he is altogether lovely.

"Furthermore, since they did not think it worthwhile to retain the knowledge of God, he gave them over to a depraved mind, to do what ought not to be done" (Rom. 1:28). "Think" in this context means to test, prove, or approve. It was a word used to refer to the testing of metals or coins to see if they were genuine. Ralph Earle explains the terrifying implication of this idea: "Humanity had tested Deity and disapproved of him. Consequently man had rejected God."[8] More than suppression of his goodness, we insinuate that God falls short of our glory. Sin seduces us to play umpire with God, to sit in judgment on his character. *The essence of sin is the belittling of God's glory.*

Adam and Eve once understood that all they needed was God and what he chose to provide for them. They once affirmed that God gave them all things richly to enjoy (Gen. 2:9; 1 Tim. 6:17; James 1:17). Then Satan weaseled into their hearts and minds, shrinking their freedom in Christ. In Galatians 1, Paul says that lies about our gospel freedom are anathema — worthy of an eternal curse. In 1 Timothy 4:1, he labels such lies "things taught by demons" — demonic doctrines.

I often ask my classes, "What are examples of demonic doctrines?" They reply the way you and I would. "Demonic doctrines deny the virgin birth of Christ." "They include denying the inspiration of Scripture." "Demonic doctrines must involve demon possession, or killing, hating."

Then we read 1 Timothy 4:1 – 2. "The Spirit clearly says that in later times some will abandon the faith and follow deceiving spirits and things taught by demons. Such teachings come through hypocritical liars, whose consciences have been seared as with a hot iron." The tension mounts. We wait to read subsequent verses that we're sure will speak about abandoning the faith through heretical teaching about the Trinity, or Christ's humanity and deity.

Then we're shocked to read Paul's description of demonic doctrine. "They forbid people to marry and order them to abstain from certain foods, which God created to be received with thanksgiving by those who believe and who know the truth. For everything God created is good, and nothing is to be rejected if it is received with thanksgiving" (1 Tim. 4:3 – 4).

What is the core lie that seduces us to abandon the faith? What is the core truth that demonic doctrine denies? "Everything God created is good, and thus God is good and generous." This is the truth to which Satan wants to blind us. Satan's seduction always comes in the form of a story offering us godness by lessening God's goodness.

Examining My Perceptions: Beliefs, Mind-Sets

Think about your perceptions/beliefs/mind-sets and a current besetting sin or a past time of surrender to temptation and prayerfully ponder and apply to your life the following heart probes:

- "As I give in to this sin, where am I pushing down evidence of God's goodness?"
- "How am I belittling God's holy love when I surrender to this sin?"
- "In association with this sin, where am I believing that God is a hoarder — a Shalt-Not God?"
- "What truths about God could deliver me from this temptation?"
- "What lies am I believing that push those truths about God out of my mind?"

Enslaved in Our Volition: Contemptuous Purposes/ Pathways of Our Will

Recall the basic process of seduction. I always pursue (volitional) what I perceive (rational) to be most pleasing (relational). I always seek what I sense is most satisfying.

The essence of seduction is the temptation to prefer other things to God's grandeur. When we surrender to seduction, then we lack God's glory as the treasure of our lives. We lack it as our passion and goal, as our all-satisfying vision.

According to Jeremiah 2:13, sin is the choice between boundless joy or broken cisterns. In the wilderness lands of the ancient Near East, water was a constant problem — a life-threatening issue. There were two primary sources of water. One was a spring of water — pure, fresh, running water from the ground. This was the preferred source and the reason why Abraham and the other patriarchs settled near springs. Here they had access to clean, cool, flowing underground water bubbling up like a modern-day artesian spring.

The other source of water was the cistern, and it was much less desirable. If you could find no spring, or if a spring ran dry, then you had to dig a cistern.

A cistern was a crude well that was not fed by underground water, but by collecting runoff water or rain. You'd dig a hole, line it with clay, and pray that the water running off from roofs, from the camel-dung-filled streets, and from the sandy, dusty hills would collect in the cistern. This less-than-appealing combination of rain water, dirt, and dung would collect in the cistern and sit, stagnating in the hot sun. Because of this, cisterns often cracked, allowing the putrid, but life-sustaining water to escape.

Satan seduces us to choose broken cisterns over spring water. He lures us to forsake Jehovah, the Spring of Living Water, and dig our own self-sufficient broken cisterns that can hold no water. And Satan knows that what entices one of us will not allure another. This is why James notes that *each one* of us is tempted when we are drawn away through *our own* desire (James 1:14). In other words, *we are tempted in or through our unique appetites.* Eve's fancy was captivated by good, pleasing, desirable fruit capable (at least she imagined) of making her godlike. Sin captured Adam's imagination when he perceived that Eve was more desirable than God.

This is why we all create our own unique and agreeable self-portraits of God. Rather than living in God's image, we create images of God that fit our distinctive personalities. The broken cistern of trusting money may be what tempts us. Yet our neighbors may care very little about money, placing their trust in personal beauty or a powerful physique. All of us change the god who captures our soul, depending on our situation and context.

Jehovah castigates Israel for this constant changing of the gods. "Why do you go about so much, changing your ways? You will be disappointed by Egypt as you were by Assyria" (Jer. 2:36). Gluttony, pride, hypocrisy, lying, power, prestige, lust, materialism, hobbies, praise, women, men, sex, pleasure — it really doesn't matter. All of these can be false gods we depend on, false lovers to whom we grant our supreme devotion.

Two repeated themes run throughout the Bible. One is God's gracious rescue of his people, as pictured in the Passover-Exodus-Redemption event. The other theme is the people's ungrateful rejection of God, as pictured by the waters of Marah, Elim, Massah, and Meribah where God's people craved other satisfactions instead of God's provision (Ex. 12 – 17). Numbers 9 – 14 brings both of these themes together. In Numbers 9, Israel celebrates the Passover, and then in Numbers 11 they complain about God's provision: "The rabble with them began to crave other food, and again the Israelites started wailing and said, 'If only we had meat to eat! We remember the fish we ate in Egypt at no cost — also the cucumbers, melons, leeks, onions and garlic. But now we have lost our appetite; we never see anything but this manna!'" (Num. 11:4 – 6).

Here is another clear picture of satanic seduction: Crave the world and the food of the world and lose your appetite for God and God's food. In seduction we face this constant interplay between demeaning God and elevating what is non-god. "We were better off in Egypt!" (Num. 11:18). "Why did we ever leave Egypt?" (Num. 11:20). Yet we are never satisfied with what we get and always end up loathing the things of this world because they can never satisfy us. "You will not eat it for just one day, or two days, or five, ten or twenty days, but for a whole month — until it comes out of your nostrils and you loathe it — because you have rejected the Lord, who is among you" (Num. 11:19 – 20). The downward spiral is clear: we loathe God, long for the world, and end up loathing the things of the world when they fail to satisfy us.

Numbers 14 further describes how this satanic seduction tempts us to loathe God. "How long will these people treat me with contempt? How long will they refuse to believe in me, in spite of all the miraculous signs I have performed among them?" (Num. 14:11). To hold someone in *contempt* means to belittle, despise, disdain, disbelieve, depreciate, and prefer lesser things to them. This is a conscious change of perception and attitude — a shift from honor to dishonor.

In the process of seduction, Satan tempts us to depreciate God and to choose lesser gods of our own making — gods that best suit our unique personality and life situation. R. Kent Hughes summarizes the progression well: "The pathology of a hard heart originates in unbelief that spawns a hardened contempt."[9] Rather than being caught up in the overflowing gladness of God — the only fountain of lasting joy — we turn to trivial pursuits, fleeting pleasures, petty resentments, and unsatisfying materialism.

And as we turn, we enslave ourselves. The pathways we pursue to find life apart from God become our gods. The bondage of our will leaves us obsessively attempting to make life work without God.

Examining My Volition: Choices, Motivations

Thinking about your volition/choices/motivations and a current besetting sin or a past time of surrender to temptation, prayerfully ponder and apply to your life the following heart probes:

+ "What cisterns am I digging to quench my relational thirsts when I cave into this sin?"

+ "What themes or patterns do I detect in these times when I am choosing this sin over Jesus?"

+ "How do I consistently, but subtly, attempt to quench my thirsts in ways that God disapproves of?"

+ "Relative to this sin, what do I do to get (demand) what I want?"

Ungoverned in Our Emotions: Fleshly Surrender of Our Mood States

Satan seduces us to pursue what we perceive will be pleasing and pleasurable. Hebrews 11:25 informs us that there is pleasure in sin for a season — for an undetermined period. In context, "pleasure" speaks of the demand that I clutch pleasure, take hold of it, cling to it, and hold on to it for dear life."

Pleasure is part of sin's seductiveness and addictiveness. Sin is seductive because it offers temporal pleasure over which I have some control. Eve not only wanted what was good, pleasing, and desirable, she also wanted the godlike status of being able to satisfy herself, of being her own self-sufficient source of pleasure.

Pleasure's temporal, finite nature makes it addictive. As we saw earlier, Jeremiah 2:23 – 24 compares giving in to sinful seduction to an animal in heat. Once we start down the path of finite pleasure, we feel a sense of urgency, an immediate craving that enslaves us. We cry out, "It's no use! I love foreign (fake, finite) gods, and I *must* go after them" (Jer. 2:25, parenthesis and emphasis added). We feel enslaved to our desires because we attempt to fill an infinite, spiritual longing with a finite, material source. Ephesians 4:17 – 19 rehearses this process of seduction:

> So I tell you this, and insist on it in the Lord, that you must no longer live as the Gentiles do, in the futility of their thinking (deceived imagination). They are darkened in their understanding (blinded perception) and separated from the life of God (enticed affection) because of the ignorance that is in them (imagination and perception) due to the hardening of their hearts (enslaved volition). Having lost all sensitivity (ungoverned emotions), they have given themselves over (volition) to sensuality (ungoverned emotion) so as to indulge in (volition and emotion) every kind of impurity, with a continual lust for more (volition and emotion). (parentheses added)

There is a strong warning in this passage. Be careful what you wish for, for your wish may be granted. If you wish to seek God, he will be found (Heb.

11:6). If you wish to seek the food of this world, then you will consume it until it gushes from your nostrils (Num. 11:18 – 20). If you wish to separate yourself from the spiritual umbilical cord that connects you to God, then you will enslave yourself to endless addictive cycles to fill your God-vacuum.

Romans 1:24, 26, and 28 offer an alarming warning. If we continue to long for God substitutes and surrender ourselves to them, God will oblige us. He will give us up to our desires. In Romans 1:26, Paul cautions that God will give us up to ungoverned lusts — to unbridled, uncontrolled appetites. When we demand to be like God, we self-sufficiently quench our thirsts and become enslaved to the things we use to satisfy our longings. Seeking to break loose from God's mastery, we enslave ourselves to Satan's sovereignty.

Examining My Emotions: Feelings, Moods

Thinking about your emotions/feelings/moods and a current besetting sin or a past time of surrender to temptation, prayerfully ponder and apply to your life the following heart probes:

- "Regarding this sin, how am I living to satisfy my immediate pleasure?"
- "Regarding this sin, where have I surrendered to my feelings?"
- "Relative to this sin, how have I become addicted to pursuing positive feelings or avoiding negative feelings?"
- "When I give in to this sin, what momentary pleasures do I experience? What lasting shame do I experience?"

Where We've Been and Where We're Headed

What's the root source of our problem? What went wrong? We've spent this chapter answering these questions, and here are two tweet-size summary answers: *The essence of sin is spiritual adultery — choosing to love anyone or anything more than God.* And: *Sin is not just a thief caught in a crime; sin is an adulterer caught in the act.*

The sinfulness of sin is not grasped in our day because the holiness of God is not grasped. Sin will be understood for what it is only when God is understood for who he is. That's why we started our biblical counseling journey before the beginning with our holy and loving triune God. By doing so, we've seen the ugliness of sin.

That's also why our biblical counseling journey next moved to the beginning — Creation — and the peace and purity of image bearers. By moving from Creation to the Fall, we see the deep impact of sin on the human personality — we learn how very far we've fallen from God's original design. And through examining the Fall, we learn why we do what we do and how to diagnose the root source of our heart problem.

Of course, we won't conclude our journey at the Fall. While we don't deny the tragedy of sin, we know that where sin abounds, grace super-abounds (Rom. 5:20). Even as we diagnose our sinful heart condition, we always keep looking to Jesus. We crop Christ back into the picture as we look at life through the lens of the cross, of the larger story of the gospel, of the redemption narrative. So as you ponder this chapter and the next, my encouragement to you comes from the words of Michael Vincent: "On my worst days of sin and failure, the gospel encourages me with God's unrelenting grace toward me."[10]

CHAPTER 9

Diagnosing the Fallen Condition of the Soul: Our Fallen Heart

There are two primary ways we can obtain medicine when we are ill. The first is from a pharmacist. I call in my prescription, and the pharmacist places my pills in a container and hands me my meds. Pharmacists rarely ask detailed questions about my medical history or condition. It's not their primary job.

A vastly different second way we can receive medicinal cures is to visit a doctor. A skilled, caring physician asks about my symptoms, explores my medical history, does a thorough exam, and orders an intensive battery of tests, blood work, X-rays, and MRIs.

Biblical counselors seek to be soul physicians, not soul pharmacists. Soul pharmacists are symptom-focused and solution-focused — dispensing verses without understanding inner-heart diagnosis. Soul physicians are root-cause-focused and *soul*-u-tion-focused — prescribing gospel-centered, comprehensive, compassionate treatment based on a careful heart diagnosis.

If we want to be part of what God is doing in the lives of people, we need to be soul physicians who understand how God originally designed us to function (chapters 6 – 7). We then need to be able to diagnose biblically what went wrong with that functioning (chapters 8 – 9).

We began that heart diagnosis in chapter 8 as we examined the dynamics of seduction, temptation, and sin. Having gained biblical insight into why we surrender to sin, now we explore the ramifications and results of sin. We'll explore what happened when sin entered the universe through entering the human heart:

+ Sin's Deep Impact on Our Relationship to God
+ Sin's Deep Impact on Our Heart Condition

Our goal is to diagnose the root source of our problems, discern why we do what we do, and learn how to pursue deep and lasting gospel-centered change.

Sin's Deep Impact on Our Relationship to God

I began my morning in a counseling meeting with a worship pastor who expressed his concern that he may be disqualifying himself from ministry due to his out-of-control temper. Even though Ray is a believer, he and I still needed to grapple with sin's deep impact on his relationship to God.

After our first meeting, I pondered a biblical grid as I thought through Ray's relationship to Christ. This Creation/Fall/Redemption model pictures how we relate to God using the imagery of four robes of Creation, four rags of the Fall, and four gowns of Redemption. Think of it as the story of our relationship to God in three acts with twelve "tweet-length" summaries.

+ **From the Robe of Righteousness to the Rag of Condemnation to the Gown of Justification**

    – *Creation*: God designed us to *rest* in him without shame in our original righteousness leading to a peaceful relationship of wholeness and shalom with him.

    – *Fall*: Sin condemned our conscience as rightfully guilty and deserving of the *penalty of sin.*

    – *Redemption*: Salvation provides *justification*, declaring us not guilty by reason of substitution — Christ paid our penalty.

+ **From the Robe of Communion to the Rag of Separation to the Gown of Reconciliation**

    – *Creation*: God designed us to *relate* like him and to commune with him.

    – *Fall*: Sin created a chasm between us and God — the *partition of sin* — that separates us from our holy and loving triune God.

    – *Redemption*: Salvation provides *reconciliation*, adopting us into our Father's forever family.

+ **From the Robe of Reflection to the Rag of Corruption to the Gown of Regeneration**

  –*Creation*: God designed us to *reflect* him through our marvelously fashioned capacities of personhood.

  –*Fall*: Sin corrupted our capacities to reflect God by invading our being with the *presence of sin* and polluting us with a perverse nature — the fallen personality structure.

  –*Redemption*: Salvation provides a new birth, *regenerating* our nature so we can live out our new life in Christ.

+ **From the Robe of Dominion to the Rag of Captivity to the Gown of Redemption**

  –*Creation*: God designed us to *representatively rule* for him and like him as under-shepherds.

  –*Fall*: Sin chained us in captivity to the *power of sin*.

  –*Redemption*: Salvation provides *redemption*, granting us freedom from sin's captivity and victory over sin.

I understand that these are just words on paper right now. So let's walk through Adam and Eve's story, Ray's story, and our story to see how robustly relevant God's Word is for life in a broken world.

From Righteousness to Condemnation to Justification

God created Adam and Eve with original innocence and righteousness. When God looked upon his children, he exclaimed, "Very good!" When Moses reflected on our first parents, he joyfully described them as "naked and unashamed." Because of their wholeness, they knew nothing but peaceful fellowship with God — walking with him in the cool of the day.

Sin changed everything. Instantly they realized they were naked — exposed spiritually as unclean. Weaving together fig leaves in their self-sufficient attempt to cover their shame, their efforts are worthless — filthy rags. No wonder they're *afraid* when they hear the sound of the LORD God approaching them in the garden. Where they once rested in their Father, they now fear his judgment. Sin condemned their conscience as rightfully guilty and deserving its penalty.

Realizing his sinful, shameful nakedness before his just Judge, Adam spoke for each of us when he said, "I was afraid." Every human being who ever lived shares this dread of standing naked before a holy God.

Jesus took on flesh and blood so that by his death he might destroy the Devil who holds the power of death and "free those who all their lives were held in slavery by their fear of death" (Heb. 2:15). Apart from Christ, we all are terrified of what we'll face the split second after we die. And no wonder. Without the peaceful assurance that God accepts us, we are left with judgment. "It is appointed unto men once to die, but after this the judgment" (Heb. 9:27, KJV).

Our ultimate fear is cosmic condemnation (Rom. 8:1 – 39). Sinners are in fearful flight from the Father while still in desperate need of him. We are terrified of spiritual separation anxiety — the shattering awareness that without Christ we will be declared "Guilty! Condemned! Rejected! Unacceptable! Banished!"

As a result of sin, you and I live in a world of shattered shalom. When we attempt to surmount our sin against God with self-sufficiency, we end up like Adam and Eve — covered in fig leaves, but naked still. We end up like the Old Testament saints who felt guilty continually, repeatedly, endlessly, year after year, day after day, again and again offering sacrifices for their sins (Heb. 10:1 – 18). Exhausted, our only hope is to confess our crime and throw ourselves on the mercy of God's court.

Shockingly, the just Judge, our Father, sheds blood, but not our own. First, he sheds the blood of innocent animals to fashion external coverings for Eve and Adam. Then he sheds the blood of his innocent Son to fashion internal robes of righteousness for us. Then he invites us to draw near in full assurance of faith with free access to his presence, cleansed from a guilty conscience. Amazing grace indeed.

As Ray and I talked about his anger, guilt, and sense of disqualification from ministry, we explored Genesis 3 (our sin and hiding) and Hebrews 10:19 – 25 (Christ's righteous sacrifice that cleanses us so we can enter God's presence). Over the course of several meetings, we pondered what fig leaves Ray typically wove in his attempt to dress himself without Christ's righteousness.

Ray diagnosed one fig leaf. "Better corporate worship! Even my leading worship is stained with self-sufficiency, with arrogant sin. I know better than this. But I keep trying to deal with my guilt without grace. I try to cover my sinful anger by creating worshipful services. My ugliest sin of all is trying to beautify myself."

I wondered with Ray, "What would it look like to take your anger and your self-sufficiency to Christ, and choose to stand stark naked before God without a shred of self-righteous clothing, clinging to Christ's righteousness alone?"

The dam burst. Tears streamed. Repentance flowed — for his sinful anger and for his sinful self-sufficiency. Ray experienced surrender, rest, peace. Ray was experiencing godly sorrow, not worldly shame. And he was experiencing freedom from condemnation, cleansing from a guilty conscience, and forgiveness of heart sin because of Christ's grace.

From Communion to Separation to Reconciliation

The Bible uses *courtroom* imagery and speaks of God as the just Judge when addressing our condemnation, guilt, and the penalty of sin. It also uses *home-family* imagery, speaking of God as our Father when addressing our relational separation from God and the partition of sin. This is the most personal of images. It's excruciating that the just Judge must declare us guilty. It's worse that the loving Father is separated from his wayward prodigal children. Our original communion with God, broken by original sin, leads to original alienation.

Experiencing condemnation, Adam and Eve *feared*. Experiencing alienation, Adam and Eve *hid*. Previously they had raced to their Father when they heard his voice in the cool of the day. Now they flee from their Father. What a great gulf Adam and Eve fixed between themselves and God when they sinned and became sinners.

As with original sin, so also our original parents bequeathed to us original alienation. "Objects of wrath," Paul labels us in Ephesians 2:3. Our holy and just God not only can't look upon sinners; he must judge sinners. David Wells succinctly explains:

> In Pauline thought, man is alienated from God by sin and God is alienated from man by wrath. It is in the substitutionary death of Christ that sin is overcome and wrath averted, so God can look on man without displeasure and man can look on God without fear.[1]

Holy love mingled. Holiness expressing wrath over sinners' sins, and love taking the initiative to appease his own righteous anger by bearing sin and judgment in our stead.

That's the good news, the gospel. Back to the bad news. What do you get when you mix human sin and divine holiness? Ruptured relationship. Separation. Alienation. Enmity. "Once you were alienated from God and were enemies in your minds because of your evil behavior" (Col. 1:21). "The sinful mind is hostile to God" (Rom. 8:7). No Father, however loving, can wink at such transgression.

As the psalmist recognized, "If you, O LORD, kept a record of sins, O Lord, who could stand?" (Ps. 130:3). None of us. So we hide. Our sins separate us from our Father. Here's Paul's picture of our condition without Christ:

> *Remember that at that time you were* separate *from Christ,* excluded from citizenship *in Israel and foreigners to the covenants of the promise,* without hope *and* without God in the world. *(Eph. 2:12, emphasis added)*

Paul describes our ultimate hopelessness as "without God in the world." Think about those words. "Without God …" Alone. Solitary. Destitute.

The author of Hebrews 10:19 – 23 pictures our predicament without Christ as inaccessibility, restricted approach, and denied access. Denied access is hard enough to handle if it means that your company has fired you and you can no longer access your computer files. However, we're not in the business realm. We're in the family realm, in the living room. It's partitioned off. We're unable to approach our Father. He's playing with his other children, partying with our brothers and sisters, but we're denied entry.

Though reconciliation obliterates that barrier so we're adopted into our Father's forever family, when we counsel Christians we need to take into account their ingrained sense of denied access. The author of Hebrews did. "Brothers, be confident! Bold. That old barrier? Christ demolished it! He opened a new living way into the living room. So what are you waiting for? Rush on in. Draw near to God in full assurance of your acceptance. You're wanted. You're cleansed. Enjoy!" (Heb. 10:19 – 23, author's paraphrase).

Ray and I trialogued about his sense of being an unwanted spiritual orphan. He noticed how he is so very like the returning prodigal son. He rehearses all the reasons why he can no longer be his Father's son, repeating to his heavenly Father why he deserves to live in the slave quarters — all the while ignoring his Father's holy hugs and kind kisses.

Ray also detected how much he tends to be like the pharisaical older brother in Luke 15:25 – 32. "We're so alike," Ray said, explaining his similarities with the older brother's thought processes. "We both say, 'I slave for you. Perfectly obey all your high and holy stipulations. Yet you never party with me.' Like him, I pout. I get angry. No matter how many times God pursues me and pleads with me to enjoy his grace and party with my family, I refuse."

Remnants of the Fall, of the chasm created by sin. Satan loves it when we live out of our old life structure. When we continue to see ourselves as sinners instead of saints and as separated instead of adopted. He loves it when we seek to bridge the canyon by our own works. With that mind-set, we don't dare come home. If we do, we do it in our own effort like the prodigal son or the pharisaical son.

The ministry of biblical counseling requires that we show believers that Christ unlocks the door to home. "Thirsty? Come drink with me. Lonely? Come celebrate with me. Welcome home!"

From Reflection to Corruption to Regeneration

Created to reflect our triune God's image, Adam and Eve corrupted, polluted, and depraved the *imago Dei*. The Bible chooses *temple* imagery to portray the corrupting *presence* of sin. Elohim, whose glory permeates the temple Holy of Holies, is pristine, pure, righteous, sinless, good, and beautiful — perfect holy love. When Adam and Eve fell, they fell short of the glory of God. They failed to reflect the immaculateness of his being, nature, and capacities.

They are now fallen image bearers with a corrupted *imago Dei*. The image remains, but it's desecrated: infected, soiled, defiled, stained, and perverted. Sin befouled our innocent parents' holy garments, contaminating every spot, warping every inch.

We need to think clearly concerning human sinfulness. Sin is not some substance, some being. It is not an impersonal force or power, nor is it a personal being eternally existing with God or coming into existence with Satan. Sin does not have a life of its own. Secular philosophers teach the duality of good and evil — two coequal, coeternal forces. The Bible does not.

Sin is what personal beings do. Or, more accurately, sin is what personal beings imagine, think, choose, do, and feel as they desire and love anything or anyone more than Christ.

Though we might wish to blame a personal or impersonal force for our evil desires and actions, the biblical truth is plain. Only personal beings sin, because sin is the personal rejection of a personal God. Sin is fundamentally relational — it is spiritual adultery committed by spiritual adulterers.

As the label "Rag of Corruption" suggests, fallen image bearers are sinners with corrupted capacities — the fallen personality structure. Created to reflect the Trinity who loves passionately, thinks wisely, chooses courageously, and experiences deeply, we now deflect his nature. Our love is carnal, selfish, and false. Our thoughts are foolish, deluded, and twisted. Our choices and actions are self-centered, compulsive, and destructive. Our emotional experiences are enslaved to fleeting pleasures.

After succumbing to seduction, Adam and Eve realized the significance of their corrupted capacities. "We're naked! Our covering of glory has departed."

Sinful capacities then kicked into gear. *Emotional* fear, based on *rational* lies about God, led them to the *volitional* choice to run and cover up while they pursued the *relational* strategy of hiding (Gen. 3:7, 10).

These corrupted capacities are a basic aspect of original sin that our first parents passed to all their offspring. Because of Adam and Eve, we're born dead.

> *As for you, you were dead in your transgressions and sins, in which you used to live when you followed the ways of this world and of the ruler of the kingdom of the air, the spirit who is now at work in those who are disobedient (volitionally defiant and unable to obey God). All of us also lived among them at one time, gratifying the cravings of our sinful nature (emotionally flesh dominated) and following its desires (relationally perverted) and thoughts (rationally deluded). (Eph. 2:1 – 3, parentheses added)*

We must grapple with ingrained tendencies of the flesh, filtered through the world and prompted by the Devil, even when working with redeemed people. These came into play as I was counseling Ray.

Regenerated, he had a decision. He could live *like* a sinner — his past identity under Satan — or he could live *as* a saint — his new identity in Christ. As we diagnosed his sin together (over the course of several meetings), we saw that when he gave in to sinful anger, it was emotionally pleasing — a quick fix, a great feeling, a release. Volitionally, it was a choice driven by the motivation to feel powerful — important, purposeful, a conquering champion. Rationally, it was a foolish belief — believing that intimidating others could somehow make him complete, manly. Relationally, it was a slap in the face to God. Ray was saying to God, "I need to be in control. My indignant anger and rage intimidates others. It allows me to get my way. I like that. Need it!"

What's Ray to desire, think, do, and feel to live like the renewed person *he already is in Christ?* (Eph. 4:17 – 24). We started with his thirsts in relationship to God. His God was someone to be obeyed, or else. Holy, but little else. His God was as intimidating as Ray was.

I asked, "So when you talk to God in prayer, what's your focus?"

Ray was quick to respond. "I'm always praying that he'll make me holy enough that he won't have to judge me."

I asked Ray to think about his prayer. "You could preach a sermon on your new nature as a saint and on your new relationship with God as a forgiven son. Yet your prayer seems to indicate that Satan is blinding you to both spiritual realities." In another meeting, we trialogued about Ray's images of God and his beliefs about God. "When you confess your sin of intimidating anger, how do you picture God responding? Does he forgive you? Embrace you? Remind you that he laid his wrath on his Son?"

We also talked about Ray's choices. Not simply the choices he made in those moments of temptation, but choices throughout his day to focus on God. It was at this point that Ray said, "I think I don't choose to get close to God because I'm terrified of surrendering fully to him, of being that close to him. I guess I've been believing that intimacy with an intimidating God is like friendship with a prison warden. I'm always one step away from solitary confinement." We wrestled with his insight in this area for some time.

Ray and I talked about his emotional life with God in light of his new identity in Christ. He said that resisting the urge to browbeat others left him feeling weak, puny, and incompetent. So we explored his true identity as a saint in Christ, how the gospel could motivate him to resist that urge, and what it would look like to take those feelings to Christ.

From Dominion to Captivity to Redemption

Law court imagery pictures God the just Judge declaring sinners "Guilty as charged." Home and family imagery pictures sinners as prodigal children separated from their Father and adulterous spouses separated from their Husband. Temple imagery shows us that sin pollutes our nature, infecting every capacity with depravity so that we no longer are like our holy God. Through a fourth image — the slave market — God teaches us that when we are dead in sin, we become the property of sin and are mastered, enslaved, and owned by it rather than servants of our sovereign Shepherd.

Though called to rule, Adam and Eve are now ruled by another. Commissioned to dominion, they are now dominated. Christened "under-shepherds" who care for creation by guiding and guarding, they now selfishly attend only to themselves. In the slave market of sin, an exchange has occurred. They've been bought and paid for so that they are now slaves to sin. Our first parents pass on their original enslavement to their offspring. Like them, we find ourselves, apart from redemption, chained in the slave market.

Paul opens our eyes to our grim captivity in Romans 6:19 when he uses a human analogy in order to depict a spiritual reality. Sin is *like a master*. Adam and Eve, pre-Fall, were innocent and free to choose either God or the Devil, good or evil. Post-Fall, Adam, Eve, and their offspring inherit a sinful disposition and are free to serve only sin. "When you were slaves to sin, you were free from the control of righteousness" (Rom. 6:20).

It is from that sorry, helpless state of slavery that Christ rescues us. He frees us from impotency to potency, from powerlessness to victory. In Romans 6:1 – 23, Paul trumpets, "Know this truth! Reckon on it! Base your Christian life on it! You are now empowered to yield to God, free to choose God's way because you've been bought from the slave market of sin and you've been given a new Master and a new nature!"

Paul's good news is the last news Satan wants us to embrace. Ray had been buying the lie that sin in him was more powerful than Christ in him. "Bob, I know I have the victory. But when the temptation comes, it feels like a monster ten times stronger than me. No matter what I do, I can't defeat it."

"You don't have to," I said quietly.

"What do you mean? You're not suggesting that I let sin win, are you?"

"No. I'm suggesting that sin already lost. Christ defeated it. He's your Master now, not sin. More than that, he's your Victor now. He fought the battle, conquered sin, crucified your old nature, and implanted a new, potent nature within you. In your deepest being you now want to reject intimidating anger, and you have the power to do so."

"Okay," Ray responded, "I hear you saying that I can't simply live by a 'try harder' mentality. So are you saying that I go the other way and just 'Let Go and Let God' do it all for me?"

"Good question. Neither of those options completely captures the biblical concept. 'Know, reckon, and yield' is a better way to convey what Paul teaches. It's progressive sanctification, a process where you first retrain and ingrain in your mind the truth — the fact that your old person with its sin-dominated capacities is dead. You are a new person now with the freedom to choose Christ's way because he implanted in you a new nature (Rom. 6:1 – 10; Eph. 4:17 – 24; Col. 3:1 – 11). Second, you have to reckon on this. In other words, you need to count yourself dead to sinful anger, but alive to God in Christ Jesus (Rom. 6:11). This needs to be your default line of thinking, the way you see yourself and your personal identity. Third, based on those truths, you will need to make a Spirit-empowered decision not to yield to sin or let sin reign so that you obey God's desires instead of sin's desires." As Ray applied the gospel to his daily life, he increasingly put off the old rags of the old man he once was and he increasingly put on the new gowns of the new man he already is in Christ.

Sin's Deep Impact on Our Heart Condition

Sin's deep impact on our relationship to God is clear. Apart from Christ we're condemned as guilty adulterous spouses and prodigal children who are dead in sin and separated from the life of God with depraved relational, rational, volitional, and emotional capacities enslaved to sin.

We now turn our attention to those fallen capacities as we examine sin's deep impact on our heart condition. As biblical counselors, when we talk about the heart, we're talking about our God-created capacities to relate, think, choose, and feel. We can think of these as the four chambers of the heart. To understand the fallen personality structure of the heart, we need to compare and contrast our original state with our fallen state.

An MRI of Our Sin-Sick Heart

Imagine Adam and Eve seconds before the Fall and seconds after. They are the same people, yet totally different.

Before the Fall, they relate passionately and live in God-dependence by sacrificing themselves to care for each other and for God's creation — enjoying and exalting God with every breath. After the Fall, everything changes. They relate selfishly and live self-sufficiently as they protect themselves by blaming God, one another, and the serpent. They cover themselves with fig leaves and worship the creature rather than their Creator. They are spiritual adulterers.

Before the Fall, they think wisely. They envision God as good and see with spiritual eyes God's beautiful plan — thinking God's thoughts after him. After the Fall, they think foolishly and arrogantly by concluding that their heavenly Father fails to know best and withholds his best. They imagine that their greatest pleasure could be in anything other than God. They are heart idolaters.

Before the Fall, they choose courageously. They move toward one another in total openness and guard the garden for God's glory — submitting their wills to God's will. After the Fall, they choose self-protectively and compulsively to follow a fallen nature enslaved to sin and to pursue what they mistakenly perceive to be most pleasing. They are enslaved destroyers.

Before the Fall, they experience deeply, feeling their loneliness when apart ("it is not good to be alone") and their joy when together. They enjoy the fullness of life offered by God and one another — experiencing all of life face-to-face with God. After the Fall, they experience fleshly and shallowly, running from their fears instead of racing to their forgiving Father. They hide and suppress their shame instead of crying out to their Father. By consuming and using others for their own gain, they are ungoverned users.

Before the Fall, they bear the *imago Dei* of the Trinity by being the Good Shepherd's under-shepherds. They give and receive freely and celebrate what they co-create — living through, to, and for God. After the Fall, the image of God within them has been depraved — they live through, to, and for self.

Our MRI provides a snapshot image of the sin-sick heart. Let's develop this image in full color and then perform exploratory open-heart surgery on the prodigal and pharisaical sons of Jesus' parable from Luke's gospel.

Fallen Heart Chamber #1: Relational Corruption — Spiritual Adulterers

When Adam and Eve fell, they retained their relational, rational, volitional, and emotional capacities. Although these capacities still existed, they were twisted. Deprived of connection with God, their capacities degenerated.

As bad as this is, there's something much worse. They were dead. The moment Adam and Eve surrendered to the serpent's seduction, they severed themselves from the umbilical cord of life in God (Eph. 2:1 – 3; 4:17 – 19). They shriveled up and died.

What a paradox! We're dead, but alive. We're zombies in the night of the living dead.

As their spiritual heirs, we are conceived with their corrupt nature. That means that relationally we are still wired for worship, but we choose to worship anything but God. We are lovers who are far too easily infatuated with a cardboard cutout of the real deal.

We can picture fallen worshipers like this:

+ We are worshiping beings created for communion with God.

+ We are dead worshiping beings separated from connection with God.

+ We are deprived and depleted: starving, hungry, thirsty worshiping beings.

+ We are depraved and decadent: crawling anywhere but to God to quench our thirst.

What is a sinner? Sinners are spiritual adulterers who reject God their Maker and Husband (Isa. 54:5) for anything but God.

Freud mistakenly hypothesized that we are psychosexual beings. He believed that the root of all issues was sexual in nature. He identified a symptom of our problem as our core problem. True, many people turn to sex and sexuality as a false god in their frantic attempt to quench their sense of alienation. However, sexual sin is simply a symptom of spiritual sin. We are worshiping beings or *psycho-spiritual* beings — souls related to God. We need God; we fear God; we reject God; we pursue non-god substitutes.

When I'm counseling someone struggling against sin, my mind is not focused on "What psychosexual issue lies beneath their cluster of symptoms?" Instead, I'm wondering, "What *worship disorder* lies beneath their cluster of symptoms? Where does Christ fit into their souls? Is he welcomed? Wanted? Feared? Dishonored?" I'm pursuing causes of their pursuit of non-God substitutes.

Looking for love in all the wrong places, sinners find nothing to fill their empty spaces. Rejecting dependence on the Holy Spirit — the stream of living water flowing within — they're parched. As Cornelius Plantinga insightfully states, "If we try to fill our hearts with anything besides the God of the universe, we find that we are overfed but undernourished."[2] Now what? Needy but empty, sinners' stomachs demand self-sufficient self-satisfaction.

Now we're ready for a comprehensive diagnosis for the fallen relational being:

- Fallen *spiritual* beings experience *alienation* from God and pursue false lovers of the soul in their desperate attempt to quench their thirst apart from God.

- Fallen *social* beings experience *separation* from one another and *manipulation* of one another and dig broken cisterns in their endless quest to use one another to quench their God-sized and God-shaped thirst.

- Fallen *self-aware* beings experience *disintegration* within their own souls and yield to destructive habits of the will and controlling passions of the affections in their futile attempts to quiet their inner restlessness and fill their inner emptiness.

So now imagine that you're providing biblical counseling for the prodigal son and the pharisaical son. Though very different from each other, they each share a fallen relational heart. You could use our MRI of the relational chamber of the fallen heart to diagnose and treat each brother. Some of your heart probes might include:

- Why and how is each son fleeing from the Father? What is each son clinging to and trusting in instead of God the Father?

+ What counterfeit lover/love is each son pursuing? What false cistern is each son trying to drink from?

+ What self-sufficient satisfaction is each son demanding? Why is each son rejecting God-satisfaction? How is each son's source of nourishment leaving him starved and poisoned? If he trusted God's good heart, how might each son be living differently?

+ How could you begin to lovingly, humbly, and boldly expose each son's false trust? How can you communicate to each son his false lover/loves?

Fallen Heart Chamber #2: Rational Corruption—Heart Idolaters

Relationally, sinners retreat from wholehearted worship of God and move to corrupt-hearted love for false gods. *Rationally*, sinners move from spiritual eyes that perceive God's good, generous, gracious heart and move to foolish lie-believers who arrogantly suppress the truth of God's holy love. We can summarize sinful *relational* capacities using the language of false love, impure affections, and spiritual adultery. We can summarize sinful *rational* capacities using the language of fleshly, foolish mind-sets and heart idolatry.

Asaph, speaking as Elohim's mouthpiece, condemns those who "thought I [Elohim] was altogether like you" (Ps. 50:21). We imagine God in our own image. We all have a golden calf (or two or more) that we bow before and worship. In our fallen state, we all worship ourselves and created reality (Rom. 1). As John Calvin famously explained, "The human mind is, so to speak, a perpetual forge of idols."[3]

To understand this process, we need to connect the links in the chain of faith, false love, foolish idols, and the fallen imagination. Faith is the core of the original human personality. God originally designed human beings as *faith-in-God-beings*, but now people are *faith-in-anything-but-God-beings*. Martin Luther provides the insightful connection:

> A god is that to which we look for all and in which we find refuge in every time of need. To have a god is nothing else than to trust and believe him with our whole heart. If your faith and trust are right, then your God is the true God.[4]

By Luther's definition, every person has a god. There is no such thing as an atheist, for everyone must put trust in something or in some combination of other persons and things, or life will disappear.

But how does my heart manufacture the *specific* idol(s) I carve and worship? First, I create sub-biblical images of God — contemptuous images that have no awe of God, no sense of the attractiveness of his beauty and awesomeness of his majesty. Then, with God dismissed, I give birth to idols in my own image to make my life work without God. Stephen Charnock connects contemptuous images of God and arrogant images of self:

> All sin is found in secret atheism. Every sin is a kind of cursing God in the heart. A man at every sin aims to set up his own will as his rule, and his own glory as the end of his actions. Every sin is an effort to turn from the worship of God to the worship of self. At root, sin is self-worship.[5]

I start by saying, "God is not good enough for me." Then I conclude, "I am sufficient for myself."

So how do these insights help us as we try to offer counsel to the prodigal and pharisaical sons? To shine a light on sin at the motivational level requires detecting the characteristic roots and shape of foolish mind-sets (Rom. 8). We need biblical wisdom to perceive the specific false route(s) each son is pursuing to satisfy the specific thirst of his soul.

This requires entering their lives, hearing their stories, and listening to their themes and plot lines. It means exploring with them what motivates them, what they believe about God, themselves, others, and their world. It means engaging their souls so deeply that you can begin to sense who they are, how they relate to you, what drives them, and what they trust in to make their lives work apart from Christ. Some of your heart probes and interventions might include:

- What faulty, foolish, and contemptuous beliefs and images about God, life, self, and others is each son believing? What fabricated subversions of God are guiding each son's mind-set? Where has each son lost his awe of God?

- What specific, unique sinful idol has each son carved in his mind? What is each son uniquely taking refuge in?

- How is each son suppressing the truth of God, Christ, grace, the gospel, the redemptive narrative?

- How could you lovingly help each son to begin to explore the foolish idols of his heart?

Fallen Heart Chamber #3: Volitional Corruption— Enslaved Destroyers

God, who freely wills and powerfully purposes, designed us with the capacity to choose—we are purposeful, *volitional*. God created us not as animals controlled by instinct, computers controlled by chips, or souls controlled by lusts.

How tragically far we've fallen. Now we're unable to have dominion over our own passions, much less God's planet. Titus describes us as enslaved destroyers. "At one time we too were *foolish*, disobedient, deceived and *enslaved* by all kinds of passions and pleasures. We lived in malice and envy, being hated and *hating one another*" (Titus 3:3, emphasis added).

Notice the first link in the chain—foolishness. *Our wills obey our minds, which obey our thirsts.* If we're convinced that God is our supreme good, then we'll pursue him with a steely will. If we're persuaded that God is not good, then we'll pursue non-god substitutes with an enslaved will.

Peter's haunting words portray that enslaved will. "For a man is slave to whatever has mastered him.... 'A dog returns to its vomit,' and, 'A sow that is washed goes back to her wallowing in the mud'" (2 Peter 2:19, 22).

Consider the enslavement cycle we've outlined here:

+ We were created for relationship with the infinite God of the universe.
+ Only God can satisfy our soul.
+ We reject God as our source of life.
+ We retain the God-shaped and *God-sized* vacuum in our soul.
+ We seek to fill that vacuum in non-God ways and through non-God means—through *finite* means.
+ Filling our soul's emptiness becomes our god.
+ It takes an infinite amount of finite "food" to fill the infinite, God-size vacuum in our soul.

We're driven to quench spiritual thirsts with physical water. We try to feed our infinitely hungry souls with finite morsels that can satisfy our stomach for only a few moments.

Picture the infinite goodness of God as a huge dotted line indicating that he is without limits, boundless, utterly immense, immeasurable, and endless. Only his infinite Being could ever quench our thirst.

Now picture our petty substitutes as puny dots, a period at the end of a sentence, a pin-prick, speck, or grain of sand. Pornography, lust, power, promotions, pleasure, money, an affair, acclaim, people pleasing — these are smaller portions than a crumb off the table. How many crumbs will it take to fill the God-sized hunger in my soul? How many grains of sand are required to fill the ocean-sized desire of my heart?

James helps us to understand the connection between our enslaved wills and our destructive relationships when he asks the age-old question, "What causes fights and quarrels among you?" (James 4:1). His answer: "Don't they come from your desires that battle within you? You want something but don't get it" (James 4:1 – 2). Since desire itself is not evil, volitional sin involves our sinful responses to our unmet desires. I want my wife to respect me. She doesn't. How do I respond?

"You kill and covet, but you cannot have what you want. You quarrel and fight" (James 4:2). What do I do with my frustrated desires? I covet. I attempt to manipulate you into meeting my need. "Perhaps my wife will respect me if I'm a successful businessman or the world's best dad." What drives such thinking? A servant's heart? No. The motivation is self-centered. "I must be respected by my wife!" As James says, "When you ask, you do not receive, because you ask with wrong motives, that you may spend what you get on your pleasures" (James 4:3).

Wrongly motivated and empty, what happens if my wife does not comply? I *kill*. I *retaliate*. "I want what I want and I want it now! Give it to me or else!" If my wife does not meet my need, then I'll retaliate against her. "I'll either get back at you or hold back from you." Perhaps I'll be cruel. Or perhaps I'll be aloof.

What's going on in my soul? "You do not have, because you do not ask God" (James 4:2). The sin in our home (human relationships) is always ultimately due to the sin in our heart (relationship with God). The root cause of all human quarrels flows from a spiritual problem. We refuse to humbly ask God; we refuse God-sufficiency.

"You adulterous people, don't you know that friendship with the world is hatred toward God? Anyone who chooses to be a friend of the world becomes an enemy of God" (James 4:4). Spiritual adultery causes every relational problem. An enslaved will is always a destructive will.

The prodigal son and the pharisaical son were both enslaved and they were both destructive — each in his own unique ways. In counseling them each biblically, you want to identify the root source of their enslavement by identifying the core thirst they are trying to quench apart from God, exposing the central foolish beliefs and images that are motivating their futile attempts, and specifying the habitual enslaved path they are following to quench their thirst. To do so you might ponder the following heart probes:

+ What cistern are they digging in their attempt to replace God, the Spring of Living Water? What God-sized and God-shaped vacuum are they each trying to fill with "finite dots"?

+ What does their pattern of behavior indicate about their beliefs about the true source of life?

+ What heart issues might be motivating their manipulation and retaliation? How are issues in their heart impacting issues in their home?

+ How could you help each son to begin to understand the root source of his enslaved and destructive behavior?

Fallen Heart Chamber #4: Emotional Corruption — Ungoverned Users

God designed our emotions to connect us with him. The psalmists illustrate repeatedly that emotions, used well and wisely, can be a thermometer helping us to assess our spiritual temperature and to encourage us to be God-dependent people who soothe our soul in our Savior. God also designed our emotions to connect us with one another. Empathy, rather than being seen as a secular psychology term, is a biblical term for shared pathos — weeping with those who weep and rejoicing with those who rejoice. God gave us the gift of emotions so we can connect with our own responses to the world — being alive to life and experiencing life with depth.

Then it all went wrong when sin entered the human heart. Paul, in Ephesians 4:17 – 19, offers a not-too-pretty picture of the four chambers of the fallen heart. Relationally we're separated from the life of God, rationally we're darkened in our understanding due to the futility of our thinking, volitionally our hearts are hardened, and emotionally we've lost all feelings and given ourselves over to sensuality.

In Ephesians 4:19, Paul chooses a very rare Greek word to describe the emotional condition of the fallen heart. The NIV translates it as "having lost all sensitivity." It means to be "past feeling" or "having ceased to care." Contrast that with God's original design. We now cease to care about our spiritual state and about soothing our soul in our Savior, preferring the pleasure of sin for a season. We cease to care about others and being sensitive to their emotions, preferring instead to use others to meet our every emotional need. We cease to care about experiencing life with depth, preferring shallow and fleeting emotional highs.

Paul's word literally means "a-pathos" — without the ability to use our passion as designed by God, without sensitivity to God and others, focused only on ourselves. When we focus our emotions only on ourselves, we become obtuse to emotional messages, we lack emotional intelligence, and we're insensitive and callous to shame. Rather than givers, we're consumers — taking anything that will make us feel better in the moment.

Paul, as a skilled spiritual heart surgeon, next diagnoses the inevitable result of emotional insensitivity. We give ourselves over to "sensuality." We're ungoverned. Out of control. Sensually trigged to indulge in every possible pleasure. We become addicted to anything that might somehow quiet the screams of emotional pain and spiritual shame. You think I'm overstating it? Paul is even more forceful. We give ourselves up to lewdness to work uncleanness in all greediness, with a continual lust for more.

Instead of using emotions to experience deeply the life God grants us, we misuse our emotions to try to suppress the pain in our soul and the sin in our heart — so that *we do not need God*. We pursue whatever pleases us for a season. We live to survive, to make it somehow. We live *as if* this world is all there is.

The prodigal son and the pharisaical son had two very different ways of handling their moods. Yet they were each, in their own way, ungoverned users. Each disrespectfully demanded of their father. Each was tone deaf to their insensitivity and dishonorable treatment toward their father. Emotional heart probes with these callous sons could include:

+ How is each son misusing emotions to quiet the pain in his soul and the sin in his heart?

+ How is each son ungoverned in the use of his emotions?

+ How is each son living an emotionally demanding life that uses and consumes others?

+ How is each son lacking emotional sensitivity?

+ How could you help each son begin to tune in to their feelings? Tune in to how they are misusing their feelings?

Where We've Been and Where We're Headed

What's the root source of our problem? We've answered that question in two tweet-size ways. First, related to sin's deep impact on our relationship to God:

Apart from Christ, we're condemned as adulterous spouses, dead in sin, separated from the life of God with depraved heart capacities enslaved to sin. Second, related to sin's deep impact on our heart condition: *Sin is what personal beings imagine, think, choose, do, and feel as they desire and love anything or anyone more than Christ.*

Sin's deep impact includes not only our personal sinfulness but also the evils we are suffering. In the next chapter, we'll learn that we live in a fallen world and it often falls on us. Even more than that, though, we'll learn how to apply the gospel to the reality of suffering through gospel-centered self-counsel.

CHAPTER 10

Applying the Gospel to Suffering: Our Gospel-Centered Self-Counsel

The gospel of Christ's grace deals thoroughly *both* with the *sins* we have *committed* and with the *evils* we have *suffered*. Somewhere along the way, some of us may have gained the mistaken notion that to address suffering means minimizing sin and capitulating to a secular psychology perspective on victimization. While I understand that concern, biblically it is unwarranted. In fact, biblical counseling that deals only with the sins we have committed is *half-biblical counseling*.

This means that it is also "half-gospel-centered" counseling. Unlike the Bible, we sometimes tend to make Christ's victory over sin predominantly individual and personal, rather than *also* corporate and cosmic. Christ died to dethrone sin and defeat every vestige of sin. Christ died to obliterate every effect of sin — individual, personal, corporate, and cosmic — including death and suffering, tears and sorrows, mourning, crying, and pain.

That's why twice in Revelation, John sees the culmination of the gospel narrative as the end of suffering and sorrow: "He will wipe every tear from their eyes. There will be no more death or mourning or crying or pain, for the old order of things has passed away" (Rev. 21:4; see also Rev. 7:17). Question 52 in the New City Catechism asks, "What hope does everlasting life hold for us?"[1] John in Revelation answers, "All our greatest sorrows will be swallowed up!" Christ died to defeat every enemy, every evil, including the Devil, who holds the power of death (Heb. 2:14 – 15), and the last enemy — suffering and death (1 Cor. 15:25; Is. 53:4).

Certainly the gospel is about payment for and forgiveness of personal sin — highlighted here in chapters 8, 9, 11, and 12. Equally certain is the gospel's eternal overthrow of the curse of sin — including suffering. That overthrow has already begun! Christ invites us to share with one another his healing hope in the midst of suffering *today*.[2]

It is only through the hope of the gospel that we can truly face suffering and find hope in suffering. Kevin Vanhoozer, in pondering the drama of redemption, explains that tragedies deal with catastrophes. The gospel, while never denying the catastrophe of sin, deals with what he calls *eucatastrophe* — Christ has accomplished something extraordinarily amazing out of something horribly evil.[3] This insight helps us to develop *a biblical sufferology* — a gospel-centered theology of suffering. We'll see that the gospel way to address suffering follows the twin paths of brutal honesty — it's normal to hurt; and radical reliance— it is possible to hope.

The Pathway to Hope Straddles the Precipice of Despair

Olaudah Equiano, a Christian and an enslaved African American, began his life story with these words, "I acknowledge the mercies of Providence in *every* occurrence of my life."[4] His words might sound trite until we realize that they introduce the narrative of his harrowing kidnapping and enslavement.

Equiano was born a free man in 1745 in the kingdom of Benin on the coast of Africa. The youngest of seven children, his loving parents gave him the name Olaudah, signifying *favored one*. Indeed, he lived a favored life in his idyllic upbringing in a simple and quiet village, where his father served as the "chief man" who decided disputes, and where his mother adored him.

At age ten, it all came crashing down:

> One day, when all our people were gone out to their works as usual, and only I and my dear sister were left to mind the house, two men and a woman got over our walls, and in a moment seized us both; and, without giving us time to cry out, or make resistance, they stopped our mouths, tied our hands, and ran off with us into the nearest woods: and continued to carry us as far as they could, till night came on, when we reached a small house, where the robbers halted for refreshment, and spent the night.[5]

His kidnappers then unbound Equiano and his sister. Overpowered by fatigue and grief, they had just one source of relief. "The only comfort we had was in being in one another's arms all that night, and bathing each other with our tears."[6]

Equiano and his sister were soon deprived of even this comfort of weeping together:

> The next day proved a day of greater sorrow than I had yet experienced; for my sister and I were then separated, while we lay clasped in each other's arms; it was in vain that we besought them not to part us: she was torn from me, and immediately carried away, while I was left in a state of distraction not to be described. I cried and grieved continually; and for several days did not eat anything but what they forced into my mouth.[7]

It was during these evil circumstances, and many more to come, that Equiano acknowledged his heavenly Father's good heart and Christ's merciful providence *in every occurrence of his life.* In his autobiography he makes the sweeping affirmation that even in the face of human evil, God is friendly and benevolent, able and willing to turn into good ends whatever may occur. Equiano believed that God squeezes from evil itself a literal blessing:

> I early accustomed myself to look at the hand of God in the minutest occurrence, and to learn from it a lesson of morality and religion; and in this light every circumstance I have related was to me of importance. After all, what makes any event important, unless by its observation we become better and wiser, and learn "to do justly, to love mercy, and to walk humbly before God!"[8]

Olaudah Equiano moved *beyond the suffering.* He faced his suffering candidly, reminding us that *it's normal to hurt.* He suffered face-to-face with God, recognizing that it's possible to hope. His story reminds us of Paul's story in 2 Corinthians 1:8 – 9:

> *We do not want you to be uninformed, brothers, about the hardships we suffered in the province of Asia. We were under great pressure, far beyond our ability to endure, so that we despaired even of life. Indeed, in our hearts we felt the sentence of death. But this happened that we might not rely on ourselves but on God, who raises the dead.*

Like Equiano and Paul, we've all endured hurt that has driven us to the precipice of despair. Unfortunately, we've likely been sent subtle messages: "Christians don't hurt." "Spiritual Christians don't talk about their struggles." Paul, inspired by God, tells us that's a lie. In fact, he shows us that when we deny our hurt, we deny our need for God. And he demonstrates that the pathway to hope often straddles the precipice of despair. Moving *beyond* the suffering first requires moving *into* the suffering.

Clinging to God Our Sustainer: Brutal Honesty

Admittedly, moving into our suffering, facing it with brutal honesty, can be terrifying. We'd all much rather pretend. But here's the good news that Paul starts with — we never have to endure suffering alone. Christ *is* always with us in our suffering and Christians *should* always be with us in our suffering. Paul says it this way, "Praise be to the God and Father of our Lord Jesus Christ, the Father of compassion and the God of all comfort" (2 Cor. 1:3).

Christ Comforts Us in All Our Troubles

We can translate the phrase "Father of compassion" as "our Father feels our pain." Saying "I feel your pain" has been used so much in our world that at times it may seem fake, phony, disingenuous. Not so with our heavenly Father.

The phrase "father of compassion" echoes Psalm 103:13 – 14: "As a father has compassion on his children, so the LORD has compassion on those who fear him; for he knows how we are formed, he remembers that we are dust." Our God is a compassionate Father.

The Greek word for "compassion" expresses the idea of feeling another person's agony. It was a word used to refer to sympathetic lament. God's compassion means that he laments our pain, aches when we ache, and weeps when we weep. Psalm 56:8 (KJV) tells us that God records our laments and collects our tears in his bottle. God mingles his lament with ours, combining his tears with ours. Isaiah 63:9 says it powerfully: "In all their distress [God] too was distressed."

Paul also tells us that God *fortifies* us in our pain — God comforts us, He co-fortifies us. Paul uses the Greek word for "comfort" ten times in five verses in 2 Corinthians 1:3 – 7 to emphasize our Father's comforting nature. In the first of these five verses, Paul tells us that God is the God of *all* comfort. All comfort is sourced in God. The flip side of that is to recognize that worldly comfort — comfort not sourced in God — is ultimately empty comfort.

The Greek word for comfort is a form of a word we've met before: *paraklasis* — one called alongside to help and empower someone in a time of need. It was used of a lawyer advocating for his client, of a mother wrapping her arms of protection around her child, and of a soldier standing back-to-back with a fellow soldier in combat. It translates into two primary English words — encouragement and comfort.

Encouragement means to put courage in someone. God comes alongside of us, envelopes us, shields us, and says, "In your suffering and pain, and the fear that goes with it, *I Am* your courage. We will be brave together." God fortifies us so we can keep on keeping on because we do not have to face suffering alone. God stands back-to-back and shoulder-to-shoulder with us, sustaining us in our suffering.

The Greek word for comfort also pictures the person in need being willing to call out for aid, summoning help, beseeching rescue. Psalm 34:17 – 18 tells us, "The righteous cry out, and the LORD hears them; he delivers them from all their troubles. The LORD is close to the brokenhearted and saves those who are crushed in spirit."

Satan wants us to think that it is spiritual to be above hurting. That's not spiritual; that's arrogant. God wants us to verbalize our suffering, our *neediness*. Paul further highlights our neediness when he tells us that when we cry out to God, he comforts us in all our *troubles*. "Troubles" literally means to press, squash, squeeze. It's used of the pressures of life that squeeze the life out of us, that crush us. It's like trying to lift weights that are more than we can possibly handle. When life overwhelms us, when it's too much to manage, that's exactly the time when we cry out for help to the God of all comfort.

Comforting Others with Our Christ-Received Comfort

The world says, "God helps those who help themselves." But based on the biblical definition of comfort, Paul says, "God helps those who admit they can't help themselves."

More than that, Paul is saying, *"Powerful biblical counselors admit their own powerlessness."* That's exactly what 2 Corinthians 1:4 teaches: "Who comforts us in all our troubles, so that we can comfort those in any trouble with the comfort we ourselves have received from God."

When we are weak — admitting our powerlessness to God, crying out for his comfort — then we are strong, empowered to empower others. God comforts and empowers us in our weakness so that we can comfort and empower others in their weakness. We miss that message sometimes because we skip the little word "can" in verse 4. It means to have the ability to, the capacity and capability to, to be empowered or strengthened, to be able to.

We falsely think that the prerequisite for helping others is always being strong, never needing help. But that's another lie of Satan. It's not the person who always has it together who is helpful — that person's not being candid anyway. It's the person who is consistently and humbly taking their struggles to God who is helpful to others. It's the person with uplifted arms and pleading eyes. If that's you and me, then God can use us to lift others up in their suffering.

There's another important biblical counseling principle tucked away in this verse. We tend to think, "For me to help another person, I have to have gone through the *same* situation or the *identical* trial." For instance, we think, "For me to help someone struggling with alcoholism, I have to have battled alcoholism in my life." But that's not what this verse teaches. Let's take another look. "Who comforts us in *all* our troubles, so that we can comfort those in *any* trouble with the comfort we ourselves have *received* from God."

Whatever our trouble is, if we've taken that trouble to Christ, then his infinite comfort in our life supplies us with the compassion and strength to comfort others with *any* trouble in their life. Our ability to help others is not based on what we've gone through; it is based on our going through suffering face-to-face with Christ.

We then become Jesus with skin on as we offer small tastes of what it is like to be comforted by Christ. As we do this, we don't point people to ourselves; we point them to Christ, who is the ultimate Comforter.

Paul teaches us another biblical counseling principle in verse 5. "For just as the sufferings of Christ flow over into our lives, so also through Christ our comfort overflows." Powerful biblical counselors understand that *shared sorrow is endurable sorrow.*

What does Paul mean when he speaks of Christ's suffering flowing into our lives? The word "suffering" means *external* misfortune, sickness, persecution, and mistreatment along with *internal* pain and sorrow. It is often used, especially with Christ, for suffering on behalf of another — sharing the same suffering, having the same feelings, suffering with, and mutual participation through a full acquaintance and joining into another person's suffering.

Christ speaks of his experiencing the sufferings of others in Matthew 25:42 – 45:

> "'I was hungry and you gave me nothing to eat, I was thirsty and you gave me nothing to drink, I was a stranger and you did not invite me in, I needed clothes and you did not clothe me, I was sick and in prison and you did not look after me.' They also will answer, 'Lord, when did we see you hungry or thirsty or a stranger or needing clothes or sick or in prison, and did not help you?' He will reply, 'I tell you the truth, whatever you did not do for one of the least of these, you did not do for me.'"

This is incarnational suffering, suffering that willingly takes on another person's abuse and agony. If you're a Christian, you've asked Jesus to take on your *sin*. Have you ever asked Jesus to take on your *suffering*? On the basis of

2 Corinthians 1:5; Matthew 25:42 – 45; and Hebrews 4:15 – 16, Jesus invites us to offer him our suffering. What amazing grace! When your suffering overwhelms you, when it brings you to the brink of despair — take it to the foot of the cross. Give it to Jesus. Say to Jesus, "Deliver me from my suffering." Humbly ask the infinite God of the universe to take on your agony.

If we want to help others who are suffering, then we need to follow Christ's model of incarnational suffering. Equiano did. In a letter of spiritual consolation addressed to his long-lost sister, he wrote, "Yes, thou dear partner of all my childish sports! Thou sharer of my joys and sorrows! Happy should I have ever esteemed myself to *encounter every misery for you*, and to procure your freedom by *the sacrifice of my own!*"[9]

What a model of incarnational suffering. Equiano does more than say, "I understand your feelings." He does more than say, "I feel what you feel." *He says, "I am willing to take on your pain — to encounter your every misery for you."*

In this, Equiano is reminiscent of Paul, who, in Romans 9:2 – 3, reveals his great empathy and unceasing anguish for his Jewish brethren. "I have great sorrow and unceasing anguish in my heart. For I could wish that I myself were cursed and cut off from Christ for the sake of my brothers."

As we share God's truth with people, are we willing to allow them to share their pain with us? Are we like Equiano, Paul, and Jesus — sharers of incarnational suffering who weep with those who weep as we take on the pain of others as our own?

I use a rather macabre image to picture this — *climbing in the casket*. When people despair even of life, when they feel the sentence of death as Paul does in this passage, we are to climb in the casket and enter their despair.

God calls us to this as the body of Christ. "There should be no division in the body, but that its parts should have equal concern for each other. If one part suffers, every part suffers with it" (1 Cor. 12:25 – 26). Paul tells us what happens when the body of Christ relates incarnationally. Together we are empowered by the fellowship of Christian endurance:

> For just as the sufferings of Christ flow over into our lives, so also through Christ our comfort overflows. If we are distressed, it is for your comfort and salvation; if we are comforted, it is for your comfort, which produces in you patient endurance of the same sufferings we suffer. And our hope for you is firm, because we know that just as you share in our sufferings, so also you share in our comfort. (2 Cor. 1:5 – 7)

We move from despair to hope, from retreating to advancing, from barely surviving to victorious thriving — together.

Our Christ-Shared Comfort Produces Courageous Endurance

Paul says that suffering on behalf of others produces *patient endurance*. It's a Greek compound word meaning "remaining under." I can remain under pressure without giving in to pressure. The word has the sense of resilience — the ability to turn setbacks into comebacks. It is more than just patience as we think of it. It is courageous endurance. It has the active significance of energetic successful resistance. It is heroism in the face of pain, the firm refusal to give in or give up. The brave determination to forge forward.

We may think that's impossible in the real world. Consider the real world of the slave church in American history. African American slaves were abused from sunup to sundown. Verbal mocking, physical whippings, sexual abuse, lack of food, worked like animals. When they went to the White church services, they heard repeatedly, "Slave don't steal from your master. Slave don't lie to your master."[10]

So Christian slaves, to enjoy real worship, met together in hiding. Rev. Peter Randolph, an ex-slave, described their powerful worship even in the midst of this horrible abuse:

> Arrangements are then made for conducting the exercises. They first ask each other *how they feel*, the *state of their minds*, etc. The male members then select a certain space, in separate *groups*, for their division of the meeting. The slave forgets all his suffering, except to remind others of the trials during the past week, exclaiming, "*Thank God, I shall not live here always!*" Then they pass from one another, shaking hands, bidding each other farewell, and promising, should they meet no more on earth, to strive to meet in heaven, where all is joy, happiness and liberty. As they separate, *they sing a parting hymn of praise*.[11]

The African American church under horribly evil circumstances and sinful abuses survived and thrived together through the intimate exchange of shared comfort and the mutual exchange of gospel hope. Today we don't need churches *with* a biblical counseling ministry. We need churches like the African American church in slavery — churches *of biblical counseling* where one-another gospel ministry saturates all that we do.

Because Paul truly believed what he wrote, he practiced what he preached. He didn't pretend that he was above despair. Recall his words: "We do not want you to be uninformed, brothers, about the hardships we suffered in the province of Asia. We were under great pressure, far beyond our ability to endure, so that we despaired even of life. Indeed, in our hearts we felt the sentence of death" (2 Cor. 1:8 – 9).

Following is a paraphrase of all the words that Paul piled on top of one another in these verses. As you read this paraphrase, ask yourself what you would think of your pastor, elder, Sunday school teacher, Christian school teacher, deacon, women's ministry director, or counselor if any of them admitted to this.

> I want you to know about the pressure, affliction, and squeezing I was under: My soul-crushing was excessively beyond my capacity to endure so that I despaired even of life. I was utterly at a loss, beyond the end of my rope, without a way of escape! Indeed, in addition, in my heart, with eyeballs only, from a human perspective, in myself, in my soul — I felt the sentence of death. I felt like a man condemned to death and told by the Supreme Court that there would be no stay of execution. I had given up and was ready to die!

Could your pastor admit to a struggle this serious, this intense, without being fired? Can you be that honest about your own struggles and suffering?

Paul did not want the Corinthians to be ignorant of what he was going through and what it was doing to him. Martin Luther wrote about two levels of suffering. Level one suffering is what happens *to* us — the external events. Level two suffering is what happens *in* us — the internal reaction. When I think of level one suffering, I often say, "The world is fallen and it often falls on us." When I think of level two suffering, I often say, "The world is a mess and it messes with our minds."[12]

We don't know what external level one suffering Paul was referring to in his letter. But we do know about the level two internal suffering he was experiencing. Whatever it was externally, internally he felt like it was beyond his ability to handle. Have you ever felt like that? He saw no human possibility of survival. Have you ever been there? He was under such weight that he felt like there was no way he had the power to lift it off. Alfred Plummer summarizes it well in his commentary: "St. Paul has many moods, and he has no wish to conceal from the Corinthians how this profoundly great trouble had depressed him."[13]

In his despair, the great apostle of hope was on the precipice of surrendering hope. As in Psalm 88 — the Psalm of the Dark Night of the Soul — Paul was brought into the pit of despair. In Paul's thinking, it was a done deal. "I'm as good as dead. I'm giving up. Bury me. Put me in a tomb."

We would be so ashamed to be so brutally honest about such deep despair and depression. That's because we glory in our strength. Paul glories in his weakness. Paul wants to be real and raw so that his followers could be real and raw. He wants them to have an opportunity to minister to him. He wants them to understand God's power that could raise him victoriously from those tomb-like feelings. He wanted them to know that we don't experience radical reliance on the God who raises the dead until we are brutally honest about our casket experiences.

Trusting in God Our Healer: Radical Reliance

In the middle of 2 Corinthians 1:9 we read one of the most important words in the Bible: "But." "But this happened that we might not rely on ourselves but on God, who raises the dead."

Why does God allow any Christian to arrive at their breaking point? We've already seen one reason — so that we become powerfully equipped to comfort others. Now we see a second reason — so that we will surrender to Christ's comfort. Paul's despair, our crashing into the breakers of life — it all comes for the express purpose that we might not trust in ourselves, but in Christ's resurrection power.

Suffering Happens So We Might Not Rely on Self, but on God

The word for "rely" contrasts trust in God with trust in human resources. For instance, in Philippians 3:4, it compares radical self-confidence with radical God-confidence. In Ephesians 3:12, Paul says that such radical reliance on God results in boldness, daring, courage, freedom, and zest for life.

How in the world did Paul move from abject despair of life to daring zest for life? What in the world could cause us to transport from the tomb to the mountaintop? Actually — nothing in *this world* has anything to do with it.

Paul moved from death to life through radical reliance on God who continually raises the dead. Paul maintains a very specific image of God, and he uses very precise wording to convey that image: God-the-*continuous*-raiser-of-the-Dead. God-the-One-*continually*-raising-the-dead. God's resurrection power is timeless and permanent.

This is why in 1 Corinthians 15:20 Paul says, "But Christ has indeed been raised from the dead, the firstfruits of those who have fallen asleep." We falsely think of the resurrection as only being about Christ. Or we falsely think of the resurrection as mattering only after our final physical death. But in 2 Corinthians 1:9, Paul clearly states that the resurrection has daily, moment-by-moment, continuous application to our lives. We die daily — we suffer daily casket experiences — the loss of a job, foreclosure on our home, betrayal by a friend, a heated disagreement with a spouse, cruel words from a child, illness, death of a loved one ... the list is endless. But for every daily casket experience, Christ promises daily resurrection experiences. He supernaturally resurrects our hope — continually.

Why do we find God's daily deliverance so hard to believe? Because when life stinks, our perspective shrinks. Our vision narrows. We look only at the earthly story of despair. And Satan is only too happy to contribute to our shrunken world. As we've seen, Satan attempts to crop Christ out of the picture. Christ is resurrected, but we aren't looking at life with spiritual eyes. Satan then goes one step farther and tries to erase Christ from the picture entirely. The Holy Spirit enters and refocuses our vision so we can see and experience Christ's daily deliverance at work in our lives.

That's exactly Paul's experience in verse 10: "He has delivered us from such a deadly peril, and he will deliver us. On him we have set our hope that he will continue to deliver us." Paul says, "God delivered me in the past. He will deliver me from my current suffering. And I am confident that he will still deliver me through all that lies ahead — because he is God-the-continuous-raiser-of-the-dead, God-the-continuous-deliverer-from-the-pit-of-despair!"

As Paul put quill to scroll, he was quite possibly meditating on Psalm 40:2–3. "He lifted me out of the slimy pit, out of the mud and mire; he set my feet on a rock and gave me a firm place to stand. He put a new song in my mouth, a hymn of praise to our God. Many will see and fear and put their trust in the LORD."

This is the gospel-centered theme of Paul's second letter to the Corinthians. Assailed inside and out, Paul survives not by self, but by God. Compare 2 Corinthians 4:7–9: "But we have this treasure in jars of clay to show that this all-surpassing power is from God and not from us. We are hard pressed on every side, but not crushed; perplexed, but not in despair; persecuted, but not abandoned; struck down, but not destroyed."

Our future resurrection has present implications. It happens every day! Whenever God raises us up again when we despair of life, he displays nothing less than his resurrection power. It is all implied in one phrase: God-the-continuous-raiser-of-the-Dead!

Healing Happens Jointly so We Might Support One Another

In 2 Corinthians 1:3–11, Paul glides back and forth between our need to depend on Christ and our need to support one another as Christians. He moves from Jesus the ultimate Soul Physician to Christians as human soul physicians. He did so once more in verse 11: "... as you help us by your prayers. Then many will give thanks on our behalf for the gracious favor granted us in answer to the prayers of many."

Paul chooses an intriguing word for "help" that means to operate together, to join in supporting. It would be easy to think that Paul is saying that mature Christians commune with Christ, but don't connect with other Christians. But that is galaxies away from Paul's point and Paul's practice. Paul's hope is firmly fixed on God *and* on his fellow believers.

Joining together as Christians doesn't mean we build some Tower of Babel in independence from God. It means exactly the opposite, and Paul highlights that when he says "as you help us by your prayers." Paul's word for "prayer" expresses personal need and intercession for others. It emphasizes utter dependence and lack of resources. In corporate prayer, human impotence casts itself at the feet of divine omnipotence.

The result of this mutual God-dependence is mutual God-worship. "Then many will give thanks on our behalf for the gracious favor granted us in answer to the prayers of many." Why was Paul so brutally honest about his utter despair? So that the body of Christ could rally around him in mutual radical reliance upon Christ, which results not in a pity party for Paul, but in a worship celebration for Christ's grace for suffering!

Acting like we have it all together doesn't prompt Christ worship or Christian fellowship. Admitting that we desperately need Christ *and* one another — that results in worship and fellowship.

Gospel-Centered Counseling Then and Now

Equiano was not alone in his hurting and hoping. Quobna Cugoano was a kindred spirit. Born in the Fante village of Agimaque in 1757, thirteen years later he was playing with other children when he was led away at gunpoint by slavers. Shoved into the hold of a slave ship, he later described his agony and that of his fellow enslaved Africans.

> The cries of some, and the sight of their misery, may be seen and heard afar; but the deep sounding groans of thousands, and the great sadness of their misery and woe, under the heavy load of oppressions and calamities inflicted upon them, are such as can only be distinctly known to the ear of Jehovah Sabaoth.[14]

Cugoano, like Equiano and Paul, practiced the spiritual art of speaking with *brutal honesty* to the "ear of Jehovah." His image of God was of an

Almighty Warrior God with ears to hear and a heart that cared and comforted those who humbly cried out to him.

Cugoano, like Equiano and Paul, also practiced the spiritual art of *radical reliance* on God and clinging trust in the "good intentions of Jehovah."

> I may say with Joseph, as he did with respect to the evil intentions of his brethren, that whatever evil intentions and bad motives those insidious robbers had in carrying me away from my native country and friends, I trust, was what the Lord intended for my good.[15]

Cugoano trusted God's goodness with radical reliance. Why? Because his image of God focused on God who continually raises the dead from the pit of despair.

As competent gospel-centered counselors who want to help others to apply the gospel to their *suffering*, we need to ask ourselves from our hearts:

- Am I brutally honest with Christ and Christians about my suffering?
- Am I climbing in the casket with my hurting friends?
- Do I acknowledge my need for *the* Soul Physician?
- Do I acknowledge my need for *a* soul physician/spiritual friend?
- Am I trusting in the God-who-continually-raises-the-dead?
- Do I cling to Christ to experience mini-resurrections every day from my mini-casket experiences?
- Am I jointly supporting others by pointing them to Christ?

Being brutally honest *with* Christ about our hurts is the pathway to radical reliance *upon* Christ who supernaturally resurrects our hope.

Where We've Been and Where We're Headed

Scripture is so comprehensive that sometimes we miss its simplicity. One way Scripture conceptualizes our struggles is to see them in two primary categories: *sin and suffering*. "Look upon my affliction and my distress and take away all my sins" (Ps. 25:18). In harmony with this, our tweet-size summary of this chapter states: *Fully biblical gospel-centered counseling deals thoroughly both with the sins we have committed and with the evils we have suffered.* The gospel deals with all of life, defeating the power of sin, Satan, and the curse.

After three realistic chapters on the Fall, we turn our focus to Redemption. The entire movement of this book and the entire movement of the biblical narrative advances relentlessly toward the gospel. What difference does the gospel make as we face and address sin and suffering? How does Christ bring us peace with God? How does Christ change people? We now turn our attention to these grand questions based on the grand narrative of the Bible.

CHAPTER 11

Prescribing God's Cure for the Soul: Part 1—Our New Nurture

If the Bible ended with the Fall, life would be hopeless and we would despair. Reflecting on life without gospel hope, Paul spoke for each of us — of all people we would be the most miserable (1 Cor. 15:19). Thankfully, God's story moves to Redemption. Paul emphasized that point in 1 Corinthians 15:3 – 4 when he reminded the Corinthians what is *of first importance* — the gospel — Christ died for our sins, was buried, and rose again on the third day.

Jesus modeled what was most important in Luke 9:51: "As the time approached for him to be taken up to heaven, Jesus resolutely set out for Jerusalem." In one of the first sermons I ever heard, I vividly recall my pastor, Bill Goode, describing this: "Jesus set his face like a flint to Jerusalem — to be crucified for our sin *and* to be raised for our salvation!"

We grasp the big-picture redemptive movement of the Bible by recognizing that the Bible is comedy, not tragedy. No, not comedy as in a modern-day situation comedy that wraps up every problem in twenty-three minutes, but comedy in the classic sense of that word in literature. The Bible would follow the literary form of tragedy if it stopped at the Fall. Tragedy moves from a wonderful beginning (picture a high point) to a horrible ending without any positive, final resolution (picture the lowest point).

The second episode in the original *Star Wars Trilogy* was tragedy. *The Empire Strikes Back* told a tale that began with the victory of the Republic (the "good guys"), but ended with their defeat at the hands of Darth Vader and the Empire (the "bad guys"). The end begged for a sequel: *The Return of the Jedi*.

That's just like the end of the Old Testament. The old covenant story of the wreckage of Yahweh's marriage to his adulterous wife, Israel, begs for completion. It begs for a New Testament, a new covenant in Christ's blood: *the return of the King*. A return that finds its consummation in the marriage supper of the Lamb (the wedding — Rev. 19:6 – 8) and the great supper of God (the final war — Rev. 19:11 – 21).

The Bible, though not denying the tragedy of the Fall, is comedic in scope. Like all classic comedy, it begins on a high note, moves to a note of despair, but ends triumphantly on the highest note imaginable — *Redemption*. The church fathers discouraged the early Christians from attending Greco-Roman dramas, not because they were PG – 13 or worse, but because they were tragedies — ending without hope. They wanted their flock to have their minds set on and renewed by the promise-filled drama of Redemption.

What Difference Does the Gospel Make?

What difference does the gospel make as we face sin and respond to suffering? To that grand question, based on the grand narrative of the Bible, we now turn our attention. In addressing that question, biblical counselors often ponder two vitally important follow-up questions, "How do we find peace with God?" "How do people change?" However, theologically and practically, we must ask those questions differently, like this: "How does *Christ bring us peace* with God?" "How does *Christ change people?*"

Evangelical theologians and biblical counselors typically answer these two questions with a single word: "Justification!" Chapters 11 and 12 offer that answer, but do not stop there. Instead they examine our *complete* salvation — *justification, reconciliation, regeneration,* and *redemption*.[1] Please do not let these theological words intimidate you. These big words carry big meaning that reveals the bigness of our God and the greatness of our salvation.[2]

In this chapter, we will explore our *new nurture* — justification and reconciliation. By *new nurture* I'm highlighting the change *in our relationship* with God that takes place because of Christ's gospel of grace. It emphasizes who we are to Christ and answers the question, "How does Christ bring us peace with God?"

Then in chapter 12, we will probe our *new nature* — our new creation in Christ. By *new nature* I'm emphasizing the truth that a real change takes place in who we are when we are made new through Christ. It highlights who we are in Christ and addresses the question, "How does Christ change people?"

Through chapters 11 and 12, our goal is to learn together how to apply the gospel truths of justification, reconciliation, regeneration, and redemption to our lives and ministries. As we learn together, we will be answering the question we have been moving toward this entire book, "What would it look like to build an approach to biblical counseling based solely on the gospel of Christ's grace?"

So Great a Salvation: Four Primary Results of Our Union with Christ

Since God designed us not only to think in words but also in images (remember the *yeser*), let's picture our complete salvation. Imagine the vilest offender — as cruel as Hitler, depraved as Manson, corrupt as Jack the Ripper. Desperately wicked. Self-deceived. Anti-social. Amoral. Mr. Mass Murderer. The day his trial begins, every major news network, Internet outlet, online and traditional magazine, and newspaper around the world join the coverage with instant updates and constant tweets.

Justification: Our New Pardon—The Judge Declares Us "Not Guilty! Forgiven!"

Shocking every reporter, spectator, member of the jury, and even his own legal team, Mr. Mass Murderer pleads guilty. Begs forgiveness. Asks for mercy.

Imagine the worldwide outrage as the judge responds, "Not guilty!"

"What a charade! Fool! He just said he was guilty. What is wrong with you? Have you gone mad? Retrial! Ethics probe! He must pay for his crimes!"

"His crimes *have* been paid for," the judge retorts. "By my son. I have judged my son in place of Mr. Mass Murderer. They've exchanged places. My guiltless son, charged with nothing — his good standing I now transfer to Mr. Mass Murderer, who is free to go."

You've not been watching *The Twilight Zone*. Not even reality TV. But reality. Spiritual reality. *New Testament reality!*

God our Judge justifies us, declaring us not guilty, forgiving us our trespasses, and reckoning his Son's righteousness to our account, and our sin and guilt to his Son's account. This is the amazing grace of *justification*.

How does Christ bring us peace with God? We must understand and apply the change in our relationship *that has already occurred* — our acceptance by

God in Christ through grace. When Satan whispers his condemning lies into our ears, we need to remember the truth of Romans 8:1: "Therefore, there is now no condemnation for those who are in Christ Jesus." Putting off Satan's lie, putting on this gospel truth, and living according to it is foundational for ongoing growth toward Christlikeness.

As amazing as the grace of justification is, we sometimes stop too soon in our understanding of amazing grace. We say, "I'm not perfect, just forgiven." But we are not *just* forgiven. To justification, God adds reconciliation.

Reconciliation: Our New Peace — The Father Says to Us, "Welcome Home!"

Imagine the spectators in the courtroom yelling, "But he's still evil through and through! A man like him can never change. He's a danger to society. He must be locked up. Looked after."

"He will live with me," the judge replies. "Enjoying all the privileges my son enjoys. I've adopted Mr. Mass Murderer into my family. He's my adult son."

God the Judge could have stopped at justification — forgiving us and then leaving us on our own. Left to our same old nurture (old relationships) we would return to our same old haunts — the world, the flesh, and the Devil. We would continue our maddening quest for relationship apart from God.

But God the Judge takes his legal robes off, replacing them with relaxed family attire, inviting us into his home, into his family, saying, "Welcome home!" — *reconciliation*. Forgiveness (justification), as amazing as it is, would have been hollow had we remained separated from the Father. The Judge becomes our adoptive Father, granting us access to his home and all the privileges of adult children — sons and daughters of God. This is the amazing grace of *reconciliation*.

How does reconciliation bring us peace with God? We must understand and apply the truth of the change in our relationship with God *that has already occurred* — our acceptance by God in Christ through grace. Imagine the difference that could take place in our lives if we applied the truth of Romans 5:1. "Therefore, since we have been justified through faith, we have peace with God through our Lord Jesus Christ."

Justification and reconciliation address our relationship to God the holy Judge and loving Father. Combined they show us who we are *to* Christ — our new *nurture*. Do we truly believe and apply the reality that we are forgiven and welcomed sons and daughters loved by the God of the universe?[3]

Regeneration: Our New Person—The Creator Says to Us, "You're a New Creation in Christ! Saints!"

The still-insistent crowd hollers, "That guarantees nothing! All your good intentions, all the love in the world, all the good nurture and best environment does not guarantee that Mr. Mass Murderer will not continue his rampage."

"I'm not finished. Hear me out," the judge insists. "I've consulted the best medical experts on the planet. Mr. Mass Murderer will receive a heart, brain, and soul transplant along with a DNA graft infusing into his very being my very nature."

The Judge of the criminal and the Father of the adult son become the Creator and Life-giver of a newborn infant — *regeneration*. Like Father, like son. We are born again of incorruptible seed. Born from above to reflect the image of our Creator. We are reborn with a new nature, a new heart — new soul, mind, will, and emotions — reborn with a renewed ability to relate (to God, others, and our self), think, choose, and feel *in Christlike ways*. God creates a new heart within us — new capacities, disposition, inclinations, purity. The old dies. The new lives. We are not only sons and daughters (reconciliation); in Christ we are *saints*. This is the amazing grace of *regeneration*.

As the story of Mr. Mass Murderer correctly indicates, new *nurture* (justification and reconciliation) without new *nature* (regeneration and redemption) is insufficient to change us. What changes us? How do people change? Christ changes us. As new creations in Christ, we are *already changed internally*, and now we help one another to live out and to grow into the new life already implanted within.

We seek to help each other to understand and apply the reality of the transformation: "Therefore, if anyone is in Christ, he is a new creation; the old has gone, the new has come!" (2 Cor. 5:17). "And we, who with unveiled faces all reflect the Lord's glory, are being transformed into his likeness with ever-increasing glory, which comes from the Lord, who is the Spirit" (2 Cor. 3:18).

Redemption: Our New Power—The Victor Says to Us, "You Are More than Conquerors through Christ! Victors!"

The shrill crowd is momentarily silenced. Totally stunned. Then a hand shoots up. "But that only means he has a clean start. What about all his old acquaintances, his old habits? They will still come around clamoring for his attention, demanding his loyalty and affection."

"Fair question," the judge agrees. "We've thought of everything. I've jailed all his old acquaintances. His foes are defeated. Plus, we've infused his new heart, brain, soul, and DNA complex with core power to remain free from and victorious over these past tempters."

This is the salvation grace of *redemption*. Freedom from the power of sin. Freedom from bondage and slavery to sin. We need victory. Resurrection power. The Judge of the criminal, the Father of the adult son, the Creator of the newborn infant, is also the Champion and Victor of the overcomer, of the empowered, freed, victorious conqueror.

How do people change? Not through our own power, but through tapping into Christ's resurrection power that has already changed us and is always available to us. We have been set free from the power of sin and death and united with the resurrection power of Christ. "But thanks be to God that, though you used to be slaves to sin, you wholeheartedly obeyed the form of teaching to which you were entrusted. You have been set free from sin and have become slaves to righteousness" (Rom. 6:17–18). We have Christ's resurrection power to be victorious over the world, the flesh, the Devil, sin, and death.

We are new creations with new power because of our new *nature*: regeneration and redemption. God has implanted a new heart into the core of our being with a new capacity to live godly lives. Do we truly believe that we are more than conquerors in Christ?[4]

Our Salvation in Christ and Our Biblical Counseling

At times we mistakenly counsel Christians as if they were non-Christians. We view our counselees only or predominantly through the lens of depravity/sin. This would be like a heart surgeon transplanting a perfectly healthy new heart into a patient, but then treating her patient as if he still has his old heart in his chest. To avoid this, the four realities of our union with Christ — justification, reconciliation, regeneration, and redemption — should guide every interaction and intervention when counseling fellow Christians.

Now we can restate our redemptive question: "*What would a biblical counseling model of change look like that was built solely on Christ's gospel of grace applied to Christians — justified, reconciled, regenerated, and redeemed people?*" Chapters 11–12 and 15–16 seek to move us toward an answer to that question, with chapters 11–12 exploring salvation by grace and chapters 15–16 exploring how we work out our salvation — progressive sanctification — by grace.

To minister effectively, we need a biblical imagination, a biblical vision, that perceives the big story God is writing and our role in it. We need to understand that we've been placed in the middle of the greatest story. We need to take these big salvation words and apply them to our daily lives together.

- Justification: "To your sin and condemnation, the gospel says, 'Not guilty! Forgiven!'"
- Reconciliation: "To your lostness and aloneness, the gospel says, 'You are accepted. Adopted. You are family — sons and daughters. Welcome home!'"
- Regeneration: "To your fallenness and heart of stone, the gospel says, 'You're a new creation in Christ. Saints!'"
- Redemption: "To your enslavement to sin and defeat at the hands of the world, the flesh, and the Devil, the gospel says, 'You are more than conquerors through Christ. Victors!'"
- Salvation and Suffering: "To your deep grief, the gospel says, 'Mourning does not have the final word. Healing does. Joy does.'"

Please stop reading and ponder, pray. What difference would it make in your life if you saw yourself in Christ, every second, as a forgiven son/daughter, saint, and victor? What difference could it make in your ministry if you whispered or shouted these words to your counselees: "Forgiven! Welcome home! New creation! Free!"

If any of this sounds overly dramatic, then perhaps we need to read our Bibles again. The cross is the climax of the Bible's relational drama where God enters the courtroom both as the Judge *and* as the aggrieved Spouse and charges his bride with adultery — marital unfaithfulness. Then God the Judge and aggrieved Spouse takes the charge upon himself in the form of his Son[5] — the act that both justifies and reconciles, and results in regeneration and redemption.

Biblical Counseling as Gospel Conversations

Is the gospel narrative truly the foundation for biblical counseling? David Powlison reacts strongly even to raising that question:

> What is the place of Christ's good news in biblical counseling? That is rather like asking, "What is the place of water and carbon in human physiology?" The gospel of Jesus is the fundamental stuff of biblical counseling. Counseling that lacks Jesus, however skillful, is not wise.[6]

The epistle to the Hebrews floods our minds with the gospel. However, sometimes we read Hebrews and miss the author's point — we miss his description of his purpose. "Brothers, I urge you to bear with my word of exhortation (*logou paraklaseos*), for I have written you only a short letter" (Heb. 13:22, parenthesis added). Hebrews is a letter of gospel consolation, of spiritual counsel encouraging weary Christians to stand firm through suffering's trials and to cling to Christ against sin's temptations.

I sovereignly stumbled upon this reality when I began examining the phrase "word of exhortation/encouragement." The synagogue rulers use the same wording when they invite Paul to share a "message of encouragement" (*logos paraklaseos*) in Acts 13:15. In response, Paul delivers a gospel conversation in Acts 13:16 – 52 that shows and tells the good news of the gospel's Creation (Acts 13:17, 20), Fall (Acts 13:18, 21), Redemption (Acts 13:19, 22 – 25), and Consummation (Acts 13:34 – 37) narrative.

Paul calls this narrative the "message of salvation" (Acts 13:26) and the "good news" (Acts 13:32) and he applies it directly to the lives of his listeners so they can enter into a relationship with God through the forgiveness and justification found only in the resurrected Christ (Acts 13:27 – 39). Paul further applies gospel truth to their lives so that even in the midst of persecution and suffering they can continue in the grace of God (Acts 13:43 – 52).

Paul's message in Acts 13 and the entire letter to the Hebrews are each biblical examples of the *personal ministry of the Word*. They model gospel consolation and counsel that present the Bible's redemptive narrative and personally apply it so that people are encouraged to continue in the grace of Christ in the midst of suffering and sin. Gospel counsel urges people to single-minded devotion to the One who is infinitely superior to all others, the One in whom all salvation, sanctification, and eternal satisfaction are found.

"Welcome Home!": A Biblical Model of Applied Justification and Reconciliation

In Hebrews 10:19 – 25, we listen in on a powerful and practical gospel-centered counseling session. This passage models how we should relate our new nurture — our justification and reconciliation — to people struggling with suffering and fighting against besetting sins.

The recipients of the letter were exhausted by their trials and were tempted to sin; they were ready to give up and give in. As they're reaching up to surrender, the author of Hebrews encourages them with these words:

Remember those earlier days after you had received the light, when you stood your ground in a great contest in the face of suffering. Sometimes you were publicly exposed to insult and persecution; at other times you stood side by side with those who were so treated. You sympathized with those in prison and joyfully accepted the confiscation of your property, because you knew that you yourselves had better and lasting possessions. So do not throw away your confidence; it will be richly rewarded. You need to persevere so that when you have done the will of God, you will receive what he has promised. (Heb. 10:32 – 36, emphasis added)

When these believers first committed their lives to Christ, their first love was so strong that they followed Jesus anywhere. They handled trials and temptations by clinging to Christ because they trusted him as their Savior, Sovereign, and Shepherd. But now they're tempted to throw away their confidence. Their trust is wavering. Everything inside screams at them to shrink back and say, *"I just can't do this, I can't go on. Following Christ is too hard."*

We have all had to battle similar temptations. Life is hard. We and the people we counsel are wrestling with emotional struggles and deep losses that break our hearts and seem to sap every ounce of energy. We and the people we love are battling sins that threaten to control and consume us and that seem to drain each speck of joy.

However, as bad as our trials are, the worst trial is our trial of faith — the temptation to give up on Christ and to give in to sin. Trials and temptations bring us to a faith point. Do we cling to Christ, or do we fling away our trust in Christ? Do we turn toward and run to Christ like we did when we first committed our lives to Christ, or do we lose confidence in Christ as our faith shrinks and our hope shrivels?

Hebrews 10:19 – 25 provides gospel encouragement to hold on to hope by reminding us who God is and what he has done for us in Christ. It's a message of peace with God — forgiveness (justification) and welcome (reconciliation) that counters the message that we receive from the world, the flesh, and the Devil — a message of condemnation and rejection.

Unforgiven and Unwelcome

Unforgiven, the classic Western starring Clint Eastwood, is a dark parable of the unforgiven and unwelcome soul. This grim and gritty film accurately portrays the despair and emptiness of the human heart in need of grace.

Eastwood plays the aging gunslinger Will Munny. In his younger, wilder days, Munny killed many men. However, as the film opens, we meet a Will

Munny who is no longer a gunslinger. He's been reformed by the love of a good woman, his wife, Claudia. She helped him give up whiskey and hang up his guns, but now Claudia is dead, killed by smallpox. Grieving, poor, and debt-ridden, Munny tries to eke out a living for himself and his two children as a pig farmer on the Kansas plains.

Then one day, a brash young gunslinger calling himself "the Schofield Kid" rides into town to remind Munny of his ugly past. "I hear tell you've killed a lot of men," the Kid tells him. "Well, up in Wyoming, there's $1,000 to be had for killing two cowboys. Seems one of 'em got mad at a woman and slashed up her face. The other ladies in that establishment have posted bounty on the heads of those two cowboys. If you come with me, we can kill those boys and split the reward."

"No," Munny replies, honoring the wishes of his dead wife. *"No more killin' for me. I ain't like that anymore, Kid."* The Kid rides off alone. But then Munny begins to think, "How are my children going to live? How will I pay off this debt? My split of that money sure would go a long way."

So he straps on his gun, and he and his friend, Ned, ride off to catch up with the Schofield Kid. As they ride together, the Kid, who is fascinated by Munny's reputation as a killer, pumps him for stories of his past. But Munny doesn't want to remember his past sins. *"I ain't like that anymore,"* he keeps repeating to Ned, the Kid, and to himself, denying the obvious question, *"If he 'ain't like that anymore,' then why is he riding off to Wyoming to kill a couple of cowboys?"*

Together they track down the two cowboys. Munny shoots one of them, a fresh-faced boy named Davey. It's a grisly scene. Later, the Kid shoots the other cowboy — Quick Mike. It's a cold-blooded killing of an unarmed man.

Later, the killings accomplished, Munny and the Kid sit under a tree outside of town waiting for their reward money. While they wait, they talk. The Kid is full of remorse and in tears. His earlier fascination with killing has evaporated now that he has actually killed a man. Munny, whose soul is stained with the blood of countless men, says, "Terrible thing, killing a man. You take away all he's got and all he's ever gonna have."

"Yeah," says the Kid, his voice choking. "Well I guess they had it comin'."

Munny looks back at him coldly and tells him, *"We all have it comin', Kid."*

It's a dark moment in a dark film. Munny's terse comment — "We all have it comin'" — is the statement of a man who can't escape his past, his sin, or his guilt. It's the statement of a damned soul. The title is fitting: *Unforgiven*, for this film is about guilt and payback. Everyone in the film is guilty: the two dead cowboys, the sheriff played by Gene Hackman, Ned, the Schofield Kid, Will Munny. In the end, *everyone is guilty, but no one is forgiven.*

Unforgiven won four Academy Awards, including best picture because it touches the very nerve center of our soul. We're all guilty. And we all need to hear the story of our Father's forgiveness. We all long to experience the thrill of our forgiving Father welcoming us into his forever family. Each of us, in our unique way, is a prodigal wandering far from home. Each of us longs for our *homecoming.*

Yet according to the letter to the Hebrews, an immovable obstacle stands in our way. Our sin blocks the door to our Father's house because unholy people cannot stand in the presence of a holy God. Our guilt requires payment and our sin requires cleansing. On our own, our situation is hopeless.

But Hebrews 10:19 – 25 tells us we are not on our own. God has a plan — he has always had a plan — a plan to showcase his amazing grace. God's grace in Christ pays for our sin, forgives our guilt, and cleanses us from all unrighteousness. The story of Hebrews, the story of our lives, does not end at a bolted door. Christ's sinless life, substitutionary death, and victorious resurrection break the chains of sin and separation. In Christ, our forgiving Father welcomes us into his forever family.

Remembering What We Have in Christ: Forgiveness and Welcome

As you hear about amazing grace, you might be thinking, "What a great message for the *unsaved* — to those who have never entered the door to the Father through Christ." And while it is a lifesaving message to those who do not yet know Christ, this message — the message of the gospel, forgiveness, and the Father's open arms — is very much a message for believers as well. Hebrews 10:19 – 25 starts with the words, "Therefore, *brothers*" — speaking of Christians. The message of our Father's forgiving, welcoming heart is a message that Christians must remind each other of daily. It is a message that all people — believers and those who do not yet believe in Christ — desperately need to hear.

Embracing Our Forgiveness in Christ: Justification

In Hebrews 10:19, the author of Hebrews introduces us to the implications of our forgiveness in Christ. "Therefore, brothers, since we have confidence to enter the Most Holy Place by the blood of Jesus …"

The truth that we can stand in the presence of a holy God is so astonishing that when we look at our sin, we find it difficult to believe. I'll never forget counseling Kim—a believer who was struggling with a besetting sin—who told me, *"Pastor Bob, some sins are so deep that even the love of God can't reach them."* Though deep in her heart Kim knew that those were lies from the pit of hell, yet in her tormented conscience, she felt that her sins were so dark that she was doomed to live an unforgiven life—even as a Christian.

Kim is not alone in believing that lie. Satan wants us to think that maybe Christ could forgive us for our sins before we were believers, but not after we come to Christ. Satan wants to keep us cringing when we think of our holy God and our sinful lives.

Rather than cringing, the author of Hebrews wants to keep us confident when we think of God and the forgiveness we have in Christ. That's why he said, "Since we have *confidence* …" The word *confidence* means holy boldness. It pictures the absence of fear in speaking to royalty, the courage to enter the King's presence.

After spending a good deal of time seeking to understand what factors in Kim's past, in her relationships, and in her thinking would lead her to doubt God's forgiveness, we turned to Hebrews 10:19–25. As Kim and I read this passage, I asked her to imagine that somehow she scored an invitation to meet the president of the United States. She agreed that she would be more than a tad intimidated by such an encounter.

Then I asked Kim to multiply that infinitely, exponentially so she could begin to feel how the recipients of this letter felt when they thought about entering God's presence. I noted that the *holy place* refers to the Holy of Holies in the Old Testament tabernacle or temple. Inside the outer courtyard was the holy place, and farther inside, separated by a veil, was the Holy of Holies—where God's presence dwelt. No one could enter into the Holy of Holies except the high priest, and he could do so just once a year to offer sacrifice for the sins of the nation. And even the high priest entered with fear and trembling.

In the Old Testament times, no one could see God and live. When personal sinfulness collided with God's infinite holiness, death was the result. So any thought of entering God's holy presence was met with dread and cowering.

Then we explored what Hebrews 10:19 is telling us. "Kim, instead of 'Stay away or die!' it's 'Come near and party!' You walk up to the president confidently and shake his hand. And you can stand confidently in the holy presence of our holy God, look him in the eyes, and know that your every sin is forgiven. Think about this: Because of Christ, you can look God in the eyes. Where normally the shame of your sin would cause you to refuse to make eye contact, now Christ lifts your chin and points your gaze to your forgiving Father's loving eyes."

As Kim and I explored that passage, we reminded ourselves that we must never forget the last words of verse 19: "*… by the blood of Jesus.*" In ourselves, in our sin, we ought to be terrified of our holy God. Without Christ's shed blood, our sin results in shame and separation. But when we accept Christ as our Savior, we're accepting his blood as the cleansing for our sin.

After much interaction around that passage, I asked Kim during the week to pen a prayer of accepting her acceptance in Christ. She returned the next week with these words:

> *Father, thank you for Jesus. Thank you for his sinless life, shed blood, and resurrection. Thank you that when your holy eyes look upon me, you see Christ and his holiness rather than my sins. Father, please keep reminding me that your love is so deep that Christ died for every sin I committed in the past, committed today, or will commit tomorrow. Help me to have confidence — holy boldness — to enter your holy presence because I know that Christ's blood reaches, cleanses, and forgives my every sin. In Jesus' cleansing name I pray, amen.*

Embracing Our Father through Christ: Reconciliation

As Kim and I rejoiced over her prayer, we discussed how truly amazing it is that we have forgiveness in Christ. But as we explored Hebrews further, we saw that it gets even more amazing. "Therefore, brothers, since we have confidence to enter the Most Holy Place by the blood of Jesus, by a new and living way opened for us through the curtain, that is, his body" (Heb. 10:19 – 20). Kim was floored to realize that because Christ opened the way home, she not only has forgiveness, she also has a Father who invites her into his forever family.

To help Kim to understand the implications of those verses, I shared my story, telling her the story I included in chapter 1 about understanding only half the picture of my salvation. How at first I saw God as only my forgiving Judge, but then came to revel in him as my welcoming Father. During the rest of our meeting, Kim and I engaged in some gospel conversations. "Kim, how would it impact you if you saw that through Christ, God is not only the Judge who forgives you but also your Father who *welcomes* you?" "What difference might it make if you truly believed that he has *always* loved you and that's why he sent his only begotten Son to die for you?" "How might it help for you to picture that now with the barrier of sin demolished, nothing stands between you and your loving heavenly Father?"

After much interaction about applying these gospel truths to her life, I asked Kim during the next week to pen a prayer of homecoming. She returned with these words:

> *Father, thank you that you are not just the holy Judge who forgives me and then sends me away. Thank you that because of Christ, I have 24/7/eternal access to you. Please help me to know that you are not the cosmic Killjoy who wants to stomp me and crush me in your holy wrath. Help me to know that you're my loving Father who already spent your wrath on your Son. There's nothing left but love and mercy! Help me to freely and confidently cry out to you, 'Abba, Father, Daddy!' In Jesus' welcoming name, amen.*

Applying What We Have in Christ

At first, we might be tempted to separate Hebrews 10:19 – 25 into two unrelated sections. The first section is about Christ and our justification and reconciliation. The second is about the body of Christ and our mutual encouragement. But if we separate these, we miss the logical, theological, and counseling connection between them: gospel conversations (Heb. 10:21 – 25) are impossible without gospel grace (Heb. 10:19 – 20).

We have forgiveness and welcome in Christ. That's our spiritual reality … now … we live like it. We apply that truth each day in how we relate to God and others through faith, hope, and love.

Drawing Near to God in Faith

The author of Hebrews emphasizes this connection in Hebrews 10:21 – 22. "And since we have a great priest over the house of God, let us draw near to God with a sincere heart in full assurance of faith, having our hearts sprinkled to cleanse us from a guilty conscience and having our bodies washed with pure water."

As Kim and I discussed this, we noted that the reason we are forgiven and welcomed is because Christ is our High Priest. We explored together how in the Old Testament the high priest represented the people before God. When the high priest, once a year, entered God's presence in the Holy of Holies, symbolically every Israelite entered with the high priest. Christ is our great

High Priest who represents us before his Father. Christ is ever present with the Father, seated on the throne of grace praying. When we enter the throne room in prayer, we're fully welcomed because our sins have been placed on our High Priest, Christ, and our Father remembers our sins no more.

I explained to Kim, "This is what the author means when he encourages us to draw near to God with full assurance of faith because our hearts have been sprinkled to cleanse us from a guilty conscience. The number one reason we don't draw near to God in prayer is because of a guilty conscience. We know we're forgiven, but we also know that we keep on sinning. Satan lies to us and says, 'You can't talk to God unless your Christian life is perfect. He doesn't want to hear from you. He's ashamed of you. You should be ashamed of yourself. Don't you dare enter God's holy presence!'

"But Kim, the author of Hebrews says, 'No. No!' He tells us that by *faith* we're to believe that when we pray, the Father sees and hears the righteousness of Christ. Yes, we do have to be perfect to enter God's presence. *In Christ* we *are* perfect."

I could tell that Kim was tracking well when she said, "So you're saying that the very action I most need to take when I'm sinning is to pray! Yet my guilty conscience and Satan's lies drive me away. But they don't have to because my guilt and my guilty conscience are cared for in Christ. So I can pray freely and confidently as a child to my Father!"

Kim, remembering a passage we explored previously, then said, "Isn't that what we're told to do in Hebrews 4:16? 'Let us then approach the throne of grace with confidence, so that we may receive mercy and find grace to help us in our time of need.' Like you said then, Pastor Bob, it's not the throne of *judgment*. In prayer we go to the throne of *grace*. So even in the midst of losing battles with sins, because of Christ I find my Father's mercy and grace to help in my most desperate times."

Holding On to Hope

The author of Hebrews seamlessly merges from *faith* to *hope*. "Let us hold unswervingly to the hope we profess, for he who promised is faithful" (Heb. 10:23). As Kim and I read those words, she compared them to Hebrews 3:1, which we had applied in an earlier meeting. "Therefore, holy brothers, who share in the heavenly calling, fix your thoughts on Jesus, the apostle and high priest whom we confess."

"Pastor Bob, I remember you saying that 'fix' was in a tense that means we're to fix our eyes *continually* on Jesus. We don't simply look once at Christ in a crisis and then turn our eyes away — that's *snapshot* Christianity, as you called it. We keep focused on Christ throughout the crisis — that's *video* Christianity."

"That's right, Kim. And here in Hebrews 10:23, the author tells us to anchor ourselves continuously to Jesus. 'Let us hold unswervingly to the hope we profess.' In the context of trials and temptation, we are to hold *unswervingly*. The Greek word means without wavering, leaning, fainting. It pictures a ship tossed at sea and needing to be securely anchored — all the time."

Kim and I noticed *who* our anchor is — Christ. He's the reason we can hold on to hope — because he who promised is faithful. What has God promised? Hebrews 13:5 tells us: "Never will I leave you; never will I forsake you." And because of that promise, what do we do? Hebrews 13:6: "So we say with confidence, 'The Lord is my helper; I will not be afraid. What can man do to me?'"

The following week Kim offered this prayer, applying these gospel truths to her life:

> *Father, two meetings in a row you've encouraged me to keep my focus fixed on Christ, my anchor of hope. When tempted to despair, remind me of the truth of my eternally secure hope in you. Remind me of John 10:28–29: 'I give them eternal life, and they shall never perish; no one can snatch them out of my hand. My Father, who has given them to me, is greater than all; no one can snatch them out of my Father's hand.' When my grip grows faint, empower me to have complete confidence in the strength of your grip. In Jesus' powerful name, amen.*

Encouraging One Another in Love

During that next meeting, Kim and I explored how in Hebrews 3, after reminding us to fix our focus on Christ, the author urges us to encourage one another. Then, in Hebrews 10:23, after reminding us to keep our hope always anchored to Christ, the author again urges us to encourage one another. We summarized the consistent message of Hebrews: *our walk with God is a community project.*

It's pictured like this in Hebrews 10:24–25. "And let us consider how we may spur one another on toward love and good deeds. Let us not give up meeting together, as some are in the habit of doing, but let us encourage one another — and all the more as you see the Day approaching."

I mentioned to Kim that when we're told to *consider* one another in 10:24, it's the same word used in Hebrews 3:1 that was translated as "fix your thoughts on." As Christians, we're not only to focus on Christ, we're also to focus on one another.

At this point, I asked Kim to summarize everything we'd been discussing. "Well, the author of Hebrews is saying, 'Since you've been given forgiveness, acceptance, peace, faith, and hope in Christ, quit focusing on yourself and start focusing on others!' A few months ago I could never have imagined myself saying that or doing that. I was so consumed with a self-focus because I was so convinced by Satan that God did not want to have anything to do with me."

Kim and I next pondered what we are to consider or focus on — *spurring one another on*. I mentioned that "spur" is a very strong word in the Greek which means to provoke, agitate, stir up, stimulate, or prod. It was used in a negative sense in Acts 15 of the sharp disagreement or contention that caused Paul and Barnabas to go their separate ways. Here it's used for the positive purpose of stirring each other up toward love and good deeds. Just because it's positive doesn't mean it's wimpy. Throughout the New Testament, we're encouraged as brothers and sisters in Christ to boldly speak the truth in love to one another."

Kim was honest in response. "Bob, it was just weeks ago that I couldn't even face my own sin. It may take some time for me to be that lovingly bold with others."

"I appreciate your honesty, Kim. You're right. As we've said, it is a *progressive* sanctification process. You're in process, like we all are. I think the final verse in this section helps us in that process." So Kim and I read Hebrews 10:25: "Let us not give up meeting together, as some are in the habit of doing, but let us encourage one another — and all the more as you see the Day approaching."

"Kim, he starts with a negative — stop abandoning each other. That's literally what the phrase 'give up meeting together' means — to abandon, forsake, let down, desert. It pictures leaving behind, leaving in the lurch."

Kim counseled me with her response. "So leaving people in the lurch is the exact opposite of how Christ treats us. In Christ we have forgiveness and acceptance. In Christ we have a throne of grace. He never leaves us or forsakes us. No wonder we shouldn't do that to each other."

Kim and I were thrilled that the author concludes on a positive note: "Let us encourage one another — and all the more as you see the Day approaching." Kim asked what *day* the author meant. I mentioned that in the Greek it's not just any day, but *The Day*. And that when the Bible talks about *The Day* it means *The Day* of Christ's return.

Kim said, "It's like the human author of this passage, the divine author of this passage, and you, Pastor Bob, have been saying to me, 'Kim, I know you're tired. But the finish line's in view. One day — *The Day* — you will see Christ face-to-face, and it will be worth it all to fall into his embrace and to hear his, "Well done, my good and faithful daughter."'"

"That's a beautiful picture, Kim," I responded. "And it fits so well with the word the author uses for *encouraging* one another, which means to come alongside and help. We're not just in the stands telling others to keep running. We're right there with them, running alongside them, stride by stride, shoulder to shoulder. All of us, with our eyes fixed on Christ and on our forgiving Father with his arms open wide saying, 'You can do it! Keep running to me and for me and in my power!'"

Where We've Been and Where We're Headed

Recall that our fifth ultimate life question is typically asked as: "How do we find peace with God?" "How do people change?" Instead, we've asked it as, "How does *Christ bring us peace* with God?" "How does *Christ change people?*"

We've noted that often the one-word answer is "justification." But we've also seen that this is just part of the answer, that we need to focus on our complete salvation. So here's this chapter's answer in a tweet: *We must build our biblical counseling models of change on Christ's gospel applied to Christians — justified, reconciled, regenerated, and redeemed people.*

Four great miracles stand at the heart of the gospel. In this chapter, we've explored the first two with a focus on our *new nurture*:

+ *Justification*: "Forgiven!" — God has taken a bunch of criminals and declared them not guilty.

+ *Reconciliation*: "Welcome home!" — God has taken prodigal children and made them his sons and daughters, and taken spiritual adulterers and made them his bride.

In chapter 12, we'll probe two more gospel miracles, with a focus on our *new nature*:

+ *Regeneration*: "You're a new creation in Christ!" — God has taken a heart of stone and made it new.

+ *Redemption*: "You're more than a conqueror through Christ!" — God has taken slaves to sin and made them free to serve righteousness.

CHAPTER 12

Prescribing God's Cure for the Soul: Part 2—Our New Nature

When the Pharisees brought the woman caught in adultery to Jesus, he invited anyone who was without sin to cast the first stone (John 8:1–11). As the Pharisees departed one by one, only Jesus was left with the woman. What great company — only Jesus.

Straightening up from where he had stooped down to write on the ground, Jesus asked, "Woman, where are they? Has no one condemned you?"

"No one, sir," she replied.

"Then neither do I condemn you," Jesus declared.

We have just witnessed the grace of *justification* and *reconciliation* — no condemnation, forgiveness, and face-to-face acceptance. We enjoy a new relationship of bold access to the Father through Christ — peace with God.

Christ's grace, as amazing as it was, did not stop there. "Go now and leave your life of sin."

To justification and reconciliation — our new *nurture* — Jesus adds the power to overcome sin through our new *nature* — *regeneration* and *redemption*. We can envision these four gospel blessings as:

+ The New *Nurture* of the New Covenant: How Christ Brings Us Peace with God

    + *Justification*: Forgiveness of Sin and Declaration of Righteousness

    + *Reconciliation*: Sonship and Adoption

- ✦ Who We are *to* Christ by Grace through Faith
- ✦ Our New Relationship: God's Heart toward Us — Peace with God
- ✦ The New *Nature* of the New Covenant: How Christ Changes People
  - ✦ *Regeneration*: Sainthood and a New Creation
  - ✦ *Redemption*: Freedom from Sin and to Righteousness
  - ✦ Who We Are *in* Christ by Grace through Faith
  - ✦ Our New Reality: A New Heart in Us — Power in Christ

Recall Kim and her haunting words, *"Pastor Bob, some sins are so deep that even the love of God can't reach them."* As Kim struggled with the guilt of her besetting sins, she desperately needed to be reminded of the gospel miracles of regeneration and redemption — her new *nurture*. She needed to remember that she was forgiven and welcomed home — by grace even in the midst of sin, she has peace with God through Christ.

However, had Kim and I stopped there, it would have been like Jesus saying, "Kim, where are your accusers? Go."

Jesus, of course, added, *" . . . and leave your life of sin."*

Kim, like the woman caught in adultery, was capable of leaving her lifestyle of sin — not in herself, not in her flesh, not by works. She was capable because she was transformed by grace in her heart — in her inner person. Kim needed the gospel reminder that, as Bryan Chapell wrote, "Christ's victory on the cross provides freedom both from the guilt *and* the power of sin."[1]

We tend to preach and counsel the gospel as if it's only about the forgiveness of sins. However, the point of having our sins forgiven is to reconnect us to God so that we can live the life he has designed us to enjoy for his glory.

Counselors and Counselees Afflicted with Gospel Amnesia

Knowing who we are in Christ is the foundation for knowing how to live like Christ and how to counsel like Christ. The apostle Peter, who knew all too well the futility of trying to change in his own power, understood the power of gospel memory. In the context of encouraging believers to grow in grace, Peter first reminds his flock of their new nature:

His divine power has given us everything we need for life and godliness through our knowledge of him who called us by his own glory and goodness. Through these he has given us his very great and precious promises, so that through them you may participate in the divine nature and escape the corruption in the world caused by evil desires. (2 Peter 1:3 – 4)

Peter then reminds them that anyone who is not growing in grace is "near-sighted and blind, and *has forgotten that he has been cleansed from his past sins*" (2 Peter 1:9, emphasis added). In their battle against sin, Peter's flock was battling spiritual amnesia about who they were in Christ.

That's why Peter prescribes a memory aid. Speaking to believers ("broth-ers — 2 Peter 1:10), he says, "So I will *always remind* you of these things, *even though you know them* and are firmly established in the truth you now have" (2 Peter 1:12, emphasis added). "These things" refers to what Peter just wrote about — their new nature in Christ. Until the day he died, Peter would never cease reminding them. "I think it is right to *refresh your memory as long as I live*" (2 Peter 1:13, emphasis added). Try telling Peter, "Stop overdoing this stuff about 'the gospel for believers' and 'reminding one another about the gospel,' and 'preaching the gospel to yourself!'"

As counselors and counselees, we too can struggle with gospel amnesia. That's why, like the flock that Peter shepherded, we need gospel memory aids.

The Counselor's Gospel Amnesia

I fear that some of the counseling we do is old covenant counseling. We coun-sel Christians as though they are still non-Christians — old creations instead of new creations in Christ (2 Cor. 5:17). We counsel saints as though they are still sinners in the core of their being and identity (Gal. 2:20). We counsel new covenant Christians as though they are still under the old covenant of law rather than the new covenant of grace through which we enjoy our new nurture and our new nature (Heb. 8:7 – 13).

Soul physicians, like physicians of the body, must know the "patient" they are operating on. Physicians of the soul, working with Christians, are working with a new "patient," a new man or woman in Christ (Col. 3:1 – 11). This is because our new covenant salvation in Christ implants within believers a new nature (Rom. 6:1 – 14). Christians are cleansed — not only forgiven their sins, but given a new heart (Heb. 9:15; Ezek. 36:26). Biblical counselors under-stand that sanctification does not involve making ourselves saints, but living out our sainthood (Eph. 1:15 – 23). Soul physicians remind counselees, like Peter reminded his flock, that central to their victory is applying the truth of their new identity in Christ (Rom. 6:9 – 14).

Let's be clear—this does not mean that there is no role for the Christian to play or that our role involves only believing. There are spiritual disciplines to engage in, imperatives to obey, biblical principles to apply, connection with the body of Christ to engage in, yielding to the Spirit to do, actions to take, and more. But we do all of this by grace on the basis of the change that has already occurred. Paul outlines the progressive sanctification process for us in Romans 6—we are to know (removal of gospel amnesia), reckon (application of gospel truth), and yield (Spirit-empowered, grace-focused growth) (see chapters 15 and 16).

The Counselee's Gospel Amnesia

I also fear that too much Christian living is old covenant living. We consume ourselves with trying to become what we already are, while our present task is to be what we already are. Someone once asked Gutzon Borglum, the creative genius behind the presidential carvings on Mount Rushmore, "How did you ever create those faces out of that rock!?" Borglum replied, "I didn't. Those faces were already in there. Hidden. I only uncovered them."

Christian, the face of Jesus is already in there. *In you!* This is the essence of regeneration. God originates within you a new disposition toward holiness. Christlikeness is etched within. The divine nature is embedded in your new nature (2 Peter 1:3 – 4; Col. 3:1 – 11).

In sanctification, we yield to and cooperate with the Holy Spirit, who uncovers the Christ who dwells within. To grow in Christ we need to understand and apply who we are in Christ. Once we are clear on the new person we are in Christ, we continue by faith active in love as we cooperate with the divine Architect who daily transforms us increasingly into the image of Christ (2 Cor. 3:18; 4:16 – 18).

Heart Change and Gospel-Changed Hearts

When we speak of our identity in Christ, we need to embed that reality in the grand gospel narrative. As Michael Horton explained, "The Good News is not just a series of facts to which we yield our assent but a dramatic narrative that replots our identity."[2] Christ's gospel story invades the very core of our life story—our new identity is a gospel identity.

To jog our memories and replot our identities as biblical counselors and as biblical Christians, we need to look beneath the surface at new creations in

Christ. We need to take some additional X-rays of the heart — this time not of the sin-sick heart (chapter 9), but of the salvation-cleansed heart.

Neonatal Saints and *Nikao* Saints: The Essence of Our New Nature

Before your mental spell-checker goes haywire, I'll define and describe two unfamiliar but crucial concepts that capture the essence of our new nature: *neonatal* saints (regeneration) and *nikao* saints (redemption).

I'm indebted to historical theologian Thomas Oden for the captivating analogy of regeneration producing neonatal saints. As Oden explained, in the new birth God imparts new spiritual life, yet it is not a perfectly mature, fully grown life:

> One reborn of God is not thereby immediately mature. Birth does not preempt but invites and enables the process of growth. One reborn of God is a neonate saint, awaiting a process of growth toward ever-fuller receptivity to the Spirit. Having been cleansed in new birth, one is drawn and called to express behavioral manifestation of the new life.[3]

The idea of being a "neonatal saint" captures the twin ideas that we are new creations in Christ and babes in Christ.

We are also *nikao* saints. *Nikao* is the English transliteration of the Greek word for victory. Paul used a superlative form of the word in Romans 8:37 when he said that in Christ we are "more than conquerors." We could translate it "we are over-conquerors in Christ." We are spiritual Olympic champions through Christ.

Think of the shoe company Nike and its motto, "Just do it!" God is telling us to claim our victory. Live out our empowered nature. Be the champion that we are in Christ. Redemption makes us *nikao* saints able to say "No" to sin and "Yes" to God (Titus 2:11 – 13). We are freed from the power of sin, freed to live under the power of God (Rom. 6:1 – 23). The gospel transferred us from an old mastery — sin, Satan, death, the flesh, the world — to a new mastery — righteousness, the Spirit, the new heart, the church.

Physicians of a New Soul

Picture a team of cardiologists joining a team of oncologists scrubbing down before surgery. "Have you ever seen a case like this?" asks the heart surgeon.

"No, and I'm glad I haven't," replies the cancer specialist. "Cancer spreading through the lungs, the chest. That's horrible enough. Add to that heart disease clogging every major artery. What a mess. Poor chap. He's rather hopeless."

"Well," counters the heart specialist, "at least he's an old man. Lived a long life. Experienced a great deal. The sad fact is he's set some patterns in place that will be hard to break. As a doctor, it's frustrating. Let's say that we eliminate the obstructions blocking his arteries. This joker is just going to return to his old way of life. Eating garbage. No exercise."

The cancer specialist adds, "I know what you mean. He's a three-pack-a-day smoker. Nothing seems to stop him, not even his diagnosis of lung cancer. Not the patch. Nothing. The second he leaves the hospital, assuming we're successful, he'll be lighting up."

Though discouraged about their patient's post-operative life, they complete their scrub down and join their teams in the operating room. Crowding around the operating table, these two crack teams work in tandem. One is to unclog diseased arteries, the other to remove diseased organs. Together they hope to give this old man a few more months, at least.

"Nurse, more light! I can't see a thing," the heart surgeon demands.

"Doctor, what do you mean?" the nurse responds. "Are you all right? Your eyes okay? I see everything."

"Then someone really fouled up this time!" the heart surgeon protests. "Of course I see everything. Everything, that is, except his obstructed arteries! This can't be my patient. Nobody move. Double-check his identity!"

Shock. Scurrying. Examining. Confirmation. "This is Mr. Olman. He's our patient. No mistake about it," confirms the head surgical nurse.

"Well, then, my work's finished," the heart surgeon replies. "This man's heart is as good as new. Better. It's as if he's had a heart transplant. But a transplant unlike any I've ever seen. Not just a better heart, but a brand-new, robust heart. Every marred part, every speck of scarred tissue, obliterated. Replaced by a heart I would die for."

Inexplicable as it is, the cancer surgeon steps in. "Well, we have Olman open. Let's remove that unhealthy lung of his." Stunned. Stops. Repeats the complaints of the first surgeon. "This is impossible. His lungs are like new. Not a trace of cancer. What's going on here?"

Days later, recovered from his open-heart "surgery," Mr. Olman leaves the hospital feeling like a new man. Saying his good-byes to his two surgeons, he thanks them profusely. "Don't thank us," the cancer doctor responds. "Thank your lucky stars."

"I'd prefer to thank my good God," Mr. Olman replies. "He healed me.

Made my heart better than new, my lungs too. More than that, he's given me a new, healthy attitude. No more junk food for me. No more cancer sticks. And I'll be working out. Have my routine planned, even started already. I'm a new man. Ha! That's funny. Mr. Olman becomes a New Man. Just call me 'Mr. Newman' from now on, docs!"

My prayer for all of us throughout this chapter is that the eyes of our hearts would be enlightened so that we may grasp together with all the saints the reality of our regeneration and redemption. This entire book has been saying in dozens of different ways that theology is practical. Now I'm adding to that and making it more specific by saying that soteriology — the theology of our salvation — is practical and essential for life and ministry.

Theology ministers understanding so that we can live out our knowledge of God. Soteriology — understanding the who, where, why, and how of our salvation — wakes us up to what is real, specifically what is real in Christ. Soteriology, gospel, grace, new nature, regeneration, redemption — these are not academic, theoretical words. There are no armchair disciples. We cannot be a disciple in theory. The doctrine of salvation tells us who we are "in Christ" as new creations and this informs how we live.

Satan seeks to capture our imagination with the lie that while we may be forgiven by grace (new nurture); we certainly are not changed by grace (new nature). He crops regeneration and redemption out of the picture. Biblical counselors crop Christ's regeneration and redemption back into every pixel of the picture. In this way, the Bible's redemptive narrative controls the stories people live by and live in — and this reality guides our biblical counsel.

Soteriology 101: Regeneration—The Spiritual Birth of Neonatal Saints

We need to get to know Kim just a little bit better. Kim was a middle-age wife and mother separated from her husband and teenage daughters. She was battling bulimia (binging and purging her food) and self-harm (cutting that left marks and caused injury but was not life threatening). Kim had been hospitalized for medical reasons and for emotional issues on several occasions before she started attending our church. Her husband and daughters were not believers. Kim made a commitment to Christ after several months of attending worship services and being actively involved in one of our women's ministry small groups. Her small group leader, Shontal, who was also a member of our biblical counseling team, came with Kim to our first appointment. On most occasions we co-counseled Kim.

As you can imagine, Kim needed truth *and* love. It's difficult on paper to describe the love component that our entire church offered Kim. Shontal and her small group loved Kim in every way possible—not an enabling love, but an encouraging love. They wept with Kim, laughed with Kim (which was a new experience for her), hung out with Kim doing "fun stuff" (also rare for her), studied and applied Scripture with Kim, helped in meeting financial needs (including a course on biblical stewardship), comforted Kim, and challenged Kim.

Several men from our church who knew Kim's husband, Rod, from work attempted to move patiently into his life. Rod was "fed up with Kim" and had insisted that she move out until "she got her act together for good." Our church connected Kim with a Christian attorney who provided *pro bono* services to assure that her rights were protected.

Now you can see why the image of God as a loving, forgiving Father who welcomed Kim home with open arms was so amazing to Kim. Christ's justifying and reconciling grace truly was life-changing for her—in ways that sometimes those of us who have been believers for years tend to forget.

Kim was seeing herself as a new person, not with renewed "self-esteem," but with new "Christ-esteem." Her awareness of who she was *to* Christ contrasted drastically with the type of love Kim experienced growing up and with how Rod and her two teen daughters related to her.

Dramatic changes were happening in how Kim saw herself in Christ and how she related to others. Shontal ministered patiently with Kim, helping her to identify and put off condemning lies from her past and present that Satan gleefully magnified. Shontal also helped Kim to renew her mind—not generically, but specifically related to her life story and her personal relationships.

However, Kim still was not consistently experiencing the power to "leave her life of sin." The hold that her bulimia and cutting had on Kim was weakening, but not defeated experientially. For Kim to experience victory, she needed to fight out of her new identity—a new identity that included both her new nurture (chapter 11) *and* her new nature (chapter 12).

Defeating Sin Out of Our New Identity

Counseling is not simply teaching. Counseling is based on understanding and applying biblical truth in the context of loving relationships. So the teaching element was a component as Shontal and I counseled with Kim. Through what Kim was hearing in Sunday morning sermons, what she was learning in her small group, and in our counseling together, she was beginning to understand that something real actually occurred at the moment of her salvation. A real change took place in Kim at regeneration. Kim began to grasp that regeneration was more than having something taken away (guilt removed through justification), more than having something added (a second nature tacked onto the first). Something new was birthed, but only after something old was crucified.

Kim, and you, and I needed regeneration because we were worse than critically ill; we were spiritually dead (Eph. 2:1 – 3). Our spiritually dead selves were incapable of seeking God, knowing God, obeying God, or being inclined toward God (Rom. 3:9 – 20). So God crucified the old dead us. "For we know that our old self was crucified with him" (Rom. 6:6).

What did God do in, for, and to Kim at salvation? In making Kim new, God did not simply remodel her, rebuild, renovate, rehabilitate, or reform Kim. He *re-birthed* Kim. Changed her. Cleansed her. Returned her to her original stance, to her original wholeness. Kim was thrilled to begin to see herself as healthy again — a healthy newborn. "Salvation" itself comes from the Latin *salvus*, meaning to securely save, to keep safe, unhurt, to make sound, whole, and healthy. For the first time in her life, Kim saw herself as an integrated, whole, healthy bearer of Christ's image (Rom. 8:29). That realization fueled and empowered much of the change process in Kim's life and relationships.

Shontal's small group was studying 1 John, and one day they focused on 1 John 3:9: "No one who is born of God will continue to sin, because God's seed remains in him; he cannot go on sinning, because he has been born of God." Shontal explained that God implanted in each of the women in the group a new disposition or inclination. They were now bent toward God instead of away from him. God gave them a new heart with right affections to love him and keep his commandments, to trust and obey him.

In summary, here's the "Regeneration 101" that Kim was beginning to understand and apply. God made Kim something that she never was before; she became someone she had never been before — a neonatal saint. That does not mean that Kim is perfect, sinless, or unable to sin. Rather, she is *now able not to sin*. In her *activity* Kim will sin (1 John 1:8 – 2:2), but in her *identity* she is not a sinner, but a saint. This new identity is not on the flesh level, but on the spirit level. Regeneration is an act so real that it is right to say that Kim, as a Christian, in her essential nature is a *saint* rather than a sinner. All other identities are lesser identities. Sinfulness is not her intrinsic state. In the deepest sense of personhood, Kim is a saint.

Neonatal saints capture this sense of a new life with a definitive change and the need for ongoing growth in Christ. This new life is lived out of a new four-chambered heart — the new cardiology of a saint.

Our New Person in Christ: The New Cardiology of a Saint

Biblical counselors talk frequently about encouraging counselees toward "heart change." Unfortunately, sometimes we do so without understanding the grand gospel narrative (chapter 1), without performing a comprehensive exam of the four chambers of the heart (chapter 6), and without taking into account the change that has already occurred (chapters 11 – 12). In thinking biblically about our new nature, we must unite all these concepts so we can provide wise counsel about heart change based on gospel-changed hearts.

We are alive in Christ, but what is the heart condition of this newborn? How healthy is the heart of the neonatal saint? First, recall the old heart that we had in our fallen state. Remember the heart disease coursing through the sick heart of the degenerate "old man" we were. That old heart was a slave to unrighteousness. The soul was selfish. The mind foolish. The will manipulative. The emotions ungoverned.

Now reflect on the new heart of the neonatal saint. The pediatrician places a stethoscope onto the new babe in Christ, smiles, and says, "A new heart! Slave to righteousness. A new soul, free to love sacrificially. A new mind, enlightened to wisdom. A new will, soft and serving. New emotions, peaceful yet deep."

God crucified our "Mr. Mass Murderer." The great Soul Physician implanted a new heart, gave us a heart transplant. In 2 Corinthians 5:17, Paul labels us "new creations." The Greek word for "creation" was used in the Septuagint for creation *ex nihilo* — out of nothing. God does not simply reorder the chaos of our old heart. He removes our old heart and gives us a totally new heart.

Kim desperately needed to understand and apply these realities. Satan was tormenting her with lies: "New creation? Right! You cut last night ... *again* ... didn't you? Your girls don't even want to see you — some *new* mom you are! If Shontal and Pastor Bob knew this *not-so-new you*, they would stop counseling you and kick you out of the church!"

Shontal wanted to help Kim crop back into her picture the biblical images of the new-Kim-in-Christ. So one evening after their small group ended, she opened her laptop and walked Kim through a PowerPoint presentation contrasting who we were apart from Christ and who we are in Christ. Together they contrasted images of the four chambers of the old heart and the four chambers of the new heart.

Renewed Heart Chamber #1: Relational — From Spiritual Adulterers to Virgin Brides

First, they looked at an image of the Scarlet Letter — an *A* for *Spiritual Adulterer.* As Shontal explained, "That's who we were *before* we came to Christ. Created to love God with all our heart, instead we love Satan, the world, the flesh, and anything but God. I'm not pointing a finger at you, Kim. I'm pointing all my fingers at *me.* That's who I *was.*"

Advancing to a second slide: "But that's not the new me or the new you in Christ." Kim and Shontal marveled at several images of pure virgin brides dressed in white. With tears streaming down her cheeks, Shontal said, "Only in Christ can a spiritual adulterer become a virgin bride of Christ. That's the *new* you, Kim!"

Then Shontal showed a third slide — this one with a picture of both the Scarlet Letter and a virgin bride. "There's something deeply and distressingly wrong with this picture, Kim. It implies that you and I are *simultaneously in the core of our being* spiritual adulterers *and* virgin brides. That's not what the Bible teaches. While I can choose to go back to my old ways, that's never the true me. I am *one new woman in Christ and so are you* — *a virgin bride of Christ* in the core of your being. It's not just that Christ *sees* you like that as if he's pretending you're something you're not. Christ *made* you like that; he changed your heart — every cell, every fiber.

"So, Kim, your new heart has new affections, longings, and desires — a new *want to!* You know how Pastor Bob talks about us as spiritual, social, and self-aware? Well, as a renewed spiritual being, we *want to* worship God in the core of our being." They viewed an image of Psalm 42 and a deer panting for water as our souls thirst for God.

Clicking to the next slide, Shontal continued, "As new social beings we *want to* sacrificially minister to others like Christ did and for Christ." Here they viewed jpegs of Christ on the cross, Christ with the woman at the well, and Christians from our church in various service projects.

Taking a drink of her cherry lemonade, Shontal advanced to the next slide, where they saw several images of women obviously contented and at peace. "As renewed self-aware beings we *want to* rest in who we are in Christ," Shontal summarized. "Kim, start with any one of these three areas — spiritual/social/self-aware — and let's talk about what it looks like for you to apply to your life the truth of that chamber of your new heart."

Renewed Heart Chamber #2: Rational—From Heart Idolaters to Grace Narrators

By the time their discussion was only halfway done, Kim and Shontal saw that it was time to wrap up. "I've got more slides! When can we go over these again?" Shontal asked excitedly. They agreed to meet in a couple days at one of Shontal's favorite restaurants that advertised itself as "quaint with Wi-Fi."

Kim had to laugh when they met. "Funny meeting at a place with food! Used to be that food was, as Pastor Bob would say, 'an idol of my heart.' Not that it's not still a battle, but at least it's a step in the right direction for me to be here and not be freaking out about whether I will purge when we leave."

After getting their orders, Shontal said, "Ironic that you'd mention idols of the heart, 'cause that's my next slide. Well, maybe not ironic, but God's 'affectionate sovereignty.'

"So, here's a pic of idols like we'd think about in the ancient world. And here are some jpegs of modern idols — money, power, and yes, food."

"And it all goes back to *this*," — Kim said as she viewed a slide with Eve and Adam eating the forbidden fruit.

"Satan conned them into believing that God does not know best and withholds his best, Shontal said. "They, like us in our fallenness, became *heart idolaters*, believing Satan's subversion of the story, buying the lie that God does not have a good heart."

Moving to the next slide, Shontal and Kim saw several pictures: building a house on the sand or on the Rock, eyeglasses aimed at the cross, an eye chart with 20/20 vision and the word "spiritual" spelled out. Shontal explained, "This one's hard to capture in one picture or one phrase, even for Pastor Bob! He changes his 'current favorite summary' all the time. Sometimes he describes the new relational heart chamber as 'Son Worshipers' — get it — 'Son,' S-O-N. Other times it's 'spiritual eyes,' or '20/20 spiritual vision,' or 'eternal mind-sets.' Lately it's been 'Grace Interpreters' or 'Grace Narrators.'"

"Some of those I get, some I'm not so sure," Kim admitted. "Are you saying that the new heart interprets all of life through the lens of grace?"

"Fist-bump time!" Shontal responded. "Exactly. It's like the description of Moses in Hebrews 11:25 – 26," using her phone Bible app to read:

He chose to be mistreated along with the people of God rather than to enjoy the pleasures of sin for a short time. He regarded disgrace for the sake of Christ as of greater value than the treasures of Egypt, because he was looking ahead to his reward. (Heb. 11:25 – 26)

Shontal continued, "Think about the pleasures and treasures that tempted Moses. Wealth. Nobility. Honor. Fine food and, yes, fine women in the Egyptian courts. How was he able to resist these allurements? Why was his imagination not captured by these seductions? He was looking ahead; he was looking away from all else to one thing — his future with God. His focus was not on the smaller, earthly, temporal story, but on the larger, heavenly, eternal story. That's the grace narrative that Pastor Bob is always talking about.

"In fact, here's how Bob says it in *Soul Physicians*," Shontal added, pulling out a dog-eared copy and leafing eventually to the right page:

Moses' mind regarded and esteemed his future reward to be of more value than his immediate benefits. "Regard" means to lead before the mind, consider, count, account, esteem, believe, regard as, interpret, and exegete. When Moses exegeted this passage of his life story, his interpretation was clear. "God is good. God is better. God is best. God is my Supreme Good."[4]

"So if I'm getting this right," Kim responded, "you're saying that my old heart was trapped in the snare that kept focusing on this life, on my works, and on how I could 'atone' for my sin of purging by cutting. But my new life, new heart, new eyes are designed to focus on the life to come, on Christ's grace, and how he's already atoned for everything. So everything I've done and everything that's been done to me ... I can look at with a new mind-set."

Renewed Heart Chamber #3: Volitional — From Enslaved Destroyers to Empowering Shepherds

Shontal and Kim discussed some of those new mind-sets and then, their meal finished, took a look at another slide. The picture was of Satan with a snare trapping people and of various humans with weapons of destruction. The header was "Enslaved Destroyers." Shontal narrated the main idea: "Our old heart chamber was dead, so our will was dead to God and enslaved to sin. Even the 'good' things we chose to do, we did self-protectively and compulsively. As Pastor Bob likes to say, 'We pursued what we mistakenly perceived to be most pleasing.'"

"I hate those pictures," Kim admitted, "not because they aren't true, but *because* they were so true of me. Let's go to the next slide!"

Obliging, Shontal advanced to a slide with two images of Christ as the Good Shepherd — one holding a little lamb close to his heart, the other of himself as the Lamb for the slaughter. This slide also had images of various Christians serving others sacrificially and courageously. The header read, "Empowered Shepherds."

"Let me try to summarize these first three chambers," Shontal said as she started to type a couple of phrases. "*Relationally*, God returns our new heart to *purity*. Rationally, he returns our new heart to *sanity*. And *volitionally*, he returns our new heart to *vitality*. We're now free and empowered to empower others. Free to serve Christ and others instead of enslaved to serving Satan and ourselves. Pastor Bob says that the volitionally mature saint says, 'I find my life by dying to myself, taking up my cross, and following Christ. I am responsible for my actions and the motivations behind them. This is my new other-centered life purpose in Christ.'"

"So, let's see if I get this right," Kim interjected. "The old me was truly a slave to food and to cutting. The new me" — pausing … choking up — "is … able … to say 'NO!' to that and 'YES!' to God. The old me was enslaved to living for me and trying to manipulate or placate my husband. The new me is empowered to choose courageously to serve my husband even if that means lovingly challenging some of his … nonsense." That led to a conversation that continued into the parking lot and spilled over into our next joint counseling session.

Renewed Heart Chamber #4: Emotional — From Ungoverned Users to Soulful Psalmists

When Kim, Shontal, and I met the next week, they filled me in on their last two conversations. Shontal showed me her slides — which were far better than mine. "Can I use those? I'll give you credit, I promise," I said. Then, more seriously, "Why don't you two keep going. I don't want to mess with the good work you've started."

Shontal advanced to her next slide. The header read, "Ungoverned Users." It had pictures of people in all states of emotional distress or emotional abuse of others. "That's chamber four of our old heart," Shontal explained. "Our fallen hearts run from our fears rather than racing to our forgiving Father. We either suppress our feelings, stuffing them instead of crying out to God, or we express our feelings indiscriminately, throwing them at others like spears."

Shontal's next slide had a picture of a gospel choir, an image of a psalm, and a third of someone crying out to God. "Notice the label on this slide," Shontal pointed out: "Soulful Psalmists."

"I like that!" I interrupted. "I used to say 'Soulful Poets,' but 'Soulful Psalmists' captures it much better. Sorry, please continue."

Shontal did. "Thanks. I think I'll copyright it and sell it to you! Where was I? Our new heart is like a singer in a gospel choir singing the wonderful African American spirituals. In one line she can be singing her heart out about grief and hurt — crying out to Christ. In the very next line she can be singing her heart out about joy and that comin' day when there will be no more tears or cryin'. Our new emotional heart chamber is not emotionless. It is emotion-full. And it is emotion-directed — directed toward God. And emotion-purposed — focused on using emotions to advance God's kingdom, not our cause. This renewed chamber of our heart feels with integrity — wholeness, honesty, candor."

This led to a full hour of joint counseling. We explored various ways in various situations where Kim could express her new emotional heart chamber in godly ways with her husband and teen daughters. In all of this, Kim, Shontal, and I were applying Kim's regeneration to her daily life and relationships.

Soteriology 102: Redemption: The Spiritual Freedom of *Nikao* Saints

To the amazing grace of regeneration, God adds for Kim, and all of us, the amazing grace of redemption. Regeneration creates in our new heart a new *want to*. Redemption creates in our new heart a new *can do*. Through our redemption in Christ we experience the spiritual freedom of *nikao* saints. We are free from sin's power, free to live holy and loving lives.

Our New Victory in Christ: *Christus Victor*

Throughout church history, passages like Colossians 2:13 – 15 have led pastors and theologians to describe Christ as *Christus Victor* — our victorious Christ:

> *When you were dead in your sins and in the uncircumcision of your sinful nature, God made you alive with Christ. He forgave us all our sins, having canceled the written code, with its regulations, that was against us and that stood opposed to us; he took it away, nailing it to the cross. And having disarmed the powers and authorities, he made a public spectacle of them, triumphing over them by the cross. (Col. 2:13 – 15)*

Paul pictures the cosmic drama of redemption. Hostile, alien powers have enslaved us. Evil taskmasters (Satan and his demons) and vicious forces (sin) have captured us. Into the fray enters *Christus Victor* to free us from our bondage to sin and our enslavement to Satan. *Christus Victor* "disarms" our enemies. He strips off their clothes. More powerfully, he strips off their arms.[5] He disarms them of the weapons they use to hold us captive.

Wanting to be sure that we grasp the message of our newfound freedom, *Christus Victor* throws a victory parade. He makes a public spectacle of our defeated foes. The Greek word for "public spectacle" pictures a victor displaying his captives as trophies in a triumphal procession. It emphasizes publishing and proclaiming the results of a decisive victory.[6]

Paul further illustrated our decisive victory by the last clause, "triumphing over them by the cross." "It was a familiar scene of a conqueror returning to Rome and leading the captured kings and warriors in chains in his triumphal procession."[7]

Greek scholar A. T. Robertson connected the dots in this picture of Christ's triumph:

> The Greek verb is *thriambeuô* to celebrate a triumph. It is derived from *thriambos*, a hymn sung in a festal procession and is kin to the Latin *triumphus* (our triumph), a triumphal procession of victorious Roman generals. God has won a complete triumph over all the fallen angelic agencies.[8]

Through *Christus Victor* we are Saints Victorious — *Nikao* Saints.

Living Victoriously in Christ

Redemption results from our co-crucifixion and co-resurrection with Christ — our union with Christ. "For we know that our old self was crucified with him so that the body of sin might be done away with, that we should no longer be slaves to sin — because anyone who has died has been freed from sin" (Rom. 6:6–7).

Having died with Christ to sin and having been raised with Christ to new life, "We know that since Christ was raised from the dead, he cannot die again; death no longer has mastery over him. The death he died, he died to sin once for all; but the life he lives, he lives to God" (Rom. 6:9–10). After emphasizing our redemption in Christ, Paul exhorts us to live our lives on the basis of our new freedom:

> *In the same way, count yourselves dead to sin but alive to God in Christ Jesus. Therefore do not let sin reign in your mortal body so that you obey its evil desires. Do not offer the parts of your body to sin, as instruments of wickedness, but rather offer yourselves to God, as those who have been brought from death*

to life; and offer the parts of your body to him as instruments of righteousness. For sin shall not be your master, because you are not under law, but under grace. (Rom. 6:11 – 14)

"Count," or "reckon" means that we live based on and consciously aware of our victory over sin. Does our victory mean that we can never sin? No. It means that we never *have* to sin.

Pastor Henry Holloman, reflecting on the implications of this passage to our daily life, urges us to ask ourselves the practical question: "'Am I staying in my casket in relation to sin, or am I walking around like a zombie committing sin?' If the latter is true, reaffirm that you died to sin with Christ. Then by God's grace get back in the casket in relation to sin."[9]

Shontal and Kim always met right after their women's small group. One evening the group had studied Romans 6, so it was natural for Shontal and Kim to discuss how these principles related to Kim's life. Shontal began, "How do you think Romans 6 connects to your battle ... let me rephrase, to your *victorious* battle with eating and cutting?"

Kim jumped in at Romans 6:12 about not letting sin reign in her mortal body, and not obeying the passions of the flesh. "God commands me to present the very members of my body — my mouth I eat with, my stomach I digest with, my hands I cut with — to God as instruments of righteousness. But how do I do that?"

Shontal noted, "When you paraphrased the verse, one important word dropped out — 'therefore.' We can't start at verse 12. Before we can present our bodies to God, we must first embrace Romans 6:11 about considering ourselves dead to sin and alive to God in Christ. This strikes at the heart of who we *are*, not just what we *do*. Because Christ is dead to sin and you died with him — you are dead to sin. And because Christ is alive to God and you were resurrected with Christ — you are alive to God."

Shontal continued, "Maybe it would help if we discussed two specific questions. First, in the moment of temptation, what difference could it make for you to see yourself co-crucified with Christ to the power of binging, purging, and cutting? Then second, in the moment of temptation, what difference could it make for you to see yourself co-resurrected with Christ so that the same power that raised him from the dead is in you and available to you to defeat binging, purging, and cutting?"

Together Shontal and Kim spent the rest of that hour discussing how — out of Kim's new identity and new victory — she could fight sin in the power of gospel grace. Grace changes us. It transforms our very being (regeneration).

And it transforms how we define ourselves in relationship to sin and to God (redemption).

Where We've Been and Where We're Headed

How does Christ change us? Here's our tweet-size answer from this chapter: *Through regeneration our new heart has a new want to; through redemption our new heart has a new can do.*

Christian, do you know who you are? Are you counting on, reckoning on, and living your Christian life based on your new nature in Christ? Do you see yourself as a new creation in Christ with four new heart chambers to love sacrificially, think wisely, choose courageously, and feel deeply? Do you see yourself as more than a conqueror through Christ? As a victor? As a spiritual champion?

Biblical counselor, do you know who your Christian counselees are? Are you counseling them based on their new nature in Christ? Based on their new heart that relates with purity, thinks with sanity, chooses with vitality, and feels with integrity? Based on the victory over sin that Christ has already won for them? Based on seeing them as spiritual champions? Are you urging them to reckon on their new life in Christ?

Typically at this point in a systematic study of Scripture, theologians move from our salvation to our sanctification. We *will* move to sanctification. However, there are two additional ultimate life questions that we must address: one about the church and one about the future. We turn our attention first to the church as we find that *growth in grace is a community project.*

CHAPTER 13

Finding a Place to Belong and Become: Our Growth in Grace Is a Community Journey

During the four years that I was in seminary, I worked at the Otis R. Bowen Center for Human Services (ORBC). It was a five-county, government-run psychiatric inpatient unit for individuals struggling with life issues.

The ORBC tried desperately to replicate a family setting with a community feel. Patients and staff shared meals together, took walks together, played games together, laughed together, and cried together. We had group therapy, individual counseling, art therapy, activity therapy, and off-site "field trips." We provided every patient a primary care team focused on their individualized treatment — a psych nurse, psychiatrist, psychologist, social worker, mental health worker, and dietician. Everyone received the best care the world could offer 24/7. The ORBC desperately tried to replicate ... the church.

While the clients at the ORBC may not have always verbalized it, they were all seeking an answer to one of life's ultimate questions, "Where can I find a place to belong and become?" The ORBC attempted to be that place. They wanted to be a place where struggling people felt accepted, loved, and cared for — a place to belong. They also wanted to be a place where struggling people could grow, overcome their struggles, and mature — a place to become.

What the ORBC was trying to be is exactly what God calls the church to be — a place to belong and become.

The world is trying to replicate what we have, so why in the world are we trying so hard to replicate the world? This is sad biblically, given that the Word of God, the Spirit of God, and the people of God provide us with all that we need for life in a broken world. It is also sad practically given the fact that the ORBC had an astronomically high rate of recidivism. Even after the best care the world could offer, patients returned repeatedly because their problems in living were never resolved.[1] Why in the world are we sending our people to the world's empty counterfeit replica of the church?

Perhaps we have forgotten the truth that God has not placed our sanctification in the hands of trained and paid professionals.[2] God's plan is that everyone in the body of Christ speaks and lives gospel truth in love so that the whole body grows up in Christ.

Why are we seeking to conform to a deformed world? Perhaps because we have also forgotten the truth that gospel-centered ministry, biblical counseling, sanctification, and the local church must be united in our thinking and in our practice. In my research for this book, I've read many excellent books on gospel-centered ministry, on biblical counseling, on sanctification, and on the local church. However, it is the rare book that provides a biblical, practical, relational strategy for uniting gospel-centered ministry, biblical counseling, sanctification, and the local church. We seem to write about and think about these biblical concepts as four separate topics rather than as one united focus.

I'll confess that I was almost guilty of making the same mistake. My original plan was to move directly from the chapters on salvation to the chapters on sanctification. Almost every systematic theology book does exactly that. However, I don't want to make the mistake of treating our growth in grace as if it was something separate from our life together in the body of Christ. That's why in this chapter we explore a biblical theology of the church — gospel communities that provide a place to belong to Christ and become like Christ.

Together with All the Saints

Ephesians 4 is perhaps the classic passage that weaves together gospel-centered ministry (Eph. 4:1 – 10), biblical counseling (Eph. 4:15 – 16), sanctification (Eph. 4:17 – 32), and the local church (Eph. 4:11 – 14). But what's fascinating about this chapter is the chapter that precedes it.

In Ephesians 3:1 – 13, Paul marvels over the gospel of Christ's grace — calling it "the unsearchable riches of Christ" (Eph. 3:8). Then Paul reminds us of God's eternal intent — that his infinite, multifaceted wisdom and grace should be made known to the on-looking universe — through the church (Eph. 3:10 – 11). That bears repeating: God has chosen to do his work — through the church.

How does the church witness to the world? First, by rejoicing in and living out the gospel indicatives of what Christ has done for us: "In him and through faith in him we may approach God with freedom and confidence" (Eph. 3:12). This is the amazing "Welcome home!" that we celebrated in chapter 11.

Second, the church bears witness to the world about Christ's great grace by grasping together with all the saints (Eph. 3:18) the infinite power and love of God in Christ. Here's how Paul prayed it, and don't neglect his phrase — *power, together with all the saints, to grasp . . .*

> *I pray that out of his glorious riches he may strengthen you with power through the Spirit in your inner being, so that Christ may dwell in your hearts through faith. And I pray that you, being rooted and established in love, may have* power, together with all the saints, to grasp *how wide and long and high and deep is the love of Christ, and to know this love that surpasses knowledge — that you may be filled to the measure of all the fullness of God. (Eph. 3:16 – 19, emphasis added)*

This is, in one prayer, gospel-centered ministry, biblical counseling, sanctification, and the local church. This is the gospel indicatives making a home in our heart as they produce gospel identify that leads, in Ephesians 4 – 6, to gospel imperatives. And how does *this* happen?

Never in isolation.

Always in community.

Always together with all the saints.

Together with all the saints we grasp the four-dimensional, infinite love of Christ — its width, length, height, and depth. "Grasp" is a fascinating word that Paul used here to mean both "to seize" and to "light upon, understand, and hold fast to *intensely with surprise*."[3] It's the soul-shocking, life-rocking, mind-boggling "Aha!" experience of "getting it," of experiencing Christ's grace in our whole being — relationally, rationally, volitionally, and emotionally.

And it happens only together with all the saints.

Paul's prayer in Ephesians 3 and his exclamatory statement about *grasping together with all the saints* is the pivot point of Ephesians. It explains how everything that goes before and everything that comes after is made real.

Everything I've written in the chapters before and after this is impossible to grasp and apply unless we do so *together with all the saints*.

That's why when we talk about biblical counseling and the local church, we are not talking simply about a church *with* a biblical counseling ministry. We are talking about a church *of* biblical counseling. That is, a church saturated with people who live and speak gospel truth to one another before church, at church, after church, away from church, in the car, at the restaurant, at work, in the neighborhood, at the sporting event, and in the midst of conflicts.

Recently, Shirley and I were singing a worship song in the middle of a Sunday morning service when a friend tapped my shoulder from behind and whispered, "Lisa and Dan just slipped out in tears." Since Shirley and I were close friends of Lisa and Dan, we quietly excused ourselves and found them in the foyer. The worship song had sparked memories of a deep loss. As Shirley and I ministered to Lisa and Dan throughout the worship service, they kept apologizing. "We're so sorry you're having to miss church to talk to us." Shirley lovingly reminded them, "We're not missing church. We are *being the church* together with you right now."

We weren't Lisa's and Dan's official biblical counseling team. We were, and are, their friends in Christ. Lisa and Dan needed more than a formal biblical counseling program (though that's wonderful, and I've written a book about developing counseling ministries in the church[4]). What Lisa and Dan needed was a church saturated with a united gospel-centered, biblical counseling, sanctification, local church mind-set — a church *of* biblical counseling.

God's Grand Vision for the Church

We need a biblical imagination that perceives the big story God is writing and our role in it as the church. We need to understand what the church has to say and do that no other institution can say and do. That starts as we understand together the résumé of Jesus, the résumé of pastors/teachers/leaders, and the résumé of God's people.

The Résumé of Jesus: The Church as a Jesus-Centered Community

Before Paul provides the ministry description for pastors and God's people, he reminds us that Jesus is the Head of the church. Paul spends the chapters and verses leading up to Ephesians 4:11 – 16 showing why Christ has the right to write our ministry description.

- He is our Redeemer in whom our full salvation is complete (Eph. 1:1 – 14). We should surrender to his will for his redeemed people.

- He is seated at God's right hand ruling over everything with all authority, appointed the Head over everything for the church, which is his body (Eph. 1:15 – 23). We should follow his directives for the church.

- We are his workmanship, created in Christ to do the beautiful work prepared for us from all eternity (Eph. 2:1 – 10). We should want to know what he prepared pastors and people for.

- He is the chief cornerstone upon whom the whole building (the church) is being built (Eph. 2:11 – 22). We should follow his architectural drawings for the church.

- He is the revelation of God's grace toward which all time and eternity have been moving (Eph. 3:1 – 15). We should yield to his infinite wisdom for his people.

- His love for us surpasses all knowledge (Eph. 3:16 – 21). We should submit to his calling on our lives.

- He ascended higher than all the heavens in order to fill the whole universe (Eph. 4:1 – 10). We should listen to the Creator, Sustainer, and Ruler of the universe.

Clearly Christ has the right to cast the vision for how his church is to function. And he has the right to expect that we will catch and implement that vision in our churches.

The Résumé of Pastors/Teachers/Leaders: The Church as a Teaching Hospital for Soul Physicians

In Ephesians 4:11 – 16, Paul highlights the Bible's most powerful, focused vision statement for the church. This passage offers Christ's ministry description for church leaders and for every member. By distilling the essence of God's call, Christ's vision captures our imagination and motivates the shift in ministry mind-set that changes everything.

Most pastoral search committees would be thrilled to read a candidate's résumé that demonstrated the ability to preach, counsel, and administer. Most seminaries would be delighted if graduate exit interviews indicated that pastoral ministry students perceived that their seminary training equipped them for preaching, counseling, and administering. Being equipped to *do* the work of the ministry seems to be everyone's ideal goal for church leaders.

Everyone but Christ. His pastoral ministry description demands the ability to *equip* others to do the work of the ministry. If seminaries followed Christ's vision for pastoral ministry, they would focus on *training trainers*. If pastoral search committees desired in a pastor what Christ desires, they would throw out every résumé that failed to emphasize experience in and passion for equipping the saints.

Instead, we listen to modern church culture that screams, "The pastor is the preacher, caregiver, and CEO!" It's time to listen to the Head of the church. "It was he who gave some to be ... pastors and teachers, to prepare God's people for works of service" (Eph. 4:11 – 12). Christ's grand plan for his church is for pastors/teachers to focus on equipping every member to do the work of the ministry.

Paul launches verse 12 with a tiny Greek word *pros*, translated by an even smaller English word "to" with giant meaning: with the conscious purpose of, in order for, for the sake of, with a view to. The word indicates the future aim and ultimate goal of a current action. That is, by definition, a vision statement — Christ's grand vision statement for every pastor/teacher.

What is the future view, the future vision to which Christ sovereignly gave his church pastors and teachers? Paul says it succinctly: *"To prepare God's people for works of service"* (v. 12). These eight words must be every church leader's reason for existence.

One central word — "prepare" — must capture every leader's passion for ministry. "Prepare" comes from the word for artist, craftsman. Local church leader — your special craft, your opus is people, equipped people, disciple-makers. Your spiritual craft or gift is to help others to scout out their spiritual gift, identify that area of ministry, and empower them to use that gift. A church is a community of gifted people, not merely a community of people with a gifted pastor.

In Paul's day, people commonly used "prepare" in the context of conditioning an athlete. Local church leader — you are a spiritual conditioning coach. Your job is not to play all the positions on the team, but to coach every player on the team, to strengthen their spiritual condition so they are able to do works of service. This fits perfectly with how Paul uses the word *prepare* — to train someone so they are fully fit and mature enough to complete their calling. The leader's calling is to help God's people to fulfill their calling.

These weren't just words for Paul. He made making disciple-makers his personal ministry description as we see in Colossians 1:28 – 29. And he made equipping equippers his personal ministry practice — Acts 20:13 – 38.

Christ's grand vision so captured Paul's ministry mind-set that at the end of his life he passed on to Timothy the vision of equipping equippers of equippers — 2 Timothy 2:2. The baton of equipping passed from Christ's hands, to Paul's hands, to Timothy's hands, to the hands of reliable disciple-makers, who passed it on yet again.

Let's not drop the baton. Let's keep Christ's grand vision alive and moving into the future.

Caring churches often talk about the church as a "hospital for the hurting." I agree with that mind-set, but I'm convinced it will not become a reality unless church leadership envisions the church as a teaching hospital for soul physicians. In any quality teaching hospital, experienced physicians mentor physicians-in-training through on-the-job training. In any Jesus-centered church, experienced soul physicians equip soul physicians-in-training through giving and receiving biblical counseling in community. For an introduction to what this looks like, we need to ponder a third résumé.

The Résumé of the People of God: The Church as a Community of Grace Sharers

Sadly, in far too many churches, the people of God are second-class citizens when it comes to the work of the ministry. If a "lay" person makes a hospital visit, that's okay, but we want to know, "Where's my pastor?" Christ's vision is so different. Pastors and teachers serve the people so God's people can serve the congregation and community. Far too many "lay" people are recruited to fill a position and to fill a need — make the coffee, cover the nursery during the service — but not to fulfill a calling.

Paul's phrase "works of service" elevates the ministry of God's people. "Works" has a sense of divine calling and meaningful purpose. We could also translate it as a vocation or a mission. The Bible uses it to describe God's own creative work. God the Creator commissions us for creative, zealous, purposeful work — work that glorifies him as we serve one another.

Paul's word for "service" highlights personal service rather than just serving for wages, serving as a slave, or serving publicly. It involves love in action through sacrificial ministry modeled after Christ's sacrifice. Christ calls his people to creative, purposeful, meaningful, sacrificial, personal ministry to one another in his name. In the context of Ephesians 4:11 – 16, that work is nothing less than making disciple-makers through the personal ministry of the Word — biblical counseling.

When leaders and members fulfill their purposes together, then the body of Christ builds itself up in two specific, cohesive ways: doctrinal unity and spiritual maturity (Eph. 4:12 – 13). When a congregation knows the truth not just academically, but personally, then their love abounds in knowledge and depth of insight (Phil. 1:9 – 11).

We often miss the vital real-life, how-to application of every-member disciple-making that Paul embedded in this text. How does the church come to unity and maturity? Exactly what are pastors equipping people to do? Specifically, how do members do the work of the ministry?

Paul's answer: by "speaking the truth in love," we grow up in Christ (Eph. 4:15). Every word in this passage funnels toward this remarkable phrase "speaking the truth in love." Christ's grand plan for his church is for every member to be a disciple-maker by speaking and living gospel truth to one another in love.

Paul selects an unusual Greek word we often translate as "speaking the truth." We should translate it both as speaking and living the truth. We might even coin the word "truthing." Paul likely had in mind Psalm 15 where the psalmist asks, "Who may dwell in your [God's] sanctuary?" He answers: "He whose walk is blameless and who does what is righteous, *who speaks the truth from his heart*" (Ps. 15:2, emphasis added). Who can serve in God's sanctuary, the church — the one who embodies the truth in relationships.

The word for "truthing" that Paul used implies being transparent, genuine, authentic, reliable, and sincere. It describes a person who ministers from a heart of integrity and Christlike, grace-oriented love. It pictures a person whose relational style is transparent and trustworthy. The tense and context indicate that the body of Christ should continually, actively, and collectively be embodying truth in love as they walk together in intimate, vulnerable connection. In one word, Paul combined content, character, and competence shared in community.

While "truthing" means more than speaking, it does not mean *less* than speaking. While it means more than sheer factual content, it does not mean *less* than the gospel fully applied. Paul used the identical word in Galatians 4:16. There he is clearly speaking of preaching, teaching, and communicating the truth of the gospel of Christ's grace (salvation) applied to daily growth in Christ (progressive sanctification).

When we combine Galatians 4:16 with Ephesians 4:16, both in context, we find an amazing description of gospel-centered biblical counseling — of the personal ministry of the Word. Speaking the truth involves:

Communicating gospel truth about grace-focused sanctification in word, thought, and action through one-another relationships that have integrity, genuineness, authenticity, transparency, and reliability, done in love to promote the unity and maturity of the Body of Christ for the ultimate purpose of displaying the glory of Christ's grace.

The normal agenda and priority of every Christian is to make disciple-makers. Christ's training strategy for disciple-making involves pastors and teachers equipping every member to embody the truth in love through the personal ministry of the Word — biblical counseling.

What happens when leaders focus their calling on equipping God's people to make disciple-makers through the personal ministry of the Word by speaking and living the truth in love? Paul shows us in Ephesians 4:16. The body in robust health grows and builds itself up in love as each part does its work. *Growth in Christ is a community journey.*

Nurturing a Unified Vision for Gospel Communities

Christ's grand vision for his church and our churches is clear. What is less clear is the extent to which our churches typically live out Christ's vision. Having read this far, you also know that the nature of God's Word is clear. The Bible is our supreme, rich, robust, relevant, and relational source for wisdom for life in our broken world.

The world sees the sufficiency of Scripture and the superiority of the church as misplaced priorities or downright foolishness. That is nothing new. But the more troubling problem is how *Christians* view the role of the Word of God and the people of God. In truth, most people don't think of the local church as the first place to look to for help. In many churches, when people in the pew look up at the pulpit, if we could hear their thoughts, we might hear something like this:

> I would go to the pastor to talk about spiritual stuff. Yeah. I'd talk to him about my prayer life, how to make godly decisions, my walk with God, and maybe, just maybe, I'd go to him to discuss my marriage, parenting, or relationships. But for *real* stuff, like if I had "emotional problems," or "mental-health issues," or was struggling with depression, anxiety, an eating disorder, PTSD, or an addiction … No, I think I'd go to a *professional* counselor.

Even more troubling is the reality that some church leaders don't seem to believe, in practice, the sufficiency of the Word of God and the superiority of the people of God in dependence on the Spirit of God. In too many churches, the Bible is preached relevantly on Sundays, but its relevant application falls woefully short in the church counseling office, in small group ministry, and in one-another care. Truth is applied to life in the pulpit, but the world's so-called wisdom is dispensed in counseling, in small group ministry, and in one-another care.

We need to reclaim biblical soul care in the local church and thoroughly equip our people to speak the truth in love. We need a theology of relating truth to life in the church. We need a theology of caring for one another in the church that unites the Word of God, the people of God, and the Spirit of God. To become a church *of* biblical counseling, our mind-set and our ministry need to change. To become a church that unites gospel-centered ministry, biblical counseling, sanctification, and the local church, we need:

+ A Unified Vision of God's Word for Life in a Broken World (the foundation that this book seeks to offer);
+ A Unified Vision of the Résumé of Pastoral Leadership and God's People (the foundation already laid in this chapter);
+ A Unified Vision of the Pulpit Ministry of the Word and the Personal Ministry of the Word;
+ A Unified Vision of One-Another Ministry; and
+ A Unified Vision of the Church and the Community.

Catching and Casting a Unified Vision of the Pulpit Ministry of the Word and the Personal Ministry of the Word

I teach pastoral counseling at a number of evangelical seminaries. In some of those schools, a small segment of students enter the course initially with "arms folded." Their mind-set is something like, "I dare you to convince me that I need to learn pastoral counseling. All my people will need is the pulpit ministry of the Word."

Notice in my quote that I say "will need." This mind-set is almost 100 percent of the time the mind-set of a pastor-to-be, not the mind-set of a student already involved in pastoral ministry. People already in pastoral ministry know that they will be asked to counsel. For them, the unstated question often is, "Prove to me that I should not refer people to the professionals after I engage in one or two quick meetings with my parishioners."

So I have two main goals in such a class. First, I want to help students to see a unified vision of the pulpit and the personal ministries of the Word.

Second, I want to help students to gain confidence in God's Word for real-life issues and to gain competence in the personal ministry of the Word.

The conviction that I want students to leave with is that the ministry of the preacher and the ministry of the counselor are not different kinds of ministry, but rather the same ministry given in different ways in different settings. The pastoral team of Kevin DeYoung (senior pastor) and Pat Quinn (counseling pastor) describe biblical preaching and biblical counseling this way:

> Both are fundamentally, thoroughly, and unapologetically Word ministries. One may be more proclamation and monologue, and the other more conversational and dialogue, but the variation in approach and context does not undermine their shared belief in the power of the Word of God to do the work of God in the people of God through the Spirit of God. What shapes our understanding of pulpit ministry is a strong confidence in the necessity, sufficiency, authority, and relevance of God's Word. The same confidence shapes our understanding of counseling ministry.[5]

This is not a book on preaching; it's not even a chapter on preaching. Instead, it is a section of a chapter seeking to communicate that Word-based ministry is always truth-to-life ministry. The same confidence we have in God's Word when we stand in a pulpit is the confidence that we can and should have when we sit across from a troubled person in our pastor's office. If the primary preaching/teaching pastor over a congregation does not have this conviction and confidence, then the church will never be a church *of* biblical counseling.

On the other hand, it is a beautiful and powerful thing to watch when a church unites the pulpit ministry of the Word and the personal ministry of the Word. Faith Church in Lafayette, Indiana, is one such example.[6] Pastor Steve Viars preaches truth to life from the pulpit on Sunday. Then, every Monday, he and twenty-five other trained biblical counselors join in truth-to-life interactive counseling conversations with one hundred troubled counselees — most of them unchurched members of the community.

More than that, in Faith's Adult Bible Fellowship classes, they relate truth to real-life issues. In Faith's Vision of Hope (a residential treatment home for women struggling with abuse issues, eating disorders, self-harm issues, addiction issues, and out-of-wedlock pregnancies) ministry, they put into practice their conviction that God's Word is robustly relevant to even the most difficult issues we face in life. In Faith's "skater park" (they have a state-of-the-art skateboard rink on their property), their trained one-another ministers engage the "outsiders," the "least of these," the "rude, rough, and rebellious" with love and truth.

It all starts because Pastor Steve Viars casts a united vision of the power of God's Word used in the pulpit, in the pastor's office, in the Vision of Hope ministry, and in the skater park. In other words, he believes in and practices biblical counseling in its many different ministerial forms. He is uniting gospel-centered ministry, biblical counseling, sanctification, and the local church.

Catching and Casting a Unified Vision of One-Another Ministry

One-another ministry comes in all shapes, sizes, and formats. There is the informal one-to-one ministry of two men iron sharpening each other over a coffee or on the work site. There is the more formal one-to-one biblical counseling ministry where a woman trained in lay counseling provides ongoing spiritual friendship, soul care, and spiritual direction to another woman dealing with life's heartaches and hardships. There is the official small group meeting that comes together for the express purpose of speaking truth in love one to another. There is the ministry or working small group, such as the worship team, the elder ministry team, the women's ministry team that gathers not simply to plan activities but also to build into each other's lives so that they become a true team, a true family, a true hospital for the hurting.

Consider each of these preceding scenarios. They could either be intentional gospel-centered, biblical counseling, sanctification, and local church oriented, or they could be something very different.

The two Christian men sipping coffee during a lunch break could simply talk shop, talk sports, or talk politics. "We're not at church, so this is not the time for 'spiritual stuff.'" Or those two men, nurtured in a church where gospel conversations are the norm, naturally move back and forth between shop talk and spiritual talk. Or, more specifically, even when they talk shop, their spiritual commitments to the gospel, to biblical counseling, to sanctification, and to the local church both color and coordinate every word they speak to each other. They are intentional about speaking truth in love so they both grow up together in Christ.

Even the formal counseling meeting between two women in the church could be intentionally biblical — relating truth to life in love — or it could be something very different. It could be care without biblical guidance. It could be biblical guidance with little love. It could be proof-texting without a focus on the grand gospel narrative. It could address suffering but not sin, or sin but not suffering — and do all the addressing without a biblical perspective on life's ultimate questions.

Small group ministries can be all over the map in their focus. Some study the Bible, but never or only rarely relate truth to life. Others are filled with polite chitchat, but rarely encourage members to address heart issues and hard relationships. Some consistently pray for each other, but the prayers are like a medical list of illnesses (fine to pray about), and rarely are those prayers like the laments or the praises of the psalmists. On the other hand, small group leaders and members might catch the vision and be trained in intentional one-another small group ministry where the group gathers each time expectantly anticipating God's Word being specifically and artfully related to their life situations.

Those working small groups, like an elder ministry team, can focus on just getting the tasks done and running the church. Or, in addition to the legitimate need to lead the church (the *product* of the meeting), they could also focus on the even greater need to be spiritual leaders of the church (the *process* during the meeting). So before they talk about a church discipline issue, they interact together about how well and wisely they are speaking truth in love to each other. Before they talk about a conflict in the church, they honestly address any "elephant in the room" unspoken conflict between members of the elder team.

This chapter is not a *how-to* chapter. To be further equipped in *how to* engage in gospel conversations that saturate the entire church, you will want to refer to the second volume in this series — *Gospel Conversations*. Instead, this chapter is a *what-to* chapter. What type of ministry mind-set can lead to a church saturated with a unified vision for gospel-centered biblical counseling that leads to growth in grace in the context of local church relationships?

Catching and Casting a Unified Vision of the Church and the Community

Churches that focus on one-another ministry, biblical counseling, and small group relationships might be perceived to be insular churches — churches that are all about believers, but little about the lost. While that could be theoretically true, it would be theologically far off the mark.

Consider Ephesians. It's all about gospel-centered, one-another mutual ministry leading to progressive sanctification centered on the body of Christ. Yet how does Paul wrap up his letter? What was the point of Ephesians? Was it all about the church being one happy family secluded behind closed doors? No. Just before his final greetings, Paul wrapped up with these outwardly focused words:

> *Pray also for me, that whenever I open my mouth, words may be given me so that I will fearlessly make known the mystery of the gospel, for which I am an ambassador in chains. Pray that I may declare it fearlessly, as I should. (Eph. 6:19–20)*

Paul, who in many places reminds his followers to follow him as he follows Christ, does not even have to state the reminder now. Paul is clearly saying that every Christian is an ambassador for Christ. As such, every Christian needs to be praying every day, "Lord, whenever I open my mouth, by your Spirit, give me words so that I will fearlessly make known the mystery of the gospel, as I should do."

Every gospel conversation we have with each other as Christians should encourage and empower us so that we can have gospel conversations with those who do not yet know Christ. The church is the place where gospel talk is so natural that it becomes the training ground for gospel talk with those who do not know the gospel.

The two rough-and-tumble mill workers talking Christ on the job site should entice their non-Christian coworkers to ask, "What's up with you guys? Your job stinks just as much as mine. So why are you two always so hope filled?"

The two Christian women engaged in a formal biblical counseling session should so change the life of the counselee (and of the counselor) that the counselee's unsaved older sister asks, "Why is your life so different? How are you now able to handle the mess that our extended family is?"

Our intentional iron-sharpening-iron, truth-relating-to-life small groups should be so impactful that unsaved neighbors ask, "What do you people do in there? Are you getting 'high' on something?" And you can answer, "No, we're not getting high, but we are lifting our eyes and our minds high to Christ, and he's making all the difference in the world. Would you like to join us next week?"

Our elder ministry team meetings should be so life-changing that our unsaved extended family members say, "I think this whole 'elder thing' is weird. Why do churches even do that? But I know this, since you joined that team, the way you respond to conflict in our extended family is so different. What's up with that? What's up with you?"

We don't divorce personal ministry in the church from personal ministry to the community. Instead, our ministry to one another in the church builds each other up in truth and love so that we can embody truth and love in our community.

Some have said that the church is the greatest superpower on earth. For this chapter, I'd word it a bit differently. The local church is *the* superior place on earth where we unite gospel-centered ministry, biblical counseling, and sanctification so that as we grow up in Christ, the body of Christ also grows numerically as others come to Christ. It is *through the church* that God has chosen to make known the glorious riches of Christ's gospel of grace.

Where We've Been and Where We're Headed

I pray that this book and this chapter are helping us to see that the Bible lays out a model of care that is superior to anything the world has to offer. And I hope that this chapter is stirring your passion concerning the unique position the local church has in giving hope, help, and healing to a broken and fallen world.

When people ask, "Where can I find a place to belong and become?" we can answer with two tweet-size responses: *Together with all the saints the church is* **the** *place to belong to Christ and the body of Christ and to become like Christ.* And: *Sanctification is a community journey.*

Where to next? To the end. No, not the end of the book, but the end of this world and the beginning of eternity. What difference does our eternal destiny make in how we live our lives today? That's our final question before we unite the first seven ultimate life questions into a foundation that provides the context for the question this entire book has been moving toward — our sanctification question, "How do we become like Jesus?"

CHAPTER 14

Remembering the Future: Our Eternal Perspective

Many sports fans, if they can't watch the big game when it's live, DVR it. Then they swear all their friends to secrecy. "Don't you dare spoil it for me! Don't tell me who won. I want to watch it and enjoy the thrill of the entire game without knowing the outcome."

I guess I'm odd. When I can't watch the big game live, I DVR it. However, I watch the end first! Especially if the big game involves one of my beloved teams. I'm a big-time fan of the Chicago Bulls. Back when Michael Jordan was leading them toward what would become the first of six NBA titles, I recorded (Beta — this was a long time ago) the NBA's final game between the Bulls and the LA Lakers. If the Bulls were victorious, they would win their first-ever world championship.

Now you have to understand something about Chicago sports fans. Chicago teams *always* choke. As a child, I lived through the epic collapse of the 1969 Chicago Cubs to the "Miracle Mets." That was just the first of many such heartbreaks as a Chicago fan. So a Chicago sports fan can never relax, no matter how sure the final outcome might *seem*.

That's why, after I recorded the Bulls game, I first watched the *end* of the game! The Bulls won! Michael Jordan and all of Chicago celebrated! Then, after watching the celebration, I rewound the tape and watched the entire game.

When the Bulls were behind by 17 points, I never panicked. Normally I would have left the room if they were behind by that much. I would have told my son to call me back into the living room only if the Bulls tied the game. I couldn't take watching them struggle. But not this time. I knew the end of the story. So I could handle the ups and downs of the game, knowing the final result.

Our Victory and Our *Victor*

Whether or not you agree with my sports-watching philosophy, you can see the benefits we gain from knowing the end of God's story — the end of *our* story. We've read the end of the gospel story. God wins! And we win! God wins the war and weds his bride. He slays the dragon and weds the damsel — his church.

Even more than revealing the victory, the end of the story reveals the *Victor*! "But we know that when he appears, we shall be like him, for we shall see him as he is" (1 John 3:2). Who is the Victor unveiled before us? The one who is both our Lion and our Lamb. The one who is our Warrior Groom of holy love. "Hallelujah! For our Lord God Almighty reigns. Let us rejoice and be glad and give him glory! For the wedding of the Lamb has come, and his bride has made herself ready" (Rev. 19:6 – 7).

Yes, the glories of heaven — no more sin, no more suffering, saints forever with perfect relationships and enduring purpose — provoke persistence today. But even more so, face-to-face relationship with the glorious One provokes Christlike and Christ-honoring living today.

Notice the order of John's description of the new heaven and the new earth. First, he describes the eternal bliss of our intimate relationship with Christ, and only then does he describe the eternal comforts of heaven.

> *"Now the dwelling of God is with men, and he will live with them. They will be his people, and God himself will be with them and be their God. He will wipe every tear from their eyes. There will be no more death or mourning or crying or pain, for the old order of things has passed away."* (Rev. 21:3 – 4)

Theology for Life

Exciting, right! Guess what? These opening paragraphs are ... get ready ... *eschatology*! That's right, you've been reading about the doctrine of the end times. Theologians call it *eschatology* from the Greek word *eschaton* for *last*, or the study of the last times.

For many of us, *eschatology* is just another big theology word that brings back either memories of detailed charts about what happens when or memories of debates between various theological camps. While I in no way want to minimize the importance of careful theological study regarding the Bible's teaching on the end times, I do want to highlight the practical implications today of end-time theology. The end of the story should guide every chapter of our life story today.

Every person has asked the questions, "Where am I headed? What is my destiny? Is there a purpose toward which my life is moving?" And the really honest person has also asked, "In the end, will I end up all alone? When all of this is over, will anyone remember me, know me, care about me?"

In our lives and ministries, these questions become even more personal, and the answers even more vital. The triumphant Christ who wins the war and weds his bride guides our every interaction in our personal ministry of the Word. We engage one another in gospel conversations, encouraging each other to ponder: "Why give up when we lose one battle, since we will know face-to-face for all eternity the One who wins the war?" "Why surrender to despair in the midst of our suffering when one day Christ himself will be the one wiping every tear from our eyes?" "Why choose mere survival when we will know face-to-face the one who will make everything new?" "Why choose the cheap thrills of the pleasure of sin for a season when in the end we wed our worthy Groom and enjoy him forever?"

This chapter brings all of these questions together by asking: "How does our future destiny with Christ make a difference today in our lives as saints who struggle against suffering and sin?" "How do I apply the end of Christ's grand redemptive story to my life story today?" This chapter addresses these questions with a simple, but biblically life-changing answer: *As saints who struggle with suffering and sin, we must remember the future.*

The Great Cloud of Witnesses Remember the Future

If we are to make any sense of the seeming madness of life in our fallen world, then we must grapple both with *before the beginning* and *after the end*. We launched our study in *Gospel-Centered Counseling* by examining what God did before he created. He related ... because he is our Trinitarian God.

The bookend of time that exists before the beginning teaches us that *reality is relational* because God is Trinitarian. It provides us with a vision from eternity past that shapes everything about our lives and ministries today. Because God is not "The-Alone-with-the-Alone," we are not alone. God is with us — Immanuel. Because of this reality from eternity past, today we minister together in community as a community with, through, and for our communitarian God. By *faith*, we look back on eternity past and remember who God is and whose we are.

God's Word provides a second bookend, a second shaping vision — this one from eternity future. We respond to this vision with hope, looking forward to and remembering our future.

Hebrews 11 and 12 describe Old Testament saints as a great cloud of witnesses whose lives we should emulate. For these Old Testament believers, the bookend of time that exists *after* the end provided a source of strength and perspective largely alien to us. The new heaven and the new earth as our eternal dwelling place *with God* was their central reference point. It was the North Star by which they navigated their lives. But today, our eternal future with God has fallen off our radar screens.

Spiritual Mathematics and Looking Forward

The great cloud of Old Testament witnesses desperately longed for their future heavenly home with God. Abraham "was looking forward to the city with foundations, whose architect and builder is God" (Heb. 11:10). Do we *look forward?* Abraham's descendants "were longing for a better country — a heavenly one" (Heb. 11:16). As Christ's followers, "here we do not have an enduring city, but we are looking for the city that is to come" (Heb. 13:14). Are we looking for what is to come?

For the great cloud of witnesses, their longing for their future home with God on the new earth impacted how they lived in their present home on this earth. Peter said they were "looking forward to a new heaven and a new earth" (2 Peter 3:13). But he doesn't stop there. "So then, dear friends, since you are looking forward to this, make every effort to be found spotless, blameless and at peace with him" (2 Peter 3:14). They practiced "so then" living in light of "looking forward living."

Paul detected "so then" living in the lives of the Colossian saints, except he called it "springing from" living. Paul thanks God for them "because we have heard of your faith in Christ Jesus and of the love you have for all the saints — the faith and love that spring from the hope that is stored up for you in heaven and that you have already heard about in the word of truth, the gospel" (Col. 1:4 – 5). Faith and love *spring from* our future gospel hope.

In Romans 8:17 – 18, Paul does some spiritual mathematics where he calculates that our present sufferings are not worthy of comparing with the future glory that will be revealed when we stand face-to-face with Christ. In Hebrews 11:24 – 26, Moses does some spiritual mathematics where he calculates, as he is looking ahead to his reward, that the pleasures of sin for a season are not worth comparing to the pleasures of eternity with Christ. As saints who struggled with *suffering* and battled against *sin*, Abraham, Peter, Paul, and Moses refused to forget to *remember the future.*

Future Amnesia and Cropping Eternity into the Picture

But we tend to forget our future, don't we? And who is responsible for our impoverished theology of our future with Christ? It's Satan, the father of lies (John 8:44). Some of his most insidious deceptions are about heaven. "He opened his mouth to blaspheme God, and to slander his name and his dwelling place and those who live in heaven" (Rev. 13:6). Just as we learned in earlier chapters that Satan tries to crop Christ out of the picture, so we learn now that he tries to crop eternity out of our mental pictures of life. He has systematically robbed us of a robust view of our future home with God. And we've let him get away with it.

That's why Paul counsels us to crop the future back into the picture as we minister to one another. As Paul writes to saints struggling with suffering and sin, he reminds them of their future. "We know that the one who raised the Lord Jesus from the dead will also raise us with Jesus and present us with you in his presence" (2 Cor. 4:14). On the basis of our future with Jesus, Paul says, "Therefore we do not lose heart" (2 Cor. 4:16). Though outwardly we are wasting away, yet inwardly we are being renewed daily (progressive sanctification).

What attitude, what mental picture leads us to not lose heart, but to keep growing in Christ? "For our light and momentary troubles are achieving for us an eternal glory that far outweighs them all" (2 Cor. 4:17). Again, we see spiritual mathematics at work where we factor in our future, where we crop our future reality into our present picture.

Imagine that your doctor told you that he had an inoculation that would heal you for the rest of your life — never, ever sick again after the medication takes hold. However, there is one catch, one temporary side effect — you will first be sick for one week. If my doctor told me that, I would do some physical mathematics, weighing one week of sickness against a lifetime of health, and I would take the shot!

That's Paul's promise — God's promise — to us in 2 Corinthians 4:17. Yes, we are afflicted in this life. But it is momentary. And our momentary sufferings are producing not a lifetime of health, but an eternity of glory!

So if Paul had one word of spiritual counsel for spiritual counselors about the personal ministry of the Word, what would it be? To encourage and exhort one another to "fix our eyes not on what is seen, but on what is unseen. For what is seen is temporal, but what is unseen is eternal" (2 Cor. 4:18). So let's take a look at what is unseen.

John Remembers the Future

Abraham, Paul, Peter, and Moses are not the only saints from that great cloud of witnesses who teach us to remember the future when facing troubling present circumstances and temptations. In Revelation, John wrote to seven churches — each of which was filled with *saints* struggling with *suffering* and *sin*. In his opening greeting, John highlights their sainthood — that Christ "has made us to be a kingdom and priests to serve his God and Father" (Rev. 1:6). He acknowledges their *sin* and emphasizes Christ's grace — "To him who loves us and has freed us from our sins by his blood" (Rev. 1:5). And he identifies with their *suffering* — "I, John, your brother and companion in the suffering and kingdom and patient endurance" (Rev. 1:9). In Revelation 2 – 3, John records Jesus addressing in the seven churches the good — saints, the bad — sin, and the hard — suffering.

Spiritual Time Travel

It is no coincidence that to saints like this (and to saints like us), John introduces God as the eternal One "who is, and who was, and who is to come" (Rev 1:4, 8; 4:8). To real people in real churches struggling with very real suffering and very real temptations to sin, John crafts a vision of a God who is eternally present and who is eternally sovereign — over our lives yesterday, today, tomorrow, and forever.

The first duty of a biblical counselor is to define reality — eternal reality — past, present, and future. We cast a vision for our counselee of God's eternality — the one who is, and was, and is to come. We help them to remember by *faith* the past and God's sovereign shepherding of it. We help them to remember with *hope* the future and God's sovereign shepherding of it. Then we help them to do some spiritual time travel, some spiritual mathematics, and some spiritual calculations that factor the end of the story into the equation of their present suffering and sin.

This is exactly what John did. "The revelation of Jesus Christ, which God gave him to *show* his servants *what must soon take place*" (Rev. 1:1, emphasis added). Revelation is a *yeser* (imagination) letter — a letter filled with portraits intended to capture the imagination, directing our minds to focus on the future and to apply that future to life today. Spiritual time travel to the future results in progressive sanctification (growth in Christlikeness) in the present.

Despite the fact that I'm a huge sci-fi fan, I realize that we can't literally travel to the future. Still, we can look to the future and look at life today in light of our future. That's why John uses the word "look" or "behold" so often in Revelation. Jesus tells us to look to the future as well: "Behold, I come like a thief! Blessed is he who stays awake" (Rev. 16:15). This is military imagery that speaks of standing guard, keeping vigil, being watchful and alert. Watching the future motivates us to keep watch today by remaining on sentry duty, faithful to the One who is faithful to us.

Scriptural Time Perspective

John, like any good biblical counselor, also repeatedly directs saints who are struggling with suffering and sin to the Scriptures — to feed their vision with biblical truth about our future reality. "[This] is, the word of God and the testimony of Jesus Christ. Blessed is the one who reads the words of this prophecy, and blessed are those who hear it and *take to heart* what is written in it, *because the time is near*" (Rev. 1:2 – 3, emphasis added). John concludes as he begins. "Behold, I am coming soon! Blessed is he who *keeps the words of the prophecy* of this book" (Rev. 22:7, emphasis added).

I resonate with the joys of dissecting the intricacies of prophecy. However, when we do this, we can easily miss the proverbial forest for the trees. We can miss the real-life application that John intended when we read a book like Revelation. John tells us exactly why he wrote Revelation — so that we would take to heart and apply its truths to our lives because the future is near. So that we would keep applying our imaginations to the reality that Jesus is coming soon! The future makes a difference today to saints struggling with suffering and sin.

What is the future picture found in the last chapters of the last book of the Bible that John wanted us to remember? It's the same message we started with in chapter 1 of *Gospel-Centered Counseling*, and the same message we started this chapter with. John wanted us to remember that life is a wedding and a war. Jesus slays the dragon (Rev. 19:17 – 21 and the great supper of God) and weds the damsel (Rev. 19:6 – 10 and the wedding supper of the Lamb).

In Revelation 19 – 22, John is saying, "Look! Look to the future. What do you see? A new heaven and a new earth. The bride beautifully dressed for her Husband. God dwelling with us. Look! What do you see? God wins the war against evil with justice and truth, and he weds his bride with purity and joy. Remember the future war and the future wedding! See with spiritual eyes your future victory and behold with faith eyes your eternal Victor!"

The believers in these seven churches easily could have thought this was too good to be true. "It's a nice dream, but not reality. It's a wonderful vision, but not an actual picture of future reality." That's why three times in these concluding chapters, we are told as plain as day, "These are the true words of God" (Rev. 19:9). "Write this down, for these words are trustworthy and true" (Rev. 21:5). "These words are trustworthy and true" (Rev. 22:6). To look into the future, we don't need a crystal ball. We have the crystal-clear, inspired, faithful, and true Word of God.

Because the end of the story seems almost too good to be true, Jesus shares with us the most glorious promise and the most clear command, "Behold, I am coming soon! Blessed is he who keeps the words of the prophecy in this book" (Rev. 22:7). Because the end of the story seems hard to fathom in the midst of our life stories in this fallen and broken world, Revelation concludes with the sternest of warnings. "And if anyone takes words away from this book of prophecy, God will take away from him his share in the tree of life and in the holy city" (Rev. 22:19).

As the saints in these seven churches are given this amazing glimpse into their future, they can't help but consider how different it will be from their present. Just a quick reading of Revelation 2 – 3 shows us that they are dealing with wicked men, enduring hardship, needing to repent of forsaking their first love, undergoing afflictions, experiencing poverty, being beaten down by slander, suffering persecution, being tempted to renounce their faith and to believe false doctrine, tolerating evil among them, having little strength, struggling with lukewarmness, and on and on goes this list of their suffering and sin.

Yet even in the midst of all of this suffering and sin, Jesus considers them saints — affirming them in numerous ways — for their perseverance, fearlessness, faithfulness even to the point of death, love, faith, works, service, keeping his words, and not denying his name. And in the midst of all their suffering and sins, Jesus repeatedly commands them to live as overcomers.

How do we live today as overcomers? By remembering the future.

Each day we must train ourselves to remember what the future reveals about our warrior King and our worthy Groom. He is the Alpha and Omega. The Almighty. The First and the Last. The Living One. The Son of God. The Holy and True One. The Ruler of God's creation. He is Holy, Holy, Holy. He is the Lord God Almighty. He is the one before whom all of creation will lay their crowns and cry out, "You are worthy, our Lord and God, to receive glory and honor and power" (Rev. 4:11). He is the One whom innumerable angels worship endlessly with the praise chorus, "Worthy is the Lamb, who was slain, to receive power and wealth and wisdom and strength and honor and glory and praise!" (Rev. 5:12). He is the One "every creature in heaven and on earth and under the earth and on the sea, and all that is in them, [sing of]: 'To him who sits on the throne and to the Lamb be praise and honor and glory and power, for ever and ever!'" (Rev. 5:13).

Jesus paints one final portrait that unites images of our future victory and our future Victor. And he does so not as a point of information, but as a personal invitation.

> *"It is done. I am the Alpha and the Omega, the Beginning and the End. To him who is thirsty I will give to drink without cost from the spring of the water of life. He who overcomes will inherit all this, and I will be his God and he will be my son." (Rev. 21:6 – 7)*

Picture it.

In your suffering that feels like it has drained out every last drop of life, picture Jesus face-to-face with *you*, inviting *you* to come to *him* and to thirst no more. Picture Jesus, his hand the hand that tenderly wipes away every last tear from your eye.

In your weariness of battling yet again that unrelenting besetting sin, picture Jesus smiling as he sees *you* walking down the aisle dressed in his righteousness — never ever to struggle with sin again.

In your loneliness, picture Jesus welcoming *you* home to your forever home with your forever family and saying "I will be your God and you will be my son."

In your sense of purposelessness or lack of meaning, picture Jesus with his arms open wide to the full expanse of the new heaven and the new earth, saying, "You've inherited all of this. Rule over it. Shepherd it. Enjoy it!"

In your suffering, come to him as the Lion, who defends you and upholds you in his glorious power and dominion. The person who hurts you or abuses you will *one day* have to stand before the Lion of God. And the ultimate abuser of God's people — Satan — will *one day* face the wrath of the Lion of God.

In your sin, come to him as the Lamb who was slain so that your sins would be forgiven. Come to him at the marriage supper of the Lamb where your ultimate and final reconciliation with God will be forever sealed.

How are we supposed to be overcomers today? By reading and applying the future gospel grace revealed in Revelation. By watching the end of the story and living in light of our victory and our eternal Victor.

Perpetua Remembers the Future

Early in the third century, when persecutions against Christians were raging like a virus in the North African city of Carthage, a young woman named Vibia Perpetua (181 – 203) was arrested along with several friends. At twenty-one, she was their leader and guiding spirit, rallying them in their last crisis and urging them to stand fast in the faith.[1] The early church preserved her journal of her martyrdom (*The Martyrdom of Perpetua*) as a martyr's relic because it is one of the oldest and most descriptive accounts of death for Christ. It is also the earliest known document written by a Christian woman.

Anyone who has ever suffered for the faith or has been oppressed by the powerful can carry on a conversation and feel a bond with Perpetua. In fact, in the introduction to her story, we read that it was "written expressly for God's honor and humans' encouragement" to testify to the grace of God and to edify God's grace-bought people.[2]

Of course, even reading the word "martyr" likely causes us to imagine that Perpetua was a spiritual "super woman" whose life and ministry we could not possibly emulate. The story of her life, however, demonstrates just the opposite.

Perpetua lived in Carthage in North Africa during the persecution of Christians under Septimius Severus. At the time of her arrest in 202 AD, she was a twenty-one-year-old mother of an infant son. Born into a wealthy, prominent, but unbelieving family, she was a recent convert with a father who continually attempted to weaken her faith and a husband who was, for reasons unknown to us, out of the picture. Nothing in Perpetua's situation or background had prepared her for the titanic spiritual struggle God would call her to face.

Perpetua, her brother, her servant (Felicitas), and two other new converts were discipled by Saturus. We learn from Perpetua that all of these faithful followers of Christ were arrested. "At this time we were baptized and the Spirit instructed me not to request anything from the baptismal waters except endurance of physical suffering. A few days later we were imprisoned."[3]

A Light in the Darkness: Experiencing the Pain of Others

Not some other-worldly super-saint, Perpetua candidly faced her fears and expressed her internal and external suffering. "I was terrified because never before had I experienced such darkness. What a terrible day! Because of crowded conditions and rough treatment by the soldiers the heat was unbearable. My condition was aggravated by my anxiety for my baby."[4]

This very human woman exuded superhuman strength. In the midst of her agony, she empathized with and consoled *others*. Her father, completely exhausted from his anxiety, came from the city to beg Perpetua to recant and offer sacrifice to the emperor. "I was very upset because of my father's condition. He was the only member of my family who would find no reason for joy in my suffering. I tried to comfort him saying, 'Whatever God wants at this tribunal will happen, for remember that our power comes not from ourselves but from God.' But utterly dejected, my father left me."[5]

On the day of her final hearing, the guards rushed Perpetua to the prisoners' platform. Her father appeared with her infant son, guilting her and imploring her to "have pity on your son!" He caused such an uproar, that Governor Hilarion "ordered him thrown out, and he was beaten with a rod. My father's injury hurt me as much *as if* I myself had been beaten. And I grieved because of his pathetic old age."[6]

Perpetua not only found in Christ the strength to empathize with her father, she also summoned Christ's power to console and encourage her family and her fellow martyrs. "In my anxiety for the infant I spoke to my mother about him, tried to console my brother and asked that they care for my son. I suffered intensely because I sensed their agony on my account. These were the trials I had to endure for many days."[7] Incredibly, Perpetua's greatest pain was her ache for others who hurt for her!

A few days passed after the hearing and before the battle in the arena commenced. During this interval, Perpetua witnessed to her persecutors and ministered to other detainees. "Pudens, the official in charge of the prison (the official who had gradually come to admire us for our persistence), admitted many prisoners to our cell so that we might mutually encourage each other."[8]

The Road to Hope: Maintaining Perpetual Persistence

Felicitas, Perpetua's servant, was in her eighth month of pregnancy at the time. As the day of the contest approached, she became very distressed that her martyrdom might be delayed, since the law forbade the execution of a pregnant woman. An eyewitness to their eventual death shared his account of their journey together. "Her friends in martyrdom were equally sad at the thought of abandoning such a good friend to *travel alone on the same road to hope*. And so, two days before the contest, united in grief they prayed to the Lord."[9] Immediately after their prayers, her labor pains began and Felicitas gave birth to a girl. After Felicitas's martyrdom, one of her sisters reared the child as her own.

The perspective we encounter in the life of Perpetua and Felicitas is far different from our own perspective on life and eternity, isn't it? Felicitas wanted to have her baby early enough so that she could be martyred *together* with her friends. Most of us would have been praying for the longest pregnancy possible so we could enjoy life in this world as long as possible. But Felicitas's hope was not in this life. She was prepared to travel the road of hope — embracing her coming death and looking ahead to the resurrection to life to come.

These eyewitnesses recorded their witness for Christ to the very end. "On the day before the public games, as they were eating the last meal commonly called the free meal, they tried as much as possible to make it instead an *agape*. In the same spirit they were exhorting the people, warning them to remember the judgment of God, asking them to be witnesses of the prisoners' joy in suffering, and ridiculing the curiosity of the crowd.... Then they all left the prison amazed, and many of them began to believe."[10]

Did you catch that? They exhorted the people to *remember the future* — to remember the judgment of God. They clung to the image of God's holy love and his and their future victory.

To the very end, Perpetua maintained her perpetual persistence. "The day of their victory dawned, and with joyful countenances they marched from the prison to the arena as though on their way to heaven. If there was any trembling, it was from joy, not fear. Perpetua followed with a quick step as a true spouse of Christ, the darling of God, her brightly flashing eyes quelling the gaze of the crowd."[11]

Consider again these words: the day of their victory, as though, as a true spouse of Christ, the darling of God. We need more eternal perspective that sees the day of our death as the day of our victory. We need more "as though" living that sees this life as a journey toward the next. We need a future vision not only of who Christ is but of who we will be in Christ — a true spouse of Christ, the darling of God. To the crowd, Perpetua was nothing but entertainment. But she knew that in Christ she was accepted in the beloved.

As these young martyrs were led through the gates to the arena, they were ordered to put on different clothes: the men the clothes of the priests of Saturn, the women the clothes of the priestesses of Ceres. "But that noble woman *stubbornly resisted* even to the end. She said, 'We've come this far voluntarily in order to protect our rights, and we've pledged our lives not to recapitulate on any such matter as this. We made this agreement with you.'

Injustice bowed to justice and the guard conceded that they could enter the arena in their ordinary dress. Perpetua was singing victory psalms *as if* already crushing the head of the Egyptian."[12]

We need more *as if* living. We need to live today in light of the fact that we've watched the video of the final victory. We need to live today *as if* we are already celebrating both the marriage supper of the Lamb (the eternal wedding) and the great supper of God (the final war). We need to sing victory songs about our Victor. "On his robe and on his thigh he has this name written: KING OF KINGS AND LORD OF LORDS" (Rev. 19:16).

We need to live like Perpetua, who provides riveting testimony to Christ's power at work in the inner life of a Christian woman whose spirit could never be overpowered. If anyone might have been able to marshal an excuse to be able to crop Christ out of her picture and crop the future out of her picture, it could have been Perpetua. Instead, she and her band of brothers and sisters of the Spirit kept reminding each other to remember the future — their future victory and their eternal Victor.

Biblical Counselors Remember the Future

We might think that the counseling application of this chapter is just to teach our counselees about the future. First, we need to recall that biblical counseling is never *just* teaching. Rather, it is speaking, living, embodying, discussing, and relating truth in love.

Second, we need to recall that in biblical counseling we face life in a fallen world honestly with our counselees. In part this involves joining our counselees in their earthly story of suffering. That's exactly what we saw John do in Revelation 1:9 where he identified with their suffering, even calling himself a brother and companion in their suffering.

We see Paul doing this also. In Romans 8, he acknowledged his own suffering and the suffering of those he ministered to (Rom. 8:17 – 19). Then, before he said that God works all things together for good, he candidly talked about how we, along with all creation, groan in pain under the agony and futility of this fallen world. Biblical counselors encourage lament and give people permission to grieve life in a fallen world.

Revelation itself models lament. Those who had been martyred called out in a loud voice, "How long, Sovereign Lord, holy and true, until you judge the inhabitants of the earth and avenge our blood?" (Rev. 6:10). Biblical counselors listen well and empathize with the earthly story of suffering and hurt. In so doing, we earn the right then to encourage our spiritual friends to listen well to God's eternal story of hope.

As this chapter emphasized, truth is best internalized in community. We *grasp together with all the saints* the holy love of God.

Jesus sends the identical message in Revelation 22:16. "I, Jesus, have sent my angel to give you this testimony for the churches." The *you* is *plural* in the Greek. The testimony in Revelation about our future victory and our eternal Victor is for all the churches to share in community. As biblical counselors, we work to keep this future vision vibrant — in our hearts, in our counselees, and in our churches. Together with all the saints we grasp, keep, and apply the reality of our future hope to our hurting and hardened hearts today.

The testimony of our future hope is a *community* testimony because it is a *cosmic* testimony. Revelation points to a cosmic battle and a cosmic victory. The last chapter in Christ's grand redemptive narrative is not simply for me and my Christian life. It's not simply for me and you together. The gospel is about reversing the curse — on a cosmic scale. The Bible is more than God's love letter to us (though it is that too). The Bible is about cosmic reconciliation. It is the message of Christ's final and universal victory over Satan, sin, and suffering.[13] That's why Jesus calls it a testimony. It is something that we share with everyone. It is the universal message of final hope in our broken and fallen world. It is the message to the entire cosmos that our triune God of holy love is alone worthy of all worship.

Where We've Been and Where We're Headed

Where is our broken world headed? How could our future impact us today as we face suffering and battle against sin? Here's our chapter-in-a-tweet answer to that ultimate life question: *As saints who struggle with suffering and sin, we must crop back into the picture our future purity (the wedding) and future victory (the final war).*

God's Word encourages us to *remember the future.* The end of the story provides hope in every chapter of our life story today.

We've asked and addressed life's first seven ultimate questions. Every question and every biblical answer has been leading toward the last two chapters of *Gospel-Centered Counseling* — chapters that address life's eighth ultimate question. "Why are we here?" "How do we become like Jesus?" "How can our inner life increasingly reflect the inner life of Christ?"

CHAPTER 15

Dispensing Grace: Our Gospel-Centered Growth in Grace

As biblical counselors, we deal with reality. We care deeply about the troubled persons sitting next to us, knowing that their struggles are real and raw. We may be counseling a woman whose husband has had an affair. We seek to compassionately help her to find God in the midst of her deep sorrow, and we want to empower her, even in her grief, to grow more like Christ. We may be counseling a young husband and father who recognizes that his rage is out of control and destructive to his wife and children. We seek to compassionately help him to find victory over his sinful anger and to become more like Christ in each of his relationships. We may be counseling the person diagnosed with clinical depression, or the person who feels enslaved to pornography. Whether facing suffering or battling sin, our focus is Christ-centered — compassionately helping people to respond to what they're facing *face-to-face with Christ* so they become *more like Christ*.

As we listen to people's stories and connect with them soul to soul, the urgency of their need for help and hope can easily drive us to the quickest route to answers. Unfortunately, the shortest route often leaves us with the wisdom of the world, which in turn leaves us without the rich depth of insight for living found in the wisdom of God's Word.

Theology for Life

We've come full circle, haven't we? We're back to the dilemma faced by the believers in Colosse regarding which source of wisdom they would turn to for life in their broken world. We're back to the pastor who wanted me to rush through the "theology stuff" in my seminar to get to the "practical stuff."

Well ... I need to let you in on a secret. You've been reading a *theology* book. Yes, even a "systematic theology" book. Historically, systematic theology books cover the following ten doctrines. Note the overlap with *Gospel-Centered Counseling*:

1. Bibliology: God's Word — Chapters 1 – 2 and Question 1 ("Where do we find wisdom for life in a broken world?")

2. Theology Proper: God the Father — Chapters 3 – 4 and Question 2 ("What comes into our minds when we think about God?")

3. Christology: God the Son — Chapters 3 – 4 and Question 2

4. Pneumatology: God the Spirit — Chapters 3 – 4 and Question 2

5. Angelology/Demonology: Satan — Chapter 5 and Question 2 ("Whose view of God will we believe — Christ's or Satan's?")

6. Anthropology: Creation — Chapters 6 – 7 and Question 3 ("Whose are we?")

7. Hamartiology: Fall — Chapters 8 – 9 – 10 and Question 4 ("What's the root source of our problem?")

8. Soteriology: Redemption — Chapters 11 – 12 and Question 5 ("How does Christ bring us peace with God?" "How does Christ change people?")

9. Ecclesiology: Church/Community — Chapter 13 and Question 6 ("Where can we find a place to belong and become?")

10. Eschatology: Consummation/Restoration/End Times — Chapter 14 and Question 7 ("How does our future destiny with Christ make a difference in our lives today as saints who struggle against suffering and sin?")

Theology *is* for life — for life in our broken world. It is an extremely secular, Christless worldview that assumes that we could possibly address life's ultimate questions apart from God's sufficient Word.

While it's sad that we race to the secular self-help shelf to find answers for living, it's equally disconcerting that too often we divorce sanctification from the rest of our Bible. We act as if all the other truths are routine background noise to get us to the real stuff of life. However, we must not ponder sanctification and Christian living in a vacuum — a biblical, theological vacuum. We must not disconnect daily Christian living from the grand gospel narrative. We must not develop approaches to counseling without the context of God-reality — theology. We must not sit down to counsel hurting people if we haven't been sitting at the feet of the Wonderful Counselor.

As biblical counselors, we care about change, and we insist that change must be gospel centered. In the end, our goal is the formation of Christ in people — all for the glory of God. This is exactly the message of Paul's biblical counselor's prayer in Philippians 1:9 – 11. We pray that our love would abound in knowledge about the gospel meta-narrative so that we have depth of gospel-centered insight into how we can help one another to grow into Christlikeness — all to the glory and praise of God. You and I counsel with this vision of transformation in view.

That's why sanctification — growth in Christlikeness for the glory of Christ — is the pinnacle toward which *Gospel-Centered Counseling* has been building. Our goal has been a unified vision of transformation by grace. Many books talk about theology, many talk about life, many talk about problems, and many talk about the gospel of grace and means of grace. Our purpose is to bring these vital life issues together by asking and answering these questions:

+ "Why are we here?"
+ "How do we become like Jesus?"
+ "How can our inner life increasingly reflect the inner life of Christ?"

Everyone has asked the question, "Why am I here?" The world offers endless answers to that ultimate life question. God's Word provides *the* answer. Our destination in the Christian life is conformity to Christ. We want our inner relational, rational, volitional, and emotional life to increasingly reflect the inner relational, rational, volitional, and emotional life of Christ. The individual might ask it like this, "How am I to pursue growth in grace?" The biblical counselor might word it like this, "How do I help people pursue sanctification?"

To understand how we increasingly reflect Christ, we have to understand and apply biblical wisdom about:

1. *The Written Word:* Because we must view the Bible accurately and use the Bible competently to find wisdom for life in a broken world,

we need to understand the Bible's story the way God tells it — as a grand gospel victory narrative.

2. *The Living Word:* Because what comes into our minds when we think about God determines everything about us, we need to grow in our knowledge of our Trinitarian God of holy love. Because life is two stories — a battle for our hearts — we must decide whether we trust Christ's image of God or Satan's subversive portrayal of God.

3. *Understanding People:* Because our goal is heart change where the whole person is whole in Christ, as biblical cardiologists we must understand God's original design for people (the *imago Dei*) as worshipers who are physically embodied, socially embedded, relational, rational, volitional, and emotional beings.

4. *Diagnosing Problems:* Because sanctification includes putting off the old way of living, we must diagnose the four chambers of the fallen heart — relationally we are spiritual adulterers, rationally we are heart idolaters, volitionally we are enslaved destroyers, and emotionally we are ungoverned users.

5. *Prescribing Soul-u-tions:* Because to grow in Christ we need to understand and apply who we are in and to Christ, we must grasp our complete salvation: justification ("Forgiven!"), reconciliation ("Welcome home!"), regeneration ("You're a new creation in Christ!" — virgin brides, grace interpreters, empowering shepherds, soulful psalmists), and redemption ("You're more than a conqueror!").

6. *God's People:* Because the body of Christ is the best soil for growth in Christ, we must understand how to become gospel communities *of* biblical counseling where everyone speaks the truth in love.

7. *The End of the Story:* Because my future destiny *with Christ* makes all the difference during my present suffering and in my current battle against sin, I must apply the end of Christ's grand redemptive story to my life story today by remembering the future.

Toward a Biblical Vision of Progressive Sanctification

So … our answers to life's seven ultimate questions make it easy to understand sanctification, right? We simply plug those summary principles into our gospel conversations at just the right moment and our counselees, parishioners, and spiritual friends morph naturally (and supernaturally) into the image of Christ, right?

Not quite. First, people are not plug-and-play objects — they are eternally valuable human beings. Second, sanctification is not a nice, neat package. Sanctification is a winding slow walk, not a light switch we turn from off to on. The Christian life is a *lifelong* journey of daily renewal of every dimension of our lives as we live out the ramifications of the gospel. Third, people helping can be like a maze. Biblical truth provides our GPS — God's Positioning Scripture — to provide us compass points, but our counseling journey with people toward Christlikeness is never a linear process from point A to point B. It zigs. It zags. It retraces. Counseling is "spaghetti relationships" — a swirled-together, messy journey as we minister to hurting people.

In this chapter, we're still a step away from the actual process of helping people in their sanctification journey (our next chapter addresses that as does the second book in this series — *Gospel Conversations*). Our current goal is to outline a biblical way of thinking about heart transformation. Even assuming that everyone agrees with the seven summary answers to life's seven ultimate life questions, there are still sanctification issues that baffle theologians and counselors alike.

Consider just a few questions about the nature of sanctification. Is sanctification (growth in holiness and spiritual maturity) for Christians simply believing more in their justification? What place does effort and discipline have to play in the sanctification process? Is the old adage "Let go and let God" a model to follow in growth in grace? Or is "Try harder" more accurate? Is our role in sanctification passive or active or something else entirely? If both salvation and sanctification are by grace, and if we play no role in our salvation, does that mean we play no role in our sanctification? If we do play a role, does that mean we grow by works and not by grace? If we do grow by grace, how are we supposed to tap into Christ's grace for our sanctification growth? Is there a place for striving in the Christian life? Does the gospel make any demands on the believer for growth in grace? Sanctification flows from a true grasp of the gospel — but how do good deeds spring up from good news?

While I want to acknowledge the complexity of growth in grace, I do not want to discourage you. I believe that the theological foundation we've laid provides tremendous help in sorting out answers to these practical sanctification questions. The rest of this chapter will introduce the difference between an either/or approach to sanctification and a both/and approach. We will address the God/believer question: "Is sanctification all of God, all of us, or does sanctification in some way involve God *and* the believer?" This discussion will allow us to see how our answers to life's seven ultimate questions help us to craft a comprehensive biblical definition of sanctification. Then we'll explore how God calls us to prepare our hearts to grow in grace by nurturing our relationship to the Trinity.

Toward a Gospel-Centered Approach to Growth in Grace

God calls biblical counselors to join the sanctification journey with saints who struggle with suffering and sin. As we commit ourselves to this relational journey and start to read the current evangelical literature, we quickly discover the debate between two either/or approaches.[1]

One approach has been labeled the *gospel indicative* approach, which in its extreme seems to emphasize that sanctification entirely or almost exclusively involves the work of God, where our only "role" is to remember and re-believe what God has already done for us in the gospel (gospel indicatives). The other approach has been labeled the *gospel imperative* approach, which in its extreme seems to emphasize that sanctification, while always initially the work of God, primarily involves our active effort to change as we obey the commands of God (gospel imperatives).

Of course, life and ministry are never so nice and neat. So it is unlikely that anyone would self-select into either of these outlier approaches to sanctification. However, these stereotypical extremes can help us to think through a both/and comprehensive approach to biblical progressive sanctification.

Comprehensive Biblical Sanctification and Gospel Indicatives

If we followed the gospel-indicative-only approach, we would be inclined to immerse ourselves in Ephesians 1 – 3 and the gospel indicatives — focusing entirely on our position in Christ and our identity in Christ. As we've seen throughout this book and in particular in chapters 11 – 13, it *is* vital that we grasp, together with all the saints, who we are in Christ. However, in this either/or approach, we would never or rarely move on to Ephesians 4 – 6 and the gospel imperatives. Perhaps we could summarize this perspective with the oft-quoted phrase, "Sanctification is the art of getting used to our justification." In church history this might have been labeled the "Let Go and Let God" approach where we are more passive and inactive as we rest in the realities of the gospel of Christ's grace.

To assess this perspective, let's see if the summarizing quote meets the test of a comprehensive biblical perspective: *"Sanctification is the art of getting used to our justification."* To be fair, before showing possible deficiencies, it helps to appreciate the intent of the quote. In Romans 6, Paul clearly highlights the truth that Christians are to know and reckon on their new identity in Christ — that our former self was crucified, that baptism into Christ is baptism into his death and resurrection, and that through our union with Christ we are dead to sin and alive to God. John Stott said it like this:

> We are to recall, to ponder, to grasp, to register these truths until they are so integral to our mindset that a return to the old life is unthinkable. Regenerate Christians should no more contemplate a return to unregenerate living than adults to their childhood, married people to their singleness or discharged prisoners to their prison cell. For our union with Jesus Christ has severed us from the old life and committed us to the new.[2]

These are wonderful truths, but perhaps incompletely stated. In Stott's quote and in the quote about "the art of getting used to …" what's highlighted and implied are knowing and reckoning (Rom. 6:1 – 11). But Paul goes on to urge that on the basis of these gospel realities, believers are to not let sin reign, but instead yield themselves to God (Rom. 6:12 – 14). "The art of getting used to" seems to truncate Paul's comprehensive biblical model in Romans 6. Paul is saying that based on what we know and what we "get used to," God calls us to a grace-empowered and grace-motivated *response*.

The definition we're assessing says that sanctification is the art of getting used to our *justification*. As amazing as our justification is, in chapters 11 – 12 we saw that justification is *not* a comprehensive biblical summary of our complete salvation. At the very least, the quote should say, "Sanctification is the art of getting used to our *justification, reconciliation, regeneration, and redemption*." In fact, Romans 6, with its emphasis on our newness in Christ, stresses regeneration more than it does justification. And since Paul highlights not letting sin reign and yielding along with "knowing and reckoning," a Pauline working definition of sanctification would at least have to include:

+ Sanctification is the art of applying our justification, reconciliation, regeneration, and redemption.

By retaining the word "art," I am communicating the unique application of universal biblical truths, the person-specific and situation-specific ways in which individuals apply gospel truth to their life. By inserting the word "applying" in place of "getting used to," I am communicating the comprehensive nature of knowing, considering, not letting sin reign, and yielding based on the realities of our complete salvation — our justification, reconciliation, regeneration, and redemption.

Comprehensive Biblical Sanctification and Gospel Imperatives

If we followed the gospel-imperative-only approach, we would be prone to skip over or fly by Ephesians 1 – 3 and our position/identity in Christ so we could race to and settle in Ephesians 4 – 6 and principles of putting off and putting on — the gospel imperatives. As we'll see in chapter 16, putting off and putting on *is* vital. However, in this either/or approach, we would separate put off/put on from their foundation in gospel indicatives. Perhaps we could summarize that perspective with, "Sanctification is the active process of putting off and putting on." In church history this might have been labeled the "Try Harder" approach, where our focus is less on our position in Christ and more on our obligation to Christ, less on our identity in Christ and more on working for Christ, less on passively resting in Christ and more on our active effort to be like Christ, and less on Christ's empowering grace and more on our effort.

To assess this perspective, let's see if the summarizing quote meets the test of a comprehensive biblical perspective: *"Sanctification is the active process of putting off and putting on."* Once again, prior to outlining possible deficiencies, it can be helpful to recognize the strengths of the quote. This description of sanctification has the advantage of communicating Paul's Romans 6 concepts of "not letting sin reign" and "yielding." It also has the advantage of communicating the Romans 6, Ephesians 4, and Colossians 3 concepts of putting off and putting on. However, left to itself, this definition seems to diminish the gospel indicatives and seems to diminish Christ's grace for sanctification.

Additionally, this definition does not address a comprehensive biblical understanding of what is to be put off and what is to be put on. Using the language of chapters 6 – 7, what is our target? What is the heart? What is heart change? We answered those questions by identifying our goal as heart change defined as our inner life increasingly reflecting the inner life of Christ. And we identified the inner life of Christ as the heart — his relational, rational, volitional, and emotional inner life.

Combining these imperative-only deficiencies with the previous indicative-only deficiencies, a biblical working definition of sanctification would at least need to say:

- Sanctification is the grace-motivated and grace-empowered art of applying our justification, reconciliation, regeneration, and redemption so that our inner life increasingly reflects the inner life of Christ (relationally, rationally, volitionally, and emotionally) as we put off the old dead person we once were and put on the new person we already are in Christ (relationally, rationally, volitionally, and emotionally).

I'll be the first to confess that in a book where I've attempted to craft tweet-size summaries, my sanctification summary is much less tweetable than:

+ Sanctification is the art of getting used to our justification.
+ Sanctification is the active process of putting off and putting on.

The good news is, I will eventually offer you a tweet-size summary. The bad news is, before I do, I need to expand my sanctification summary even more. Our primary goal is not brevity, not even "balance," but biblical accuracy for real-life biblical counseling.

Comprehensive Biblical Sanctification and Gospel-Centered Counseling

I introduced this chapter by noting that we must build our response to our sanctification question on our comprehensive response to our first seven ultimate life questions. So, to my previous working definition, I now add components from our theological answers to each of those questions:

+ Sanctification is the grace-motivated and grace-empowered art of applying our justification, reconciliation, regeneration, and redemption to our daily lives and relationships through wisdom from the Word of God, through relational dependence on our triune God, through the encouragement of the people of God, and through the motivation from our future with God so that our inner life increasingly reflects the inner life of Christ (relationally, rationally, volitionally, and emotionally) as we put off the old dead person we no longer are and put on the new person we already are in Christ (relationally, rationally, volitionally, and emotionally) for God's glory.

I admit it — that's almost five tweets. However, it *is* comprehensive. It *does* incorporate gospel indicatives and gospel imperatives as well as elements from our answers to all of life's ultimate questions and from all ten of systematic theology's classic categories.

If some confusion remains, we can ask a simple question and respond with a succinct biblical answer. How do we become like Jesus? We work out our sanctification as God works in us (Phil. 2:12). Those are the two truths we must protect: the grace gift of God in sanctification and our role in sanctification. Kevin DeYoung united both of these realities:

> We ought to positively glory in the indicatives of the gospel. The indicatives ought to fuel our following of the imperatives. Our obedience must be grounded in the gospel. Sanctification is empowered by faith in the promises of God. We need to be reminded of our justification often and throughout our Christian lives. Our pursuit of personal righteousness will not go anywhere without a conviction that we are already reckoned positionally righteous in Christ.[3]
>
> The New Testament gives us commands, and these commands involve more than remembering, revisiting, and rediscovering the reality of our justification. We must also put on, put off, put to death, strive and make every effort ... Yes this effort is always connected to gospel grace. But we cannot reduce effort to simply believing in justification.[4]

Sanctification involves knowing and reckoning on our identity in and union with Christ — gospel indicatives. Much of *Gospel-Centered Counseling* has focused on helping us to know and reckon on these truths. Sanctification also involves applying those truths — yielding, through the Spirit's empowerment, to gospel imperatives. Our tweet-size summary captures this twin reality: *Sanctification is the art of applying our complete salvation by God's grace, Spirit, Word, people, and future hope so we increasingly reflect Christ.*

Toward a Biblical Understanding of How Growth in Grace Blossoms

Because we care deeply about people and about gospel-centered change, we need to address another question: "How do God's role and the role of the counselee connect?" As saints struggling with suffering and sin, and with the goal of sanctification, what is the process by which growth in grace takes place? What is the process by which Christ's power rests upon and works within us? Here are our tweet-size answers:

- Sanctification involves gospel truth applied to life along with active elements of heart change motivated and empowered by grace as we commune with our triune God.
- God calls us to prepare our hearts to grow in grace by nurturing our relationship to the Trinity.

Sometimes we learn best how to do something by first being shown the wrong ways to do it. The apostle Paul seems to have such a learning and teaching style. In many passages he teaches us how *not* to live the Christian life. His teaching dovetails well with our study of the either/or approaches to growth in grace and with our study of a comprehensive both/and approach.

Do *Not* Grow in Grace by "Trying Harder"

Paul teaches us not to grow in grace by dependence on our own power, works, or our flesh. In Galatians, he wondered who had bewitched the saints in Galatia. Having been saved by faith apart from human effort, why were they now trying to sanctify themselves by works — through the power of the flesh, through human self-sufficiency?

As we've seen in Colossians, Paul wonders what human philosophy has taken captive and deceived the saints in Colosse. Having been saved by faith, why would they attempt to live their Christian lives based on rules, rituals, regulations, and self-righteous works?

In Philippians, Paul makes it more personal, using himself in his illustration of the wrong way to live the Christian life. Speaking to "brothers" (Phil. 3:1), that is, to believers, he warned them not to have confidence in the flesh. If anyone could have confidence in the flesh, it would be Paul. "Circumcised on the eighth day, of the people of Israel, of the tribe of Benjamin, a Hebrew of the Hebrews; in regard to the law, a Pharisee; as for zeal, persecuting the church; as for legalistic righteousness, faultless" (Phil. 3:5 – 6). However, Paul counted all his human effort, both for salvation and for sanctification, as loss, as rubbish, literally, as camel dung. Good for nothing. Human effort apart from God's power is worthless for sanctification.

Knowing how *not* to live out our sanctification, Paul informs us *how to* grow in grace. What is powerful enough to produce the final product envisioned in progressive sanctification? "I want to know Christ and the power of his resurrection ... becoming like him in his death" (Phil. 3:10). To grow in grace, to become conformed to Christ's image, *we need Christ's resurrection power.*

Paul underscored the same truth in Ephesians 1:15 – 23. Having spoken of the Ephesians' positional sanctification in verses 1 – 14, Paul moved to their progressive sanctification as he prayed that they might know Christ intimately and avail themselves of his infinite power. He spoke of "his incomparably great power for us who believe. That power is like the working of his mighty strength, which he exerted in Christ when he raised him from the dead and seated him at his right hand in the heavenly realms" (Eph. 1:19 – 20).

Pauline sanctification does not follow the paradigm of "Try harder!" It is not about works and human effort. It *is* about connecting with Christ's resurrection power.

Do *Not* Grow in Grace by "Doing Nothing"

However, that does not mean that Pauline sanctification shifts to the other pole and says, *"Do nothing!"* There is a role for us to play. We do have a responsibility. Paul wrote:

> *Not that I have already obtained all this, or have already been made perfect, but I press on to take hold of that for which Christ Jesus took hold of me. Brothers, I do not consider myself yet to have taken hold of it. But one thing I do: Forgetting what is behind (works-based righteousness, self-effort sanctification, "trying harder") and straining toward what is ahead,* I press on *toward the goal to win the prize for which God has called me heavenward in Christ Jesus. All of us who are mature should take such a view of things.* (Phil. 3:12–15, emphasis and parenthesis added)

Paul is not "letting go and letting God." He's straining, pressing on, and working hard to work out the salvation that God worked in him.

How do we live out our sanctification in Christ? How do we grow in grace? It is not by "trying harder." Not by human effort. Nor is it by "doing nothing," by "letting go and letting God." It is not freedom from responsibility. Instead, it is by "communing with God," by "connecting with Christ and his grace," by "tapping into Christ's resurrection power," by "yielding to God's Spirit," and by developing a "transforming relationship with God."

Do Grow in Grace by "Communing with God"

Since the power to grow in grace is itself a grace gift from Christ, since Paul connects that power to Christ's resurrection power, and since we have a role to play in keeping our hearts receptive to his power, we need to understand our faith role in spiritual growth. Our faith role relates to, and relates us to, each member of the Trinity.

+ Trust in the Father: Faith through Grace
+ Abide in the Son: Union with Christ
+ Yield to and Be Filled with the Spirit: Empowered by the Spirit

J. I. Packer noted that for the Puritans' *communion with God* was the "comprehensive reality that is central to Christian existence."[5] We grow in grace only through a relationship with God the Father, a relationship of mutual interchange, joint participation, and fellowship — *koinônia*: receiving and responding to our Father's grace-love. Our soul must be captured by our forgiving Father, our heart enraptured by his narrative of grace-love, our will surrendered to his good and generous will, and our emotions fully open to his good heart.

Sanctification, just as much as salvation, begins with faith (Gal. 3:1 – 14). Faith is our victory that overcomes the world, the flesh, and the Devil (1 John 4:4 – 5; 5:4 – 5; Rom. 6:1 – 8:14). We entrust ourselves to the good work that God has already accomplished in our heart. As Richard Lovelace emphasized, "The counselor who is attempting to move people further in sanctification should therefore begin with a strong emphasis on justification and reiterate this often in the course of his work" (I would add reconciliation, regeneration, and redemption to justification).[6] By faith, we reckon on our new nurture and new nature. In sanctification, we depend on God's power, the power at work when he raised his Son (Eph. 1:15 – 23; 3:14 – 21) — God's resurrection power.

Sanctification requires *trust in God the Father*, and it also demands *abiding in God the Son*. We are delivered from the bondage of sin through the power of our union with the indwelling Christ. Lovelace wrote, "As Romans 6 makes clear, the ground of sanctification is our union with Christ in his death and resurrection, in which the old nature was destroyed and a new nature created with the power to grow in newness of life."[7]

Just as we received Christ Jesus as Lord, so we continue to live in him, rooted and built up in him, strengthened in the faith (Col. 2:6 – 7). We are united theologically and actually in Christ's death and resurrection. We need to abide in Christ, remaining in, residing in, and sharing in him intimately, in active, practical spiritual union. Puritan pastor Thomas Boston described our growth in grace using the biblical imagery from John 15 of Christ as the Vine:

> This sanctifying Spirit, communicated by the Lord Jesus to His members, is the spiritual nourishment the branches have from the stock into which they are ingrafted; whereby the life of grace, given them in regeneration, is preserved, continued, and actuated. It is the nourishment whereby the new creature lives, and is nourished up towards perfection. Spiritual life needs to be fed, and must have supply of nourishment: and believers derive the same from Christ their Head, whom the Father has appointed the Head of influences to all His members.[8]

Boston concludes his discussion of the new nature with words of counsel for growth in grace through communion.

> To you that are saints, I say, strive to obtain and keep up actual communion and fellowship with Jesus Christ; that is, to be still deriving fresh supplies of grace from the fountain thereof in Him, by faith, and making suitable returns of them, in the exercise of grace and holy obedience.[9]

Sanctification also requires that we be *filled with the Spirit*. The Holy Spirit is the resident counselor in every believer. He's our spiritual caregiver serving as our source, guide, and enabler of new life in Christ. He operates in our affections, thoughts, wills, and emotions.

In what power, or better, in whose power do I live? The person in Romans 7 is trying to live the good life in his own power. We need to live the good life from a good heart, from the good power of the Spirit. We need to walk according to the Spirit; we need to be filled with the Spirit. When we're told to yield to the Spirit, be led by the Spirit, keep in step with the Spirit, and be controlled by the Spirit, we're being told to actively appropriate and personally depend on the Spirit in our daily lives. True spirituality is not achieved in our own energy.

To be filled with the Spirit means to saturate ourselves with the spiritual so that we are under the Spirit's influence. Filling with the Spirit requires supplanting the old influence (putting off the flesh) and being filled up with the Spirit. It is a present tense imperative: we're commanded to be continually emptying ourselves of the flesh's influence and continually being filled with the Spirit. It is a passive voice word: we are filled — but we must open ourselves to, desire to be filled, thirst for, and respond to the invitation to drink.

Resurrection Power Multipliers

The concept of connection with our triune God is not novel. However, I've found that we infrequently think through the "how to" of that connection or what we might call *spiritual fellowship*. We even less frequently ponder how the process of communion with God relates to the sanctification process of *spiritual formation*. And we almost never map out the connection between spiritual fellowship, spiritual formation, and the *spiritual disciplines*. Finally, we rarely relate these concepts to *spiritual counsel* — how we help others to grow in grace.

Since we grow in grace through communion with the Father, Son, and Holy Spirit, we need to understand how to connect with God. We must learn how to use the means of Trinitarian connecting that God has graciously put at our disposal. I label these means *RPMs — Resurrection Power Multipliers* (from Phil. 3:10 and Paul's desire to know the power of Christ's resurrection).

Our path to victory is humble dependence (faith) on God to connect his resurrection power to the depths of our being. God's strength is made perfect in our conscious human weakness and conscious human dependence. As Paul repeatedly reminds us in 2 Corinthians, "But this happened that we might not rely on ourselves but on God, who raises the dead" (2 Cor. 1:9). "But we have this treasure in jars of clay to show that this all-surpassing power is from God and not from us" (2 Cor. 4:7). "But he said to me, 'My grace is sufficient for you, for my power is made perfect in weakness.' Therefore I will boast all the more gladly about my weaknesses, so that Christ's power may rest on me" (2 Cor. 12:9).

The power to grow comes from Christ, but we are to avail ourselves of it. In progressive sanctification we need to ask, "What is the biblical process by which Christ's power rests on and works within us?" The RPMs are the means by which we never sever our spiritual umbilical cord. The RPMs continually nourish us in our inner person as we "eat" right and "exercise" right spiritually (John 4:34; 6:35 – 69; 7:37 – 39; 1 Cor. 9:24 – 27; 2 Cor. 3:17 – 18; 4:16 – 18; 1 Tim. 4:7 – 8). Spiritual victory demands the dependent, contingent, connected, cooperative life (John 5:30; 6:53; 15:1 – 5).

Paul says that we receive grace for living the abundant life daily the same way that we receive grace for living the eternal life — by faith (Gal. 3 – 5; Col. 2). So the question becomes, "How do we receive grace by faith in our daily life to live the abundant life?" So what does it mean to do this? How did Jesus do this? Paul? The early Christians? Is there a pattern to follow? What does it look like in daily life to abide in Christ?

What we need is biblical insight into our practical relationship with God in sanctification. We must develop a theology of the spiritual life that can guide us into constant interaction with the grace of God as a real part of our daily lives.

Understanding Our Transforming Friendship with God

We develop a transforming friendship with God by grace through faith. We obtain transforming power by working out our own salvation with fear and trembling — with utmost seriousness — with grace-empowered and inspired spiritual discipline.

In the Fall, we died spiritually. We broke our connection to God and became separated from the life of God (Eph. 4:18). Life became deformed from the top down. Being separated from the life of God, we are not only wrong, we are wrung out. Robbed of the vital nutrient of grace relationships — connection — we become depraved *and* depleted. We experience spiritual weakness caused by spiritual starvation.

In salvation, we are reconnected to God, reconciled to him. This opens the way of access to him. This new nurture, this new connection, fills our previously depleted souls. Our grace relationship with God through Christ transforms us by reconnecting us to the Spirit. We are transformed by contact with God.

Spiritual victory requires transforming ingrained heart tendencies through living out our regeneration — the impartation of new life. The seed of our new life has germinated. Now it needs to blossom as we connect with Christ's grace by faith active in love. Spirituality is cooperative, dependent interaction with God. We are spiritual to the extent that we are connected to God and dominated by God's grace. The RPMs bring our total being back into effective, contingent cooperation with Christ and his resurrection power.

Enjoying Spiritual Formation through the Spiritual Disciplines

To grow in grace we need spiritual formation through the spiritual disciplines that disconnect our embodied personalities from the old flesh patterns and connect us to Christ. The flesh is habituated to the entrenched ways of the past inherited from Adam and ingrained through life before Christ. It is incited by the world and enticed by the Devil to act in independence from God. We find the power to put off these old habits and to put on the new person we already are in Christ by connecting with Christ through the RPMs (see fig. 15:1).

Throughout church history, Christians have used terms like "the spiritual disciplines" and "spiritual formation" to explain this process of connecting with Christ and his resurrection power so that we can put off the old and put on the new. The historical practice of the spiritual disciplines of spiritual formation moves us to a spiritual responsiveness and openness that empowers our embodied personalities toward a readiness and an ability to connect with Christ's resurrection power.

The spiritual disciplines are activities of mind and body that help to bring our whole selves into cooperation with God and his grace so we can connect

Figure 15:1

RPMs: Resurrection Power Multipliers
Spiritual Foundation: Change through Christ's Word • Spiritual Theology: Preaching, Teaching, Bible Study, Personal Study, Our New Identity in Christ
Spiritual Formation: Communion with Christ/Conformity to Christ • Spiritual Disciplines: The Individual and Corporate Disciplines
Spiritual Friendship: Compassionate Discernment from Christ's Ministers • Spiritual Counseling: Individual Biblical Counseling
Spiritual Fellowship: Connection with Christ's Body • Spiritual Discipleship: Small Group Ministry and Large Group Fellowship and Worship
Spiritual Filling: Control by the Holy Spirit • Spiritual Empowerment: The Filling of the Spirit
Spiritual Fruit: Character and Competence in Christ • Spiritual Ministry/Maturity: Service, Evangelism, Discipleship, Stewardship
Spiritual Family: Completing One Another in Christ • Spiritual Homes: Godly Marriages, Shepherding Parents
Spiritual Fighting: Conquering Christ's Enemies (The World, the Flesh, and the Devil) • Spiritual Warfare/Victory: The Whole Armor of God

with him and his resurrection power. They empower us to actively appropriate and depend on God's Spirit in our lives: to live by, be led by, yielded to, filled with, controlled by, walking in, and keeping in step with God's transforming and indwelling Holy Spirit.

The spiritual formation categories that I provide in figure 15:1 offer one way to classify the various means of connecting ourselves with Christ's resurrection power. As I have studied the Word, pastored churches, shepherded believers, counseled people, and taught about the spiritual life, I have developed these categories as a helpful way to conceptualize the individual and corporate disciplines of the sanctified life.

By *spiritual foundation*, I mean change through the preaching, teaching, and personal study of God's Word. Through these we learn who we are in Christ and to Christ. We cannot grow in God's grace apart from immersion in God's Word. We connect to him as we feed on his living and active Word, which nourishes our spiritual life.

I am using *spiritual formation* both for the entire process and for one aspect of the process. Spiritual formation is the classical name given for the practice of spiritual disciplines, both individual and corporate. These include such individual disciplines as prayer, meditation, silence, solitude, fasting, frugality, and many more. They include the corporate disciplines of mutual confession, body life, fellowship, worship, and many others. We grow in our receptivity and openness to Christ's resurrection power through these historic Christian disciplines of the faith.

My third category of resurrection power multipliers is *spiritual friendship*. By this I am highlighting the ministry of soul physicians and the arts of soul care, spiritual direction, mentoring, encouraging one another, one-to-one discipleship, and biblical counseling. We connect to Christ as we connect to Christians. We grow in grace as spiritual friends help us to sustain, heal, reconcile, and guide our faith in Christ.

Though this is a book on biblical counseling, I do *not* believe that counseling is the only way or even the primary way of growing in grace. Biblical counseling is simply one means of promoting growth in grace. Effective soul physicians disciple their spiritual friends in the practice of all of the RPMs. In my pastoral ministries, I never counsel believers until they have agreed to commit themselves to the full ministry of the local church — a ministry that embodies the RPMs.

Spiritual friendship is a companion to *spiritual fellowship*. Whereas spiritual friendship recognizes how connection with one other Christian prompts connection with Christ, so spiritual fellowship discerns that connection with the body of Christ in group settings also nourishes our relationship to our Savior. This can include small group ministry as well as large group fellowship and worship. Spiritual friendship and spiritual fellowship remind us that relationships are the greatest spiritual disciplines.

Spiritual filling is yet another powerful means of tapping into Christ's resurrection power. It is our responsibility to yield our human spirit to the Holy Spirit. We are to walk in step with the Spirit and be filled with the Spirit — controlled by his passions and evidencing his fruit — the character of Christ.

The category of *spiritual fruit* (not to be confused with the fruit of the Spirit) indicates that ministry for Christ is another avenue for connecting to Christ. Evangelism, teaching, serving, discipling — these all motivate us to be strong in the grace of our Lord Jesus Christ. Doing ministry for Christ in a fallen world is draining. As we pour ourselves out for others, we learn how frail and needy we are. So we cling to Christ to empower us and connect with Christ to equip us.

Spiritual family recognizes that the godly relationships in our homes are another form of resurrection power multipliers. Relationships with those who love us enhance our receptivity to the love and power of our heavenly Father.

Spiritual fighting reflects the truth that part of our responsibility in the sanctification process includes availing ourselves of the whole armor of God. Through the whole armor and by God's Spirit, we defeat the world, the flesh, and the Devil.

Taken together, I intend these eight categories to represent the types of activities Paul undertook and that we are to undertake as we press toward the mark of the prize of the high calling of Christlikeness. These eight categories of responsibility answer the questions, "How do we remain vitally connected to Christ who is the umbilical cord of our spiritual life? Who is the nutrient that sustains, heals, reconciles, and guides us?"[10]

The key to growth in grace is tapping into Christ's resurrection power by means of communing with the Trinity. This has been recognized throughout church history. The Westminster Confession of Faith reminds us:

> They, who are once effectually called, and regenerated, having a new heart, and a new spirit created in them, are further sanctified, really and personally, through the virtue of Christ's death and resurrection, by His Word and Spirit dwelling in them.[11]

We *are further sanctified* as we tap into the resurrection power that already dwells within us.

Where We've Been and Where We're Headed

We've been asking, "How do we become like Jesus?" "How can our inner life increasingly reflect the inner life of Christ?" You've already seen my tweet-size answer: *Sanctification is the art of applying our complete salvation by God's grace, Spirit, Word, people, and future hope so we increasingly reflect Christ.*

Now, in our final chapter, we need to see what it looks like to put this all together in our lives and ministries. To do that, we'll walk through a dozen journey markers in a biblical heart-change model of progressive sanctification.

CHAPTER 16

Putting Off and Putting On: God's Heart-Change Model of Progressive Sanctification

Imagine Kevin and Elyse sitting across from you and your spouse. As a husband and wife biblical counseling team, you've worked with Kevin and Elyse for some time. They came to you because, "Lately, we always seem to be at each other's throat. If it weren't for our fights (verbal, not physical), we'd never communicate." You've counseled them separately and jointly, connecting with them, listening to them, and exploring their heart struggles biblically.

Through your counseling relationship, both Kevin and Elyse have come to understand themselves and each other more biblically — who they are, how they relate, and *whose* they are. They're coming to grips with their respective heart issues that are behind the serious symptom of mutual verbal abuse. They're beginning to grasp who they are in Christ, and this reality is providing not only encouragement but also conviction. They're recognizing that their current pattern of relating is miles away from a marriage that reflects Christ and the church. In their conviction, they've received Christ's grace as they've repented to Christ and confessed heart sin to each other.

All of this is motivating Kevin and Elyse to change, to grow, to become more like Jesus. They understand that they can't change on their own. They are beginning to "get" that they have already been changed by Christ, and that to grow in Christ they need to connect with Christ and the body of Christ.

They are, to use the language of chapter 15, "communing with Christ" and "connecting to his resurrection power that is at work within them." They are yielding to and cooperating with the Holy Spirit, who daily transforms them increasingly into the image of Christ (2 Cor. 3:18; 4:16 – 18).

By God's empowerment, the four of you have laid the gospel-centered, gospel-indicative, grace-motivated, grace-empowered foundation. So is counseling over? Do Kevin and Elyse naturally/supernaturally live out their married life in Christ without any further counsel? If they say to you, "What next?" do you interpret that to mean that Kevin and Elyse have not truly come to know and reckon on their identity in Christ? If they say, "You've talked about heart change and reflecting Christ. What is the process like?" have they returned to works and the law?

I'm sure you know my answer. Biblical counsel does *not* end with the gospel indicatives — as vital as they are. Biblical counsel does *not* shy away from gospel imperatives. Biblical counselors do *not* simply talk about heart change and Christlikeness and then leave people to guess at what Christlike heart change looks like and how it occurs. Recall one of our tweet-size definitions of the sanctification process:

+ Sanctification involves gospel truth applied to life along with active elements of heart change motivated and empowered by grace as we commune with our triune God.

Knowing how Christ changes people provides the foundation for knowing what the biblical heart change process involves. Communion with our triune God provides the relational motivation and the spiritual power that prepares our hearts to grow in grace.

But what does heart change look like? What does Christlikeness look like? What is it that we are to put off and put on? These are the legitimate questions that Kevin and Elyse are asking. In the biblical counseling world, we have not always provided a comprehensive biblical description of the heart. Nor have we always provided a real-world depiction of what Christlikeness means or what we are to put off and put on. *Gospel-Centered Counseling* has sought to address this need by specifically defining the heart as our relational (spiritual, social, self-aware), rational, volitional, and emotional capacities. Our comprehensive definition of sanctification addresses the heart, Christlikeness, and putting off/putting on:

+ Sanctification is the grace-motivated and grace-empowered art of applying our justification, reconciliation, regeneration, and redemption to our daily lives and relationships through wisdom from the Word of God, through relational dependence on our triune God, through the encouragement of the people of God, and through the motivation from our future with God so that our inner life increasingly reflects the inner life of Christ (relationally, rationally, volitionally, and emotionally) as we put off the old dead person we no longer are and put on the new person we already are in Christ (relationally, rationally, volitionally, and emotionally) for God's glory.

Heart Change: From Root to Fruit

The Holy Spirit knows how to make resurrection power active in our lives as we respond to suffering and sin, with the goal of progressive sanctification. As Kevin and Elyse nurture their relationship with God the Father, Son, and Spirit, connecting to Christ's resurrection power, the Spirit empowers them to live out their new life in Christ from their new heart through a two-part process:

+ Co-Crucifixion with Christ: Mortification — Putting Off
+ Co-Resurrection with Christ: Vivification — Putting On

Throughout the history of sanctification, pastors, theologians, and lay people have used the terms "mortification" and "vivification" to describe the practical outworking of our new life in Christ. In my studies, I've located 94 New Testament passages related to the putting off/mortification and putting on/vivification process.

We are co-crucified with Christ and therefore dead to sin. This is our theological reality. Mortification is the practical application of our co-crucifixion in which we put off our old grave clothes. We quit living like the old dead person we once were. We make actual in our practice what is already actual in our regeneration. United with Christ in his crucifixion, we died to sin. Our old man has been crucified. Mortification is putting off the vestiges of sin so sin no longer exercises dominion over us because we are no longer sin's slaves.

We are also co-resurrected with Christ and therefore alive to righteousness. This is our second theological reality. Vivification is the practical application of our co-resurrection in which we put on our new wedding attire. We start living like the new alive person that we now are in Christ. We make actual in practice what is already actual in our regeneration. United with Christ in his resurrection, we came alive to righteousness. Vivification is putting on, clothing ourselves with, and living out all the aspects of our new nurture and new nature.

Putting Off and Putting On a Heart-Shaped Manner of Life

Paul uses two terms in Ephesians 4:17 – 24 to teach us what we put off and put on. First, we are to put off "walking" as we did when we were unsaved (Eph. 4:17 KJV). "Walk" describes our typical way of life, our accustomed lifestyle, and our normal manner of conduct. Second, we are to put off our "former way of life" (Eph. 4:22). "Way of life" refers to our habitual conduct, our routine conversation or manner of life, our customary way of living.

The old life of the flesh, attuned to the world and tempted by Satan, was driven by our spiritually adulterous and relationally idolatrous habituated resistance to the Spirit. Our new spiritual life in Christ grows out of our new heart with renewed affections, mind-sets, purposes, and mood states. Paul is teaching us that we work out our sanctification in the power of the Spirit as we put off those old sinful habits of fleshly life patterns and as we put on new godly patterns that increasingly reflect Christ.

What exactly is it that Kevin and Elyse are to put off and put on? In chapter 6, I introduced the four chambers of the heart and the lifestyle themes or patterns associated with them:

+ Relational Beings: Affections
+ Rational Beings: Mind-Sets
+ Volitional Beings: Pathways/Purposes
+ Emotional Beings: Mood States

Putting off and putting on relate to the lifestyle themes and patterns of our heart — affections, mind-sets, purposes, and mood states — that we live out in our relationships. As regenerate people, Kevin and Elyse operate out of a new heart — a characteristic lifestyle, walk, or manner of life controlled by the Spirit. However, the ingrained (habituated) flesh, incited by the fallen world and enticed by the Devil, tempts Kevin and Elyse to live according to their old lifestyle themes and patterns.

So for Kevin and Elyse, *mortification* is the process of putting off or de-habituating themselves from those old fleshly patterns that reflect who they once were when they were separated from the life of God. *Vivification* is the process of putting on or re-habituating themselves to new patterns that reflect who they already are in Christ.

For Kevin and Elyse, "putting off and putting on" is no mere amputation of surface manifestations, but disturbing, disrupting, uprooting, and replacing the roots of inner characteristics, patterns, and life themes in our relational, rational, volitional, and emotional capacities. Speaking of the old person we were without Christ, God says, "Don't carry around that corpse! It's rotten. Dead. Disgusting. Put off the old habits, the old grave clothes, the rags of corruption, the old conduct that was so characteristic of the old, dead you. Instead, continually be putting on the new manner of life that is now characteristic of the new you."

Putting Off and Putting On a Heart-Shaped Motivational Structure

So, as we think through transformation theologically with Kevin and Elyse, what does the spiritual formation process look like? First, we don't want to leave Kevin and Elyse with the impression that the process of progressive sanctification is some "nice neat package." It is not. Though the Bible provides us with all that we need for life and godliness, it never offers an outline. The Bible engages us relationally, connecting our life story to Christ's gospel story.

Second, while the process is always a unique relational journey, the Bible does provide wisdom about the motivational structure of the heart. As we learned in chapters 6 – 9, we pursue (volitional) what we perceive (rational) to be pleasing (relational), which prompts reaction (emotional). Rational direction determines relational motivation, which directs volitional interaction, which influences emotional reaction. This is why the heart change model of progressive sanctification in figure 16:1 moves from rational, to relational, to volitional, to emotional.

Theologically and practically, we can envision the motivational structure of the heart like this. If I conclude (rational direction) that God is not my Supreme Good (relational motivation), then I will follow a self-centered lifestyle (volitional interaction) and end up emotionally out of control (emotional reaction). On the other hand, if I live out of my new nurture/nature and conclude (rational direction) that God is my Spring of Living Water (relational motivation), then I will follow an other-centered lifestyle (volitional interaction) and learn to soothe my soul in my Savior (emotional reaction).

Figure 16:1

The Heart Change Model of Progressive Sanctification
The Putting Off/Mortification Journey with Christ
• Journey Marker 1: Rational Mortification Putting Off Our Old Foolish Mind-Sets: "I Repent of the Insane Idols of My Heart"
• Journey Marker 2: Relational/Spiritual Mortification Putting Off Our Old Disordered Spiritual Affections: "I Divorce the Adulterous False Lovers of My Soul"
• Journey Marker 3: Relational/Self-Aware Mortification Putting Off Our Disordered Old Self-Aware Affections: "I Reject the Ugliness of My Self-Beautification"
• Journey Marker 4: Relational/Social Mortification Putting Off Our Old Disordered Social Affections: "I Uproot My Self-Centered Using of Others"
• Journey Marker 5: Volitional Mortification Putting Off Our Old Self-Centered Purposes/Pathways: "I Put to Death My Enslaved Destructive Self-Gratification"
• Journey Marker 6: Emotional Mortification Putting Off Our Old Ungoverned Mood States—"I Crucify My Addictive Passions"
The Putting On/Vivification Journey with Christ
• Journey Marker 7: Rational Vivification Putting On Our New Wise Mind-Sets: "I Renew My Mind by Being Transformed by the Truth of Christ's Grace Narrative"
• Journey Marker 8: Relational Spiritual Vivification Putting On Our New Purified Spiritual Affections: "I Enjoy and Exalt God My Spring of Living Water"
• Journey Marker 9: Relational Self-Aware Vivification Putting On Our New Purified Self-Aware Affections: "I Reckon On the Truth of Who I Am to and in Christ"
• Journey Marker 10: Relational Social Vivification Putting On Our New Purified Social Affections: "I Nourish My New Shepherding Love for Others"
• Journey Marker 11: Volitional Vivification Putting On Our New Other-Centered Purposes/Pathways: "I Fan into Flame My New Freed Will Empowered to Empower Others"
• Journey Marker 12: Emotional Vivification Putting On Our New Managed Mood States: "I Soothe My Soul in My Savior"

The Journey of Growth in Grace

The Heart Change Model of Progressive Sanctification gives you a grid, guide, or map for thinking through how you will *journey with* Kevin and Elyse. In chapter 7, we journeyed in and journeyed out with Mike. Now we can journey "off" and journey "on" with Kevin and Elyse.

"Journey" coincides nicely with Paul's word "walk" — a manner of life. Progressive sanctification is a lifelong journey where our inner life increasingly reflects the inner life of Christ. These twelve putting off/putting on journey markers of transformation in Christ represent repeatable paths that we walk as we apply the victory that Christ has already won for us.

I've purposely chosen to use the continuous tense language of "putting off" and "putting on" as opposed to "put off" and "put on." We were saved once for all. Sanctification, however, is ongoing, progressive. We do not once for all repent of an old way of thinking, never to have to face that lie again. Instead, we must continually gird up the loins of our minds, continually allow God's Spirit to transform our thinking, continually live according to the new person we are in Christ, and continually count ourselves dead indeed to sin, but alive to God. Daily we are being transformed more and more into Christ's image (2 Cor. 3:17 – 18; 4:16 – 18).

These twelve journey markers offer a logical and theological process for helping others with heart change. In counseling, we must apply them idiosyncratically. Each counselee, parishioner, and spiritual friend is uniquely complex. Though these twelve categories are useful handles that shepherd our interactions, they are a guide, not a straitjacket.

Through Christ's empowerment (that's why it's called a journey *with Christ*), each individual is personally, individually, and uniquely responsible to put off his or her old characteristic manner of living, replacing it with the new lifestyle in Christ. The consistent practice of putting off and putting on leads to new patterns so that more and more the person's characteristic affections, mind-sets, purposes, and mood states are set on God and not on the world.

The Putting Off/Mortification Journey with Christ

When Paul selected the phrase "putting off," he chose a clothing metaphor that suggests stripping off and laying aside an old set of clothes that symbolizes the old manner of life, the old set of characteristics associated with the old person. Clothing represents an outward symbol of what is inside. In Paul's day, when slaves were freed, they changed their attire, no longer wearing a slave's wardrobe. Thus "putting off" suggests ceasing to live in a certain way, stripping off, being done with, and terminating everything associated with the old unregenerate person.

But Paul goes further. He speaks not simply of putting off slave clothes; he speaks of putting off grave clothes — the clothing that the "old man" wore. That old man is now dead. Paul describes the old set of clothes as "corrupt" (Eph. 4:22 KJV), indicating that they are putrid, crumbling, like the rotting waste of cadavers, stinking, and ripe for being disposed of and forgotten.

Mortification is the habitual weakening of the flesh, of those vestiges of the old dead you. It involves the ongoing crippling of your old fleshly inclinations, putting off your old dead false lovers, foolish mind-sets, self-centered pathways, and ungoverned mood states.[1]

Journey Marker 1: Rational Mortification—Putting Off Our Old Foolish Mind-Sets

Stop the madness! That's what putting off foolish mind-sets does. It says, "No more!" to the insanity of Satan's lying, works narrative. It repents of the "God-is-not-good" falsehood. It rejects all non-God reality, stamping out the eyeballs-only thinking that crops Christ out of the picture and suppresses the reality of the Trinity's holy love.

What is a foolish mind-set? It is the smaller story, the earthly perspective of life that says, "Curse God and die!" It clamors for our attention, claiming that anything other than God is our supreme good. The foolish mind-set is captured and captivated by fleshly imaginations that scream from Jeremiah 2, "God is a land of great darkness! He's a desert. He's not your Spring of Living Water, so dig cisterns of your own making."

When Kevin and Elyse put off their old mind-sets, they repent of the insane idols of their heart. They put off their old contemptuous images of God and refuse to think like the old arrogant fools that they used to be. They dismiss all fabricated subversions of reality that entice them to doubt God and trust themselves. They put off dethroning God. In summary, putting off foolish mind-sets requires that Kevin and Elyse repent of the idols of their hearts that capture their imagination.

Facing *suffering* and wondering if God is good, they put off all images of God as a shalt-not God. Kevin and Elyse each say to God, "I put off my blindness to Christ's worth. I cease finding fault with you — perceiving injustice in you. I reject all contemptuous views of you. I refuse to think little of you. I cast off all images of you as a cosmic Killjoy. I discard my loss of awe of you — my loss of all respect for you that causes me to no longer detect your holy love, to no longer appreciate your majestic beauty."

Facing *sin* and wondering whether they should choose the pleasure of sin for a season or pleasing God forever, Kevin and Elyse put off fleshly pictures, images, stories, and narratives that control their convictions and direct their actions. They each say to God, "I put off the satanic strongholds that captivate my imagination. I disavow the lies of the earthly, temporal stories of reality that I've been believing. I take off the foolish frame of reference, lenses, and eyeglasses through which I have been viewing life."

Journey Marker 2: Relational Mortification — Putting Off Our Old Disordered Spiritual Affections

Remember Satan's strategy. He belittles Christ, then exalts himself, all in the sick hope of causing us to be unfaithful to Christ. He attempts to tempt us with foolish mind-sets about God so he can allure us toward false lovers of the soul. Satan shrinks Christ so that we end up with a God so small that we fail to relentlessly worship him.

Rationally, Kevin and Elyse must put off their old foolish mind-sets by saying, "I repent of the insane idols of my heart." *Relationally*, they must put off their old false lovers by saying, "I divorce the adulterous false lovers of my soul." We can no longer live like the ugly whores we used to be (see Jer. 2) because Christ has returned us to the purity of virgin brides who are motivated by gratitude to passionately love God.

Affections, longings, thirsts, delights, and desires are "where the action is." Modern Christianity reduces life to the externals of behavior while the significance of motivating desire is insufficiently emphasized. Our old flesh was habituated not simply to *do evil* but also, and more insidiously, to *love evil*. Our flesh is ingrained toward patterns of false lovers from its years of disconnection from God. In Christ we have put off these patterns and must daily rid ourselves of any remnants.

When faced with *suffering*, Kevin and Elyse are tempted to think, "Life is bad and so is God." If they surrender to this fleshly mind-set, they're easy game for the allure of false lovers who seem to promise protection, comfort, ease, or at least enough pleasure to cause them to temporarily forget their pain. In divorcing the adulterous false lovers of their soul, they each cry out to their Father, "I've been a relational prodigal. I now reject my past pattern of fearful flight from you. and I put on faith in you as my forgiving Father. When life is bad, I cling to you as my supreme good. I say, 'My flesh and my heart may fail, but God, you are the strength of my heart and my portion forever.' I confess as sin my pursuit of false lovers of the soul and put on sole devotion to you. I put off my whoredom and spiritual adultery. When life is bad, I remind myself, 'Whom have I in heaven but you? And earth has nothing I desire besides you.'"

When faced with a *besetting sin* that yanks them here and there like a yo-yo and tosses them about like a rag doll in a Doberman's mouth, Kevin and Elyse must mortify their fleshly desires. They each confess, "I've allowed my religious affections to grow cold, my love to become lukewarm. I've rejected God as my highest joy, my greatest delight. I've replaced God with false lovers. I've not related to you as a good God with a supremely good heart. I confess as sin my denial of Christ-sufficiency. My broken cisterns are filthy and useless. I've sinned by forsaking my Spring of Living Water, and I now acknowledge this for what it is — spiritual adultery. So right now in Christ's resurrection power, I put off my false passions, my delighting in lesser gods, my sinfully misdirected longings, and my pursuit of God-designed desires in God-prohibited ways."

Journey Marker 3: Relational Mortification—Putting Off Our Old Disordered Self-Aware Affections

We follow foolish mind-sets fanned into flame by Satan and his lying narratives about God as a shalt-not God. Believing these, we choose to love any lover other than Christ. Doubting God while still being designed to trust someone or something, we trust ourselves. Turning from God's love while still being designed to receive infinite love, we crave love in all the wrong places.

Augustine defined abnormality as a soul caved in on itself. That describes perfectly our old self-aware false lovers. We live fleshly in this area to the degree that we are ruled by internal dispositions toward radical self-centeredness, self-sufficiency, self-protection, self-hatred, selfishness, and self-beautification.

For Kevin and Elyse, the flesh-oriented conscience is an evil conscience that replaces their identity in Christ with a shameful identity in self. It rejects grace in favor of works. They see themselves as shameful since they've failed to reckon on who they are in Christ because they've refused to live by grace, choosing instead to live their lives and see themselves according to Satan's lying narrative of works. Their shame leads to self-hatred, which they foolishly attempt to deal with through self-sufficiency.

When bombarded by *suffering*, Kevin and Elyse believe Satan's fairy tale. "Life is bad, so is God, and so are you." His penetrating arrows pierce their conscience. "These bad things must be happening to me because my tit-for-tat God is displeased with me. If only I could please him. The only way to please him is by doing good works and by beautifying myself. I have to make myself pretty enough that he'll want me. I must cover my shame."

Mortification counters these lies. Kevin and Elyse each say to Christ, "I reject the ugliness of my self-beautification. Every time I beautify myself, I deny you. I demean your grace. I act as if the cross was foolishness. I confess as sin my living according to Satan's works narrative. I confess as sin refusing to base my sense of self on my new nurture in Christ. I put off all my self-sufficient attempts to become acceptable. I put on my new grace identity in Christ."

Facing suffering without shame is hard enough. Sometimes it seems almost impossible to honestly face our *sinfulness* without capitulating to shame. We load our conscience with guilt, and we forget to lighten our conscience with grace. We remind ourselves how horrible it is to sin, but we neglect how wonderful it is to be forgiven. We believe yet another of Satan's myths. "You are evil and God is unforgiving." His piercing lies whisper into our tender consciences, "God hates sin. You are a sinner. God hates you. Some sins are so deep that even the love of God cannot reach them." Now we double-time it trying desperately to become something we already are: saints and sons/daughters.

Mortification counters these lies. Kevin and Elyse each say to their forgiving Father, "I reject the ugliness of self-beautification. I've sinned against you by doubting your graciousness and by seeing myself according to Satan's condemning narrative. I've hated myself and therefore attempted to beautify myself. I've begun by faith, but tried to continue by works. This is an abomination to you, but I am never an abomination to you. I've swallowed Satan's mental cyanide, allowing myself to be implanted and imprinted with questions about your heart toward me. I confess as sin questioning the depth of your holy love and pardoning grace. I've dethroned your grace, replacing it with my works. What a denial of Christ's gospel of grace."

Journey Marker 4: Relational Mortification—Putting Off Our Old Disordered Social Affections

Adam rejected God's sufficiency and satisfaction (foolish mind-sets), followed Satan (spiritual false lovers), hid and covered up (self-aware false lovers), then shamed and blamed his wife (social false lovers). Like father, like son. Cain jealously hated his brother, refusing to be his keeper/shepherd, instead being his judge, jury, and executioner.

Our old disordered social affections epitomize the opposite of the Trinity. The Trinity is radically other-centered. Adam, Cain, Kevin and Elyse, and you and I, when we live according to the flesh, are radically self-centered. More than that, we are fueled by a drive that uses others for our own well-being.

In mortification, we put off our old flesh-oriented way of relating to others. Caved in on ourselves because we've rejected God as our Fountain of Life, we desperately crave, and therefore demand, that others fulfill longings and thirsts that only our infinite God can fill.

Finding ourselves in this hopeless state, James tells us that we frenetically race between manipulation and retaliation (James 4:1 – 4). Battling unmet desires, we first attempt to manipulate others to meet our needs. "I want what I want and I want it now and I want it from you!" When they don't come through for us, we retaliate. "If you won't make me feel better about me, then I will make you feel worse about you!"

In *suffering*, Kevin and Elyse feel thirsty because no one seems to be coming through for them. Rather than turn *to* Christ, they turn *on* each other. In times like these, they each must return to God saying, "Father, forgive me. I'm running on empty because I'm not turning to you. I'm discarding your invitation to drink whenever I am thirsty. So now I'm sinfully drinking from my spouse, demanding that he/she make me feel good. I put off my shaming and blaming way of relating to my spouse. I confess as sin my manipulation of my spouse, using him/her to fill me."

Kevin and Elyse are responding to their suffering by sinfully causing each other to suffer. They must take their *sinful* self-centeredness to Christ. "Lord Jesus, I'm using my spouse. My jealous hatred of my spouse is a reflection of the old me and more a mirror of Satan than any image or reflection of you. I confess as sin my non-Trinitarian way of relating. I put off my radically self-centered orientation."

Journey Marker 5: Volitional Mortification — Putting Off Our Old Self-Centered Purposes/Pathways

Pathways are products of the will, and the will is our ability to choose, decide, and create. Our decisions and actions flow from our will. Pathways are our patterned and purposeful behaviors, actions, motivations, and interactions as we respond to our world.

Designed by God, our wills were free to choose courageously to create good and to empower and shepherd others. Depraved by sin, our wills became enslaved to compulsive, cowardly, and destructive choices. Redeemed by

Christ, our wills are released to choose sacrificially to shepherd others. Living to empower and shepherd others is the essence of Christlike character. Volitionally, we are mature to the degree that our pathways (patterns of willing) are other-centered.

Yet we can return to the old way, the old willing, the old fleshly, self-centered pathways of volitional purposing. Theologically, we label these "enslaved acts of the flesh" — characteristic ways we will to live, habitual patterns of behavior that pursue the purpose of destructive self-gratification.

When Kevin and Elyse are convinced that God is their supreme good and they turn to him as the lover of their soul, then their wills are free to serve others in love (Gal. 5:13). However, when they doubt God's goodness and turn away from him as their Spring of Living Water, then their wills become enslaved to the flesh and they live to indulge their own needs, cravings, desires, and wants (Gal. 5:13 – 15). Because they follow spiritual false lovers, they live an empty life from an empty spiritual reservoir. In their emptiness, Kevin and Elyse live to protect themselves from any more pain. As they look to each other, they try to siphon from each other, stealing "gasoline" to fuel their depleted souls.

Kevin and Elyse can respond to *suffering* with enslaved acts of the flesh, with habituated cowardly, compulsive, destructive choices. They don't get what they want, or they get what they want and it's not enough. They feel empty. Thirsty. They might choose the pathway of the sluggard who gives up on life and never tries again. Or they might select the way of debauchery and try to drown their sorrows. Or they may journey down the path of rage, always angry at their spouse for letting them down. When they recognize these fleshly character patterns, then they each can turn to their Father, saying, "Dear Lord, forgive me. Instead of coming to you in my suffering, I've taken matters into my own hands. What a mess I've made. I've shamed your name, hurt my spouse, and disgraced myself. I choose to put off these old self-centered pathways. I reject my cowardly choices designed only to make me feel good."

Or, totally apart from any obvious area of suffering, Kevin and Elyse might compulsively choose to *sinfully* follow any number of godless lifestyles. When they find themselves entangled in such sins, they can each return to Christ. "Lord Jesus, I have no excuse. You've given me everything I need for life and godliness. I have misused my freedom to indulge my flesh. I wouldn't have done so if I hadn't first discarded you as my source of life. I wouldn't have done that if I had been living according to my renewed mind-set. Forgive me. In your strength, I put off my fleshly behavior. I reject my characteristic pattern of responding to life."

Journey Marker 6: Emotional Mortification—Putting Off Our Old Ungoverned Mood States

Feelings are a blessing and a problem for human life. We cannot live without them and we can hardly live with them. Nonetheless, feelings were and are God's idea. Created to feel life deeply, sin transformed us into moody addicts, while salvation restores us to soulful psalmists. We are saints returned to emotional integrity by Christ, enlivened to experience life honestly in all its grief and hope.

Yet the battle continues. The flesh attempts to rule our emotionality through ungoverned mood states. Emotions are hauntingly present, like a ghostly power possessing us. We require an emotional exorcist, not to eradicate all feelings, but to put off our old ungoverned mood states and to put on our new managed mood states.

My mood states are bound to my volitionality (pathways of the will), my rationality (mind-sets of my heart), and my relationality (lovers of my soul). In the flesh, I surrender to Satan's lie that "God is not good," and I solicit false lovers who seem better. Then I develop characteristic strategies that I pursue to deal with my starving soul.

Given such a state of affairs, is it any wonder that emotionally I obey addictive passions that seek to make my belly god? Casting off any hope of true soul satisfaction, of course I settle for a semblance of sensual satisfaction. I deaden my pain through feeling pleasure.

When Kevin and Elyse endure *suffering*, pain screams at them. They ache. Thirst. Hurt. Their flesh impels them toward emotional stoicism: "Repress your feelings, don't face them!" Or toward emotional sensationalism: "Express your feelings indiscriminately. You hurt. Hurt your spouse too!" Or toward emotional sensualism: "Anesthetize your moods. Find pleasure. Drown your sorrows." To put off these fleshly emotional responses, Kevin and Elyse each need to say to their Father, "I've sinned against you by surrendering to ungoverned mood states. I put off my self-centered response to my feelings. I refuse to make feeling good the idol of my heart. Instead, I take my pain to you. Teach me to soothe my soul in my Savior."

In struggling against besetting *sin*, everything within Kevin's and Elyse's fleshly self wants to enjoy the pleasure of sin for a season. Wants to just feel good for one moment. Putting off these sinful emotional passions, they each say to Christ, "I put off my addictive passions. I crucify the flesh and my demand for instant gratification. My demand that I feel good. I confess my refusal to face the sorrow of life and my hunger for heaven face-to-face with Christ. I put off my ungoverned mood states. I confess my hate, despair, and terror. Empower me to put on compassion, enjoyment, and rest in Christ."

The Putting On/Vivification Journey with Christ

Progressive sanctification has a dual aspect. Its negative side is mortification — the weakening, defeating, and killing of the flesh. Its positive side is vivification — the growing, maturing, and enlivening of the regenerate person. Paul urges us to "put on" the new self, using another common clothing metaphor. "Putting on" pictures wrapping a tunic around your chest. Figuratively, it speaks of taking on, acting like, and putting on in activity what is already true internally. "Take on the characteristics of the new person you already are. Clothe yourself with the virtues Christ implanted in your new nature."

In vivification, I put on what I already am. I stir up and fan into flame the new me. I count and reckon on my new nature and new nurture. I put on in my lifestyle, my walk, and my manner of life what is already inwardly true of me. I put on my new want to and can do.

Paul clearly explains the process in Colossians 3. You're already dead, so crucify the remnants of that old dead you (Col. 3:1 – 5). More than that, you've been raised with Christ (Col. 3:1). You have already put on the new self that is daily being renewed in knowledge in the image of Christ (Col. 3:10). "Therefore, as God's chosen people, holy and dearly loved, clothe yourselves with compassion, kindness, humility, gentleness and patience. And over all these virtues put on love, which binds them all together in perfect unity" (Col. 3:12, 14). Put your new position into practice through continually clothing yourself with new lovers, mind-sets, pathways, and mood states so that you are increasingly transformed into the image of God in Christ.

Journey Marker 7: Rational Vivification — Putting On Our New Wise Mind-Sets

If rational mortification stops the madness, then mental *vivification* returns us to sanity. In light of the cross, it is insane to doubt God's goodness. Christ's cry, "It is finished!" is our proclamation to Satan. "Your old lying narrative is finished! Rejected." Paul's words become our motto. "If God is for us, who can be against us? He who did not spare his own Son, but gave him up for us all — how will he not also, along with him, graciously give us all things?" (Rom. 8:31 – 32).

What is a new mind-set? It's the larger gospel story, the eternal heavenly perspective on life that says, "Trust God and live!" Our new mind-sets come complete with new vision. Our divine Physician performed totally success-ful laser surgery on our spiritual eyes so that we no longer look at life with eyeballs only, but with faith eyes.

Having put off the insane idols of their heart, Kevin and Elyse now put on God's version of their life story. They filter every life event through the lens of Christ's grace narrative, through the screen of God's gospel goodness. The reality of God's larger story invades their smaller story, enlightening them to what is really real.

Facing *suffering coram Deo*, Kevin and Elyse put on their new mind-set. When disappointed by their spouse, they ache, groan, and are sad, but they consent to grace truth. "God is not against me. He's not my enemy. God is good. He works all things, even marital disappointment, together for good because he is good." They receive their plotline from Christ, not Satan.

In the midst of their *suffering*, Kevin and Elyse each pray, "Father, through the pain in my marriage, I surrender my mind to you. I consent to the truth of Christ's grace narrative. I allow you to transform me by the renewing of my mind-set. Moment by moment, fill my thought life with images of God-reality. Enlighten me to know you and the power of your resurrection and the fellow-ship of your suffering. Enlighten me together with all the saints to grasp how high and deep and wide and long is your love. I commit to being a spiritual mathematician, adding life up from your perspective. As I face suffering in my marriage, I believe that though life is bad, you are my supreme good."

In the midst of our suffering, we often must face our *sinning*. We struggle. Doubt. Satan steps up to the plate and says, "And you call yourself a Chris-tian? Oh, yeah, when things are going good, then you trust God. But when your marriage is rocky, you turn away from God. Maybe that's why God lets your marriage be such a mess. You're doubting God and God hates doubters, so God hates you!"

In the midst of such temptations to doubt God's goodness, we must put on the spiritual image of the cross that deciphers every narrative we ponder. We must live according to renewed images of the Trinity's holy love. So Kevin and Elyse each pray to God, "Father, I've sinned in doubting you. But I won't pile doubt upon doubt. I know that even when I'm sinful; you're gracious. I surrender to you to renew my mind through grace narratives. I receive your forgiveness. I accept my acceptance in Christ. I put on the mind of Christ. Like Christ, I believe that you alone satisfy the spiritual appetites of my soul. I put on Trinitarian images of you. You are the eternal community of love and admiration. You are holy love."

Journey Marker 8: Relational Vivification—Putting On Our New Purified Spiritual Affections

Our eighth sanctification journey marker builds on a basic premise of *Gospel-Centered Counseling*: We pursue what we perceive to be pleasing. Through the ongoing process of journey marker 7, we're putting on the truth that God is our supreme good. It's based on this conviction that we're drawn toward God. Made to know good with our minds, we were also created to pursue good with our souls. Re-created to know Christ's supreme worth, we put on our new purified spiritual affections. We put on loving God supremely out of recognition of his supreme good and flowing from gratitude for his amazing grace.

Rationally, we put on our new wise mind-sets by saying, "I consent to the truth of Christ's grace narrative." *Relationally*, we put on our new purified spiritual affections by saying, "I enjoy and exalt Christ as my supreme good." Our chief end is to glorify God and enjoy him forever.

When facing *suffering*, the new Kevin and Elyse face God. Their deepest longing is not relief from suffering (as wonderful as that might be), but communion with God in the fellowship of Christ's suffering. So they entrust their soul to God, handing it over to him for safe keeping. They each say to God, "I hate suffering, yet I thank you for it. Thank you for teaching me through suffering that I cannot live by bread alone, that I cannot live alone. Thank you for teaching me that I need every word that proceeds from your mouth. That I need you. In my suffering, help me to find you, know you, cling to you. Draw me to yourself in my emptiness."

When struggling against *sin*, Kevin and Elyse pursue God as their purest pleasure, rather than pursuing the pleasure of sin for a season. Friendship with God becomes their one holy longing, rather than friendship with the world. The deepest affection of their soul is to know God and to make him known. So they each pray to their Father, "As the deer pants for the water, so my soul longs after you. You alone are my true joy giver and the apple of my eye. Orient me to you. Help me to entrust myself to you, enjoy you, and exalt you as my Spring of Living Water, as my Thirst Quencher. I cling to you as your child."

Journey Marker 9: Relational Vivification—Putting On Our New Purified Self-Aware Affections

We follow wise mind-sets fanned into flame by Christ's grace narrative about God as a rewarder, not a hoarder. Convinced by Christ, we pursue our soul's sole lover. Entrusting ourselves to our good God, we rest knowing who we are *in* Christ and who we are *to* Christ. Therefore, our renewed self-awareness is grace based and Christ focused. By grace we gain Christ-esteem. Christ-shalom.

In Romans 12, Paul begins to apply the truth he has taught in Romans 1–11 concerning our salvation in Christ. His first two points of application are about *rational renewal* (being transformed by the renewing of our minds) and about *relational spiritual renewal* (offering ourselves to God in a spiritual act of worship). His third application highlights our *relational self-aware renewal.* "For by the grace given me I say to every one of you: Do not think of yourself more highly than you ought, but rather think of yourself with sober judgment, in accordance with the measure of faith God has given you" (Rom. 12:3). Paul is saying, "Be wise minded about yourself. Be in your right mind about yourself, about who you are in Christ."

What does this look like? How are we to evaluate ourselves? Paul begins and ends verse 3 with the answer: "For by the grace given me ... in accordance with the measure of faith God has given you." My sense of self must be grace based. "I am who I am because of the great I Am."

Kevin and Elyse put on their new self-awareness in the midst of *suffering* by accepting the new grace-love view of themselves that is in accordance with Christ's grace narrative. This counters Satan's law/works narrative that says, "You're suffering because you're bad." They eschew diabolical deception and place their faith, hope, and love in Christ's love for them. So they each say to God, "This suffering tempts me to doubt you and your love for me. Yes, I will search my heart to see if there is any secret sin in me, because I do know that in your holy love you discipline me. More than that, I understand that not all suffering is a direct fault of mine. I live in a fallen world, and right now it's falling on me. But that doesn't mean that you've fallen on me, that you want to crush me. Break me so that I depend on you more? Yes. Crush me so I give up hope? Never! By faith, I accept my acceptance in Christ. I make it the prayer of my life to grasp how long, high, deep, and wide Christ's love is to me."

Facing the reality of their struggle with *sin,* Kevin and Elyse maintain a sober self-assessment. They realize that they are not perfected, glorified saints. Yet they also understand that they are not unregenerate sinners. Even in the midst of sin, they put on and reckon on the theological reality that they are regenerated, justified, redeemed, and reconciled. So they each say to God, "Father, I've sinned against you. Thank you for forgiving me. Empower me to be victorious over this sin. Defeat Satan as he attempts to cause me to think that you are against me. Seeing you in all your holy love, I see myself holy and loved. I rest happy, calm, safe in Christ. I receive my new nurture. I hear you saying to me, 'Forgiven!' 'Welcome home!' I accept my new identity as your adult child. I clothe myself with my new standing in Christ."

Journey Marker 10: Relational Vivification—Putting On Our New Purified Social Affections

Our renewed communion with Christ equips us to experience a new content-ment with who we are in and to Christ. Communing with Christ and content in Christ, now we are free to connect to others. We're empowered by a godly passion to epitomize Trinitarian relationships that are radically other-centered.

When we put on our new social grace-love, we involve ourselves in the process of stirring up our new love for others. We fan into flame the spirit of power, *love*, and wisdom implanted in our soul at salvation (2 Tim. 1:6 – 7). We love others with authenticity that flows from our new heart.

This moves Kevin and Elyse not simply to focus on their own *suffering*, but to *suffer* alongside one another. They each cry out to God, "Father of all compassion and God of all comfort, as I've received compassion and comfort from you, please give me the courage to join with my spouse in his/her time of need. Empower me to climb in the casket with my spouse. I want to connect with him/her and help him/her to connect with you. And connecting, please give us comfort, give us co-fortitude, strength together as we connect in Christ. Help me to die to self so he/she can experience your resurrection power."

When walking alongside each other in their *sin*, they each cry out to God, "Father, as you have granted me grace, help me to grant my spouse grace. Not cheap grace, but costly grace. Help me to enter his/her battle. Help me to relate in a spirit of meekness. Empower me to equip my spouse to know that he/she can be victorious because of you. May I walk with him/her along his/her jour-ney, down into the valleys of the shadow of defeat and up the hills of victories."

Journey Marker 11: Volitional Vivification—Putting On Our New Other-Centered Purposes/Pathways

We are purposeful beings with a will that chooses to follow characteristic pathways and patterns as we engage life. Our renewed wills are freed and empowered so we can courageously create good for God's glory by sacrificially empowering others.

But what does it mean, what does it look like, to move from putting off self-centered pathways to putting on new other-centered pathways? And what resources has God provided to empower us to fulfill this calling?

Volitional maturity starts as we fan into flame a new answer to the age-old question, "Why am I here?" In Adam, we're here to *survive*. To take care of ourselves. At best, we're here to build a tower of power that boosts our ego. At worst we're here to huddle in the corner of our domicile, hoping we'll be safe from the storms of life.

In Christ, we are here to *thrive*. We're not here for ourselves. We're here for God. We're here to fulfill his Creation Mandate. Here to be our brother's keeper. Here to be like Jesus.

With this renewed purpose, Kevin and Elyse will each be able to face *suffering*, saying, "Father, these defeats are hard. Devastating. I feel like quitting. Not sure how much more I can take. But I believe your promise. You will never give me more than I can handle. You'll always provide a way of escape. More than that, You always have your reasons. Your plan. I don't want only the good; I want the best. I want Christlikeness. So, Father, whatever shattered dreams you find necessary to polish me, I accept. In your gentleness, make me strong. Strong in you. Strong for others."

With this renewed purpose, Kevin and Elyse will be able to believe that God can even use their *sin* to bring about his purposes. "Father, I hear Satan's insidious whisper: 'Now you've done it. Blown it good. For good. You've thwarted your Master's purposes for your life. You're cast off. Adrift. Disqualified.' Make it stop, Father. Can it be true that where sin abounds, grace much more abounds? Please forgive me. Please renew me. Please take this mess I've made and create beauty from ashes. Renew within me a right spirit. In my brokenness, use me for your glory."

Journey Marker 12: Emotional Vivification—Putting On Our New Managed Mood States

As new creations in Christ, we can face our feelings and experience life with all its joys and sorrows. God has given us all that we need for emotional life and emotional maturity so that we can put off unmanaged moods and put on new managed mood states. So that we can put off emotional hypocrisy and put on emotional integrity.

As new emotional beings, we are soulful psalmists who can ingeniously integrate our inner experiences. As a spiritual being experiencing intense emotion, we can soothe our soul in our Savior. As a self-aware being sensing profound moods, we can admit, understand, label, and accept our mood states. As a social being sensing emotion in others, we can empathize with others, sustaining and healing them. As a rational being, we can bring rationality to our emotionality, understanding with wisdom the causes and nature of our feelings and envisioning with spiritual eyes imaginative ways to handle our moods. As a volitional being, we can consciously and courageously choose to creatively respond to our emotional states. As an emotional being, we can openly experience whatever we are feeling, being responsive to God and God's world.

Facing *suffering* as an emotional being, Kevin and Elyse can each cry out to God, "I wish I didn't have emotions, but I do. Tons of them. Right now, Father, I'm feeling _____, and _____, and _____. Knowing what I know, I think I'm normal. Groaning is our lot until glory. Thank you for giving me the courage to face what I feel. Now I ask for the insight to understand what my emotions are suggesting about who I am and how I am relating to you and others. And, to be honest, I ask to feel better. Peace. Joy. Contentment. But regardless of how I feel, I ask for self-control. Help my responses to my emotions to be you-honoring."

Facing personal *sin* as an emotional being, Kevin and Elyse can each cry out to God, "Some of my feelings are godly conviction, godly sorrow. Some of my feelings are worldly shame. Help me to face both. I've grieved you. That grieves me to the core. I want to please you. Want to bring you joy. It amazes me that I can impact you. Grieve you. Please you. Help me to sort out my mingled myriad of moods. Most importantly, help me to surrender to you. Cling to you. Obey you. Soothe my soul in you."

Where We've Been and Where We're Headed

How do we become like Jesus? What does the theological and practical sanctification journey look like in real life? Here's a tweet-size summary: *Gospel-motivated/empowered heart change puts off and puts on affections, mind-sets, purposes, and mood states so we increasingly reflect the heart of Christ.*

Where are we headed? Well, I'll save that for the book's conclusion.

Living Life Empowered by Christ's Changeless Gospel Truth

Recall "Brother Theophilus" and his letter to "Dear Brother Paul" from chapter 1. Theophilus and his fellow Christians in Colosse were saints struggling with suffering and sin — straining to understand how their Christianity made a difference in their daily lives and relationships.

Paul responded with a 1,577-word letter. Think about that. Paul's response was about the size of one modern blog post. But what wisdom Paul packed into those few words. It was the wisdom of Christ — in whom are hidden *all* the treasures of wisdom and knowledge.

Gospel Wisdom for Life Abundant and Eternal

As we've seen, that wisdom is wisdom for living our Christian lives by applying the gospel to our suffering and sin so that we increasingly reflect the image of Christ and thus increasingly glorify God. Not so coincidentally, that's also the end goal, the purpose of gospel-centered biblical counseling. Paul says it like this in Colossians 2:6 – 7, which is Paul's summary application of the CCFRCC Narrative of the Drama of Redemption that he presents in Colossians 1:1 – 2:5: "So then, just as you received Christ Jesus as Lord, continue to live in him, rooted and built up in him, strengthened in the faith as you were taught, and overflowing with thankfulness."

"So then," Paul says. In other words, Paul's tweet-size summary of the Christian life is:

+ Live life today in light of Christ's gospel victory narrative.

Throughout *Gospel-Centered Counseling*, you've encountered my tweet-size summaries. Here they are, all in one place. Combined, they encapsulate my thinking on biblical counseling that is gospel centered.

Question 1: The Word—"Where do we find wisdom for life in a broken world?"

+ Chapter 1: Tweet-Size Summary

   –To view the Bible accurately and use the Bible competently, we must understand the Bible's story the way God tells it — as a gospel victory narrative.

+ Chapter 2: Tweet-Size Summaries

   –The supremacy of Christ's gospel, the sufficiency of Christ's wisdom, and the superiority of Christ's church provide the wisdom we need for counseling in a broken world.

   –We discover wisdom for how to live life in a broken world from the wisest person who ever lived — Christ!

Question 2: The Trinity/Community—"What comes into our mind when we think about God?" "Whose view of God will we believe—Christ's or Satan's?"

+ Chapter 3: Tweet-Size Summary

   –We must know the Trinitarian Soul Physician personally to be a powerful soul physician.

+ Chapter 4: Tweet-Size Summary

   –To know the God of peace and the peace of God, we must know our triune God in the fullness of his holy love demonstrated in the cross of Christ.

+ Chapter 5: Tweet-Size Summary

   –Because Satan attempts to plant seeds of doubt about God's good heart, God calls us to crop the Christ of the cross back into the picture.

Question 3: Creation—"Whose are we?" "In what story do we find ourselves?"

+ Chapter 6: Tweet-Size Summary

  –The whole, healthy, holy person's inner life increasingly reflects the inner life of Christ—relationally, rationally, volitionally, and emotionally.

+ Chapter 7: Tweet-Size Summaries

  –Theology matters.

  –Understanding people biblically matters.

  –Biblical counselors pursue compassionate and wise counseling where our love abounds in depth of knowledge about the heart in the world.

Question 4: Fall—"What's the root source of our problem?" "What went wrong?"

+ Chapter 8: Tweet-Size Summaries

  –The essence of sin is spiritual adultery—choosing to love anyone or anything more than God.

  –Sin is not just a thief caught in a crime; sin is an adulterer caught in the act.

+ Chapter 9: Tweet-Size Summaries

  –Apart from Christ, we're condemned as adulterous spouses, dead in sin, separated from the life of God with depraved heart capacities enslaved to sin.

  –Sin is what personal beings imagine, think, choose, do, and feel as they desire and love anything or anyone more than Christ.

+ Chapter 10: Tweet-Size Summary

  –Fully biblical gospel-centered counseling deals thoroughly both with the sins we have committed and with the evils we have suffered.

Question 5: Redemption—"How does Christ bring us peace with God?" "How does Christ change people?"

+ Chapter 11: Tweet-Size Summary

  –We must build our biblical counseling models of change on Christ's gospel applied to Christians—justified, reconciled, regenerated, and redeemed people.

+ Chapter 12: Tweet-Size Summary

  –Through regeneration our new heart has a new want to; through redemption our new heart has a new can do.

Question 6: Church—"Where can we find a place to belong and become?"

+ Chapter 13: Tweet-Size Summaries

  –Together with all the saints, the church is *the* place to belong to Christ and the body of Christ and to become like Christ.

  –Sanctification is a community journey.

Question 7: Consummation—"How does our future destiny with Christ make a difference in our lives today as saints who struggle against suffering and sin?"

+ Chapter 14: Tweet-Size Summary

  –As saints who struggle with suffering and sin, we must crop back into the picture our future purity (the wedding) and future victory (the final war).

Question 8: Sanctification—"Why are we here?" "How do we become like Jesus?" "How can our inner life increasingly reflect the inner life of Christ?"

+ Chapter 15: Tweet-Size Summary

  –Sanctification is the art of applying our complete salvation by God's grace, Spirit, Word, people, and future hope so we increasingly reflect Christ.

+ Chapter 16: Tweet-Size Summary

  –Gospel-motivated/empowered heart change puts off/puts on affections, mind-sets, purposes, and mood states so we increasingly reflect the heart of Christ.

A Summary of the Summaries

I can summarize all those tweets with an even smaller tweet:

+ *Theology matters.*

If we're going to be gospel-centered biblical counselors, if our biblical counseling is truly biblical, then we have to understand and apply the theological gospel narrative of the Bible. That's our foundation for *how Christ changes lives*.

How to Care Like Christ

In the introduction, I pictured two extremes in people helping. One extreme is all love/relationship and no truth — we don't know what to do after the hug. The other extreme is all theology/truth and no love/relationship — we don't know how to relate truth to life lovingly. We don't know how to care like Christ.

To the theological foundation in *Gospel-Centered Counseling*, as biblical counselors we need to add relational maturity and relational compassion so that we speak and live gospel truth in loving wisdom. That's our target in book two in this equipping series — *Gospel Conversations* — where we seek to grow in twenty-two biblical counseling *relational competencies*. They are not "skills" or "techniques." Relational competencies flow from a gospel-changed heart. Then they overflow as we compassionately journey with fellow saints who struggle with suffering and sin. We take the gospel-centered wisdom from God's Word, apply it to our lives, and then lovingly and wisely help our brothers and sisters apply that same gospel-centered wisdom to their lives. That's biblical counseling. That's caring like Christ. I hope you'll join me in *Gospel Conversations*.[1]

Notes

Introduction

1. Jared Wilson, *Gospel Wakefulness*, 213.
2. Robert Kellemen, *Soul Physicians*, 3.
3. The Biblical Counseling Coalition Confessional Statement: http://biblicalcoun-selingcoalition.org/about/confessional-statement/.
4. Michael Horton, *The Gospel-Driven Life*, 111.
5. Ibid.
6. Ibid., 116.

Chapter 1: Mining the Richness of God's Word: God's Treasures of Wisdom

1. I develop Ashley's story and a biblical counseling response in *Sexual Abuse: Beauty for Ashes*.
2. Robert Kellemen, *Soul Physicians*.
3. The Biblical Counseling Coalition Confessional Statement: http://biblicalcoun-selingcoalition.org/about/confessional-statement/.
4. Paul Tripp, *Instruments in the Redeemer's Hands*, 1.
5. *Gospel Conversations*, volume 2 in this series, equips you in this process of relating God's story to our life stories.
6. Jay Adams, *A Theology of Christian Counseling*, ix.
7. For the role of the church in God's grand narrative, see Kevin Vanhoozer, *The Drama of Doctrine*.
8. Ibid.

Chapter 2: Discovering Wisdom for Life in a Broken World: Our Treasure Hunt for Wisdom

1. F. F. Bruce, *The Epistles to the Ephesians and Colossians*, 167.
2. Edmond Hiebert, *The Pauline Epistles*, 222 – 28.
3. William Hendriksen, *Philippians, Colossians, and Philemon*, 17.
4. Martha Nussbaum, *Therapy of Desire*, 13 – 28.
5. Consider the following historical insights into the connection between ancient philosophy and modern psychology. "The philosophers in ancient Greece took over from religion the moral direction of daily life.... In ancient times the healer of the soul who emerges in advancing cultures is not typically a member of the medical guild. In Greece he belongs instead to *the fraternity of philosophers*. Socrates was, and wished to be, *iastros tes psuches*, a healer of the soul. These Greek syllables have been recast to form the word 'psychiatrist.'... Socrates understood himself as a religious doctor of the soul. It is primarily as the *physician of the soul* that Socrates regarded himself.... Socrates was a great forerunner of the many who

have searched out and sifted the thoughts of men for the healing and well-being of their souls." From McNeill, *A History of the Cure of Souls*, 17, viii, 20, 41. Epicurus wrote: "Empty is that philosopher's argument by which no human suffering is therapeutically treated. For just as there is no use in a medical art that does not cast out the sicknesses of bodies, so too there is no use in philosophy, unless it casts out the suffering of the soul." Quoted in Nussbaum, *Therapy of Desire*, 13. Speaking of first- and second-century culture, Thomas Oden wrote, "The study of psychology was included in what Clement called philosophy — for it included the study of motivation, perception, passion, habit, and behavior modification." Thomas Oden, *Pastoral Counsel*, 228.

6. Bruce, *Epistles*, 166 – 67.
7. Ibid., 219.
8. Hendriksen, *Philippians, Colossians, and Philemon*, 17, emphasis in the original.
9. Bruce, *Epistles*, 166 – 67.
10. Nussbaum, *Therapy of Desire*, 102 – 39.
11. Ibid., 115 – 26. These first-century secular counselors even practiced their own brand of secular nouthetic counseling — often using the word *nouthetein* for their need to share strong reproof and correction to express passionate disapproval of their counselees' beliefs and conduct.
12. Consider passages such as Proverbs 1:2 – 3, 20 – 21, 33; 2:11, 16, 21 – 22; 3:8, 16.
13. See chapters 6 – 7, which examine a comprehensive biblical understanding of people.
14. Nussbaum, *Therapy of Desire*, 127 – 30.
15. Ibid., 119.
16. Ibid., 353 – 57.
17. See chapters 6 – 7.
18. See chapter 13 for a fuller development of the role of God's people in addressing life in a broken world.
19. James Bratt, ed., *Abraham Kuyper*, 488.
20. Steve Viars, " 'Brian' and Obsessive-Compulsive Disorder," in *Counseling the Hard Cases*, 65.
21. See chapters 6 – 7.
22. These concerns are not limited to the biblical counseling world. Psychiatrists such as Allen Frances and Edward Shorter believe that the right medication prescribed in the right dosage at the right time can save a life. However, we've convinced ourselves that a variety of merely human experience — temporary bouts of sadness or excitement or distraction — are in fact pathologies that need to be blasted with drugs. See Allen Frances, *Saving Normal*, and Edward Shorter, *How Everyone Became Depressed*.
23. For a nuanced perspective on the state of psychotropic interventions, see Charles Hodges, *Good Mood Bad Mood*.
24. For a comprehensive approach to understanding biblical counseling, medication, and the complex mind/body issues, see Laura Hendrickson, "The Complex Mind/Body Connection" in James MacDonald et al., eds., *Christ-Centered Biblical Counseling*, 409 – 22.
25. Robert Kellemen, *God's Healing for Life's Losses*.
26. John Frame, *Doctrine of the Word of God*, 331.

Chapter 3: Knowing the Creator of the Soul: Our Great Soul Physician

1. A. W. Tozer, *Knowledge of the Holy*, 1.
2. Alexander Pope, *Essay on Man*, 2.1, 43.
3. Michael Reeves, *Delighting in the Trinity*, 9.
4. C. S. Lewis, *Mere Christianity*, 174.
5. Robert Letham, *Holy Trinity*, 1.
6. John MacArthur, *Ephesians*, 273.
7. Ibid., 316.
8. Ibid.
9. For specifics of how our church responded, see Robert Kellemen, *Equipping Counselors*, 31 – 52.
10. Because there was evidence of physical abuse, we worked through the proper channels and developed a plan for the daughter to stay for a period of time in the home of a family in our church — a family equipped to minister biblically and lovingly. And, given the issue of depression, we consulted with medical personnel.
11. Letham, *Holy Trinity*, 82.
12. Ibid., 80.
13. "Appendix: Letter to Nathaniel Hawthorne, June 1851," from H. Melville, http://xroads.virginia.edu/~ma96/atkins/cmletter.html.
14. Christopher Hitchens, interview on *Hannity and Colmes*, Fox News, May 13, 2007.
15. Michael Reeves, *Delighting in the Trinity*, 110.
16. Ibid., 111.
17. Ibid., 110.
18. Kevin Vanhoozer, *Drama of Doctrine*, 21 – 24, 224.
19. Michael Horton, *Gospel-Driven Life*, 59.
20. John Stott, *Message of Romans*, 311.
21. Jack Miles, *God: A Biography*.
22. Thomas Torrance, *Christian Doctrine of God*, ix – x.
23. Jonathan Edwards, "The End for Which God Created the World," 4.

Chapter 4: Recognizing the Most Important Fact about Us: Our View of God

1. J. I. Packer, *Knowing God*, 201 – 202, emphasis added.
2. Matt Chandler, Josh Patterson, and Eric Geiger, *Creature of the Word*, 154 – 55.
3. Justin Holcomb and Lindsey Holcomb, *Rid of My Disgrace*, 73, 75.
4. Jared Wilson, *Gospel Wakefulness*, 69.
5. John Stott, *Cross of Christ*, 132.
6. Ibid., 130.
7. Cited in William P. Farley, *Gospel-Powered Parenting*, 24.
8. Eric Rust, *Covenant and Hope*, 78.
9. Stott, *Cross of Christ*, 131.
10. G. C. Berkouwer, *Work of Christ*, 277.
11. Emil Brunner, *Mediator*, 450, 470.
12. Stott, *Cross of Christ*, 133.
13. Ibid., 159.
14. Ibid., 274.

15. Ibid., 329.
16. Ibid.
17. "Trialogued" is a term I introduced in chapter 3 and develop fully in *Gospel Conversations*. The word communicates that biblical counseling is not a monologue, not even just a dialogue, but a trialogue — three people are always involved in every gospel conversation: the counselor, the counselee, and the divine Counselor through God's Word and Spirit.
18. Stott, *Cross of Christ*, 335.
19. Sinclair Ferguson, *Grow in Grace*, 56, 58.

Chapter 5: Engaging the Battle for Our Soul: Our Spiritual Warfare in Spiritual Friendship

1. Ken Wuest, *Word Studies*, 141.
2. Jay Adams, *Theology of Christian Counseling*, 5.
3. Michael Horton, *Gospel-Driven Life*, 112.
4. Ibid., 116.
5. Thomas Brooks, *Precious Remedies*, 29.
6. Martin Luther, "Sermon on John 18:28," #983, 333 – 34.
7. Martin Luther, "Sermon on the Mount," 42.
8. C. S. Lewis, *The Chronicles of Narnia*.
9. Greg Gilbert, *What Is the Gospel?*, 89, 98.
10. Daniel Montgomery and Mike Cosper, *Faith Mapping*, 38.
11. Elyse Fitzpatrick, *Idols of the Heart*, 116.
12. John Piper, *Future Grace*, 9 – 10.
13. Matthew Henry, *Commentary on the Whole Bible*, 1096.

Chapter 6: Examining the Spiritual Anatomy of the Soul: Our View of People

1. For additional insight on how I worked with Mike, see Robert Kellemen, *Anxiety: Anatomy and Cure*.
2. For an extensive biblical development of the *imago Dei*, see Robert Kellemen, *Soul Physicians*, 117 – 59.
3. Philip Butin, *Revelation, Redemption, and Response*, 68.
4. For an extensive theology of biblical counseling regarding the comprehensive nature of human nature see, Robert Kellemen, *Soul Physicians*, 150 – 213.
5. Jonathan Edwards, *Religious Affections*.
6. R. Laurin, "Concept of Man as Soul," 131.
7. Hans Wolff, *Anthropology of the Old Testament*, 8 – 11.
8. Franz Delitzsch, *System of Biblical Psychology*, 242.
9. John Piper, *Pleasures of God*, 48.
10. Henry Scougal, *Life of God in the Soul of Man*, 108.
11. Jonathan Edwards, *Religious Affections*, 9.
12. Ibid., xxviii.
13. John Owen, *Temptation and Sin*, ix.
14. Jonathan Edwards, *Freedom of the Will*, 13.
15. Richard Baxter, *Christian Directory*, 85.
16. Timothy Keller, "Puritan Resources for Biblical Counseling," 11 – 44.

17. Thomas Boston, *Human Nature in Its Fourfold State*, 62.
18. For a comprehensive approach to understanding biblical counseling and the body, see Laura Hendrickson, "The Complex Mind/Body Connection," 409–22.
19. Kellemen, *Anxiety*, 39–40.
20. For a comprehensive approach to understanding biblical counseling and physical and social influences on the heart, see Jefery Forrey and Jim Newheiser, "The Influences on the Human Heart," 123–37. Also see Kellemen, *Anxiety*, 39–42.
21. Ed Welch, "Who Are We? Needs, Longings, and the Image of God in Man," 31.
22. Jay Adams, *Theology of Christian Counseling*, 39.
23. Sam Williams and Bob Kellemen, "The Spiritual Anatomy of the Soul," 120.

Chapter 7: Journeying into the Heart: Our Role as Soul Physicians and Biblical Cardiologists

1. *Everlasting being* is not a specific part of the conversational sketch because it encompasses the entire spiritual conversation. Our *coram Deo* existence is the context, circumference, and container that encircles every aspect of every counseling relationship.

Chapter 8: Exploring Serpentine Seduction to Sin: Our Spiritual Adultery

1. J. C. Ryle, *Gospel of Luke*, 54.
2. William Wilson, *Wilson's Old Testament Word Studies*, 428.
3. John Murray, *Principles of Conduct*, 126.
4. Jay Adams, *Theology of Christian Counseling*, 6.
5. Milton Vincent, *Gospel Primer*, 17.
6. Elyse Fitzpatrick, *Idols of the Heart*, 80–81.
7. Augustine, *City of God*, 12.
8. Ralph Earle, *Word Meanings in the New Testament*, 139.
9. R. Kent Hughes, *Hebrews*, 100.
10. Vincent, *Gospel Primer*, 20.

Chapter 9: Diagnosing the Fallen Condition of the Soul: Our Fallen Heart

1. David Wells, *Search for Salvation*, 29.
2. Cornelius Plantinga, *Not the Way It's Supposed to Be*, 122.
3. John Calvin, *Institutes of the Christian Religion*, 55.
4. Martin Luther, *Large Catechism*, 1.
5. Stephen Charnock, *Existence and Attributes of God*, 171.

Chapter 10: Applying the Gospel to Suffering: Our Gospel-Centered Self-Counsel

1. New City Catechism, http://www.newcitycatechism.com/.
2. For a fuller development of a biblical approach to biblical counseling for suffering, see Robert Kellemen, *God's Healing for Life's Losses*.
3. Kevin Vanhoozer, *Drama of Doctrine*, 38.
4. Olaudah Equiano, *Life of Olaudah Equiano*, 4.

5. Ibid., 24.
6. Ibid., 25.
7. Ibid.
8. Ibid., 254.
9. Ibid., 30.
10. For a comprehensive description of how the African American church provided sustaining, healing, reconciling, and guiding Christian care for one another *in the midst of enslavement*, see Robert Kellemen and Karole Edwards, *Beyond the Suffering.*
11. Peter Randolph, *From Slave Cabin to Pulpit*, 112 – 13, emphasis added.
12. See Robert Kellemen, "Spiritual Care in Historical Perspective," 107 – 20.
13. Alfred Plummer, *Second Epistle of Saint Paul to the Corinthians*, 17.
14. Quobna Cugoano, *Evil of Slavery*, 16.
15. Ibid., 17.

Chapter 11: Prescribing God's Cure for the Soul: Part 1 — Our New Nurture

1. The Bible provides many terms related to salvation, such as "adoption" and "union with Christ." I am suggesting that one way we can subsume all the various aspects of our salvation is with the four broad terms *justification, reconciliation, regeneration*, and *redemption*. For example, I would include "adoption" as an aspect of the theological category of "reconciliation." And it is because of our "union with Christ" — being "in Christ" that we enjoy the benefits of *justification, reconciliation, regeneration*, and *redemption.*
2. Anthony Carter, *Blood Work*, 23.
3. See Kellemen, *Soul Physicians*, 363 – 65 for my collation and paraphrase of more than 150 New Testament passages about our new nurture.
4. See Kellemen, *Soul Physicians*, 379 – 84 for my collation and paraphrase of more than 150 New Testament passages about our new nature.
5. Kevin Vanhoozer, *Drama of Doctrine*, 51 – 52.
6. David Powlison, *Speaking Truth in Love*, 44.

Chapter 12: Prescribing God's Cure for the Soul: Part 2 — Our New Nature

1. Bryan Chapell, *Christ-Centered Worship*, 243, emphasis added.
2. Michael Horton, *Gospel-Driven Life*, 12.
3. Thomas Oden, *Life in the Spirit*, 168.
4. Robert Kellemen, *Soul Physicians*, 412.
5. Ralph Earle, *Word Meanings*, 356.
6. Ibid.
7. Ibid.
8. A. T. Robertson, *Word Pictures*, 498.
9. Henry Holloman, *Forgotten Blessing*, 42 – 43.

Chapter 13: Finding a Place to Belong and Become: Our Growth in Grace Is a Community Journey

1. For research into the effectiveness, or the lack thereof, of professional counseling/psychology, see: J. S. Berman and N. C. Norton, "Does Professional Training Make a Therapist More Effective?" 401 – 7; J. Durlak, "Comparative Effectiveness of Paraprofessional and Professional Helpers," 80 – 92; J. A. Hattie, C. F. Sharpley, and H. J. Rogers, "Comparative Effectiveness of Professional and Paraprofessional Helpers," 534 – 541; Keith Herman, "Reassessing Predictors of Therapist Competence," 29 – 32.
2. Paul Tripp, *Instruments in the Redeemer's Hands*, xi.
3. G. Delling, s.v. "katalambano."
4. Robert Kellemen, *Equipping Counselors for Your Church*.
5. Kevin DeYoung and Pat Quinn, *Scripture and Counseling*.
6. To learn more about Faith Church, visit: http://www.faithlafayette.org/.

Chapter 14: Remembering the Future: Our Eternal Perspective

1. Marcelle Thiébaux, *Writings of Medieval Women*, 3.
2. "The Martyrdom of Perpetua" in Patricia Wilson-Kastner, *Lost Tradition*, 19.
3. Ibid., 20.
4. Ibid.
5. Ibid., 22.
6. Ibid., emphasis added.
7. Ibid., 20.
8. Ibid., 23.
9. Ibid., 26 – 27, emphasis added.
10. Ibid., 27.
11. Ibid., 28.
12. Ibid., emphasis added.
13. This does *not* mean that everyone universally is saved. See Robert Kellemen, *Soul Physicians*, 534 – 37, for the biblical contrast between the saint's everlasting rest and the sinner's everlasting misery. Jesus, in the midst of His offer to quench our thirsts eternally, reminds us that those whose robes are not washed in His cleansing blood remain outside His saving grace (Rev. 22:10 – 15).

Chapter 15: Dispensing Grace: Our Gospel-Centered Growth in Grace

1. For a well-developed both/and approach that contrasts with these either/or approaches, see Stuart Scott, "The Gospel in Balance," in James MacDonald, Bob Kellemen, and Steve Viars, eds., *Christ-Centered Biblical Counseling*, 167 – 80.
2. John Stott, *Romans*, 180.
3. Kevin DeYoung, "Glorying in Indicatives and Insisting on Imperatives," The Gospel Coalition, http://thegospelcoalition.org/blogs/kevindeyoung/2011/08/16/glorying-in-inidactives-and-insisting-on-imperatives.
4. Kevin DeYoung, "Gospel-Driven Effort," The Gospel Coalition, http://thegospel-coalition.org/blogs/kevindeyoung/2011/06/14/gospel-driven-effort.
5. J. I. Packer, *Quest for Godliness*, 201.

6. Richard Lovelace, *Dynamics of Spiritual Life*, 114.

7. Ibid., 104.

8. Thomas Boston, *Human Nature in Its Fourfold State*, 296.

9. Ibid., 316.

10. For a biblically based presentation of the spiritual disciplines, see Donald Whitney, *Spiritual Disciplines for the Christian Life*.

11. *The Westminster Confession of Faith*, Chap. XIII, Section I, Center for Reformed Theology and Apologetics, http://www.reformed.org/documents/wcf_with_proofs/.

Chapter 16: Putting Off and Putting On: God's Heart-Change Model of Progressive Sanctification

1. For a more detailed description of the putting-off process, including an expanded description of the journey, see Robert Kellemen, *Soul Physicians*, 449 – 75.

Conclusion: Living Life Empowered by Christ's Changeless Gospel Truth

1. Robert Kellemen, *Gospel Conversations: How to Care Like Christ*.

Bibliography of Works Cited and Consulted

Adams, Jay. *The Christian Counselor's Manual.* Grand Rapids, MI: Zondervan, 1973.

_____. *Competent to Counsel.* Grand Rapids, MI: Zondervan, 1970.

_____. *A Theology of Christian Counseling: More Than Redemption.* Grand Rapids, MI: Zondervan, 1979.

Alexander, Donald, ed. *Christian Spirituality: Five Views of Sanctification.* Downers Grove, IL: InterVarsity, 1988.

Augustine. *The City of God.* New York: Modern Library, 2000.

Baxter, Richard. *A Christian Directory.* Philadelphia: Soli Deo Gloria, 1997.

Berkouwer, G. C. *Work of Christ.* Grand Rapids, MI: Eerdmans, 1965.

Berman, J. S., and N. C. Norton. "Does Professional Training Make a Therapist More Effective?" *Psychology Bulletin* 98, no. 2 (1985): 401 – 7.

Bigney, Brad. *Gospel Treason.* Phillipsburg, NJ: P&R, 2012.

Boston, Thomas. *Human Nature in Its Fourfold State.* Carlisle, PA: Banner of Truth Trust, 1997.

Bratt, James, ed., *Abraham Kuyper.* Grand Rapids, MI: Eerdmans, 1998.

Brooks, Thomas. *Precious Remedies Against Satan's Devices.* Carlisle, PA: Banner of Truth Trust, 1997.

Bruce, F. F. *The Epistles to the Ephesians and Colossians.* Grand Rapids, MI: Eerdmans, 1979.

Brunner, Emil. *The Mediator.* London: Westminster, 1947.

Butin, Philip. *Revelation, Redemption, and Response.* New York: Oxford University Press, 1995.

Calvin, John. *Institutes of the Christian Religion.* Translated by Henry Beveridge. Peabody, MA: Hendrickson, 2007.

Carson, D. A., and Timothy Keller, eds. *The Gospel as Center.* Wheaton, IL: Crossway, 2012.

Carter, Anthony. *Blood Work.* Sanford, FL: Reformation Trust, 2013.

Chandler, Matt. *The Explicit Gospel.* Wheaton, IL: Crossway, 2012.

Chandler, Matt, Josh Patterson, and Eric Geiger. *Creature of the Word: The Jesus-Centered Church.* Nashville: B&H, 2012.

Chapell, Bryan. *Christ-Centered Worship.* Grand Rapids, MI: Baker, 2009.

Charnock, Stephen. *The Existence and Attributes of God*. Grand Rapids, MI: Baker, 1996.

Chester, Tim. *You Can Change*. Wheaton, IL: Crossway, 2010.

Cugoano, Quobna. *Thoughts and Sentiments on the Evil of Slavery*. New York: Penguin, 1999.

Delitzsch, Franz. *A System of Biblical Psychology*. Eugene, OR: Wipf & Stock, 1861.

Delling, G. s.v. "katalambano." In *Theological Dictionary of the New Testament*, edited by Geoffrey Bromiley, 496. Grand Rapids, MI: Eerdmans, 1985.

DeYoung, Kevin. *The Hole in Our Holiness*. Wheaton, IL: Crossway, 2012.

DeYoung, Kevin, and Pat Quinn. *Scripture and Counseling*.

DeYoung, Kevin, and Pat Quinn. "The Preacher, the Counselor, and the Congregation." Introduction in *Scripture and Counseling: God's Word for Life in a Broken World*, Bob Kellemen and Jeffery Forrey, editors. Grand Rapids, MI: Zondervan, 2014.

Dodson, Jonathan K. *Gospel-Centered Discipleship*. Wheaton, IL: Crossway, 2012.

Durlak, J. "Comparative Effectiveness of Paraprofessional and Professional Helpers." *Psychological Bulletin* 86, no. 1 (1979): 80–92.

Earle, Ralph. *Word Meanings in the New Testament*. Peabody, MA: Hendrickson, 2000.

Edwards, Jonathan. "The End for Which God Created the World." In *The Works of Jonathan Edwards*. Peabody, MA: Hendrickson, 1998.

_____. *Freedom of the Will*. Philadelphia: Soli Deo Gloria, 1998.

_____. *Religious Affections*. New Haven, CT: Yale University Press, 2009.

Emlet, Michael. *CrossTalk*. Greensboro, NC: New Growth, 2009.

Equiano, Olaudah. *The Interesting Narrative of the Life of Olaudah Equiano*. New York: Modern Library, 2004.

Eyrich, Howard, and William Hines. *Curing the Heart: A Model for Biblical Counseling*. Fearn, Tain, Scotland: Christian Focus, 2007.

Farley, William P. *Gospel-Powered Parenting: How the Gospel Shapes and Transforms Parenting*. Phillipsburg, NJ: P&R, 2009.

Ferguson, Sinclair. *Grow in Grace*. Carlisle, PA: Banner of Truth, 1989.

Fitzpatrick, Elyse. *Idols of the Heart*. Phillipsburg, NJ: P&R, 2001.

Forrey, Jeffery, and Jim Newheiser. "The Influences on the Human Heart." Chapter 8 in *Christ-Centered Biblical Counseling: Changing Lives with God's Changeless Truth*, edited by James MacDonald, Bob Kellemen, and Steve Viars, 123–37. Eugene, OR: Harvest House, 2013.

Frame, John. *The Doctrine of God*. Phillipsburg, NJ: P&R, 2002.

_____. *The Doctrine of the Word of God*. Phillipsburg, NJ: P&R, 2010.

Frances, Allen. *Saving Normal*. New York: William Morrow, 2013.

Gilbert, Greg. *What Is the Gospel?* Wheaton, IL: Crossway, 2012.

Greear, J. D. *Gospel: Recovering the Power That Made Christianity Revolutionary.* Nashville: B&H, 2011.

Grudem, Wayne. *Systematic Theology.* Grand Rapids, MI: Zondervan, 1994.

Hattie, J. A., C. F. Sharpley, and H. J. Rogers. "Comparative Effectiveness of Professional and Paraprofessional Helpers." *Psychological Bulletin* 95, no. 3 (1984): 534 – 41.

Hedges, Brian. *Christ Formed in You: The Power of the Gospel for Personal Change.* Wapwallopen, PA: Shepherd, 2010.

Hendrickson, Laura. "The Complex Mind/Body Connection." Chapter 28 in *Christ-Centered Biblical Counseling,* edited by James MacDonald, Bob Kellemen, and Steve Viars, 409 – 22. Eugene, OR: Harvest House, 2013.

Hendriksen, William. *Philippians, Colossians, and Philemon.* Grand Rapids, MI: Baker, 1979.

Henry, Matthew. *Commentary on the Whole Bible.* Vol. 2. Old Tappan, NJ: Revell.

Herman, Keith. "Reassessing Predictors of Therapist Competence." *Journal of Counseling and Development* 72 (September/October 1993): 29 – 32.

Hiebert, Edmond. *The Pauline Epistles.* Vol. 2 of *An Introduction to the New Testament.* Chicago: Moody, 1977.

Hitchens, Christopher. Interview on *Hannity and Colmes.* Fox News, May 13, 2007.

Hodges, Charles. *Good Mood Bad Mood.* Wapwallopen, PA: Shepherd, 2013.

Holcomb, Justin, and Lindsey Holcomb. *Rid of My Disgrace.* Wheaton, IL: Crossway, 2011.

Holloman, Henry, *The Forgotten Blessing.* Nashville: Word, 1999.

Horton, Michael. *The Gospel-Driven Life.* Grand Rapids, MI: Baker, 2009.

Hughes, R. Kent. *Hebrews.* Vol. 1. Wheaton, IL: Crossway, 1993.

Kellemen, Robert. *Anxiety: Anatomy and Cure.* Phillipsburg, NJ: P&R, 2012.

_____. *Equipping Counselors for Your Church: The 4E Ministry Training Strategy.* Phillipsburg, NJ: P&R, 2011.

_____. *God's Healing for Life's Losses: How to Find Hope When You're Hurting.* Winona Lake, IN: BMH, 2010.

_____. *Gospel Conversations: How to Care Like Christ.* Grand Rapids, MI: Zondervan, 2015.

_____. *Sexual Abuse: Beauty for Ashes.* Phillipsburg, NJ: P&R, 2013.

_____. *Soul Physicians: A Theology of Soul Care and Spiritual Direction.* Winona Lake, IN: BMH, 2007.

_____. "Spiritual Care in Historical Perspective: Martin Luther as a Case Study in Christian Sustaining, Healing, Reconciling, and Guiding." PhD dissertation, Kent State University, 1997.

_____. *Spiritual Friends: A Methodology of Soul Care and Spiritual Direction.* Winona Lake, IN: BMH, 2007.

Kellemen, Robert, and Karole Edwards. *Beyond the Suffering: Embracing the Legacy of African American Soul Care and Spiritual Direction.* Grand Rapids, MI: Baker, 2007.

Kellemen, Robert, and Susan Ellis. *Sacred Friendships: Celebrating the Legacy of Women Heroes of the Faith.* Winona Lake, IN: BMH, 2009.

Kellemen, Robert, and Jeffery Forrey, editors. *Scripture and Counseling: God's Word for Life in a Broken World.* Grand Rapids, MI: Zondervan, 2014.

Keller, Timothy. "Puritan Resources for Biblical Counseling," *Journal of Pastoral Practice* 9, no. 3 (1998): 11–44.

Lane, Tim, and Paul Tripp. *How People Change.* 2nd ed. Greensboro, NC: New Growth, 2008.

Laurin, R. "Concept of Man as Soul." *Expository Times* 72 (Feb. 1961): 131–34.

Letham, Robert. *The Holy Trinity.* Phillipsburg, NJ: P&R, 2004.

_____. *Union with Christ.* Phillipsburg, NJ: P&R, 2011.

Lewis, C. S. *The Chronicles of Narnia.* Reprint ed., New York: HarperCollins, 1994.

_____. *Mere Christianity.* San Francisco: Harper, 1960.

Lovelace, Richard. *Dynamics of Spiritual Life.* Downers Grove, IL: InterVarsity, 1979.

Luther, Martin. *Large Catechism.* Translated by Robert Fischer. Philadelphia: Fortress, 1981.

_____. "Sermon on John 18:28." In *What Luther Says.* Vol. 1. Edited by E. Plass. St. Louis: Concordia, 1959.

_____. "The Sermon on the Mount." In *Luther's Works.* Vol. 21. St. Louis: Concordia, 1953.

MacArthur, John, ed. *Counseling: How to Counsel Biblically.* Nashville: Thomas Nelson, 2005.

_____. *Ephesians: MacArthur New Testament Commentary.* Chicago: Moody, 1986.

MacDonald, James, Bob Kellemen, and Steve Viars, editors. *Christ-Centered Biblical Counseling: Changing Lives with God's Changeless Truth.* Eugene, OR: Harvest House, 2013.

McNeill, John T. *A History of the Cure of Souls.* New York: Harper & Row, 1951.

Miles, Jack. *God: A Biography.* New York: Vintage, 1995.

Montgomery, Daniel, and Mike Cosper. *Faith Mapping: A Gospel Atlas for Your Spiritual Journey.* Wheaton, IL: Crossway, 2013.

Murray, John. *Principles of Conduct.* Grand Rapids, MI: Eerdmans, 1957.

Nussbaum, Martha. *The Therapy of Desire: Theory and Practice in Hellenistic Ethics.* Princeton, NJ: Princeton University Press, 1994.

Oden, Thomas. *Life in the Spirit*. Vol. 3 of *Systematic Theology*. San Francisco: Harper, 2001.

_____. *Pastoral Counsel*. Vol. 3 of *Classical Pastoral Care*. Grand Rapids, MI: Baker, 1987.

Owen, John. *Temptation and Sin*. Evansville, IN: Sovereign Book Club, 1958.

Packer, J. I. *Knowing God*. Downers Grove, IL: InterVarsity, 1973.

_____. *A Quest for Godliness*. Wheaton, IL: Crossway, 1990.

Piper, John. *Future Grace*. Sisters, OR: Multnomah, 1995.

_____. *The Pleasures of God*. Sisters, OR: Multnomah, 2000.

Plantinga, Cornelius. *Not the Way It's Supposed to Be: A Breviary of Sin*. Grand Rapids, MI: Eerdmans, 1995.

Plummer, Alfred. *Second Epistle of Saint Paul to the Corinthians*. Edinburgh: T & T Clark, 1975.

Pope, Alexander. *Essay on Man, and Other Poems*. Dover, DE: Dover, 1994.

Powlison, David. "Affirmations & Denials: A Proposed Definition of Biblical Counseling." *The Journal of Biblical Counseling* 19, no. 1 (Fall 2000): 18 – 25.

_____. *Seeing with New Eyes*. Phillipsburg, NJ: New Growth, 2003.

_____. *Speaking Truth in Love*. Winston-Salem, NC: Punch, 2005.

Randolph, Peter. *From Slave Cabin to Pulpit*. Chester, NY: Anza, 2004.

Reeves, Michael. *Delighting in the Trinity*. Downers Grove, IL: InterVarsity Academic, 2012.

Robertson, A.T. *Word Pictures in the New Testament*. Nashville: Holman, 2000.

Rust, Eric. *Covenant and Hope*. Waco, TX: Word, 1972.

Ryle, J. C. *The Gospel of Luke*. San Francisco: Bottom of the Hill, 2012.

Scott, Stuart. "The Gospel in Balance." Chapter 11 in *Christ-Centered Biblical Counseling*. Edited by James MacDonald, Robert Kellemen, and Steve Viars, 167 – 180. Eugene, OR: Harvest House, 2013.

Scott, Stuart, and Heath Lambert, eds. *Counseling the Hard Cases*. Nashville: B&H Academics, 2012.

Scougal, Henry. *The Life of God in the Soul of Man*. Ross-Shire, Scotland: Christian Focus, 1948.

Shorter, Edward. *How Everyone Became Depressed*. Cary, NC: Oxford University Press, 2013.

Smith, David. *With Willful Intent*. Wheaton, IL: Victor, 1994.

Stott, John. *The Cross of Christ*. Downers Grove, IL: InterVarsity, 1986.

_____. *The Message of Romans*. Downers Grove, IL: InterVarsity Academic, 2001.

_____. *Romans*. Downers Grove, IL: InterVarsity, 1994.

Thiébaux, Marcelle. *The Writings of Medieval Women*. New York: Garland, 1994.

Torrance, Thomas. *The Christian Doctrine of God*. Edinburgh: T & T Clark, 1996.

Tozer, A. W. *The Knowledge of the Holy*. New York: HarperCollins, 1978.

Tripp, Paul. *Instruments in the Redeemer's Hands: People in Need of Change Helping People in Need of Change*. Phillipsburg, NJ: P&R, 2002.

Vanhoozer, Kevin. *The Drama of Doctrine: A Canonical Linguistic Approach to Christian Doctrine*. Philadelphia: Westminster John Knox, 2005.

Viars, Steve. "'Brian' and Obsessive-Compulsive Disorder." Chapter 3 in *Counseling the Hard Cases*. Edited by Stuart Scott and Heath Lambert, 57 – 84. Nashville: B&H Academics, 2012.

Vincent, Milton. *A Gospel Primer for Christians*. Bemidji, MN: Focus, 2008.

Welch, Ed. "Who Are We? Needs, Longings, and the Image of God in Man," *Journal of Biblical Counseling* 13, no. 1 (1994): 25 – 38.

Wells, David. *The Search for Salvation*. Downers Grove: IL, InterVarsity, 1972.

Whitney, Donald. *Spiritual Disciplines for the Christian Life*. Colorado Springs: NavPress, 1991.

Williams, Sam, and Bob Kellemen. "The Spiritual Anatomy of the Soul." Chapter 7 in *Christ-Centered Biblical Counseling*. Edited by James Mac-Donald, Bob Kellemen, and Steve Viars, 107 – 122. Eugene, OR: Harvest House, 2013.

Wilson, Jared C. *Gospel Wakefulness*. Wheaton, IL: Crossway, 2011.

Wilson, William. *Wilson's Old Testament Word Studies*. McLean, VA: MacDonald, n.d.

Wilson-Kastner, Patricia. *Lost Tradition: Women Writers of the Early Church*. Washington, DC: University Press of America, 1981.

Wolff, Hans. *Anthropology of the Old Testament*. London: SCM, 1974.

Wuest, Ken. *Word Studies in the Greek New Testament*. Vol. 1. Grand Rapids, MI: Eerdmans, 1953.

Scripture Index